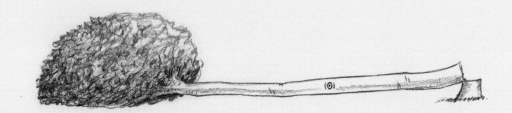

Part One

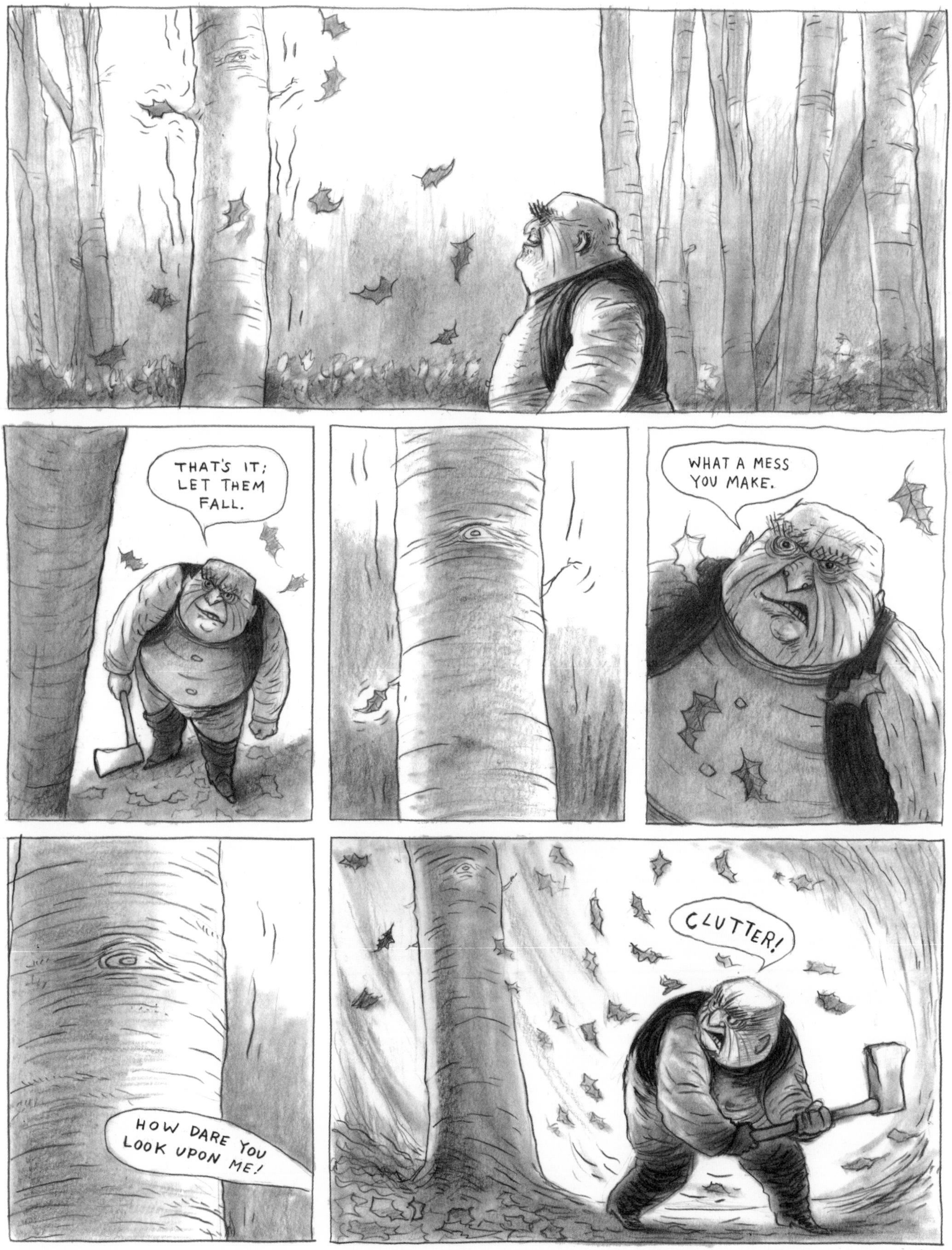
THAT'S IT; LET THEM FALL.
WHAT A MESS YOU MAKE.
HOW DARE YOU LOOK UPON ME!
CLUTTER!

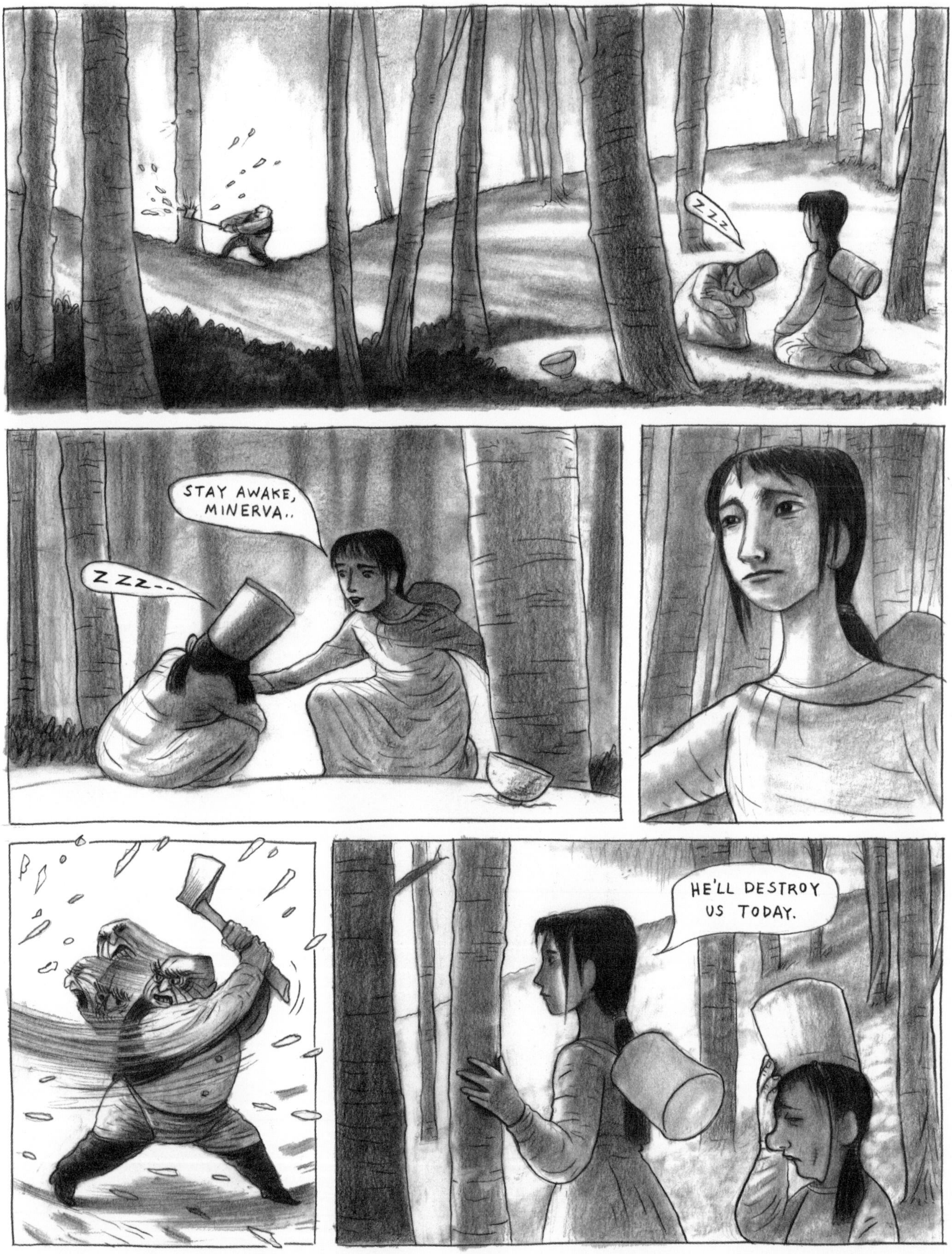
Z Z Z
STAY AWAKE, MINERVA..
Z Z Z..
HE'LL DESTROY US TODAY.

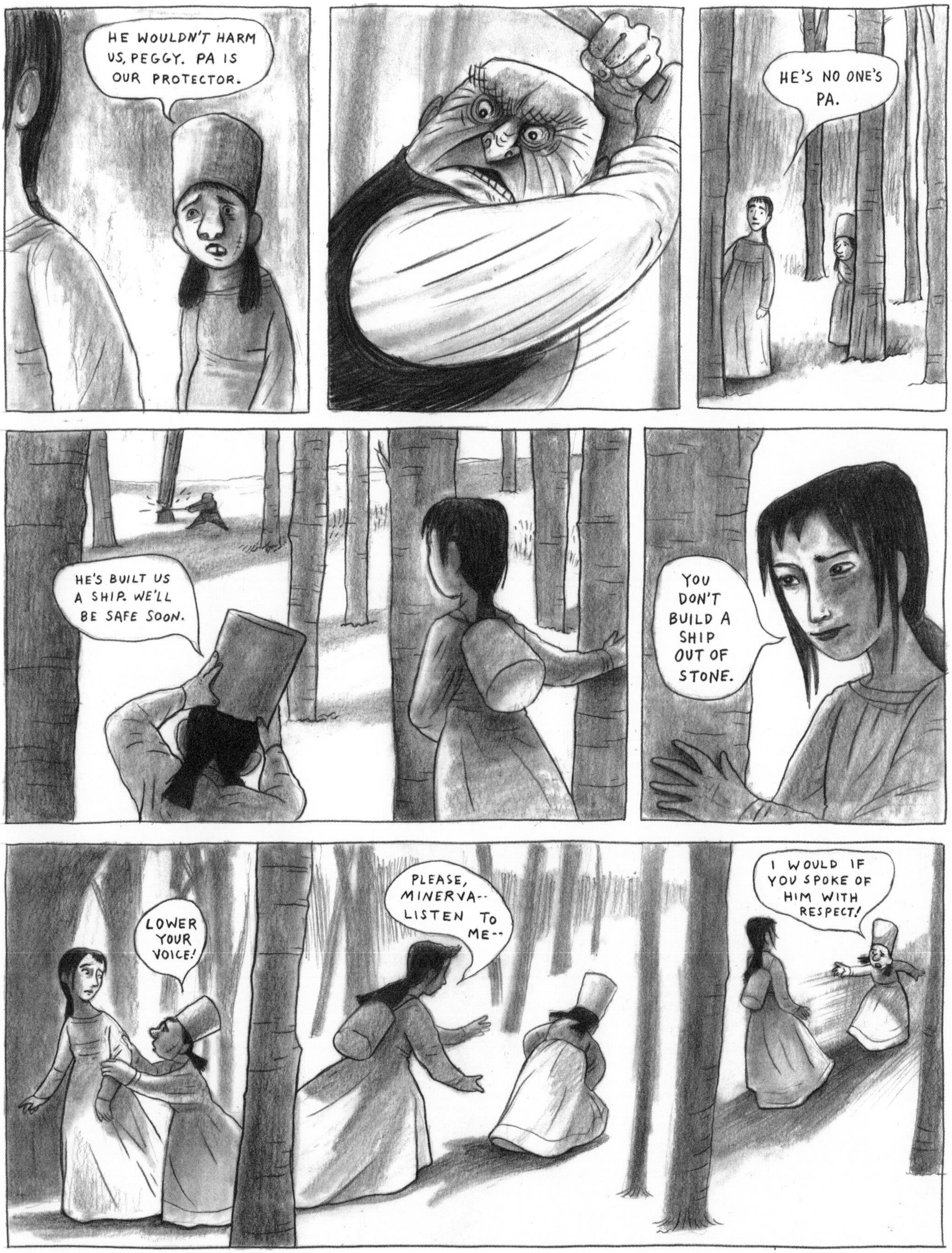
HE WOULDN'T HARM US, PEGGY. PA IS OUR PROTECTOR.
HE'S NO ONE'S PA.
HE'S BUILT US A SHIP. WE'LL BE SAFE SOON.
YOU DON'T BUILD A SHIP OUT OF STONE.
LOWER YOUR VOICE!
PLEASE, MINERVA-- LISTEN TO ME--
I WOULD IF YOU SPOKE OF HIM WITH RESPECT!

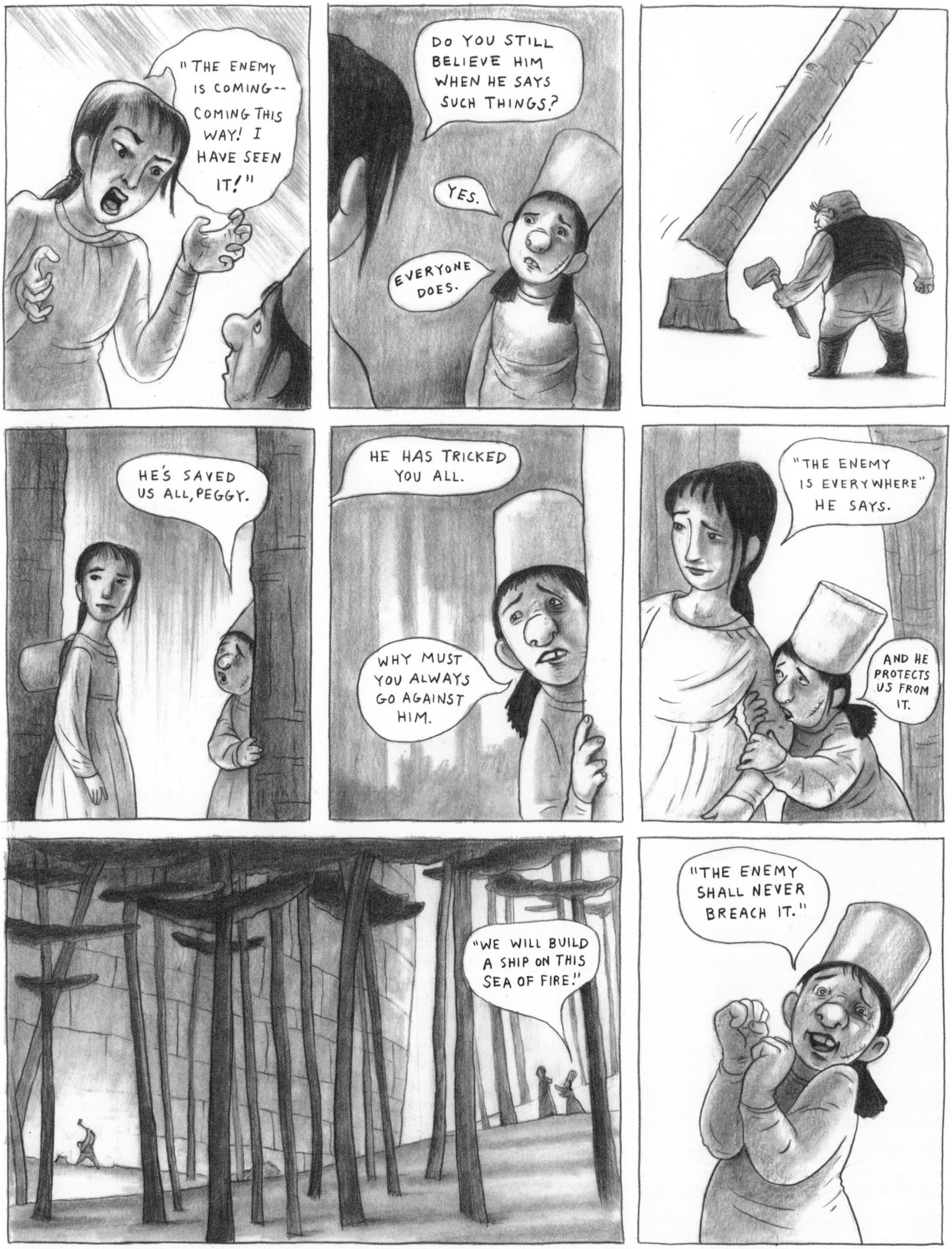
"THE ENEMY IS COMING-- COMING THIS WAY! I HAVE SEEN IT!"
DO YOU STILL BELIEVE HIM WHEN HE SAYS SUCH THINGS?
YES.
EVERYONE DOES.
HE'S SAVED US ALL, PEGGY.
HE HAS TRICKED YOU ALL.
WHY MUST YOU ALWAYS GO AGAINST HIM.
"THE ENEMY IS EVERYWHERE" HE SAYS.
AND HE PROTECTS US FROM IT.
"WE WILL BUILD A SHIP ON THIS SEA OF FIRE!"
"THE ENEMY SHALL NEVER BREACH IT."

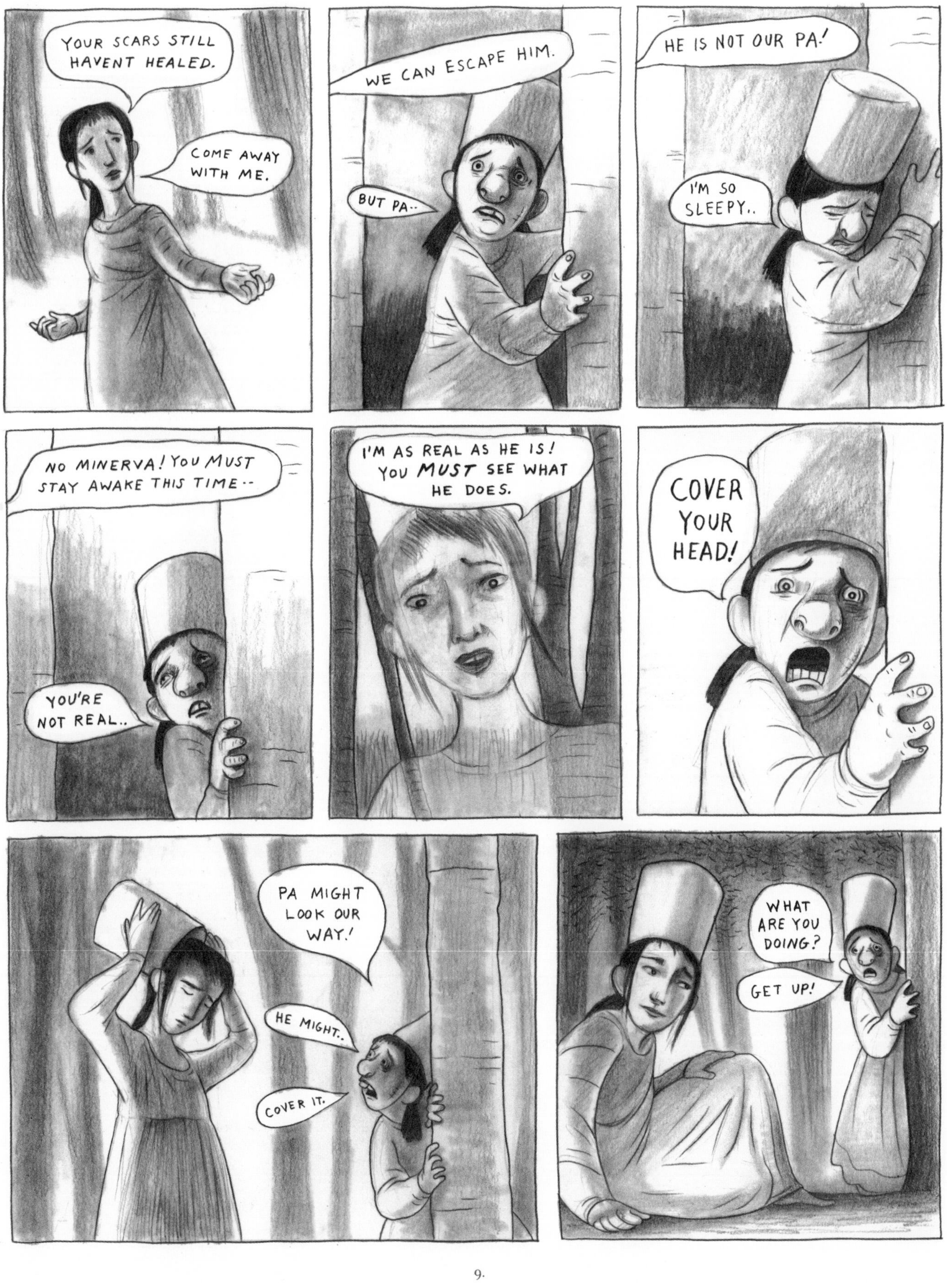
YOUR SCARS STILL HAVENT HEALED.
COME AWAY WITH ME.
WE CAN ESCAPE HIM.
BUT PA..
HE IS NOT OUR PA!
I'M SO SLEEPY..
NO MINERVA! YOU MUST STAY AWAKE THIS TIME--
YOU'RE NOT REAL..
I'M AS REAL AS HE IS! YOU MUST SEE WHAT HE DOES.
COVER YOUR HEAD!
PA MIGHT LOOK OUR WAY!
HE MIGHT..
COVER IT.
WHAT ARE YOU DOING?
GET UP!

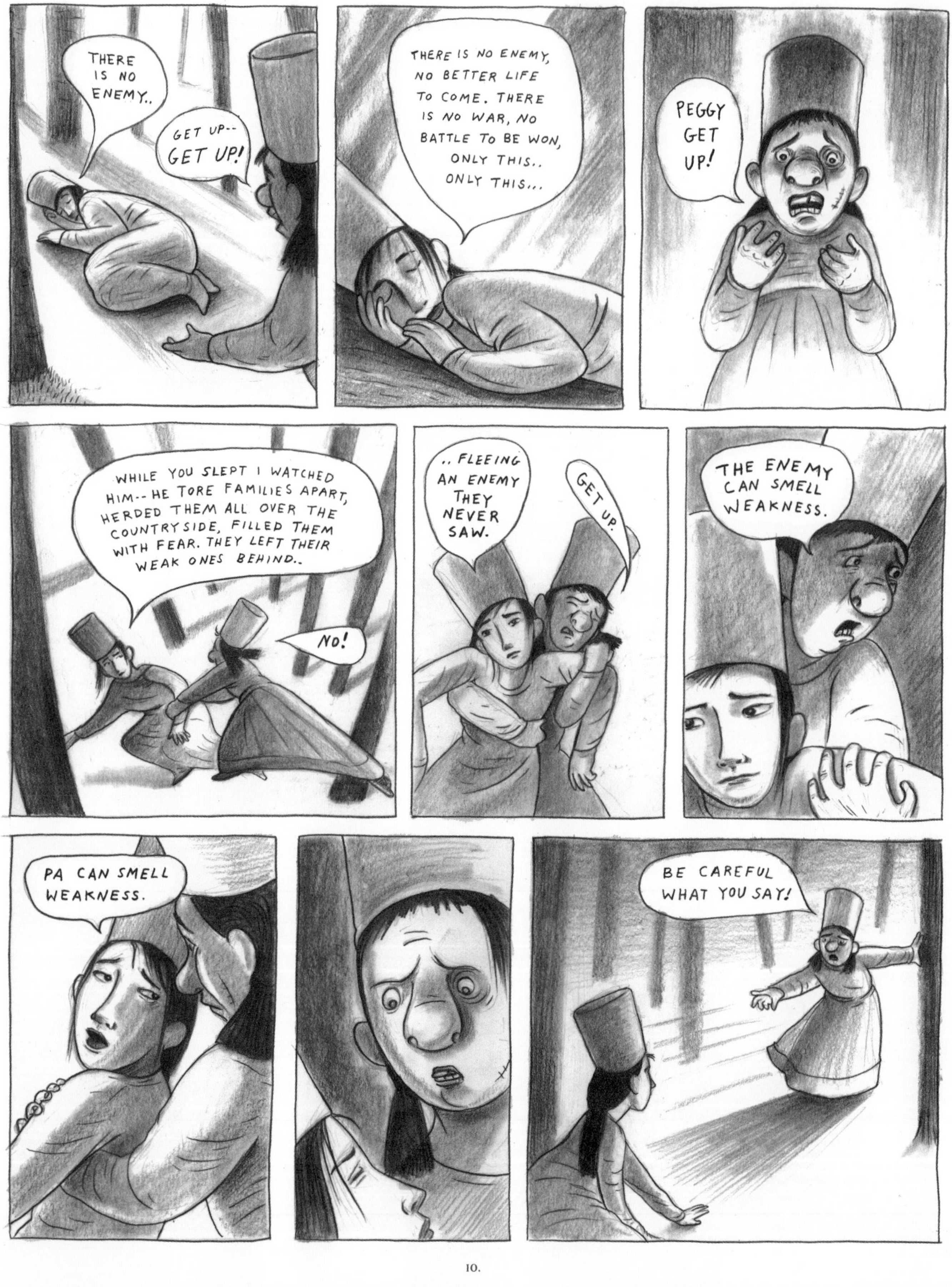
THERE IS NO ENEMY..
GET UP-- GET UP!
THERE IS NO ENEMY, NO BETTER LIFE TO COME. THERE IS NO WAR, NO BATTLE TO BE WON, ONLY THIS.. ONLY THIS...
PEGGY GET UP!
WHILE YOU SLEPT I WATCHED HIM-- HE TORE FAMILIES APART, HERDED THEM ALL OVER THE COUNTRYSIDE, FILLED THEM WITH FEAR. THEY LEFT THEIR WEAK ONES BEHIND..
NO!
.. FLEEING AN ENEMY THEY NEVER SAW.
GET UP.
THE ENEMY CAN SMELL WEAKNESS.
PA CAN SMELL WEAKNESS.
BE CAREFUL WHAT YOU SAY!

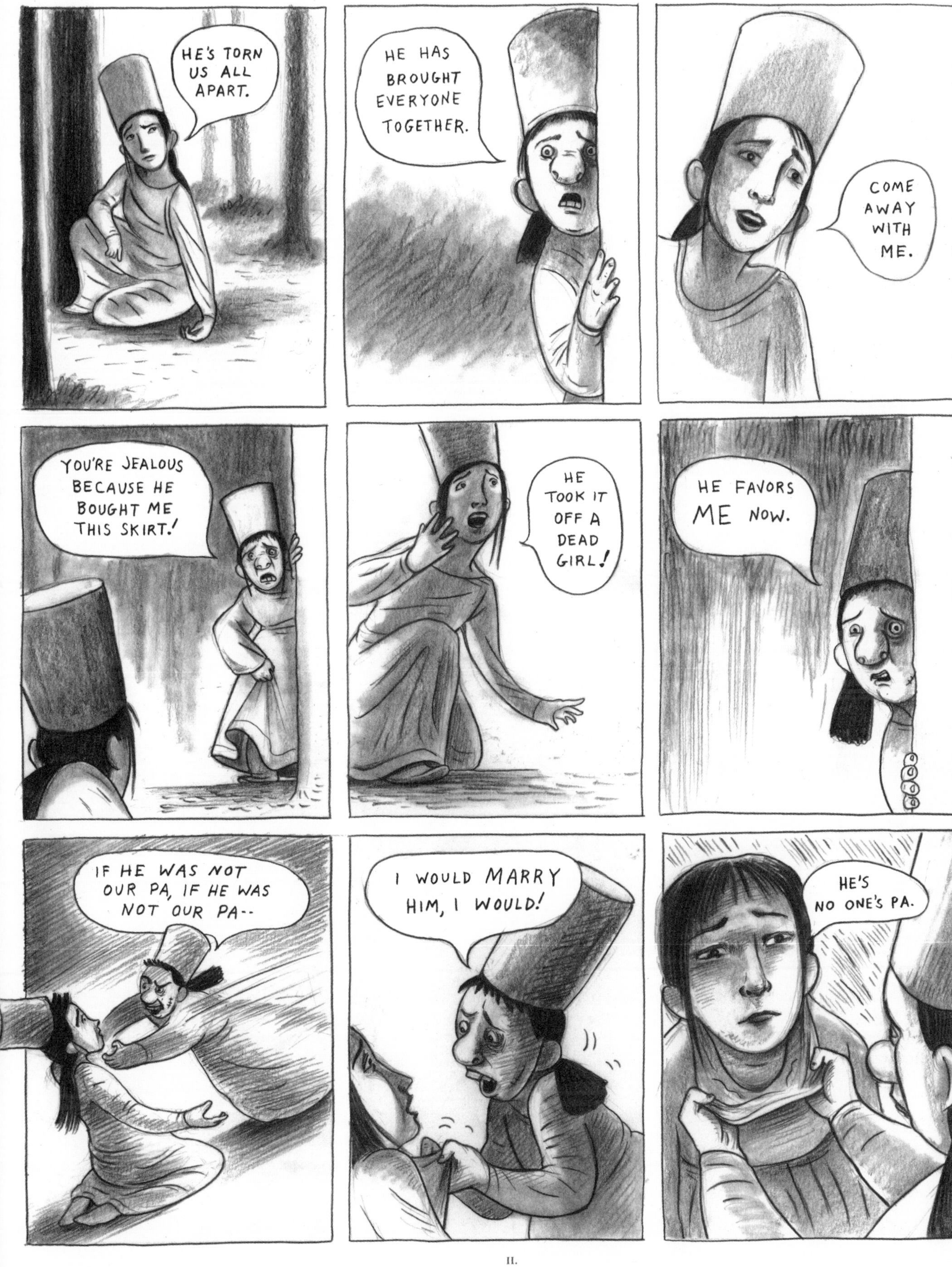
HE'S TORN US ALL APART.
HE HAS BROUGHT EVERYONE TOGETHER.
COME AWAY WITH ME.
YOU'RE JEALOUS BECAUSE HE BOUGHT ME THIS SKIRT!
HE TOOK IT OFF A DEAD GIRL!
HE FAVORS ME NOW.
IF HE WAS NOT OUR PA, IF HE WAS NOT OUR PA--
I WOULD MARRY HIM, I WOULD!
HE'S NO ONE'S PA.

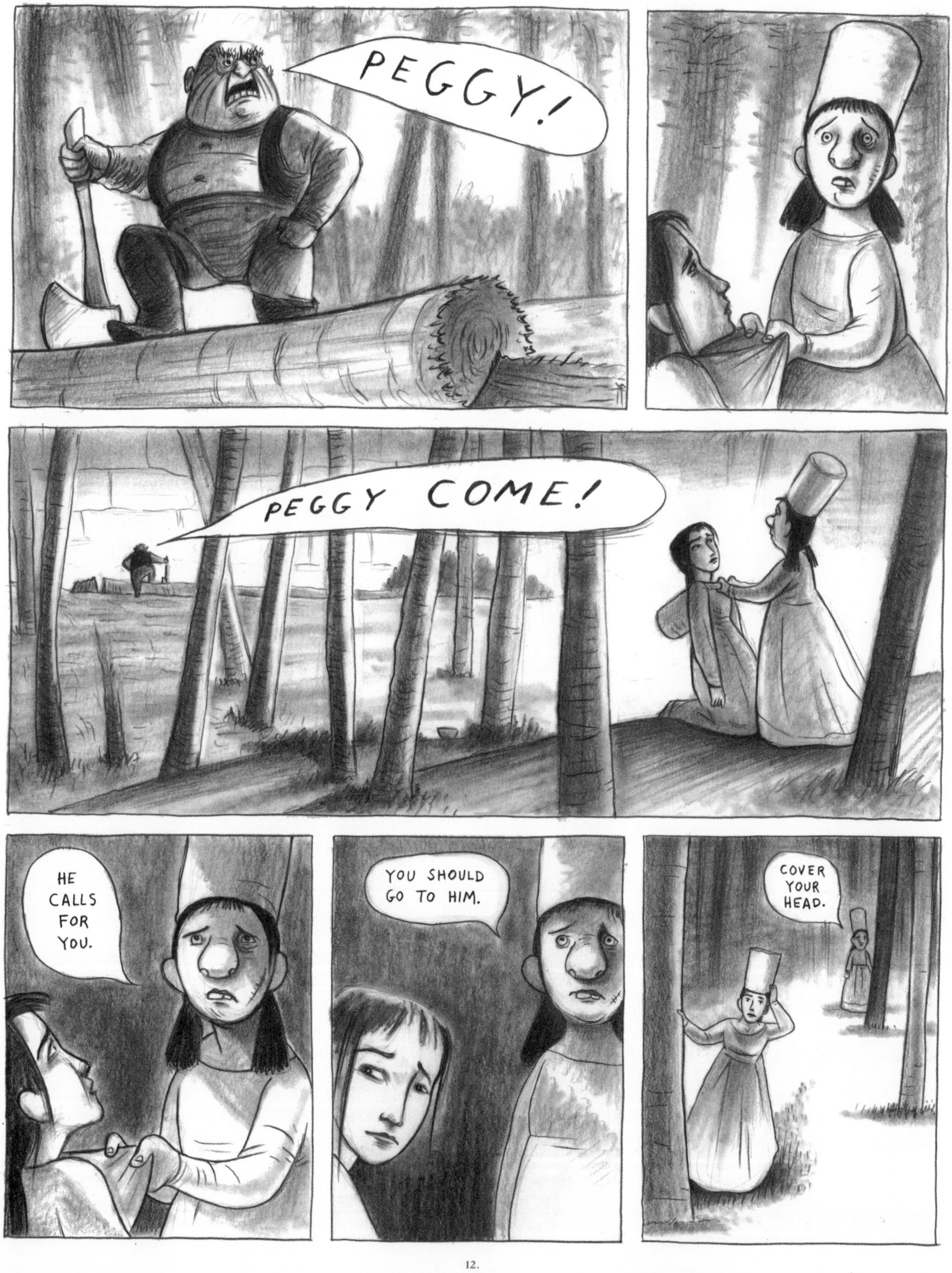
PEGGY!
PEGGY COME!
HE CALLS FOR YOU.
YOU SHOULD GO TO HIM.
COVER YOUR HEAD.

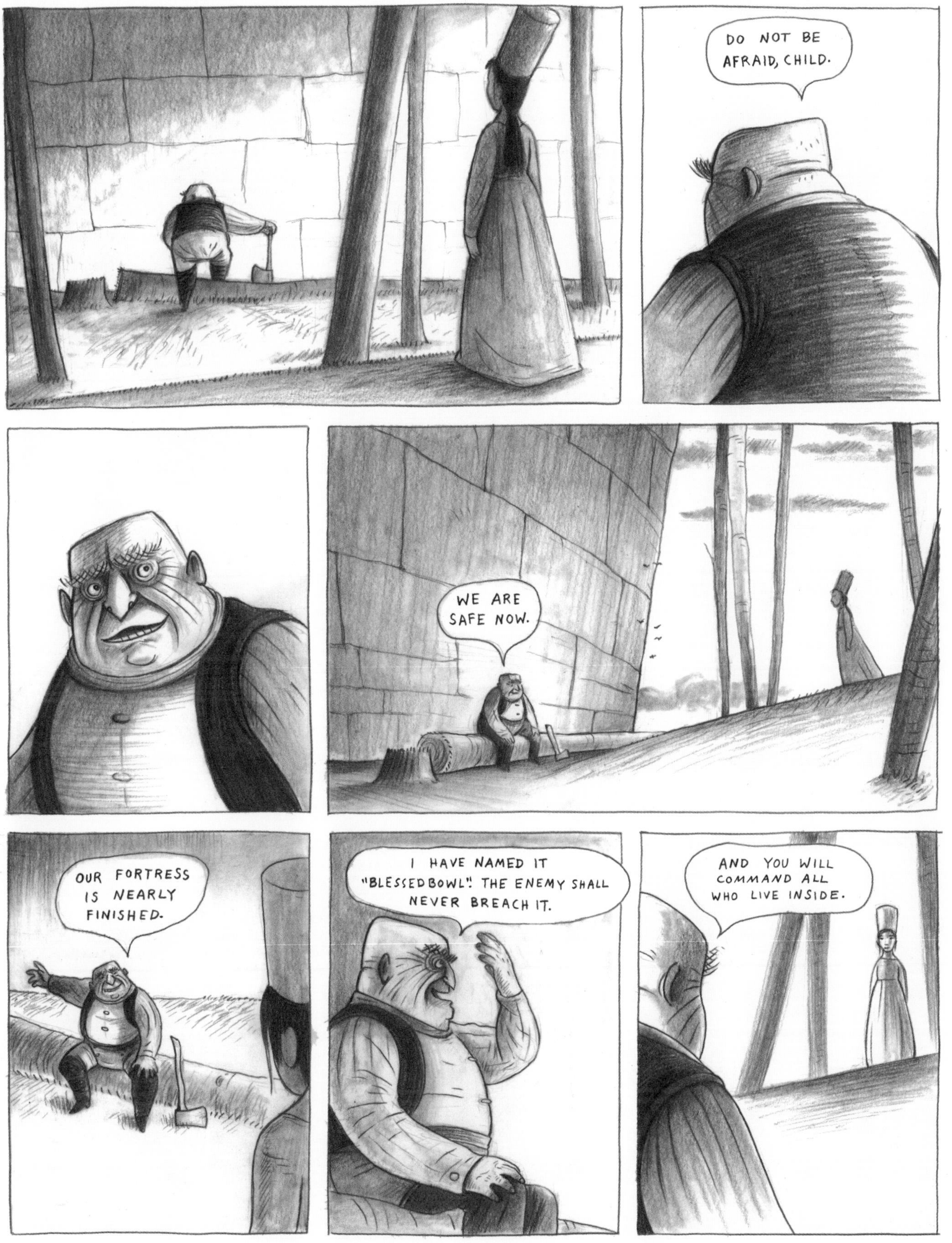
DO NOT BE AFRAID, CHILD.
WE ARE SAFE NOW.
OUR FORTRESS IS NEARLY FINISHED.
I HAVE NAMED IT "BLESSEDBOWL". THE ENEMY SHALL NEVER BREACH IT.
AND YOU WILL COMMAND ALL WHO LIVE INSIDE.

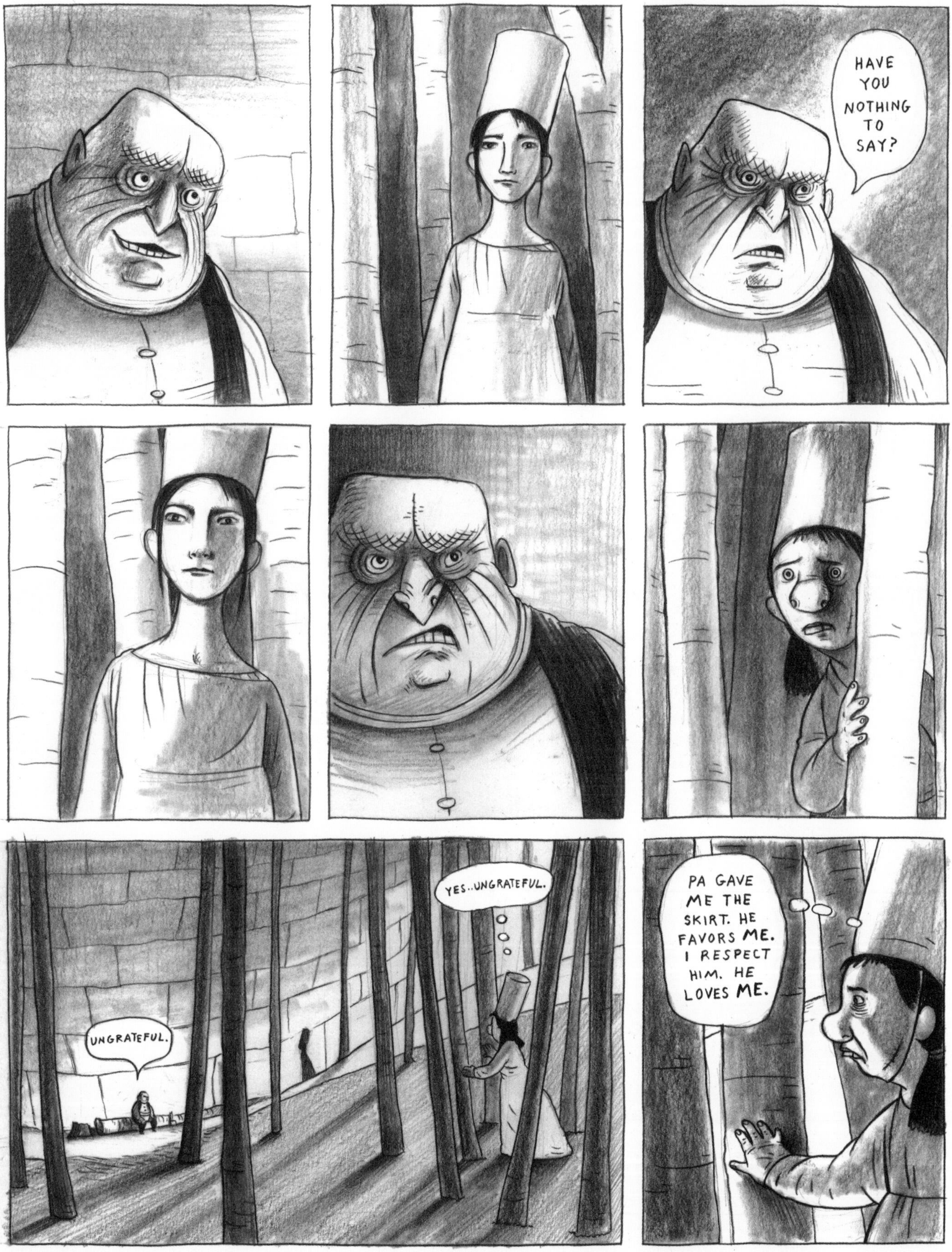
HAVE YOU NOTHING TO SAY?
YES..UNGRATEFUL.
UNGRATEFUL.
PA GAVE ME THE SKIRT. HE FAVORS ME. I RESPECT HIM. HE LOVES ME.

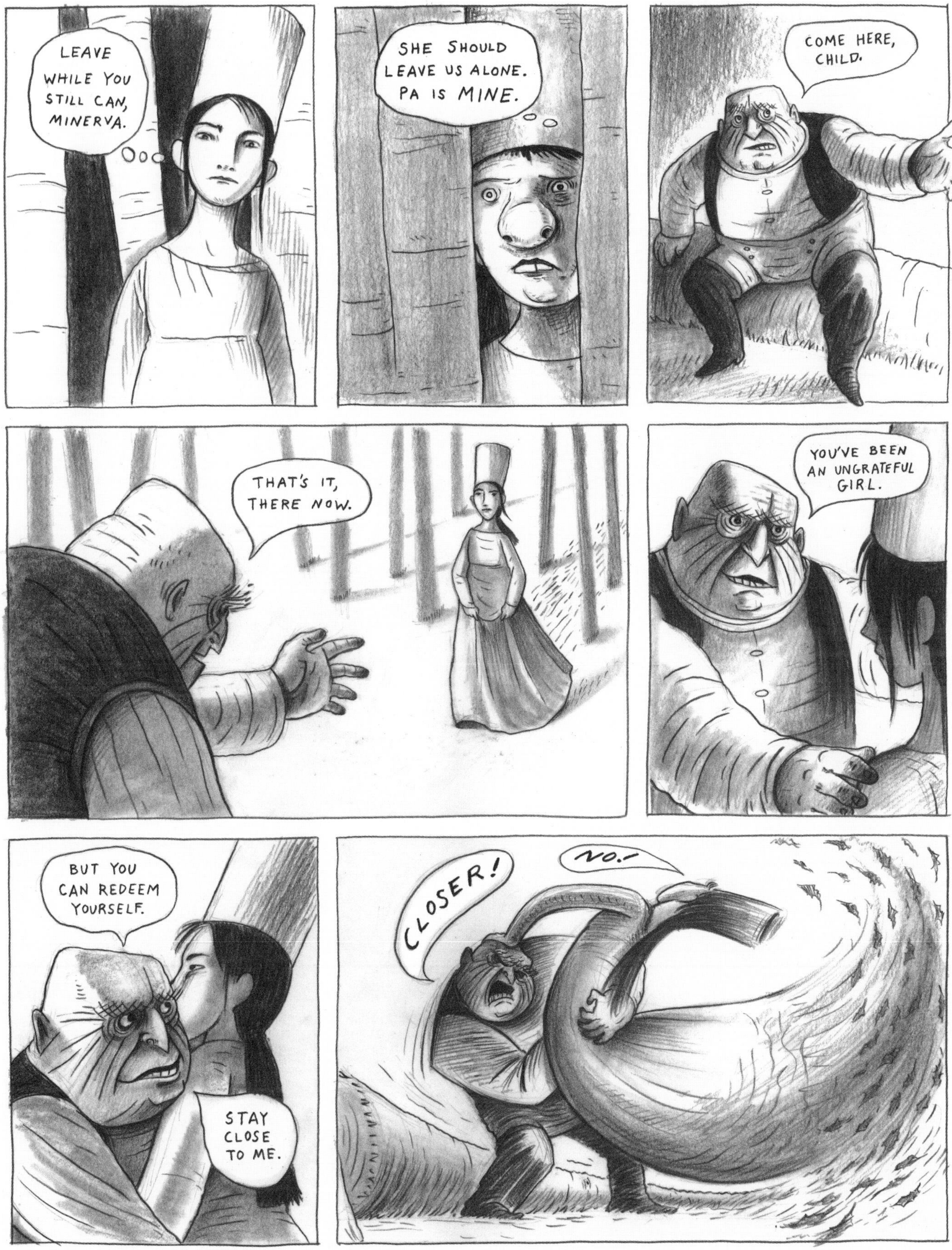
LEAVE WHILE YOU STILL CAN, MINERVA.
SHE SHOULD LEAVE US ALONE. PA IS MINE.
COME HERE, CHILD.
THAT'S IT, THERE NOW.
YOU'VE BEEN AN UNGRATEFUL GIRL.
BUT YOU CAN REDEEM YOURSELF.
STAY CLOSE TO ME.
NO.!
CLOSER!

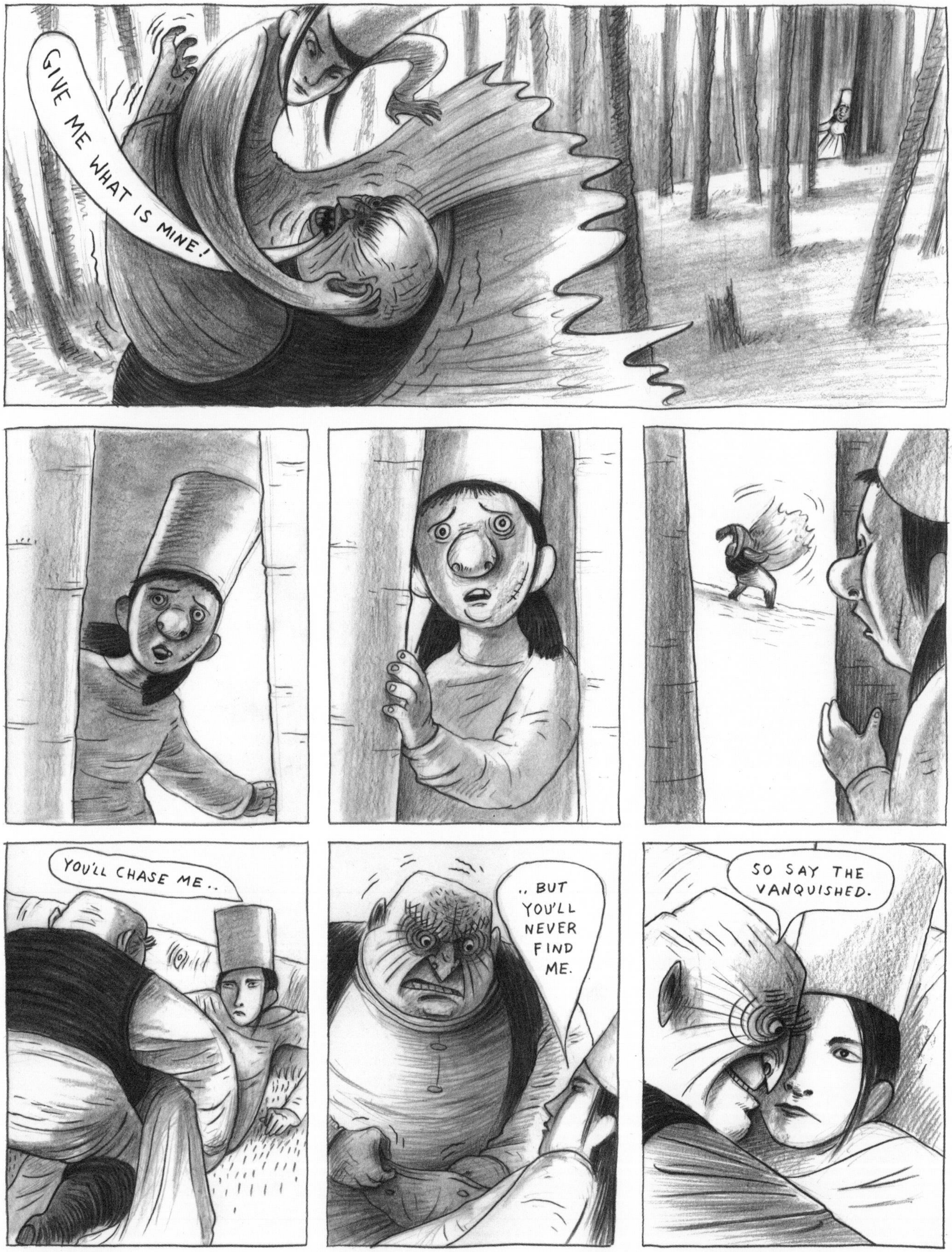
GIVE ME WHAT IS MINE!
YOU'LL CHASE ME..
.. BUT YOU'LL NEVER FIND ME.
SO SAY THE VANQUISHED.

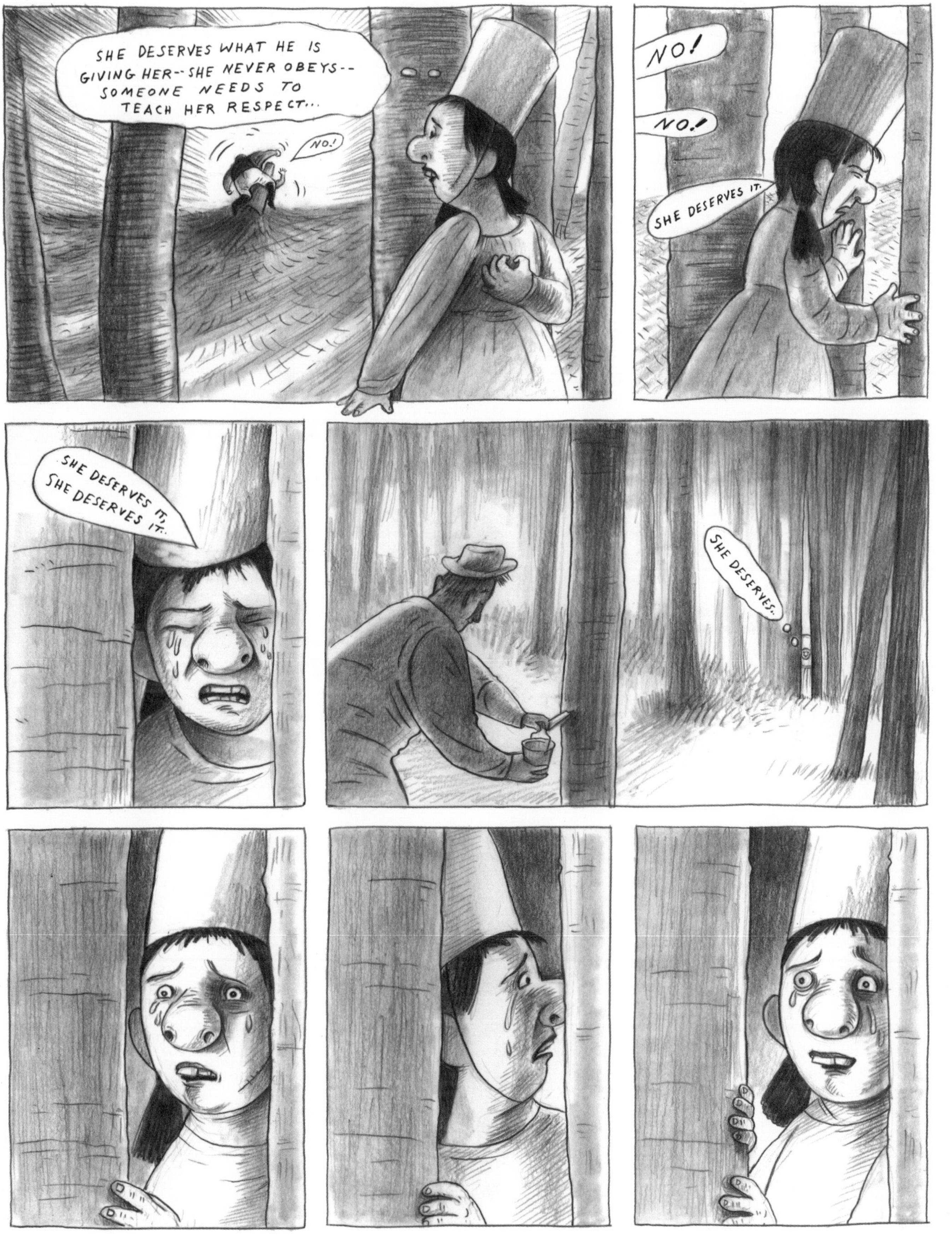
SHE DESERVES WHAT HE IS GIVING HER-- SHE NEVER OBEYS-- SOMEONE NEEDS TO TEACH HER RESPECT...
NO!
NO!
NO!
SHE DESERVES IT.
SHE DESERVES IT, SHE DESERVES IT.
SHE DESERVES.

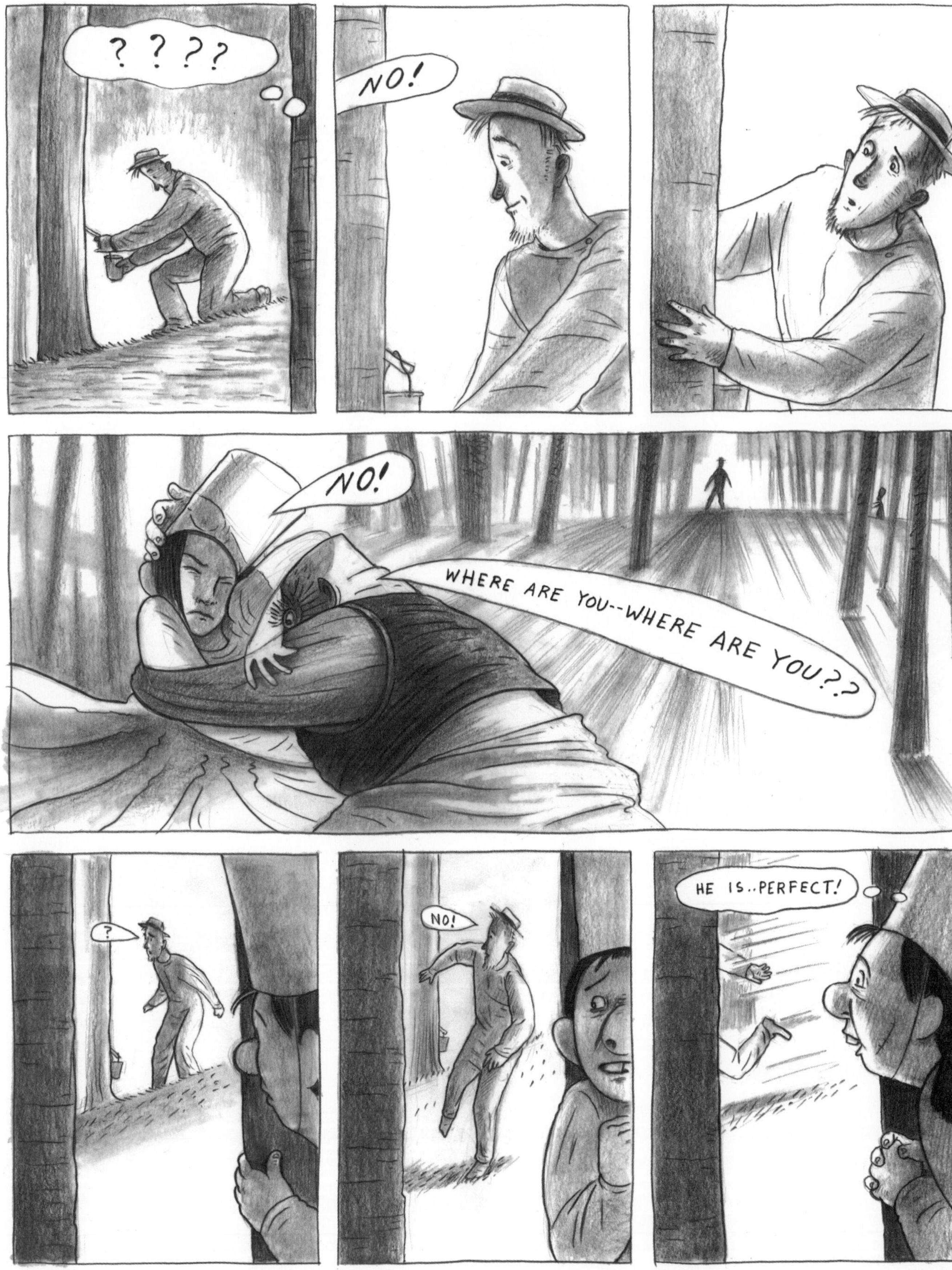
? ? ? ?
NO!
NO!
WHERE ARE YOU--WHERE ARE YOU??
?
NO!
HE IS..PERFECT!

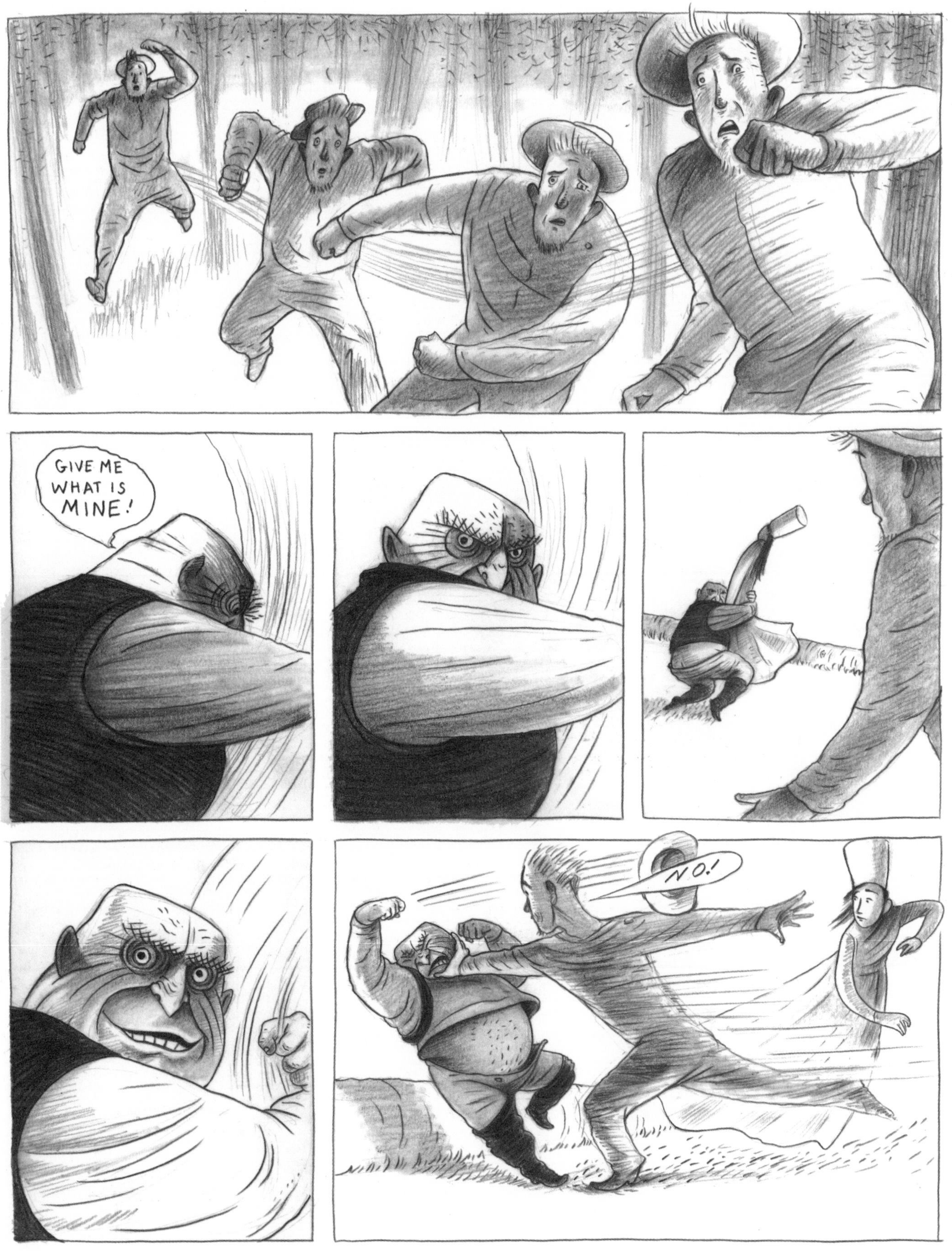
GIVE ME WHAT IS MINE!
NO!

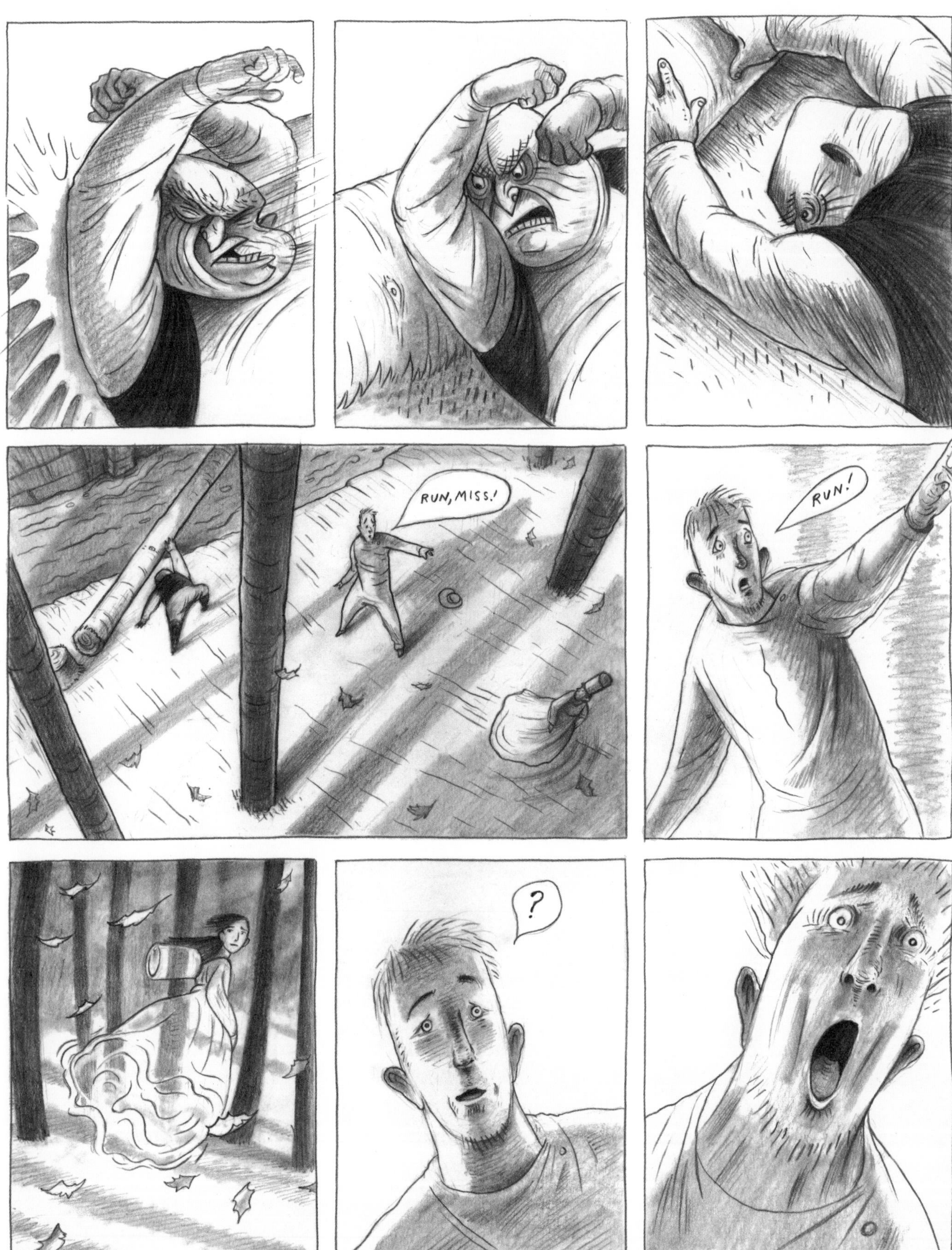
RUN, MISS!
RUN!
?

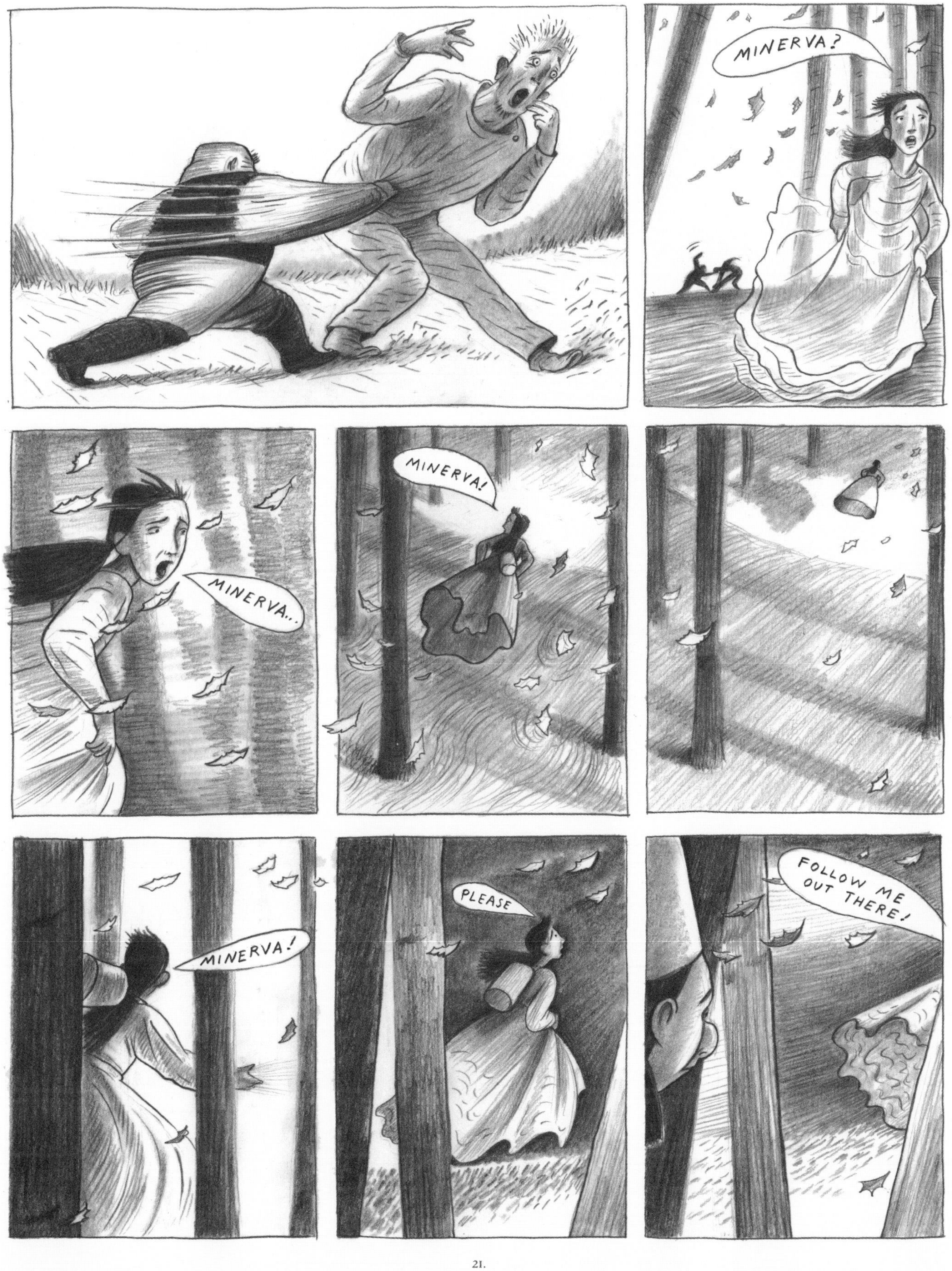
MINERVA?
MINERVA...
MINERVA!
MINERVA!
PLEASE
FOLLOW ME OUT THERE!

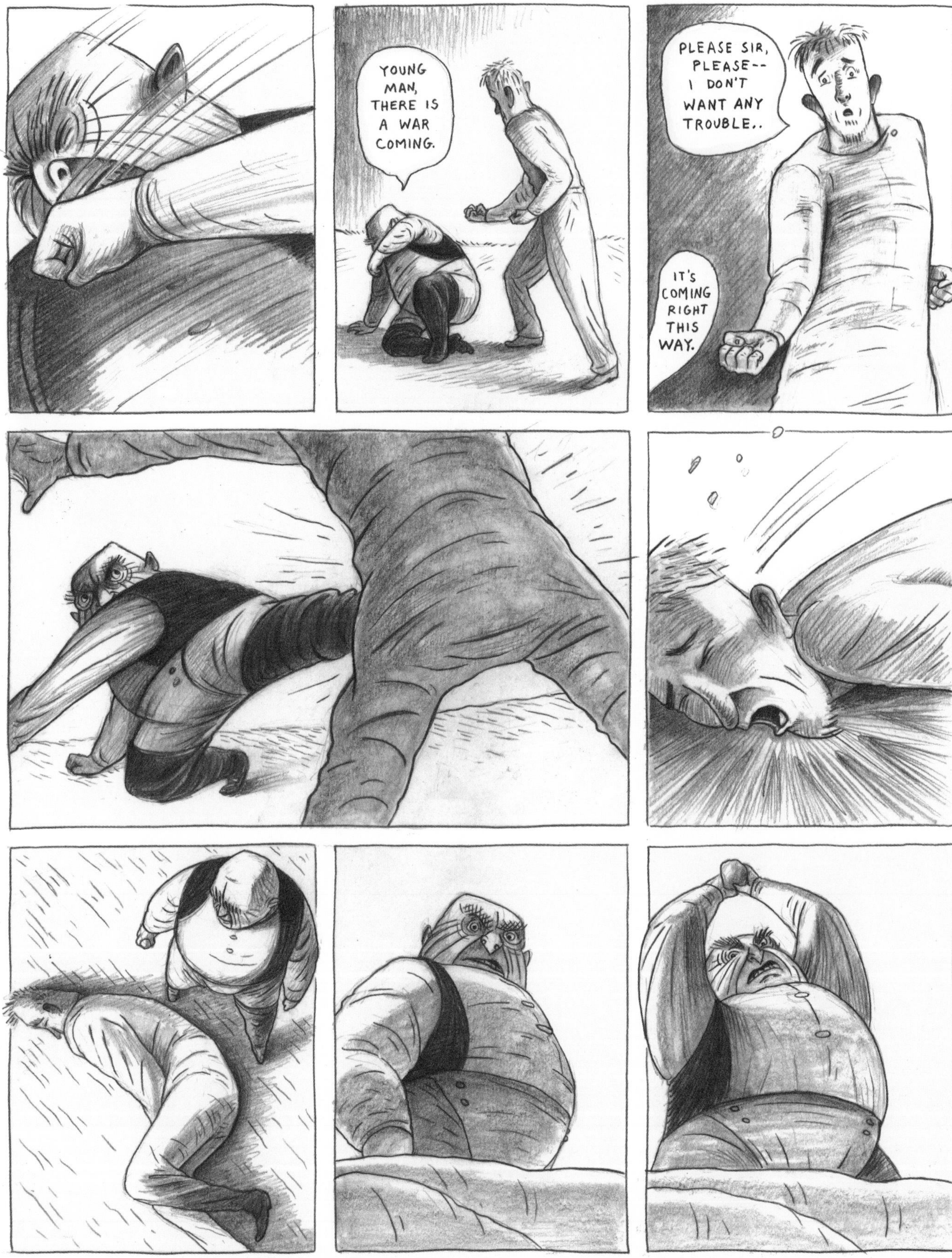
YOUNG MAN, THERE IS A WAR COMING.
PLEASE SIR, PLEASE-- I DON'T WANT ANY TROUBLE..
IT'S COMING RIGHT THIS WAY.

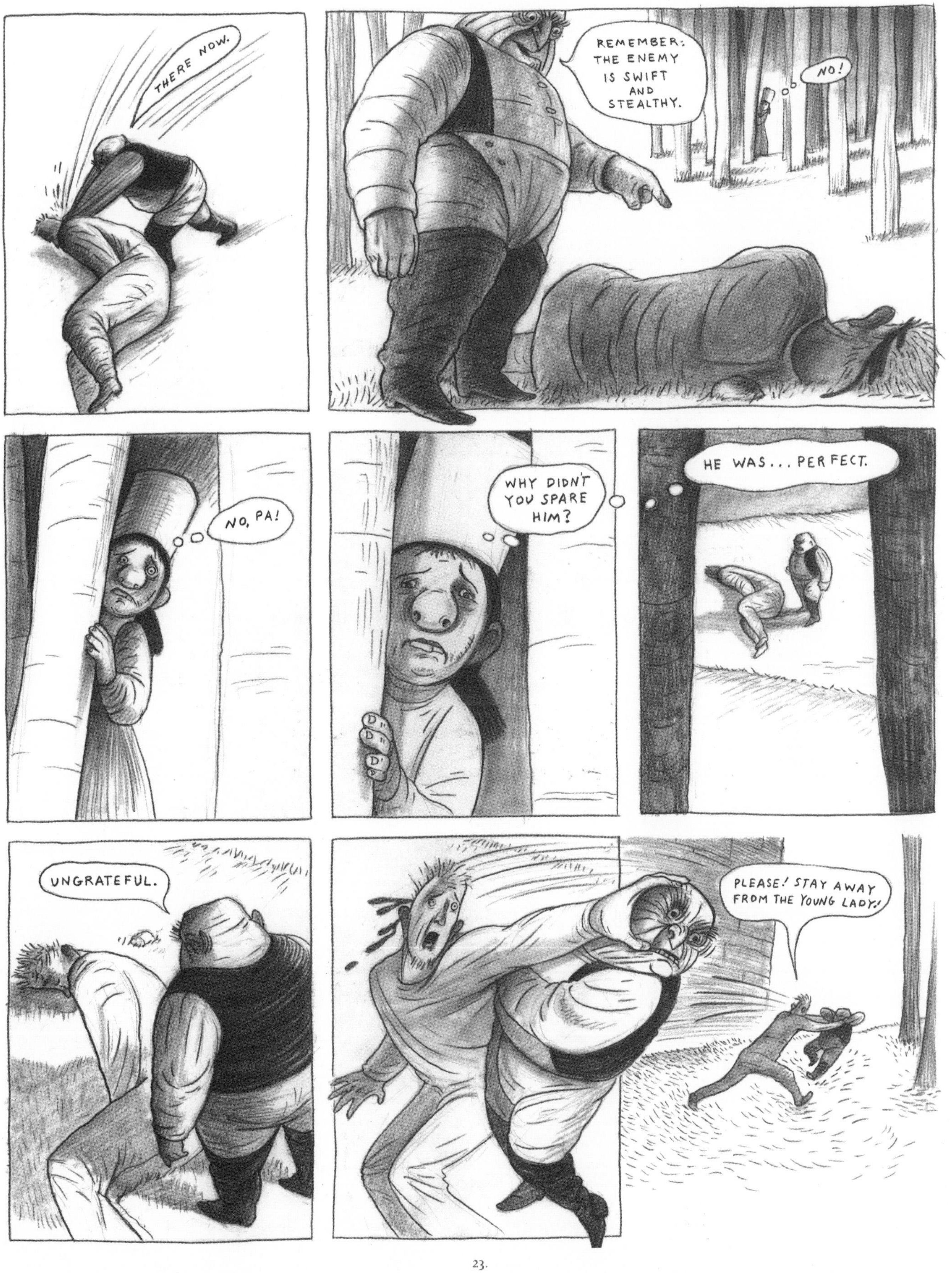
THERE NOW.
REMEMBER: THE ENEMY IS SWIFT AND STEALTHY.
NO!
NO, PA!
WHY DIDN'T YOU SPARE HIM?
HE WAS... PERFECT.
UNGRATEFUL.
PLEASE! STAY AWAY FROM THE YOUNG LADY!

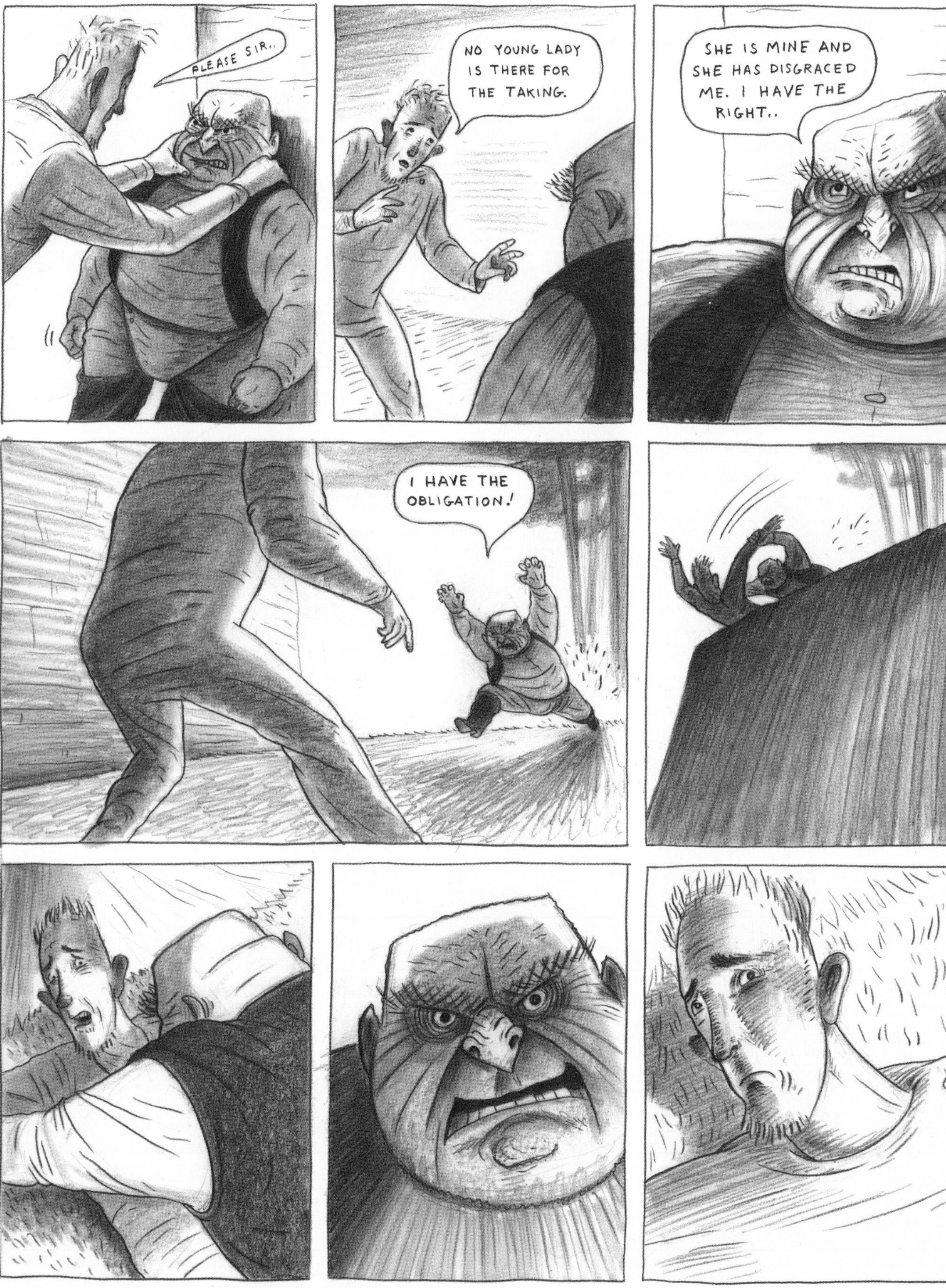
PLEASE SIR..
NO YOUNG LADY IS THERE FOR THE TAKING.
SHE IS MINE AND SHE HAS DISGRACED ME. I HAVE THE RIGHT..
I HAVE THE OBLIGATION!

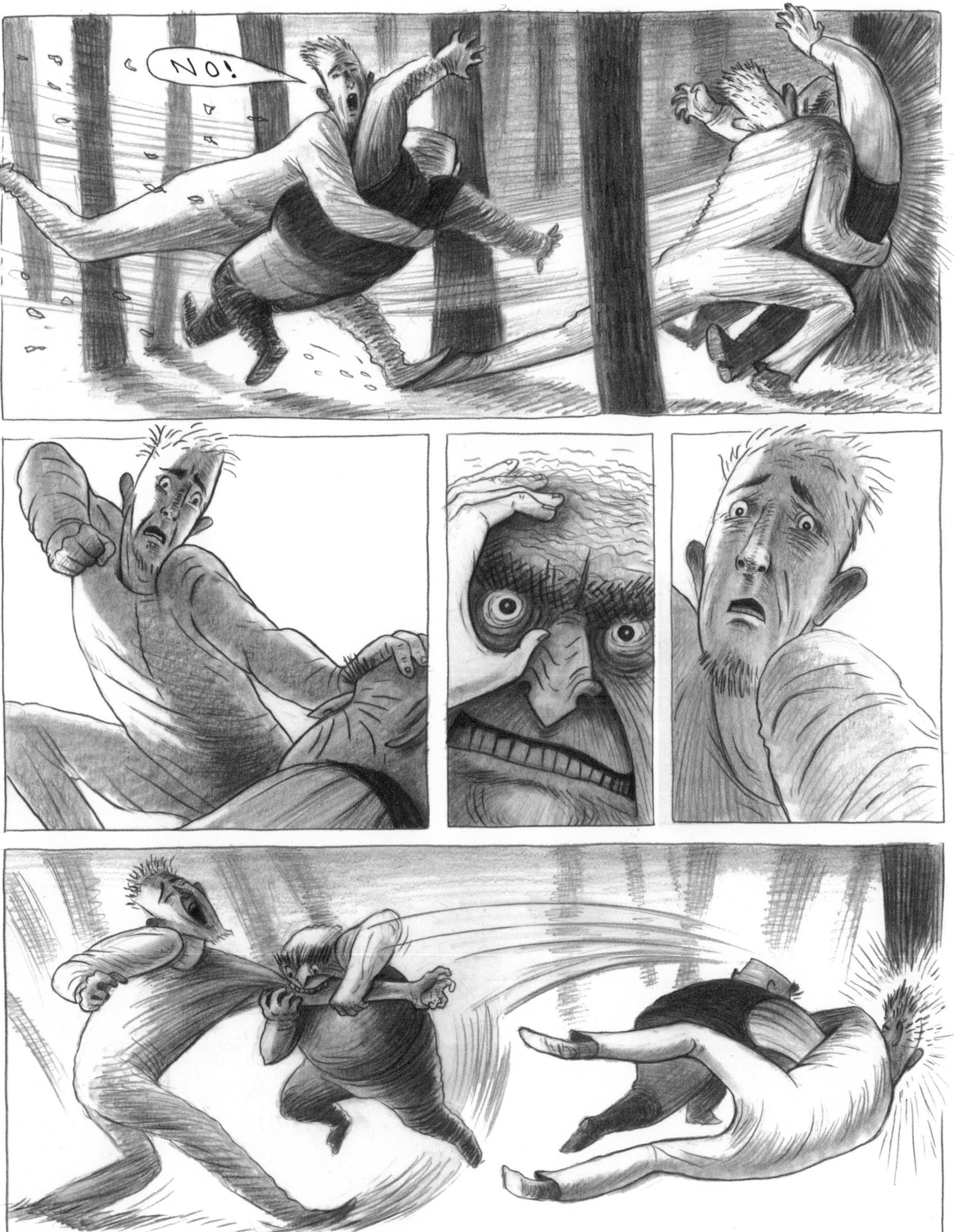
NO!

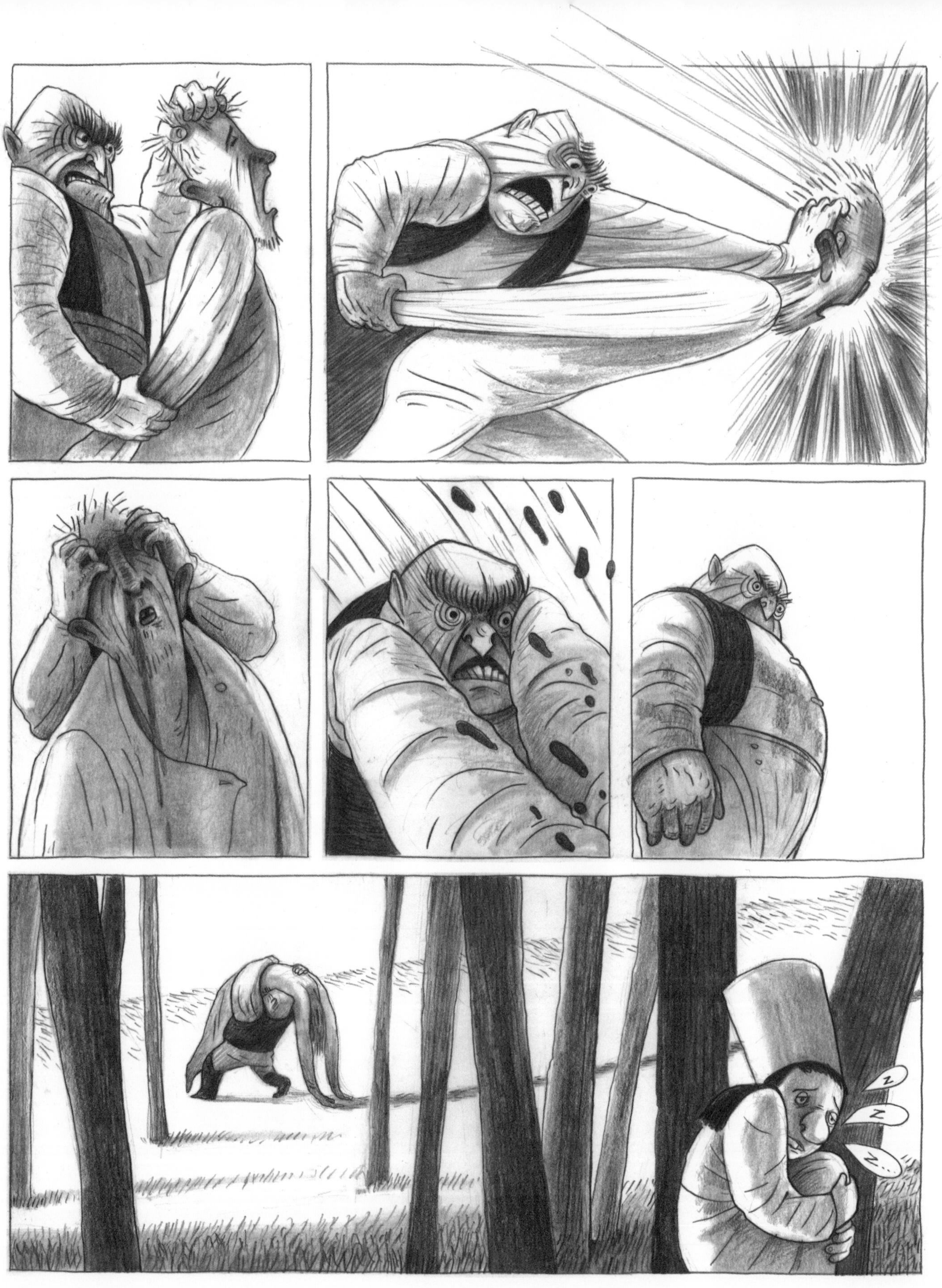
Z
Z
Z...

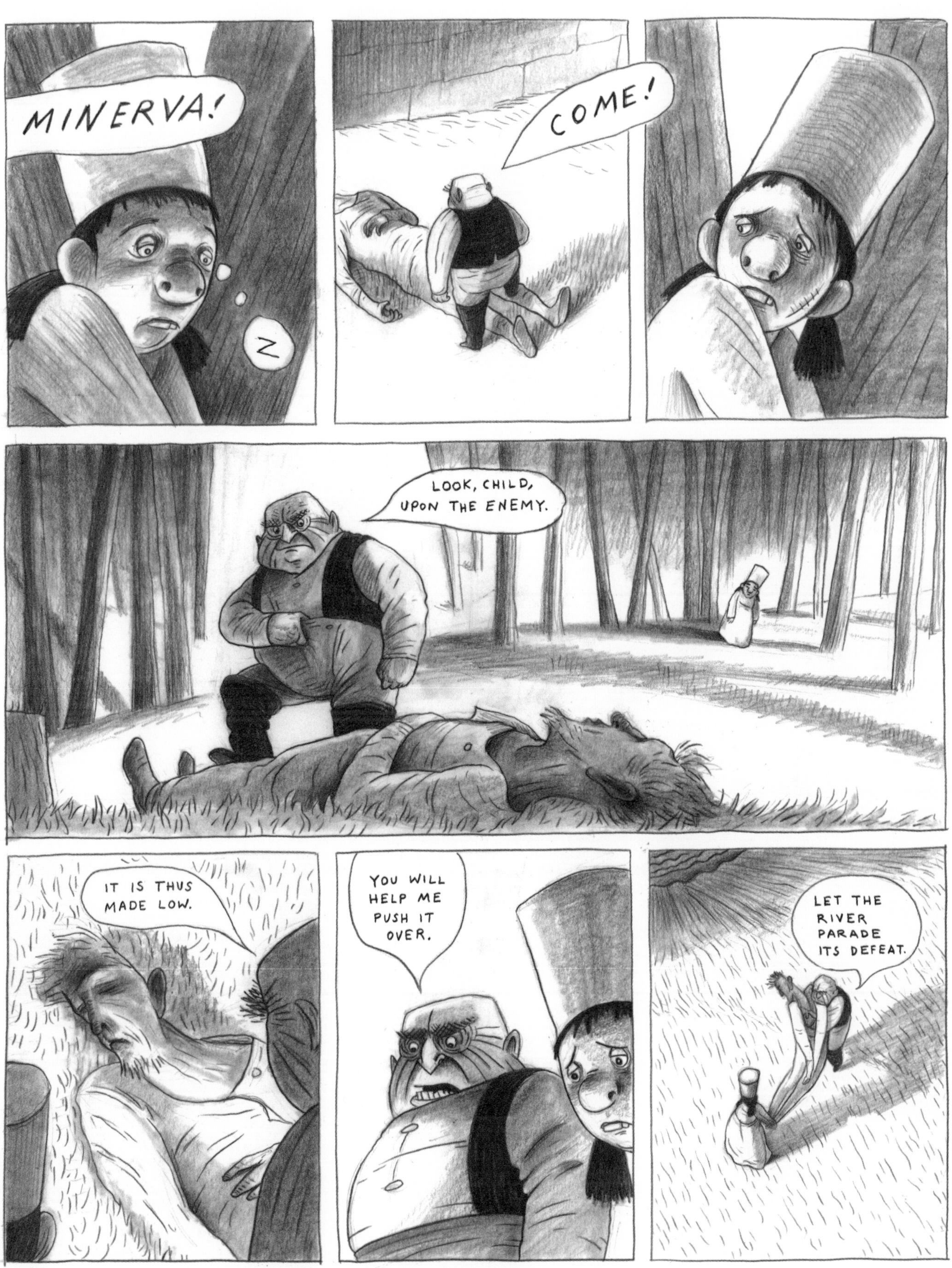

MINERVA!
Z
COME!
LOOK, CHILD, UPON THE ENEMY.
IT IS THUS MADE LOW.
YOU WILL HELP ME PUSH IT OVER.
LET THE RIVER PARADE ITS DEFEAT.

THERE ARE MORE LIKE THIS; MANY MORE.
HE.. WAS.. PERFECT..
WE SHALL VANQUISH THEM ALL..
YOU HAVE A LOOK OF WEAKNESS, CHILD.

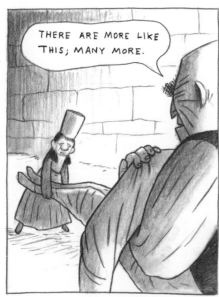

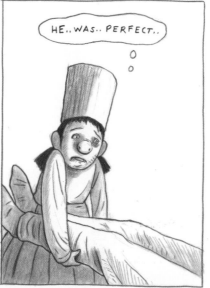

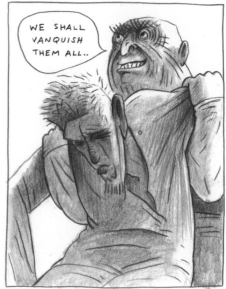

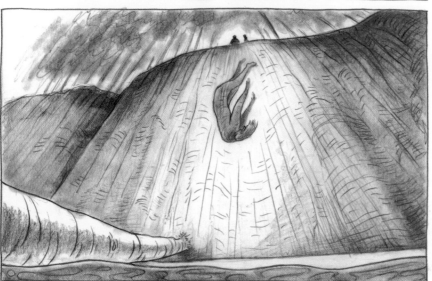

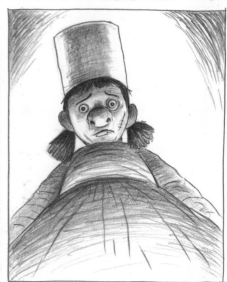

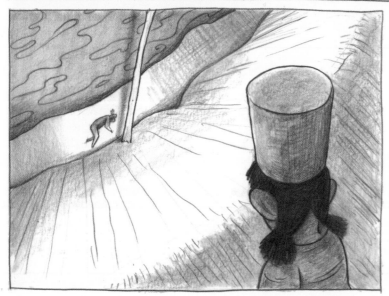

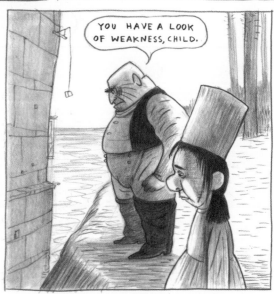

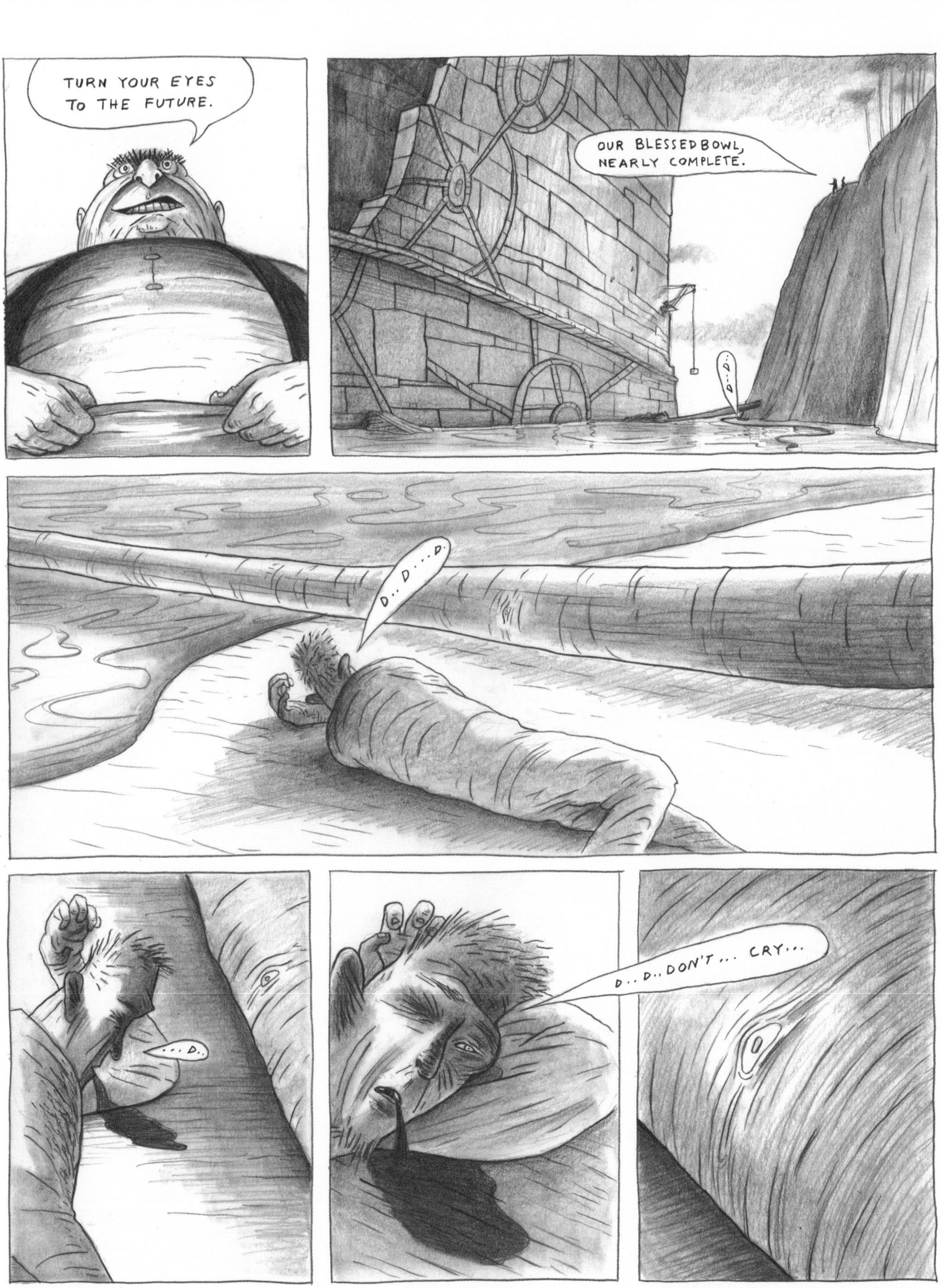
TURN YOUR EYES TO THE FUTURE.
OUR BLESSEDBOWL, NEARLY COMPLETE.
D..D...D.
...D.
D..D..DON'T... CRY...

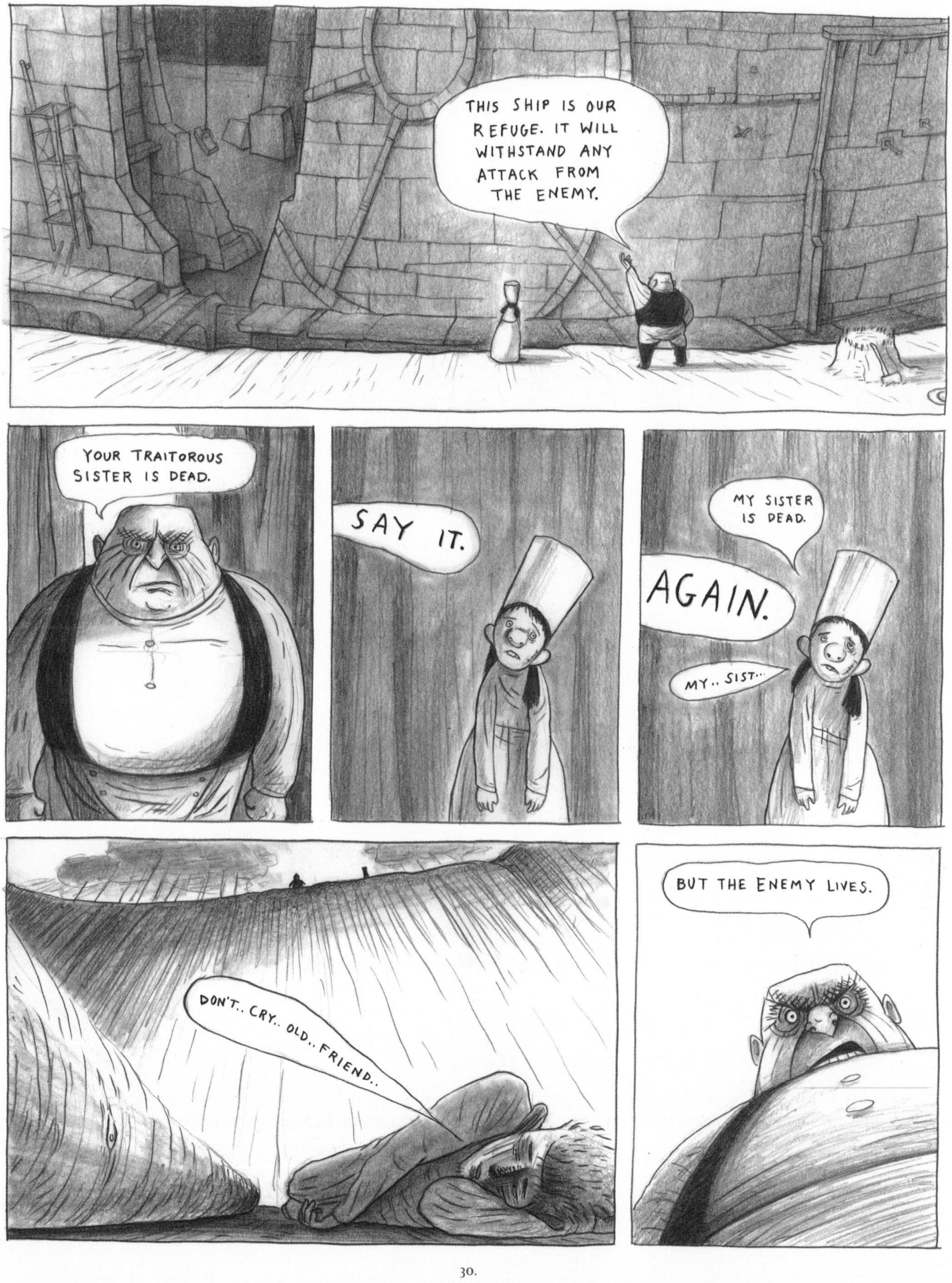
THIS SHIP IS OUR REFUGE. IT WILL WITHSTAND ANY ATTACK FROM THE ENEMY.
YOUR TRAITOROUS SISTER IS DEAD.
SAY IT.
MY SISTER IS DEAD.
AGAIN.
MY.. SIST...
DON'T.. CRY.. OLD.. FRIEND..
BUT THE ENEMY LIVES.

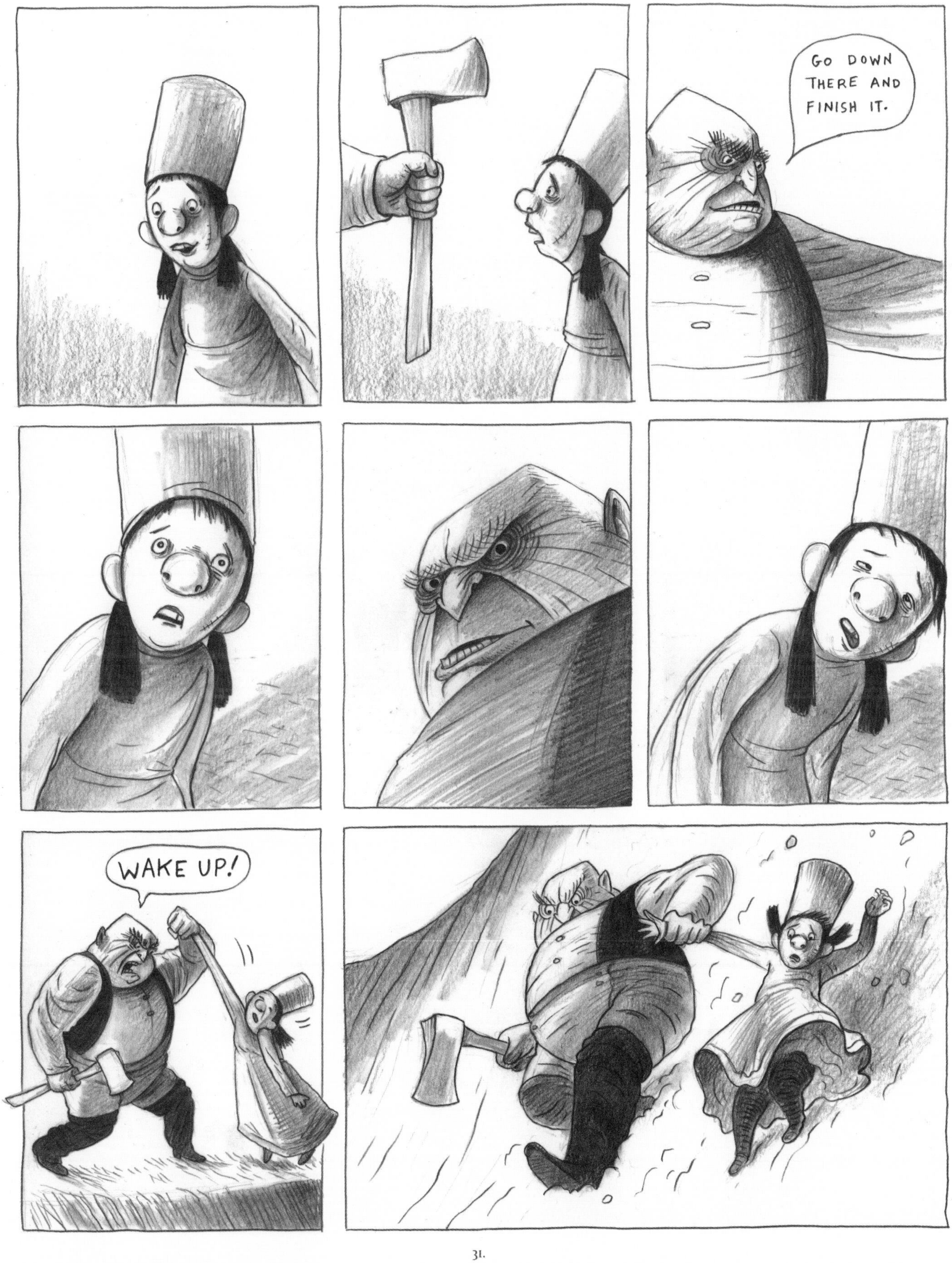
GO DOWN THERE AND FINISH IT.
WAKE UP!

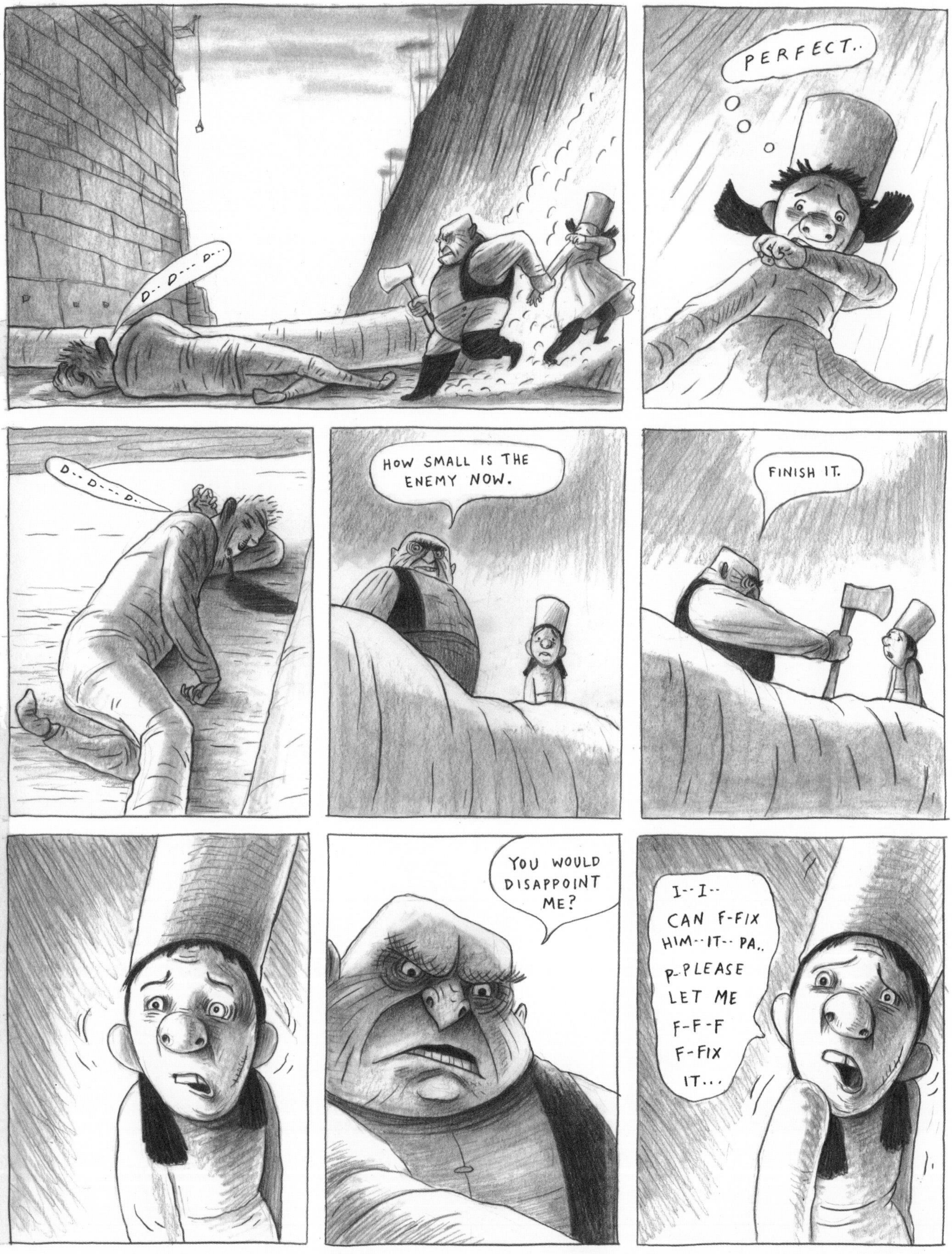
D-- D--- D---
PERFECT..
D-- D--- D-
HOW SMALL IS THE ENEMY NOW.
FINISH IT.
YOU WOULD DISAPPOINT ME?
I-- I-- CAN F-FIX HIM-- IT-- PA.. P-PLEASE LET ME F-F-F F-FIX IT...

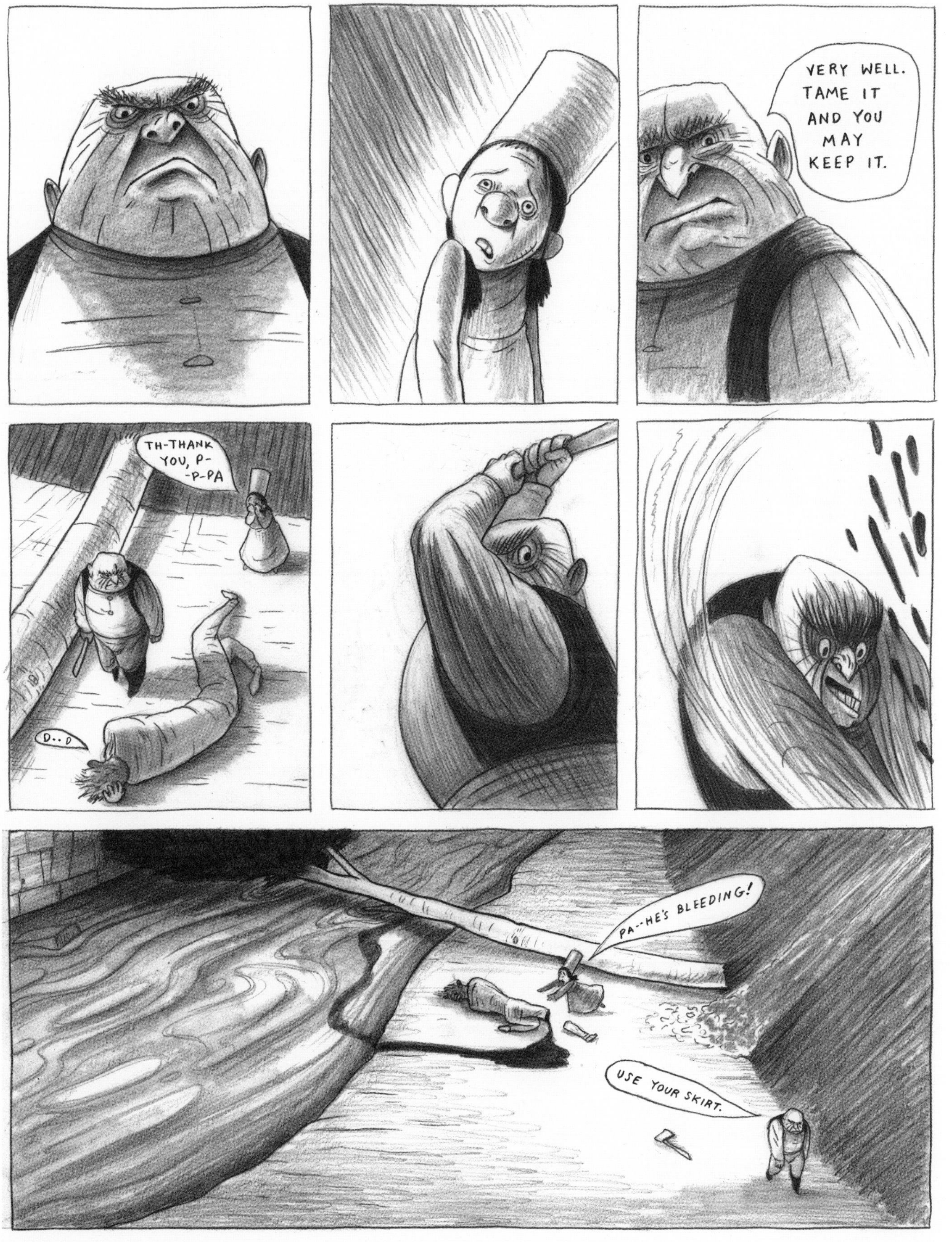
VERY WELL. TAME IT AND YOU MAY KEEP IT.
TH-THANK YOU, P- -P-PA
D..D
PA--HE'S BLEEDING!
USE YOUR SKIRT.

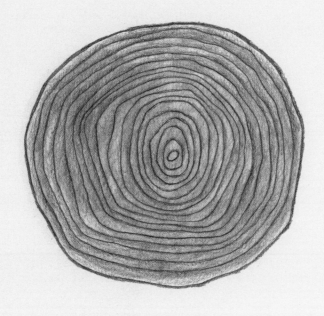

Part Two

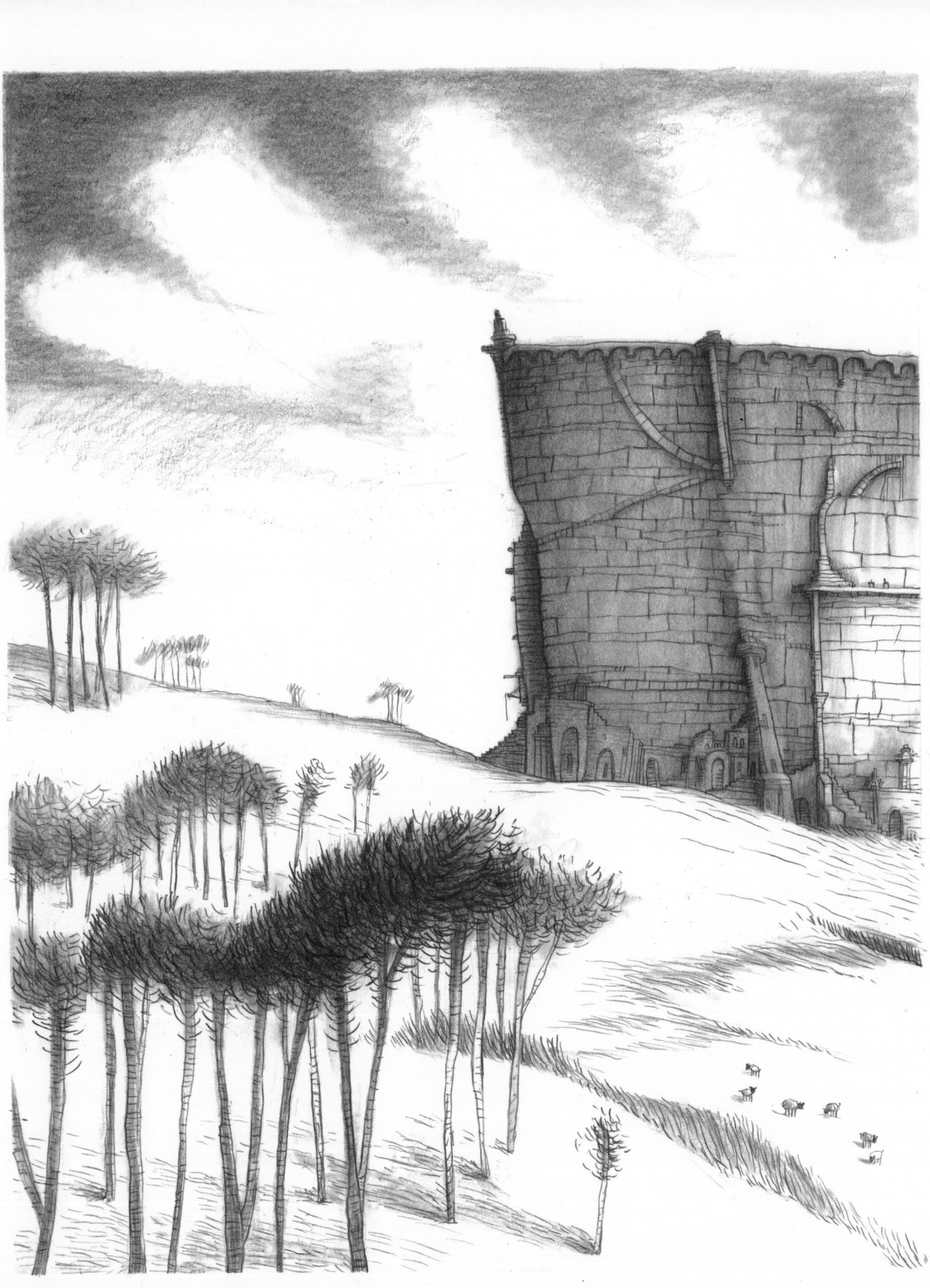

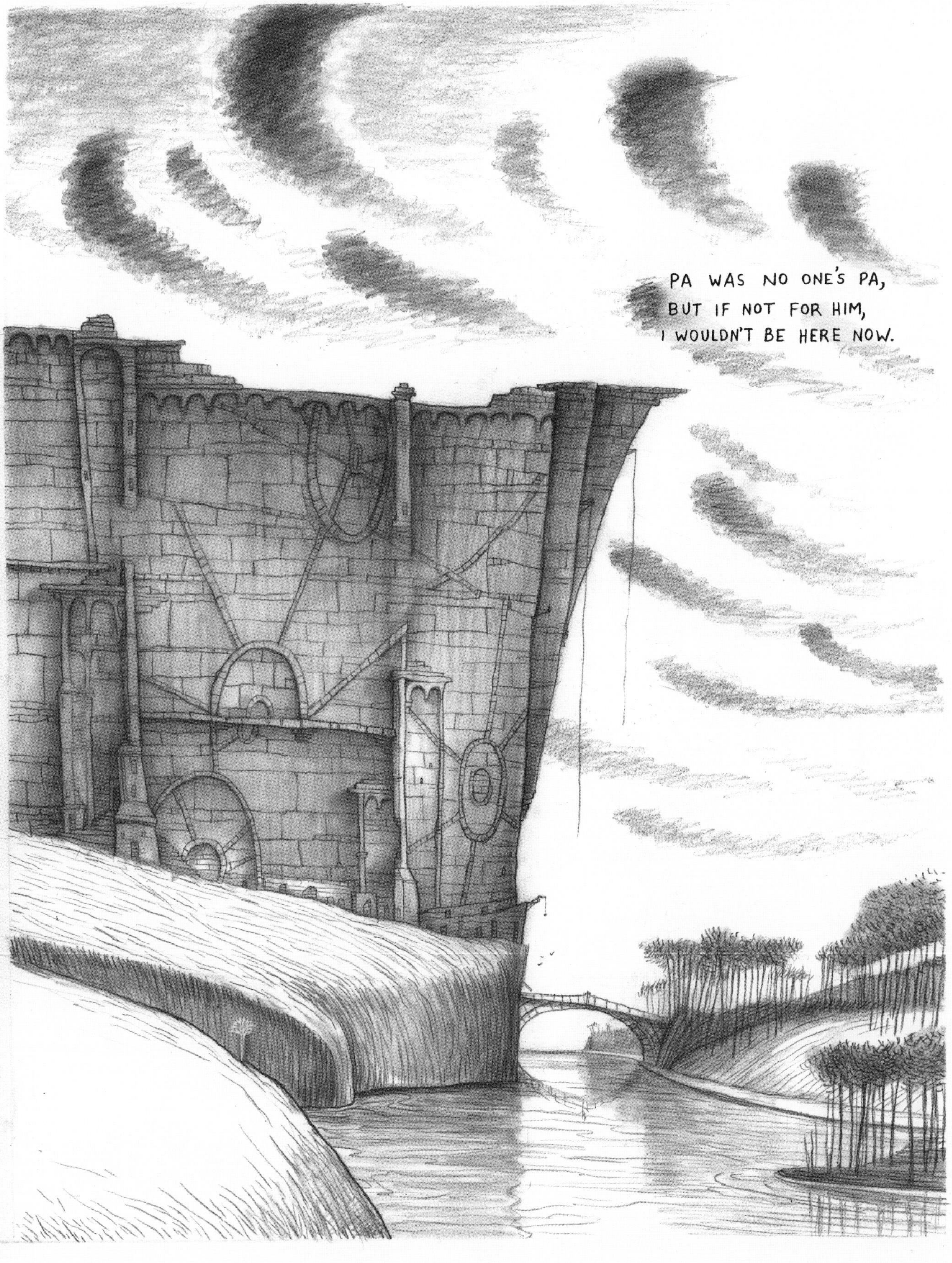
PA WAS NO ONE'S PA,
BUT IF NOT FOR HIM,
I WOULDN'T BE HERE NOW.

IT WAS GOOD THAT HE CUT ME DOWN.

AS A TREE I HAD ALWAYS BEEN TROUBLESOME..

..SHAKING, MAKING A MESS..

THINKING BACK, WHAT I MISSED MOST WERE THE BIRDS. THEY WERE FINE GOSSIPS.

I CRAVED THEIR NEWS AS MUCH AS I ENVIED THEM..

..STUCK, AS I WAS, IN THAT SPOT.

BLESSEDBOWL WAS NOT QUITE FINISHED BACK THEN.

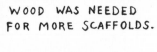

WOOD WAS NEEDED FOR MORE SCAFFOLDS.

I WAS ENLISTED.

38.

.. BUT MY SHAKING PROVED TROUBLESOME..

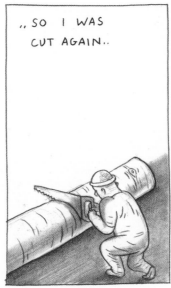

.. SO I WAS CUT AGAIN..

.. AND STORED FOR FUEL.

BUT EVERYTHING HAS A WAY OF COMING BACK AROUND.

I WAS PLUCKED FROM THERE TO SERVE ANOTHER PURPOSE..

I LEARNED TO CONTROL MY SHAKING..

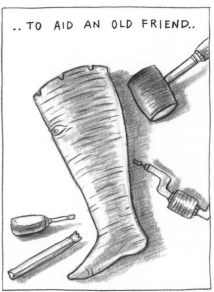

.. TO AID AN OLD FRIEND..

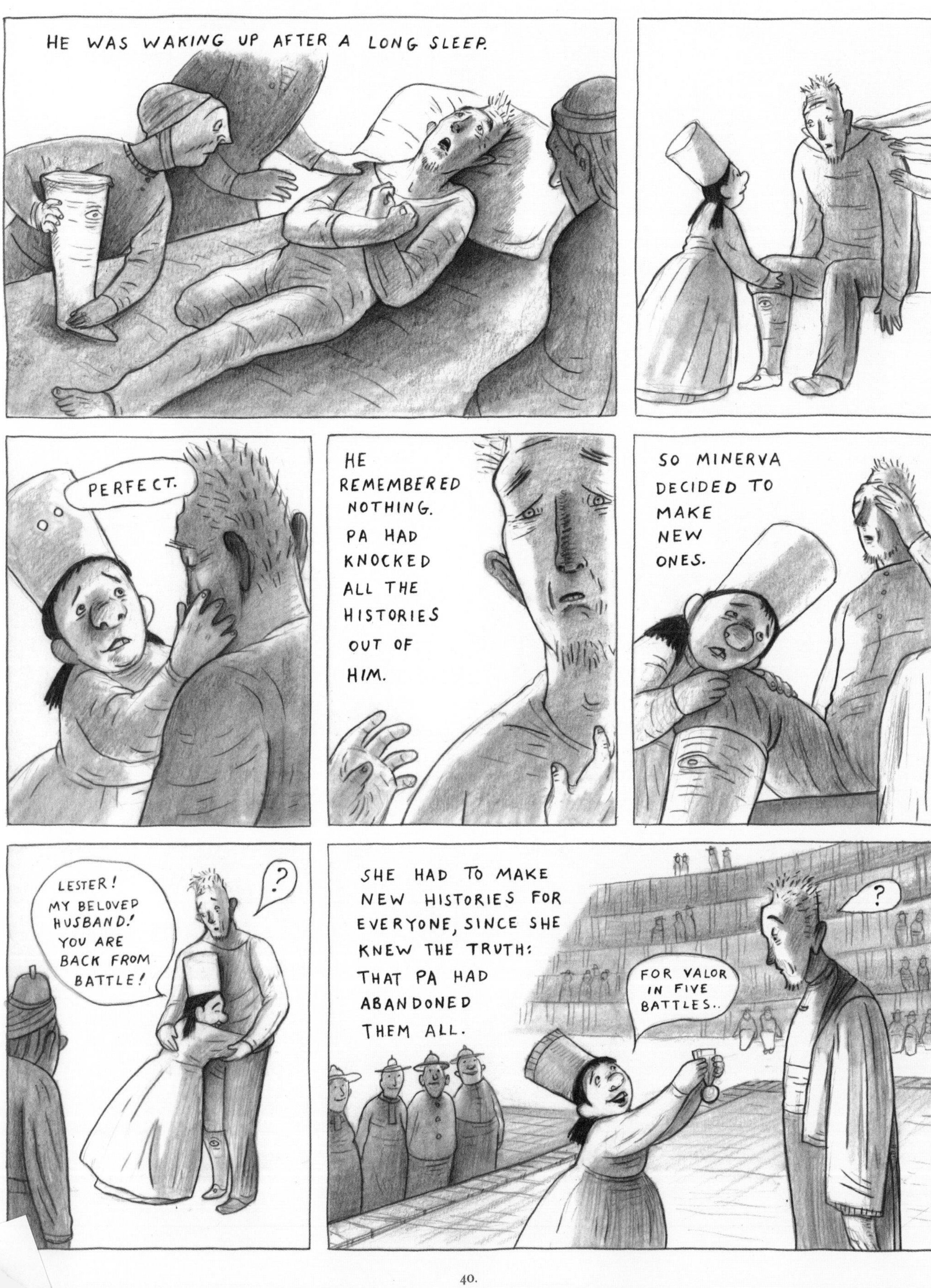
HE WAS WAKING UP AFTER A LONG SLEEP.
PERFECT.
HE REMEMBERED NOTHING. PA HAD KNOCKED ALL THE HISTORIES OUT OF HIM.
SO MINERVA DECIDED TO MAKE NEW ONES.
LESTER! MY BELOVED HUSBAND! YOU ARE BACK FROM BATTLE!
?
SHE HAD TO MAKE NEW HISTORIES FOR EVERYONE, SINCE SHE KNEW THE TRUTH: THAT PA HAD ABANDONED THEM ALL.
FOR VALOR IN FIVE BATTLES..
?

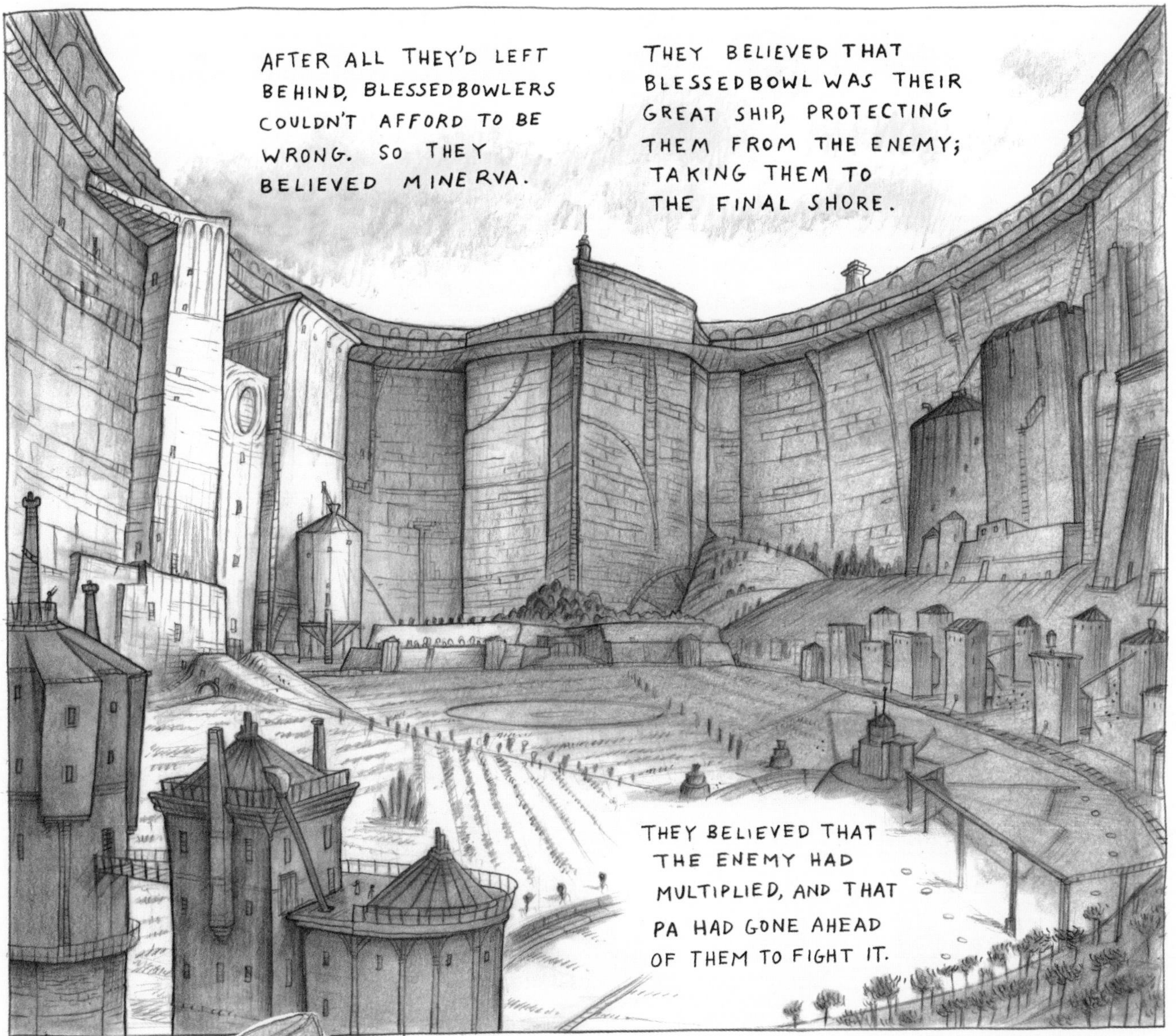
AFTER ALL THEY'D LEFT BEHIND, BLESSEDBOWLERS COULDN'T AFFORD TO BE WRONG. SO THEY BELIEVED MINERVA.
THEY BELIEVED THAT BLESSEDBOWL WAS THEIR GREAT SHIP, PROTECTING THEM FROM THE ENEMY; TAKING THEM TO THE FINAL SHORE.
THEY BELIEVED THAT THE ENEMY HAD MULTIPLIED, AND THAT PA HAD GONE AHEAD OF THEM TO FIGHT IT.

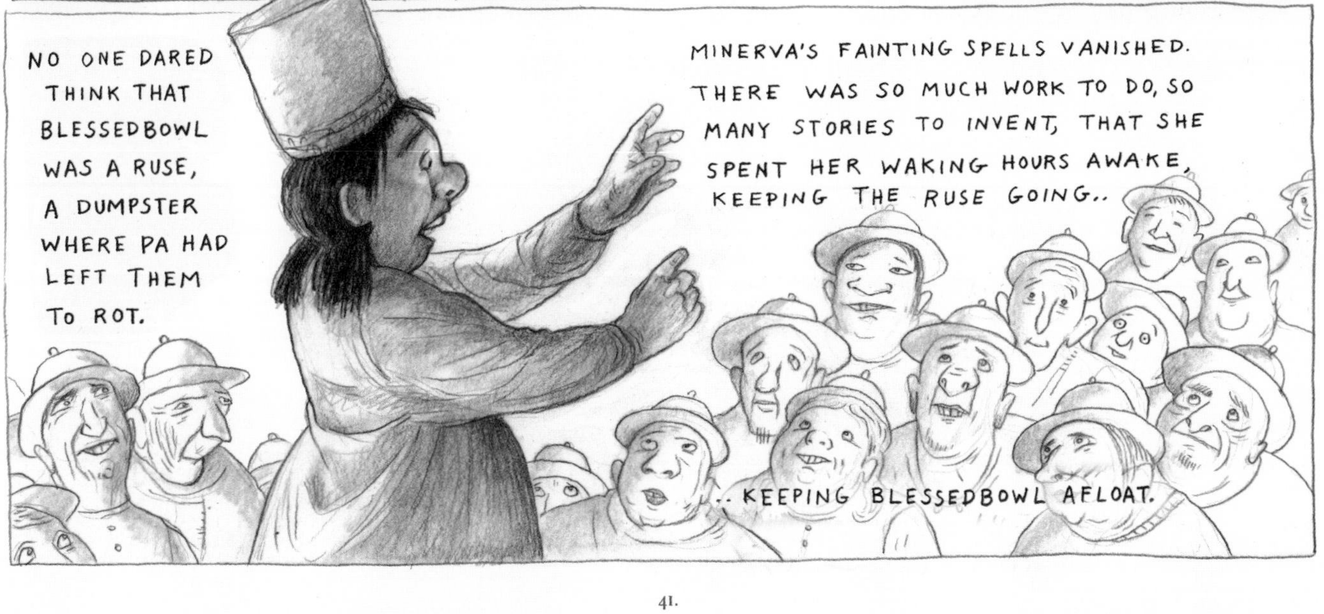
NO ONE DARED THINK THAT BLESSEDBOWL WAS A RUSE, A DUMPSTER WHERE PA HAD LEFT THEM TO ROT.
MINERVA'S FAINTING SPELLS VANISHED. THERE WAS SO MUCH WORK TO DO, SO MANY STORIES TO INVENT, THAT SHE SPENT HER WAKING HOURS AWAKE, KEEPING THE RUSE GOING..
.. KEEPING BLESSEDBOWL AFLOAT.

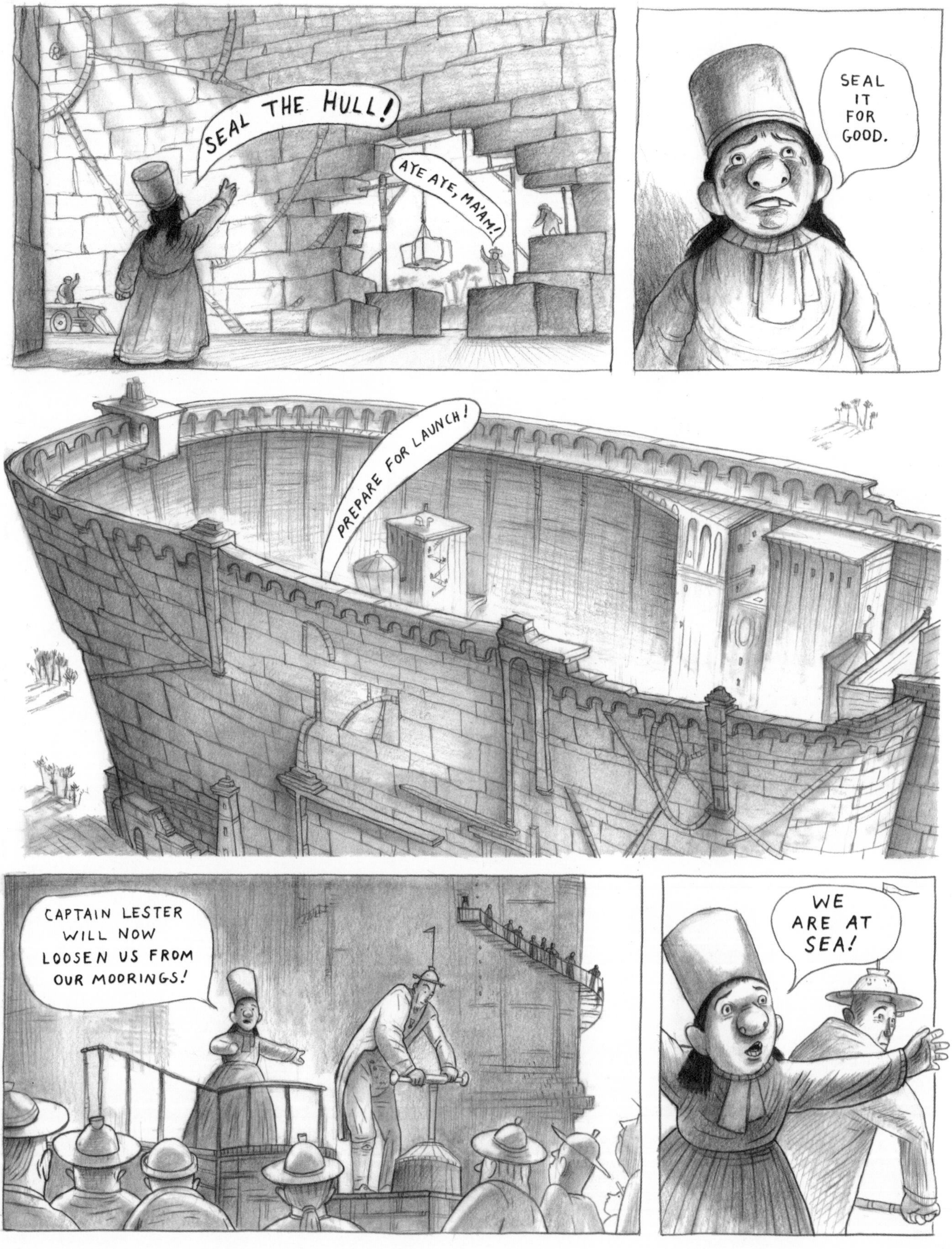
SEAL THE HULL!
AYE AYE, MA'AM!
SEAL IT FOR GOOD.
PREPARE FOR LAUNCH!
CAPTAIN LESTER WILL NOW LOOSEN US FROM OUR MOORINGS!
WE ARE AT SEA!

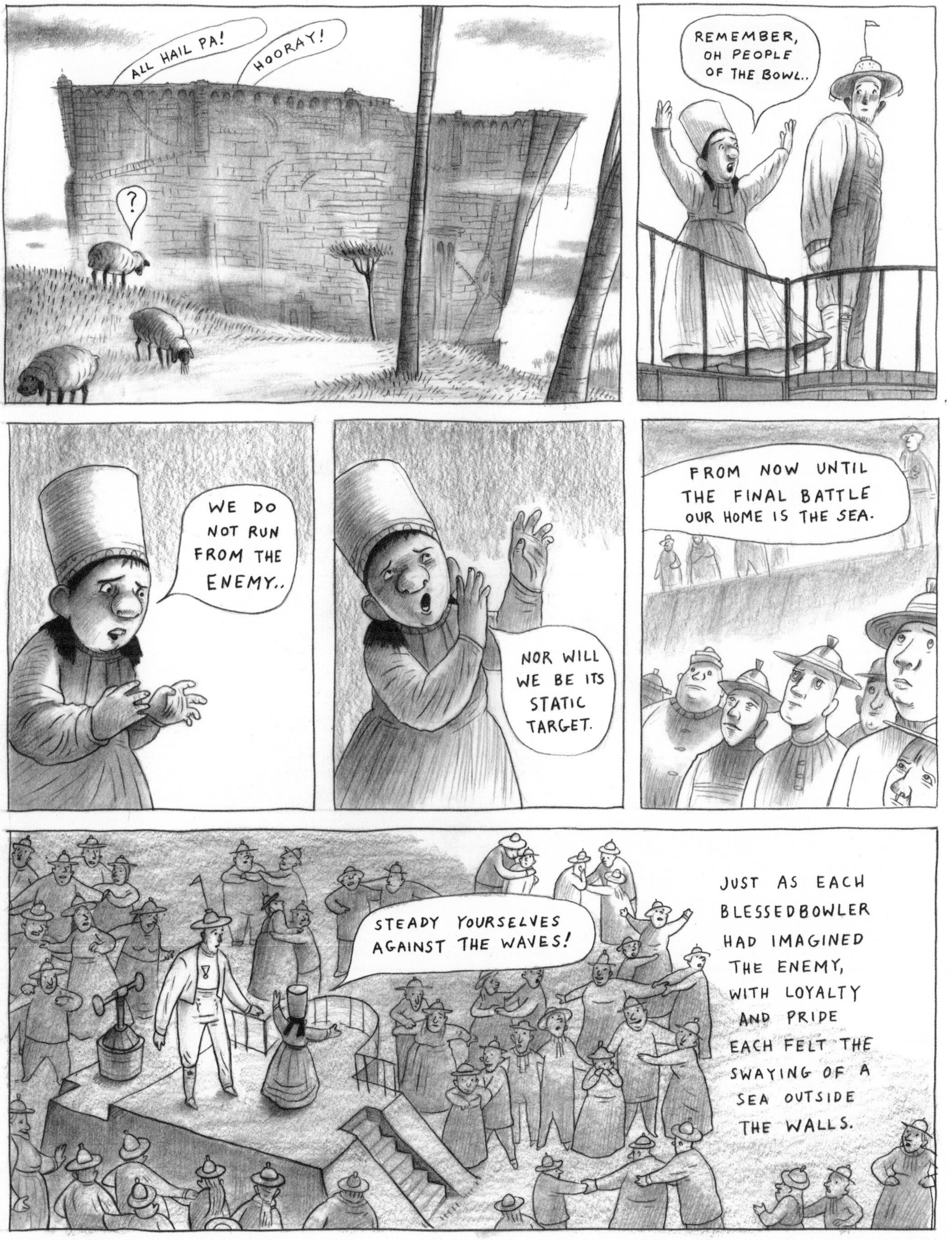
ALL HAIL PA!
HOORAY!
?
REMEMBER, OH PEOPLE OF THE BOWL..
WE DO NOT RUN FROM THE ENEMY..
NOR WILL WE BE ITS STATIC TARGET.
FROM NOW UNTIL THE FINAL BATTLE OUR HOME IS THE SEA.
STEADY YOURSELVES AGAINST THE WAVES!
JUST AS EACH BLESSEDBOWLER HAD IMAGINED THE ENEMY, WITH LOYALTY AND PRIDE EACH FELT THE SWAYING OF A SEA OUTSIDE THE WALLS.

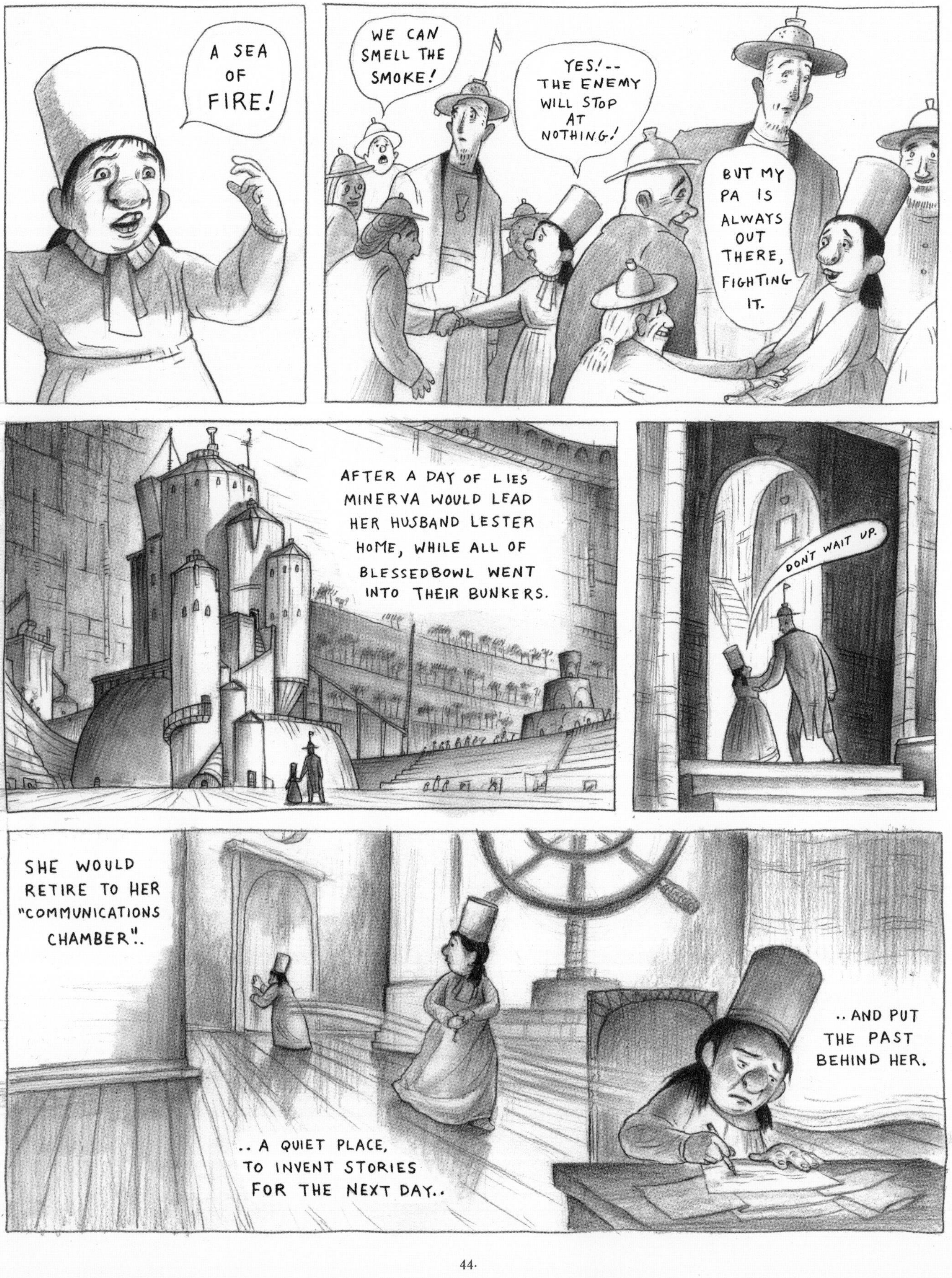
A SEA OF FIRE!
WE CAN SMELL THE SMOKE!
YES!-- THE ENEMY WILL STOP AT NOTHING!
BUT MY PA IS ALWAYS OUT THERE, FIGHTING IT.
AFTER A DAY OF LIES MINERVA WOULD LEAD HER HUSBAND LESTER HOME, WHILE ALL OF BLESSEDBOWL WENT INTO THEIR BUNKERS.
DON'T WAIT UP.
SHE WOULD RETIRE TO HER "COMMUNICATIONS CHAMBER"..
.. A QUIET PLACE, TO INVENT STORIES FOR THE NEXT DAY..
.. AND PUT THE PAST BEHIND HER.

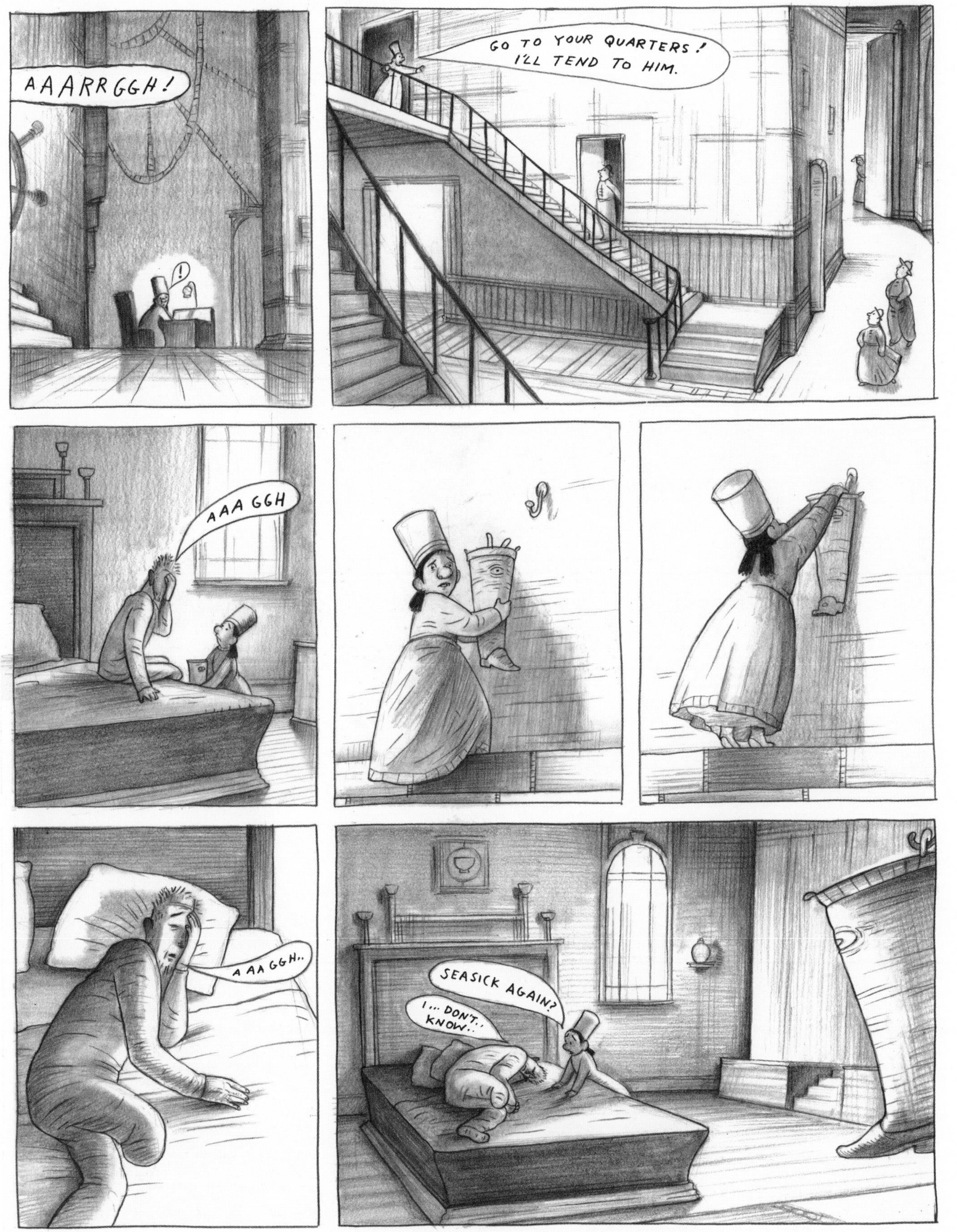
AAARRGGH!
!
GO TO YOUR QUARTERS! I'LL TEND TO HIM.
AAAGGH
AAAGGH..
SEASICK AGAIN?
I... DON'T. KNOW..

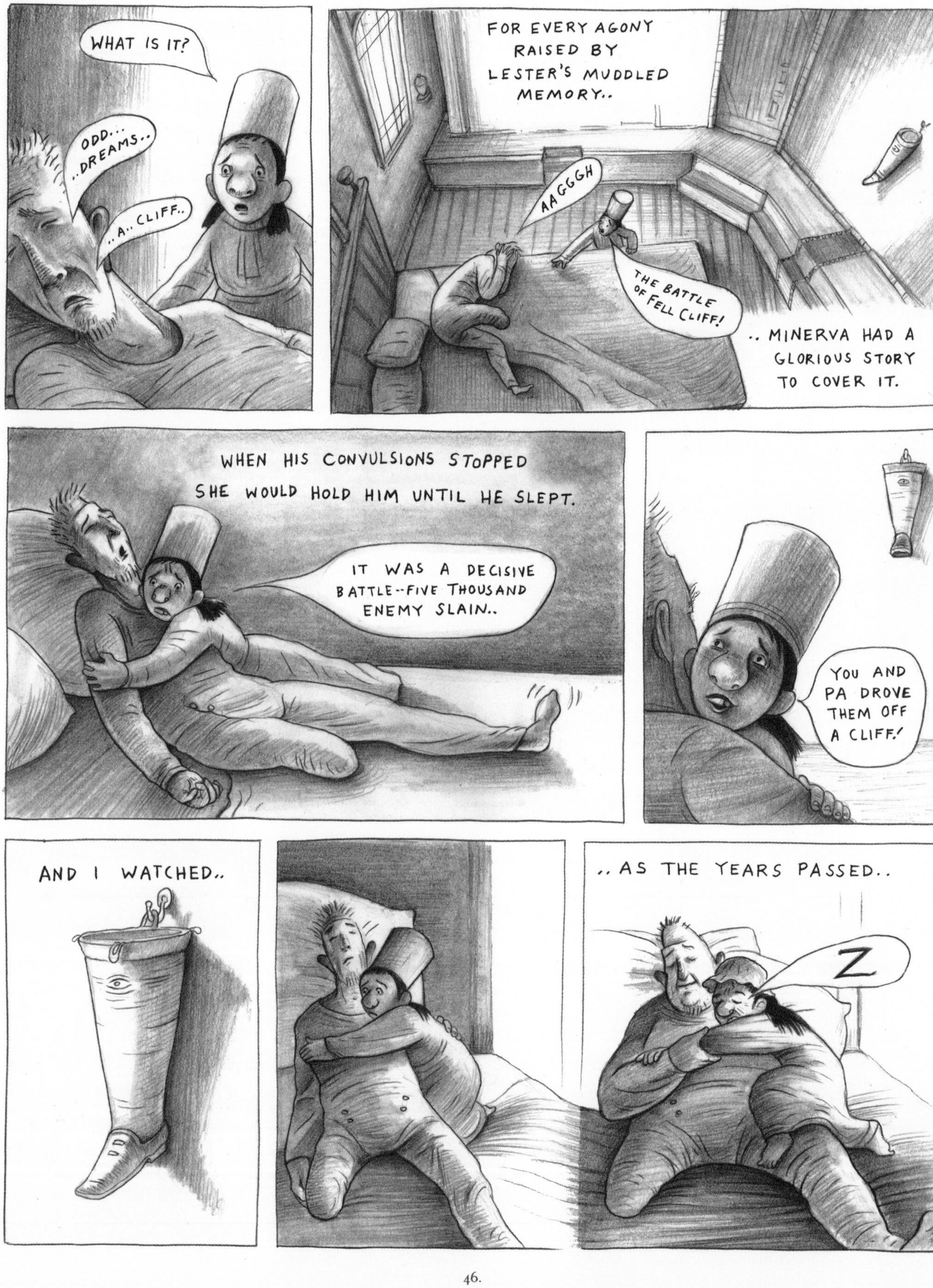
WHAT IS IT?
ODD... ..DREAMS..
..A.. CLIFF..
FOR EVERY AGONY RAISED BY LESTER'S MUDDLED MEMORY..
AAGGGH
THE BATTLE OF FELL CLIFF!
.. MINERVA HAD A GLORIOUS STORY TO COVER IT.
WHEN HIS CONVULSIONS STOPPED SHE WOULD HOLD HIM UNTIL HE SLEPT.
IT WAS A DECISIVE BATTLE--FIVE THOUSAND ENEMY SLAIN..
YOU AND PA DROVE THEM OFF A CLIFF!
AND I WATCHED..
.. AS THE YEARS PASSED..
Z

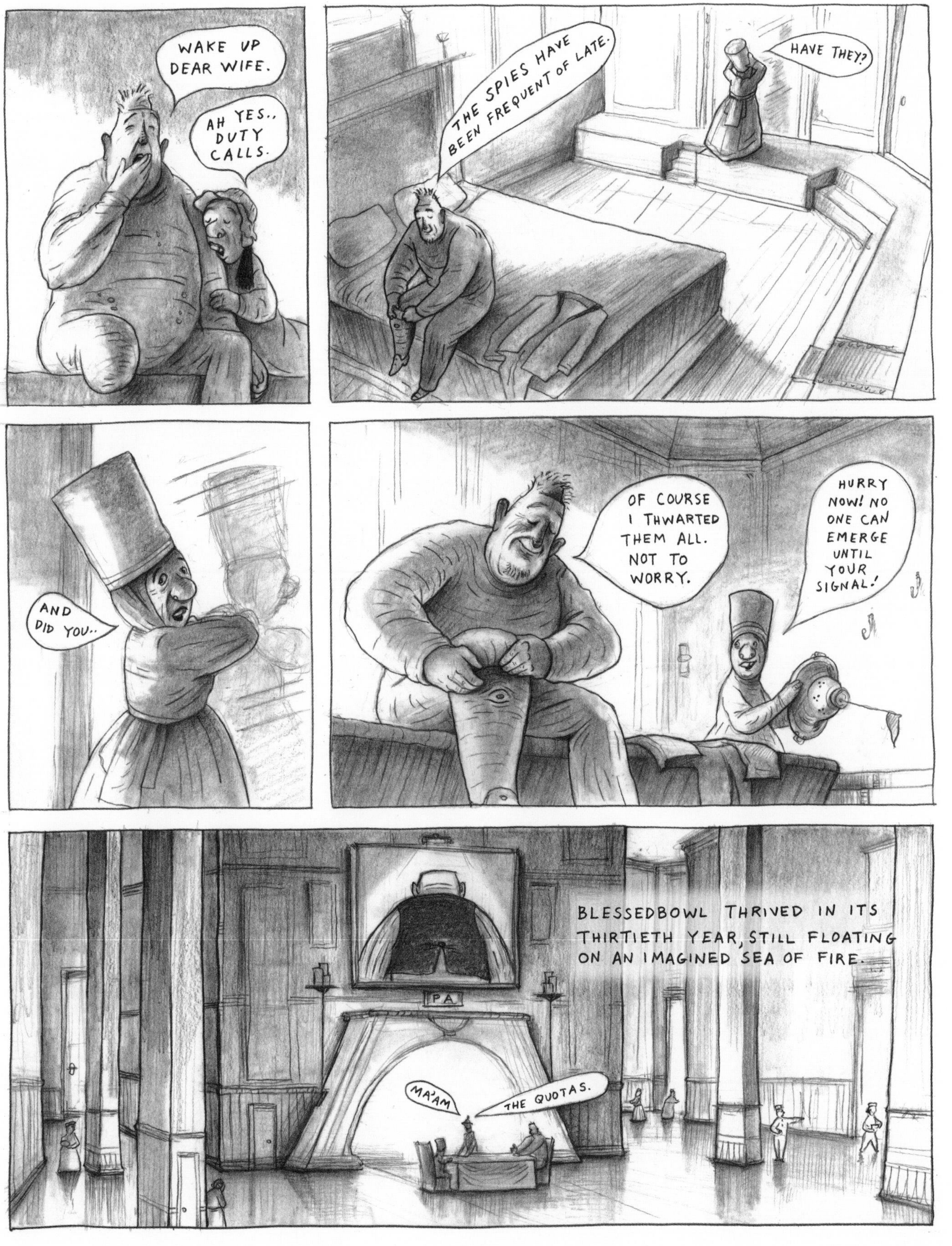
WAKE UP DEAR WIFE.
AH YES.. DUTY CALLS.
THE SPIES HAVE BEEN FREQUENT OF LATE.
HAVE THEY?
AND DID YOU..
OF COURSE I THWARTED THEM ALL. NOT TO WORRY.
HURRY NOW! NO ONE CAN EMERGE UNTIL YOUR SIGNAL!
BLESSEDBOWL THRIVED IN ITS THIRTIETH YEAR, STILL FLOATING ON AN IMAGINED SEA OF FIRE.
PA
MA'AM
THE QUOTAS.

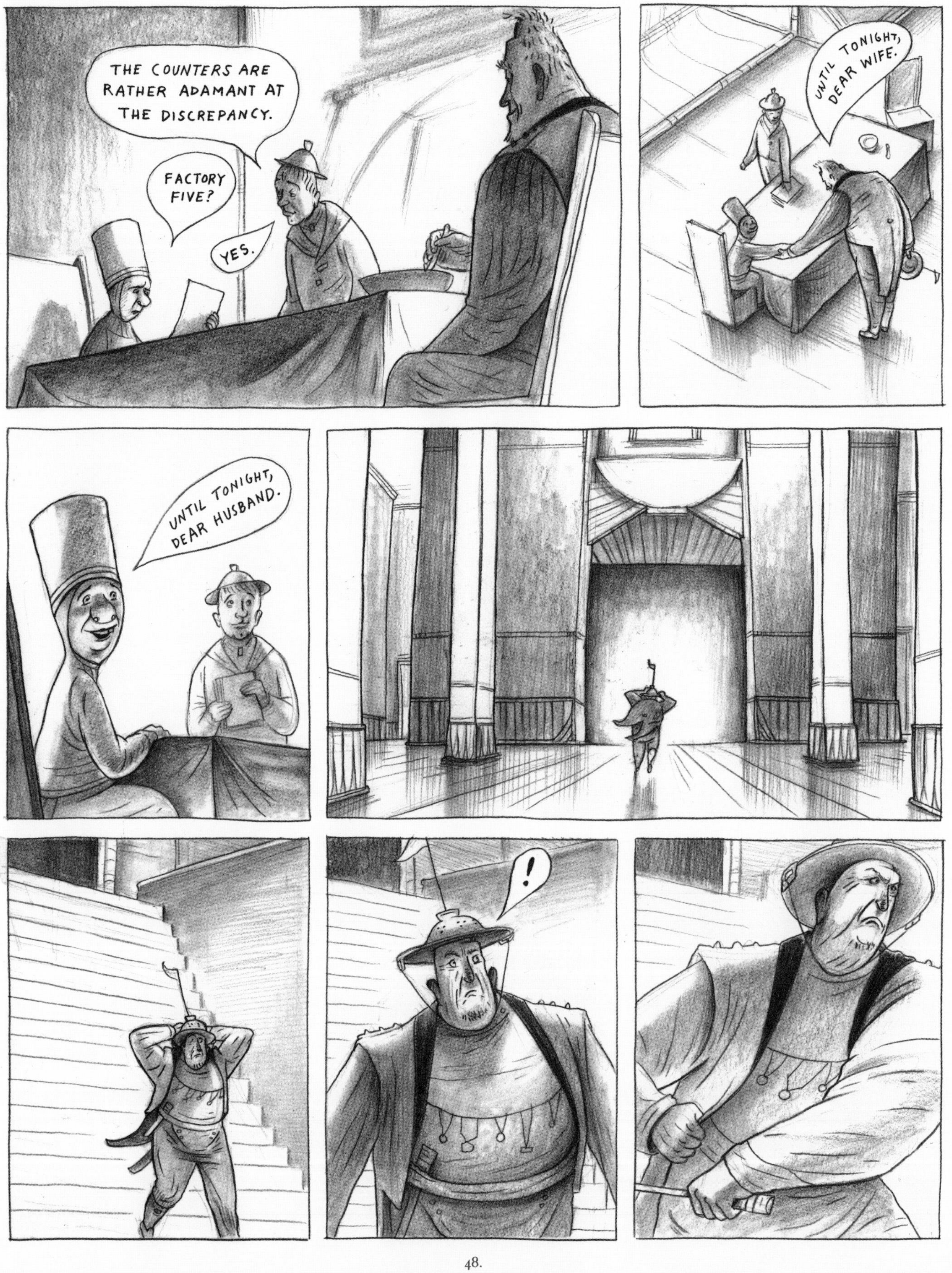
THE COUNTERS ARE RATHER ADAMANT AT THE DISCREPANCY.
FACTORY FIVE?
YES.
UNTIL TONIGHT, DEAR WIFE.
UNTIL TONIGHT, DEAR HUSBAND.
!

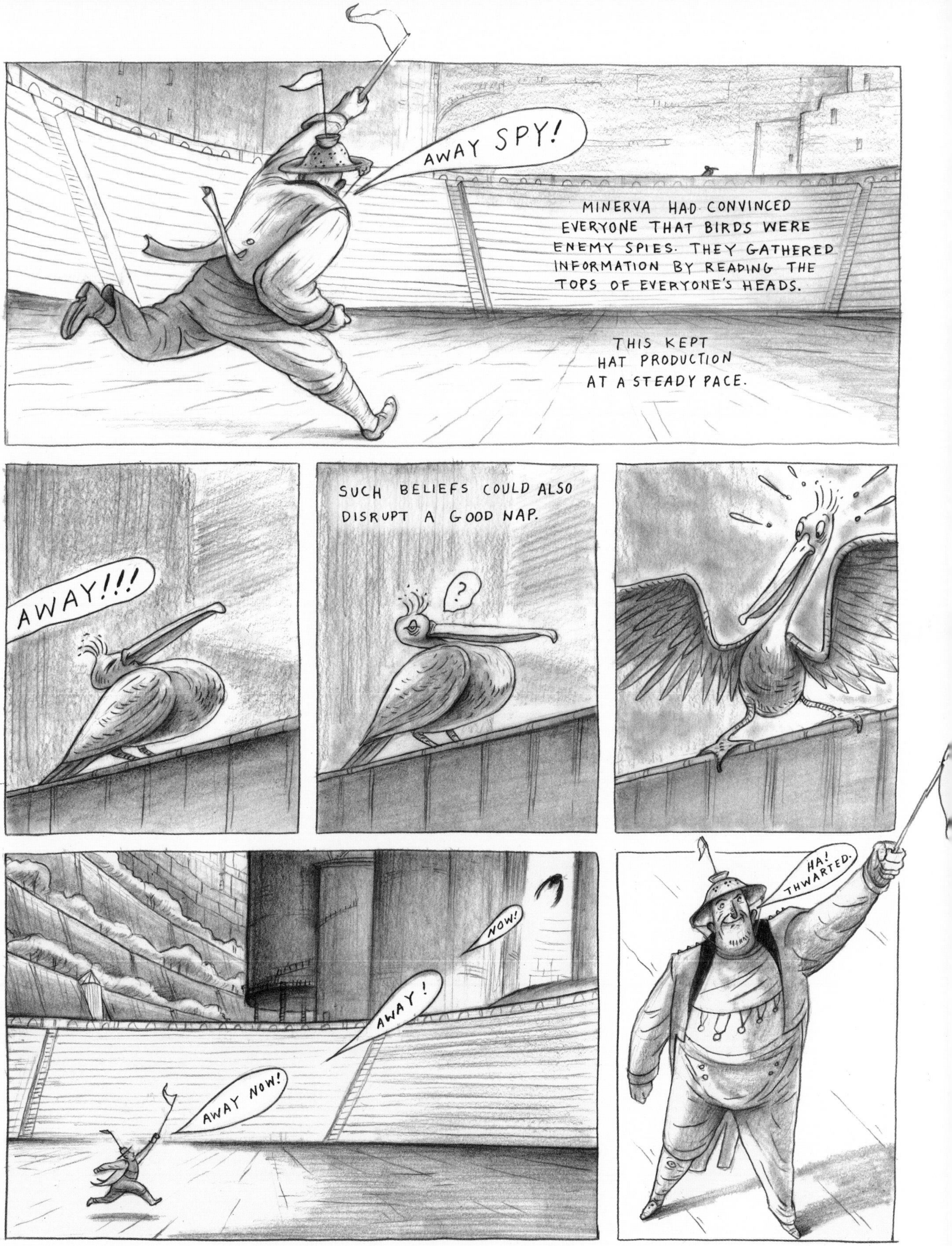
AWAY SPY!
MINERVA HAD CONVINCED EVERYONE THAT BIRDS WERE ENEMY SPIES. THEY GATHERED INFORMATION BY READING THE TOPS OF EVERYONE'S HEADS.
THIS KEPT HAT PRODUCTION AT A STEADY PACE.
AWAY!!!
SUCH BELIEFS COULD ALSO DISRUPT A GOOD NAP.
?
AWAY NOW!
AWAY!
NOW!
HA! THWARTED.

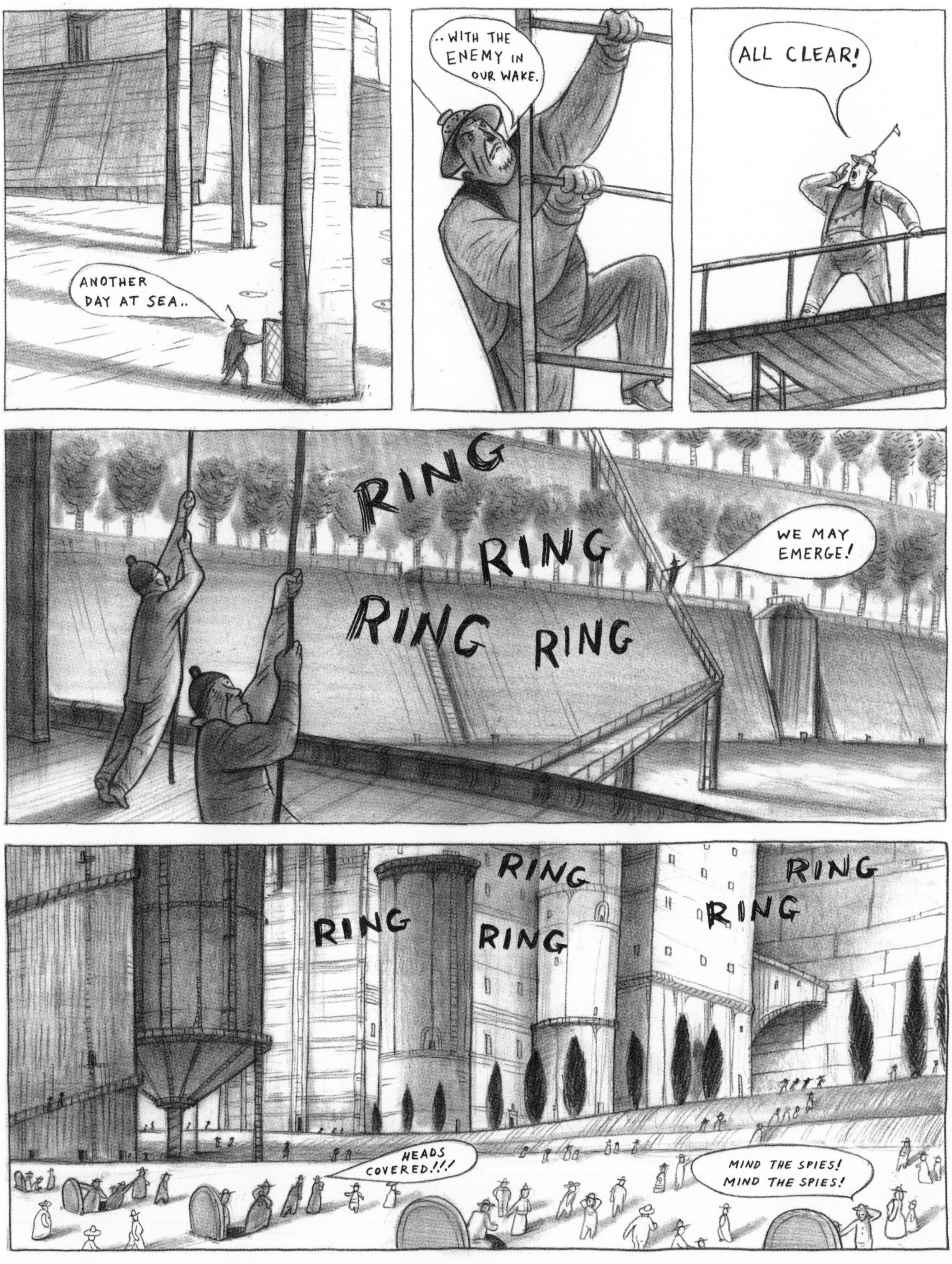
ANOTHER DAY AT SEA..
..WITH THE ENEMY IN OUR WAKE.
ALL CLEAR!
RING
RING
RING RING
WE MAY EMERGE!
RING
RING
RING
RING
RING
HEADS COVERED!!!
MIND THE SPIES! MIND THE SPIES!

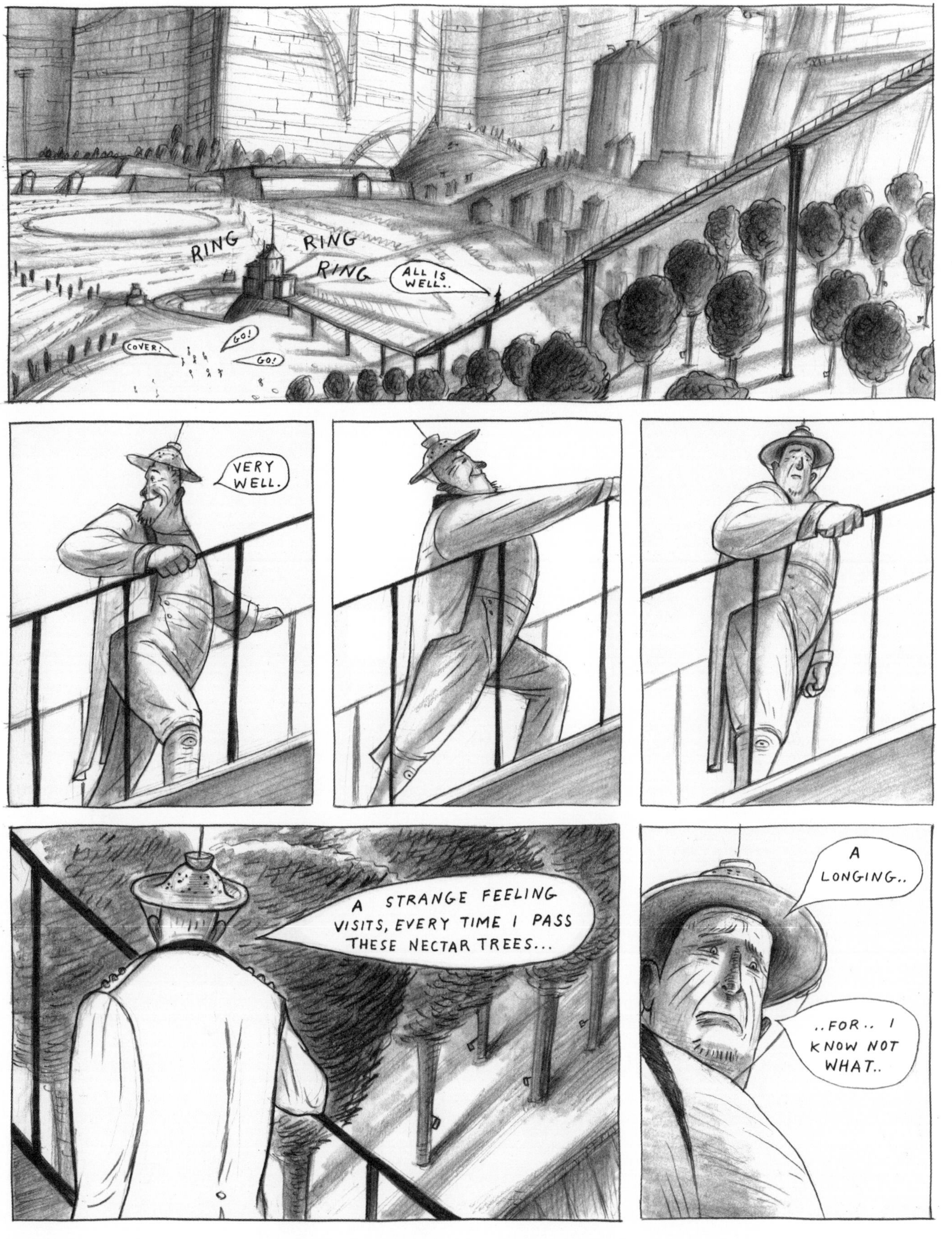
RING
RING
RING
ALL IS WELL..
COVER!
GO!
GO!
VERY WELL.
A STRANGE FEELING VISITS, EVERY TIME I PASS THESE NECTAR TREES...
A LONGING..
..FOR.. I KNOW NOT WHAT..

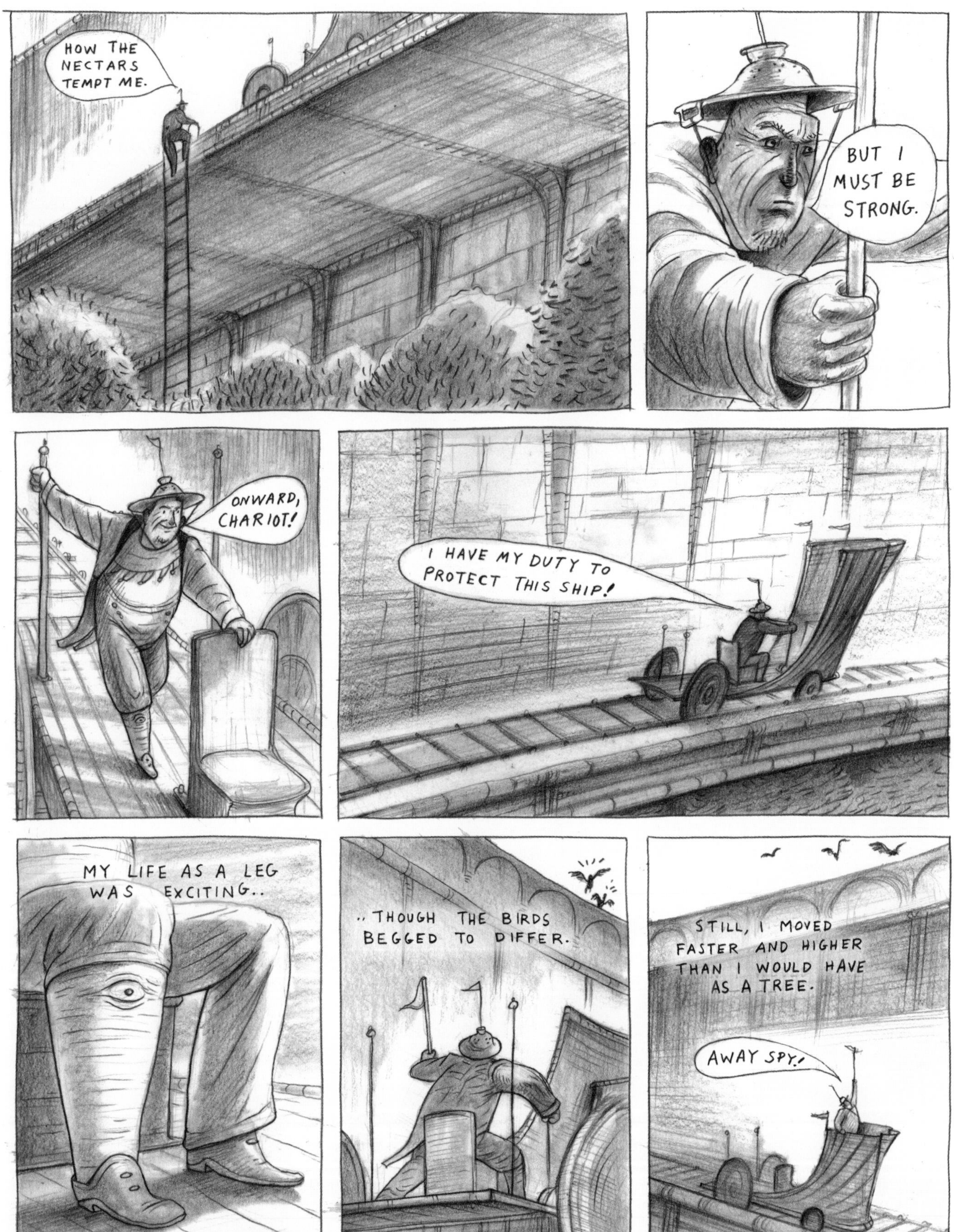
HOW THE NECTARS TEMPT ME.
BUT I MUST BE STRONG.
ONWARD, CHARIOT!
I HAVE MY DUTY TO PROTECT THIS SHIP!
MY LIFE AS A LEG WAS EXCITING..
..THOUGH THE BIRDS BEGGED TO DIFFER.
STILL, I MOVED FASTER AND HIGHER THAN I WOULD HAVE AS A TREE.
AWAY SPY!

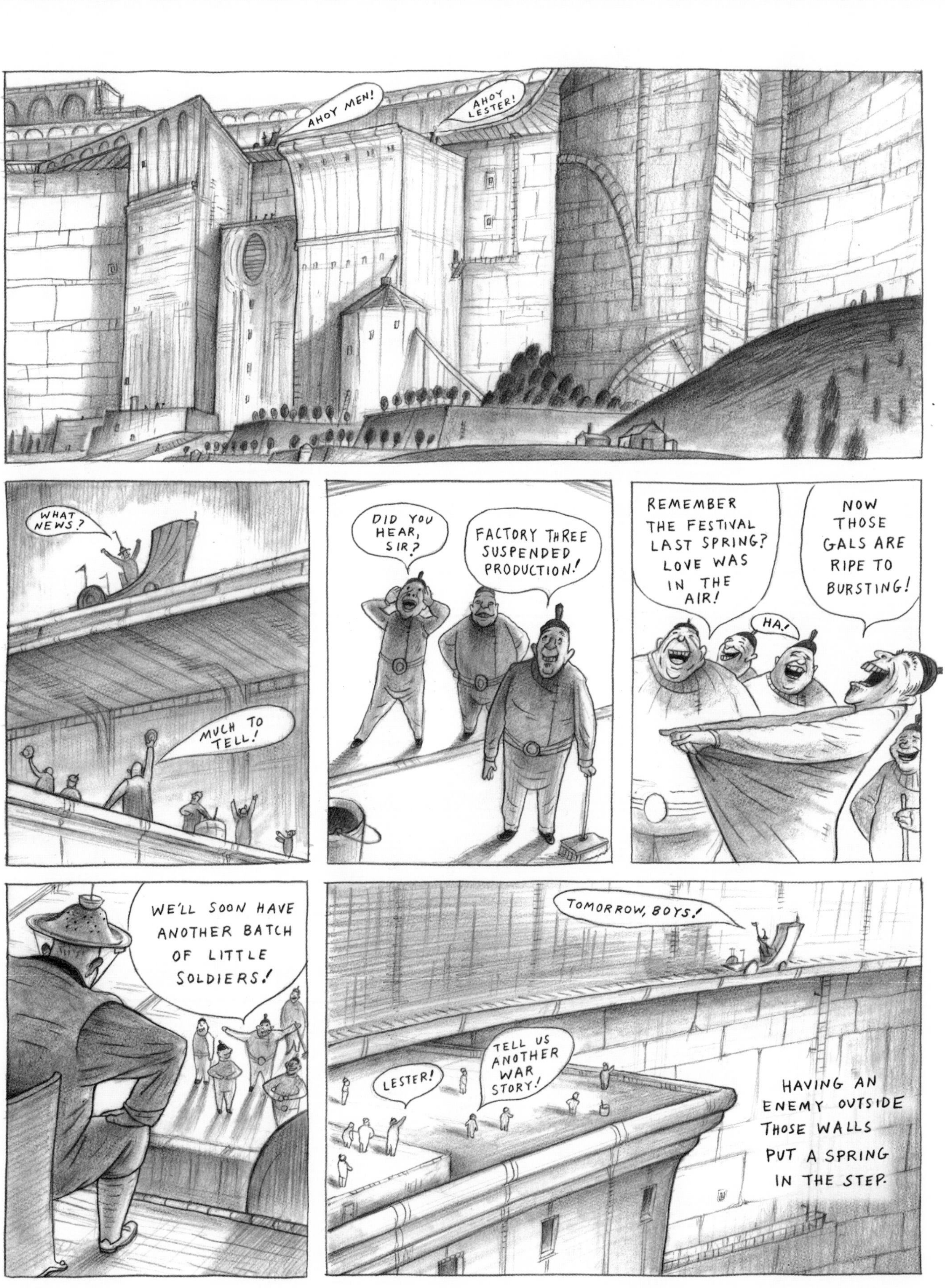
AHOY MEN!
AHOY LESTER!
WHAT NEWS?
MUCH TO TELL!
DID YOU HEAR, SIR?
FACTORY THREE SUSPENDED PRODUCTION!
REMEMBER THE FESTIVAL LAST SPRING? LOVE WAS IN THE AIR!
HA!
NOW THOSE GALS ARE RIPE TO BURSTING!
WE'LL SOON HAVE ANOTHER BATCH OF LITTLE SOLDIERS!
TOMORROW, BOYS!
LESTER!
TELL US ANOTHER WAR STORY!
HAVING AN ENEMY OUTSIDE THOSE WALLS PUT A SPRING IN THE STEP.

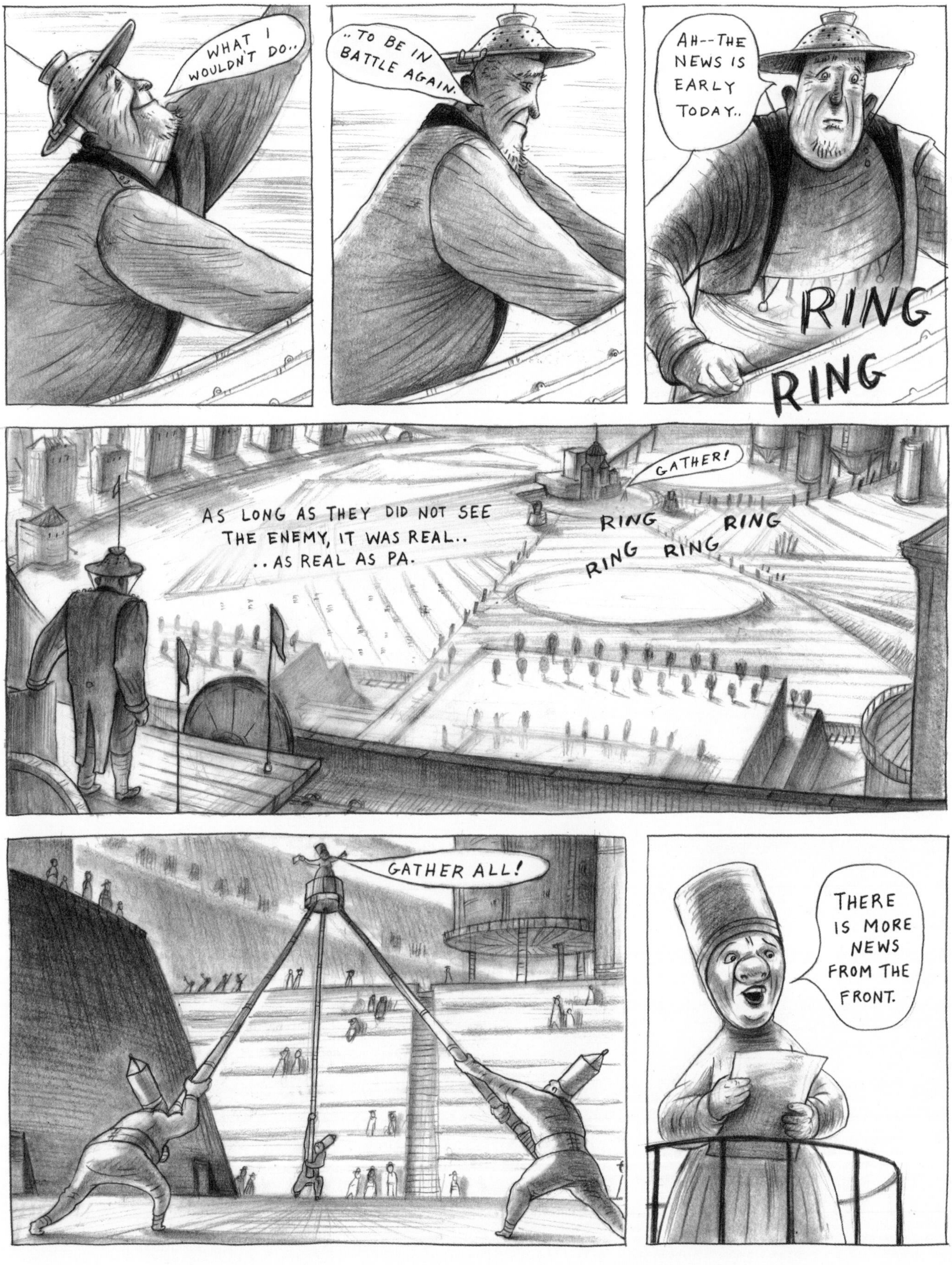
WHAT I WOULDN'T DO..
..TO BE IN BATTLE AGAIN.
AH--THE NEWS IS EARLY TODAY..
RING
RING
GATHER!
AS LONG AS THEY DID NOT SEE THE ENEMY, IT WAS REAL..
..AS REAL AS PA.
RING
RING
RING
RING
GATHER ALL!
THERE IS MORE NEWS FROM THE FRONT.

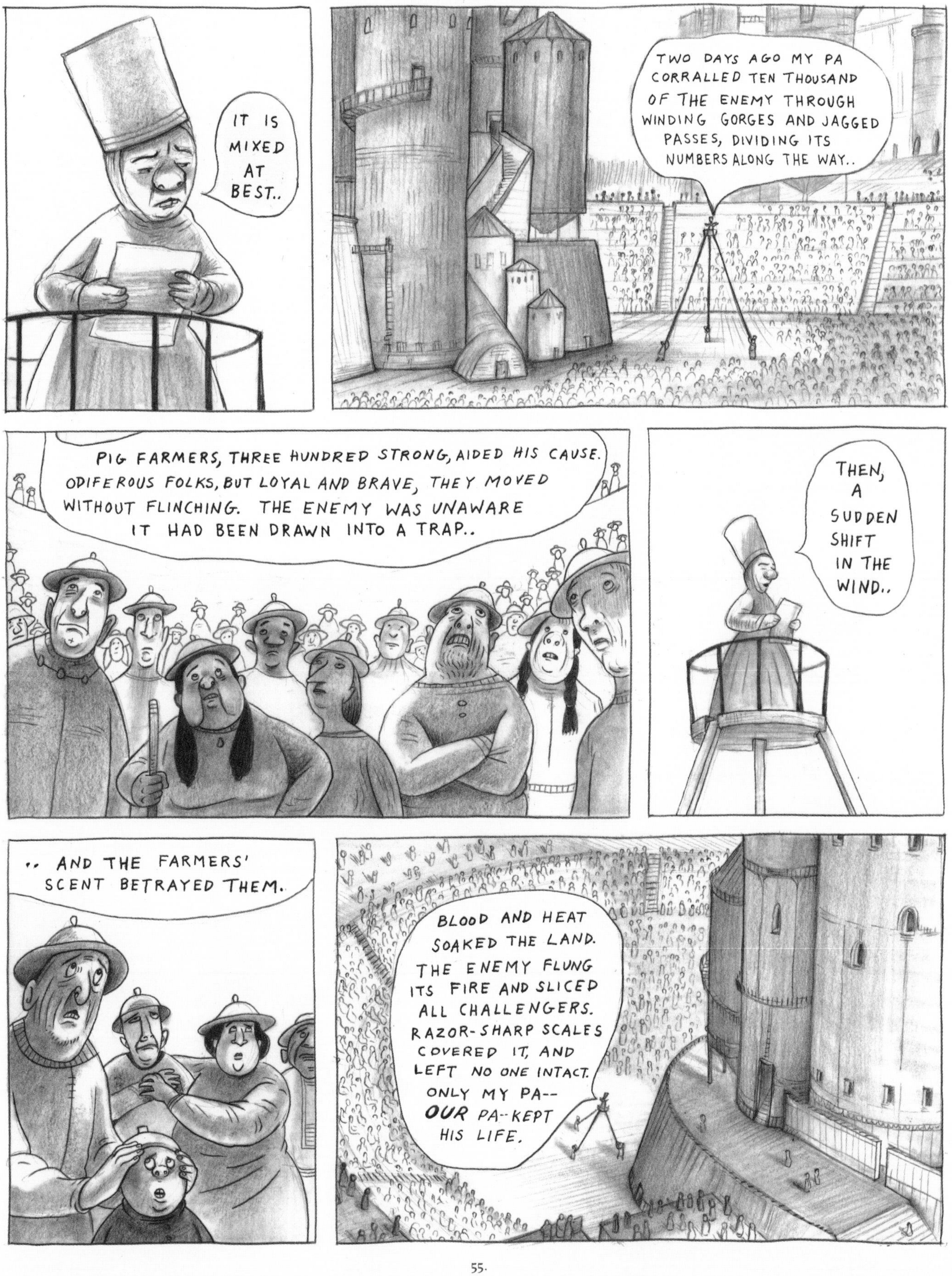
IT IS MIXED AT BEST..
TWO DAYS AGO MY PA CORRALLED TEN THOUSAND OF THE ENEMY THROUGH WINDING GORGES AND JAGGED PASSES, DIVIDING ITS NUMBERS ALONG THE WAY..
PIG FARMERS, THREE HUNDRED STRONG, AIDED HIS CAUSE. ODIFEROUS FOLKS, BUT LOYAL AND BRAVE, THEY MOVED WITHOUT FLINCHING. THE ENEMY WAS UNAWARE IT HAD BEEN DRAWN INTO A TRAP..
THEN, A SUDDEN SHIFT IN THE WIND..
.. AND THE FARMERS' SCENT BETRAYED THEM..
BLOOD AND HEAT SOAKED THE LAND. THE ENEMY FLUNG ITS FIRE AND SLICED ALL CHALLENGERS. RAZOR-SHARP SCALES COVERED IT, AND LEFT NO ONE INTACT. ONLY MY PA-- OUR PA--KEPT HIS LIFE.

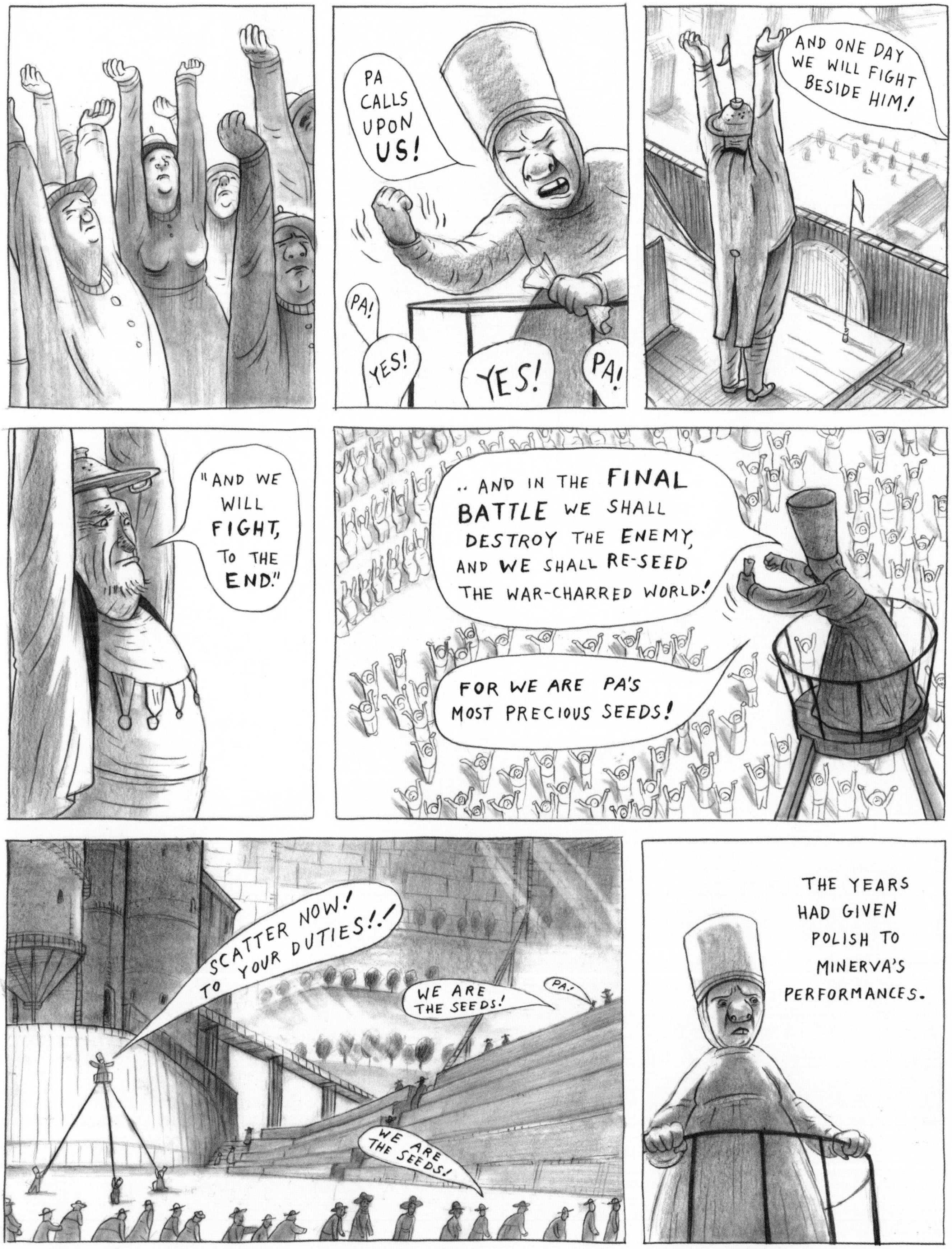
PA CALLS UPON US!
PA!
YES!
YES!
PA!
AND ONE DAY WE WILL FIGHT BESIDE HIM!
"AND WE WILL FIGHT, TO THE END."
.. AND IN THE FINAL BATTLE WE SHALL DESTROY THE ENEMY, AND WE SHALL RE-SEED THE WAR-CHARRED WORLD!
FOR WE ARE PA'S MOST PRECIOUS SEEDS!
SCATTER NOW! TO YOUR DUTIES!.!
WE ARE THE SEEDS!
PA!
WE ARE THE SEEDS!
THE YEARS HAD GIVEN POLISH TO MINERVA'S PERFORMANCES.

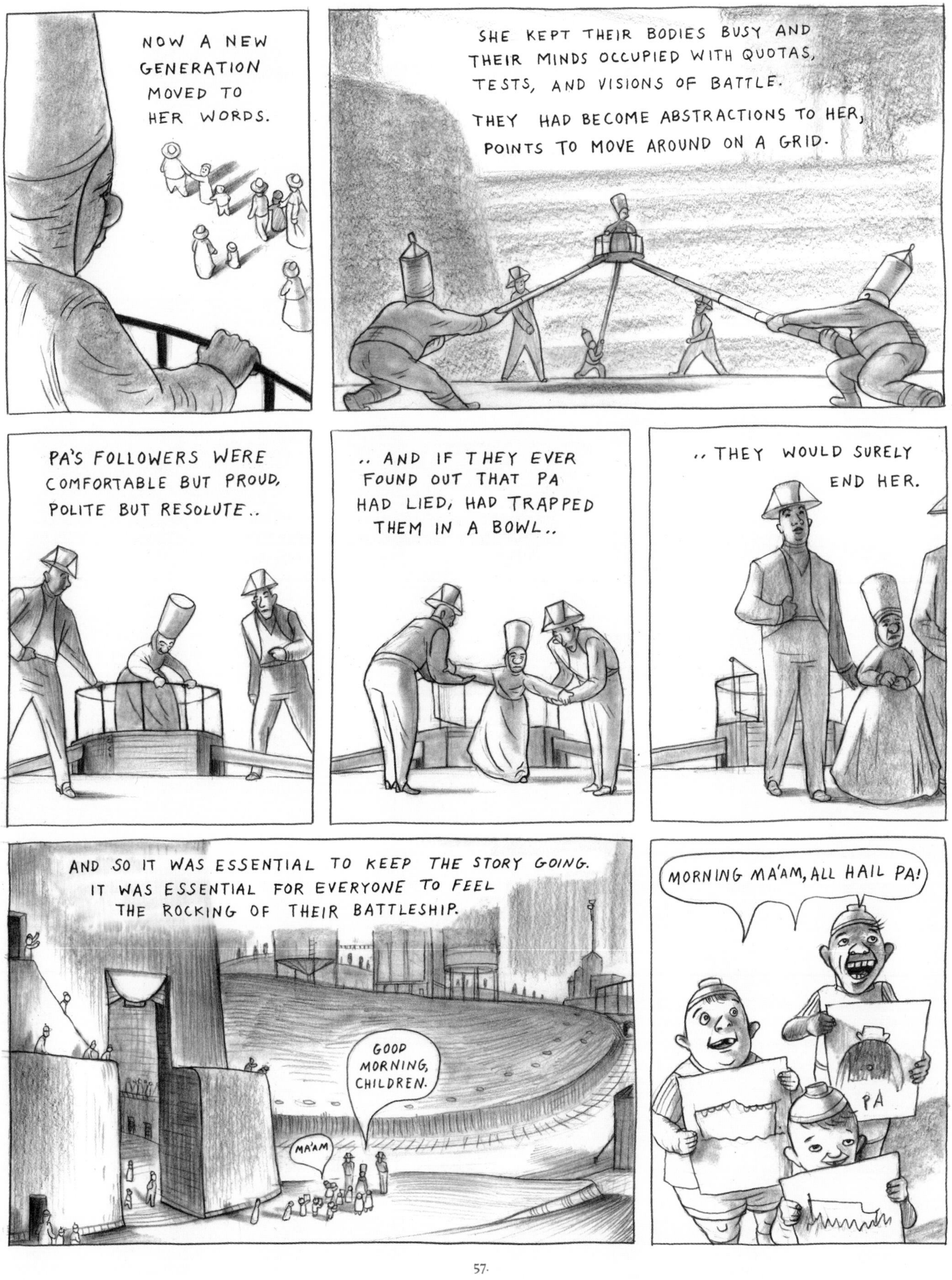
NOW A NEW GENERATION MOVED TO HER WORDS.
SHE KEPT THEIR BODIES BUSY AND THEIR MINDS OCCUPIED WITH QUOTAS, TESTS, AND VISIONS OF BATTLE.
THEY HAD BECOME ABSTRACTIONS TO HER, POINTS TO MOVE AROUND ON A GRID.
PA'S FOLLOWERS WERE COMFORTABLE BUT PROUD, POLITE BUT RESOLUTE..
.. AND IF THEY EVER FOUND OUT THAT PA HAD LIED, HAD TRAPPED THEM IN A BOWL..
.. THEY WOULD SURELY END HER.
AND SO IT WAS ESSENTIAL TO KEEP THE STORY GOING. IT WAS ESSENTIAL FOR EVERYONE TO FEEL THE ROCKING OF THEIR BATTLESHIP.
GOOD MORNING, CHILDREN.
MA'AM
MORNING MA'AM, ALL HAIL PA!
PA

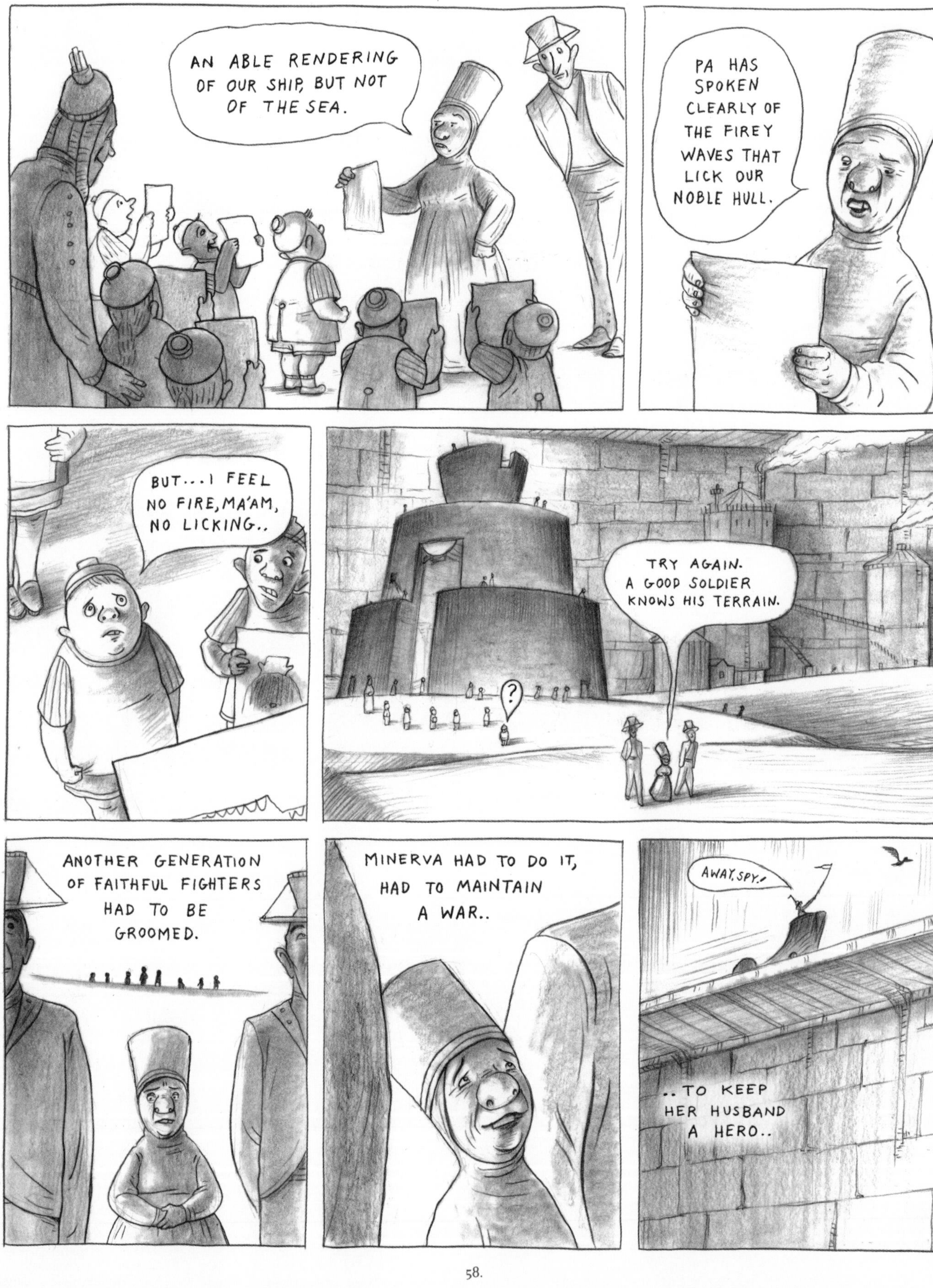
AN ABLE RENDERING OF OUR SHIP, BUT NOT OF THE SEA.
PA HAS SPOKEN CLEARLY OF THE FIREY WAVES THAT LICK OUR NOBLE HULL.
BUT... I FEEL NO FIRE, MA'AM, NO LICKING..
?
TRY AGAIN. A GOOD SOLDIER KNOWS HIS TERRAIN.
ANOTHER GENERATION OF FAITHFUL FIGHTERS HAD TO BE GROOMED.
MINERVA HAD TO DO IT, HAD TO MAINTAIN A WAR..
AWAY, SPY!
..TO KEEP HER HUSBAND A HERO..

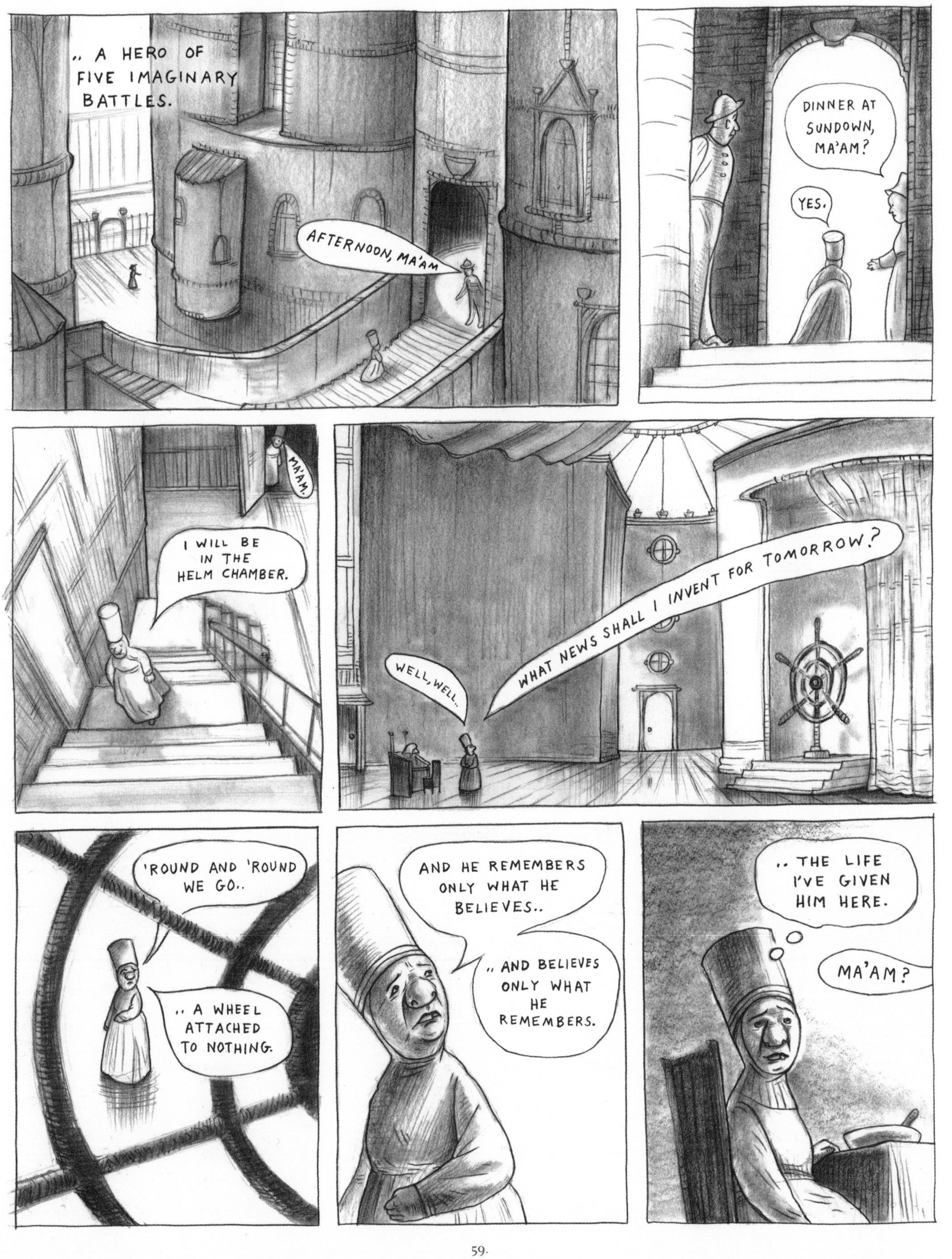
.. A HERO OF FIVE IMAGINARY BATTLES.
AFTERNOON, MA'AM
DINNER AT SUNDOWN, MA'AM?
YES.
MA'AM.
I WILL BE IN THE HELM CHAMBER.
WELL, WELL..
WHAT NEWS SHALL I INVENT FOR TOMORROW?
'ROUND AND 'ROUND WE GO..
.. A WHEEL ATTACHED TO NOTHING.
AND HE REMEMBERS ONLY WHAT HE BELIEVES..
.. AND BELIEVES ONLY WHAT HE REMEMBERS.
.. THE LIFE I'VE GIVEN HIM HERE.
MA'AM?

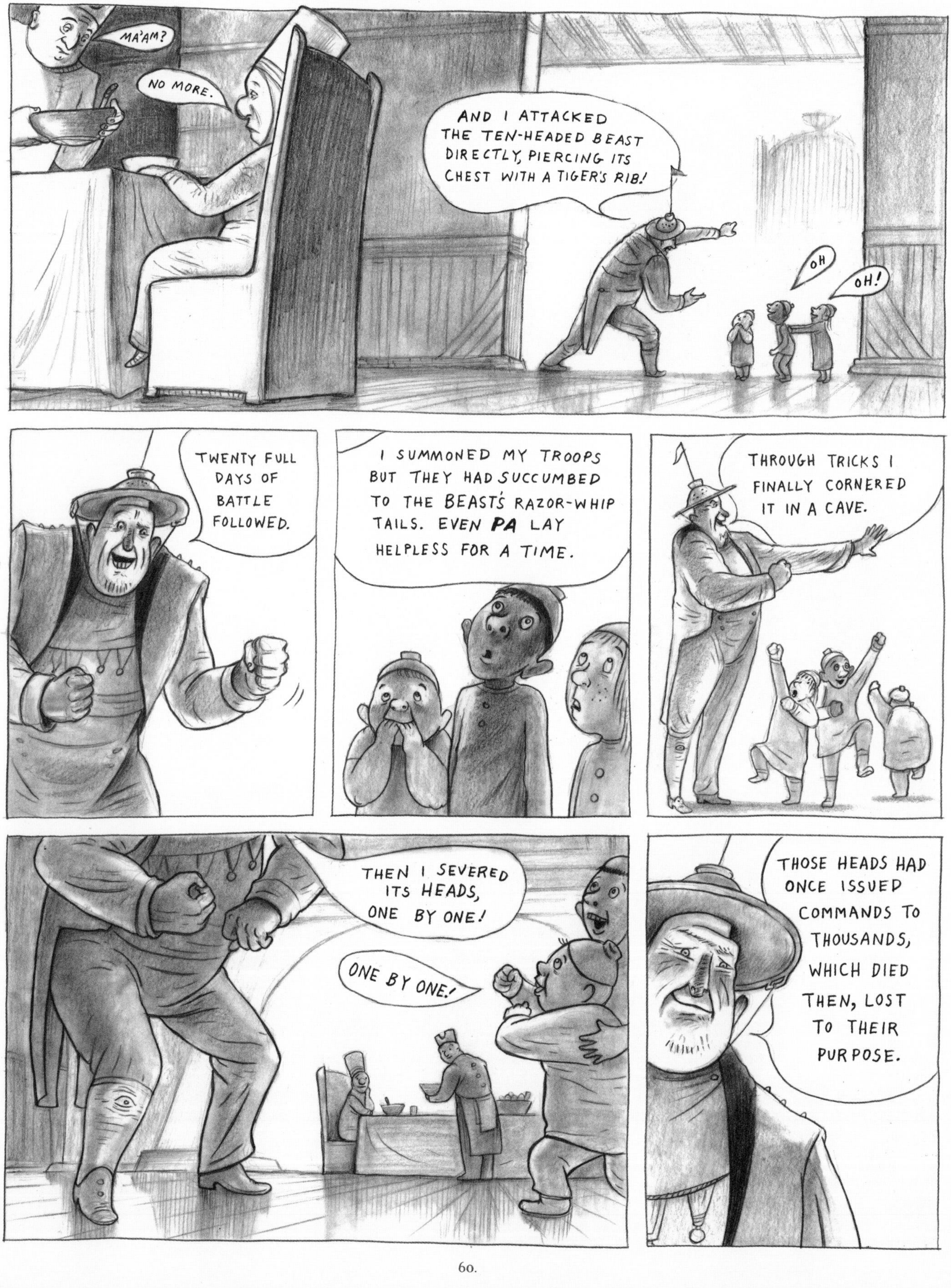
MA'AM?
NO MORE.
AND I ATTACKED THE TEN-HEADED BEAST DIRECTLY, PIERCING ITS CHEST WITH A TIGER'S RIB!
OH
OH!
TWENTY FULL DAYS OF BATTLE FOLLOWED.
I SUMMONED MY TROOPS BUT THEY HAD SUCCUMBED TO THE BEAST'S RAZOR-WHIP TAILS. EVEN **PA** LAY HELPLESS FOR A TIME.
THROUGH TRICKS I FINALLY CORNERED IT IN A CAVE.
THEN I SEVERED ITS HEADS, ONE BY ONE!
ONE BY ONE!
THOSE HEADS HAD ONCE ISSUED COMMANDS TO THOUSANDS, WHICH DIED THEN, LOST TO THEIR PURPOSE.

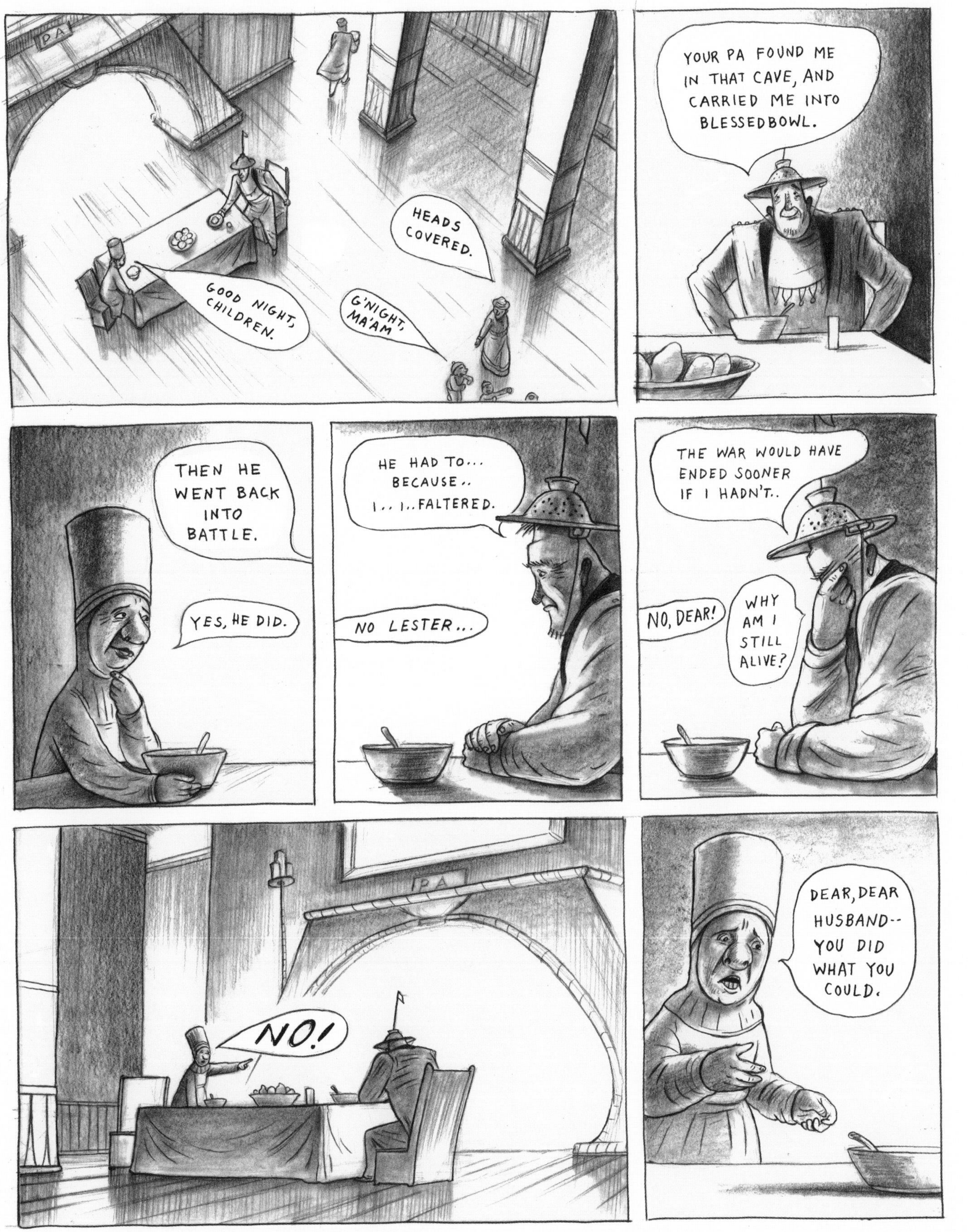
HEADS COVERED.
GOOD NIGHT, CHILDREN.
G'NIGHT, MA'AM
YOUR PA FOUND ME IN THAT CAVE, AND CARRIED ME INTO BLESSEDBOWL.
THEN HE WENT BACK INTO BATTLE.
YES, HE DID.
HE HAD TO... BECAUSE.. I.. I..FALTERED.
NO LESTER...
THE WAR WOULD HAVE ENDED SOONER IF I HADN'T..
NO, DEAR!
WHY AM I STILL ALIVE?
NO!
DEAR, DEAR HUSBAND-- YOU DID WHAT YOU COULD.

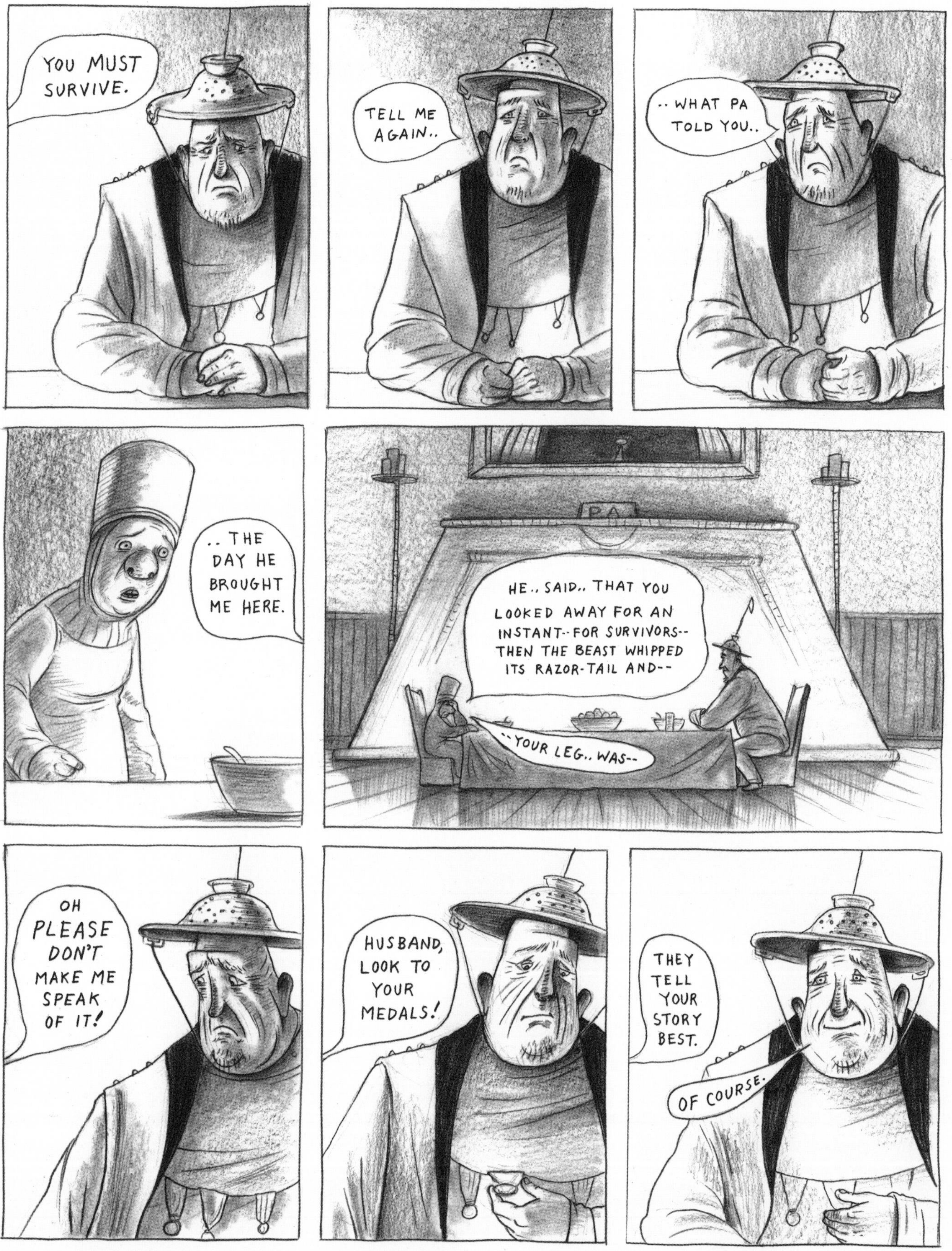
YOU MUST SURVIVE.
TELL ME AGAIN..
.. WHAT PA TOLD YOU..
.. THE DAY HE BROUGHT ME HERE.
PA
HE.. SAID.. THAT YOU LOOKED AWAY FOR AN INSTANT--FOR SURVIVORS--THEN THE BEAST WHIPPED ITS RAZOR-TAIL AND--
--YOUR LEG.. WAS--
OH PLEASE DON'T MAKE ME SPEAK OF IT!
HUSBAND, LOOK TO YOUR MEDALS!
THEY TELL YOUR STORY BEST.
OF COURSE.

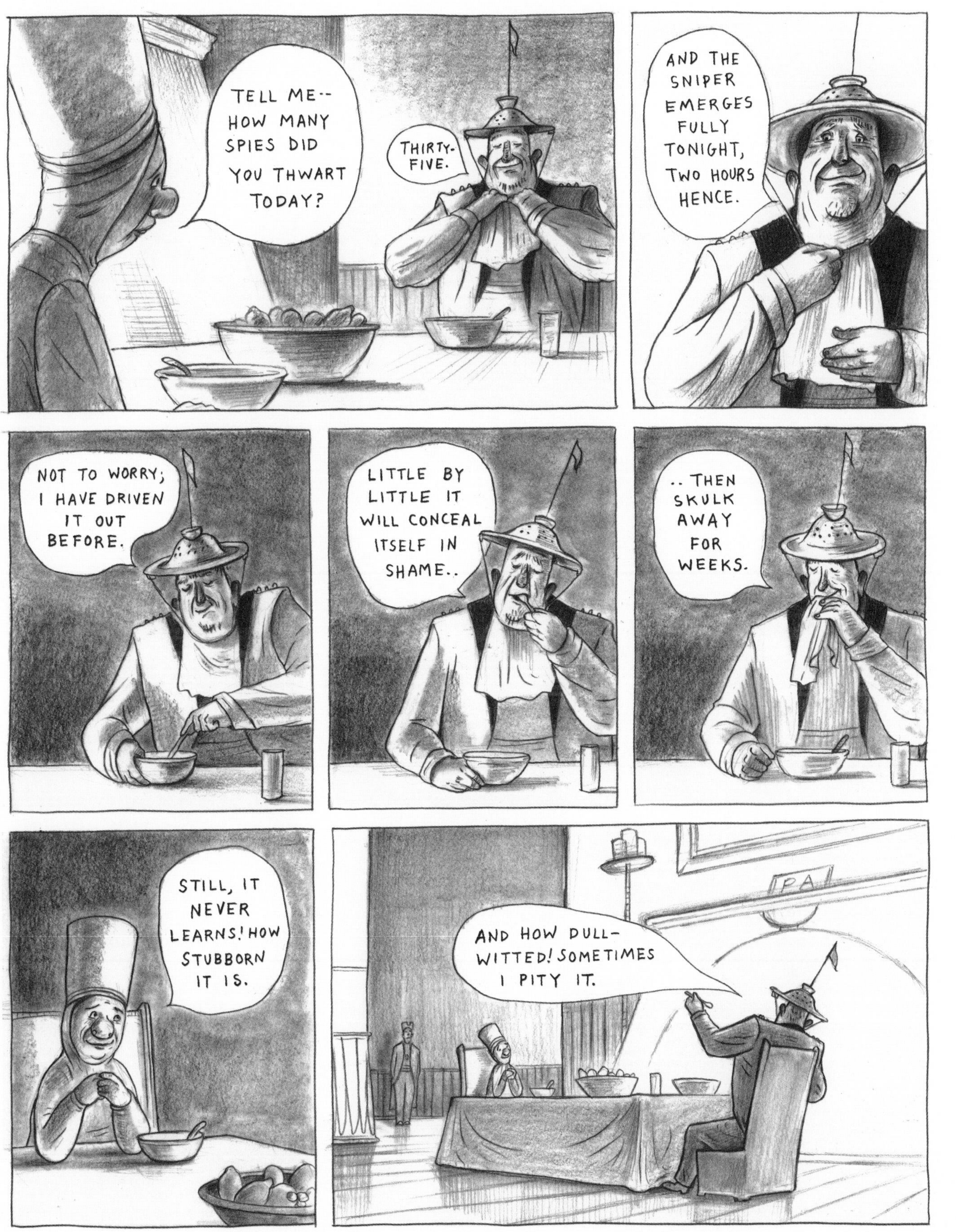
TELL ME-- HOW MANY SPIES DID YOU THWART TODAY?
THIRTY-FIVE.
AND THE SNIPER EMERGES FULLY TONIGHT, TWO HOURS HENCE.
NOT TO WORRY; I HAVE DRIVEN IT OUT BEFORE.
LITTLE BY LITTLE IT WILL CONCEAL ITSELF IN SHAME..
.. THEN SKULK AWAY FOR WEEKS.
STILL, IT NEVER LEARNS! HOW STUBBORN IT IS.
PA
AND HOW DULL-WITTED! SOMETIMES I PITY IT.

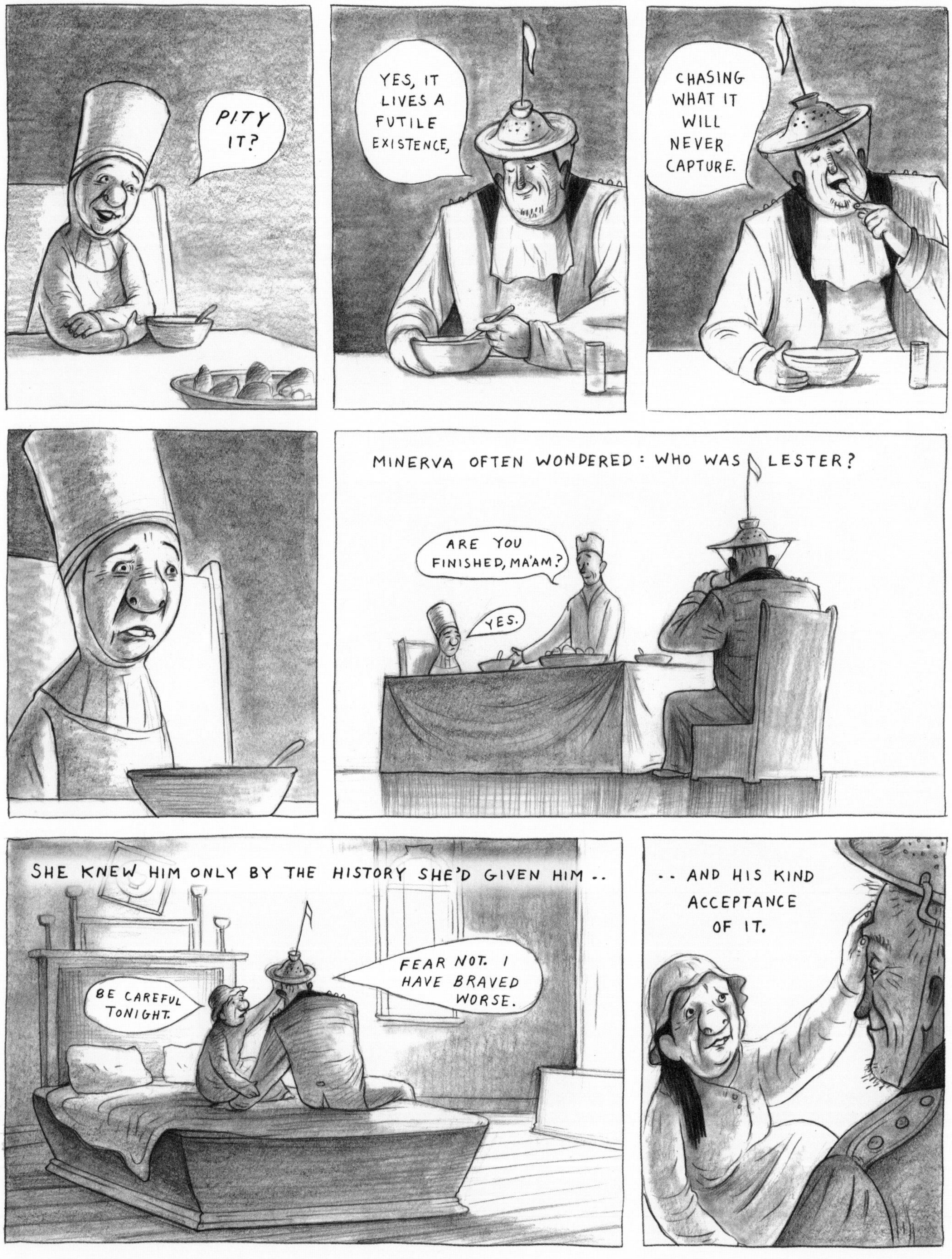
PITY IT?
YES, IT LIVES A FUTILE EXISTENCE,
CHASING WHAT IT WILL NEVER CAPTURE.
MINERVA OFTEN WONDERED: WHO WAS LESTER?
ARE YOU FINISHED, MA'AM?
YES.
SHE KNEW HIM ONLY BY THE HISTORY SHE'D GIVEN HIM ..
BE CAREFUL TONIGHT.
FEAR NOT. I HAVE BRAVED WORSE.
.. AND HIS KIND ACCEPTANCE OF IT.

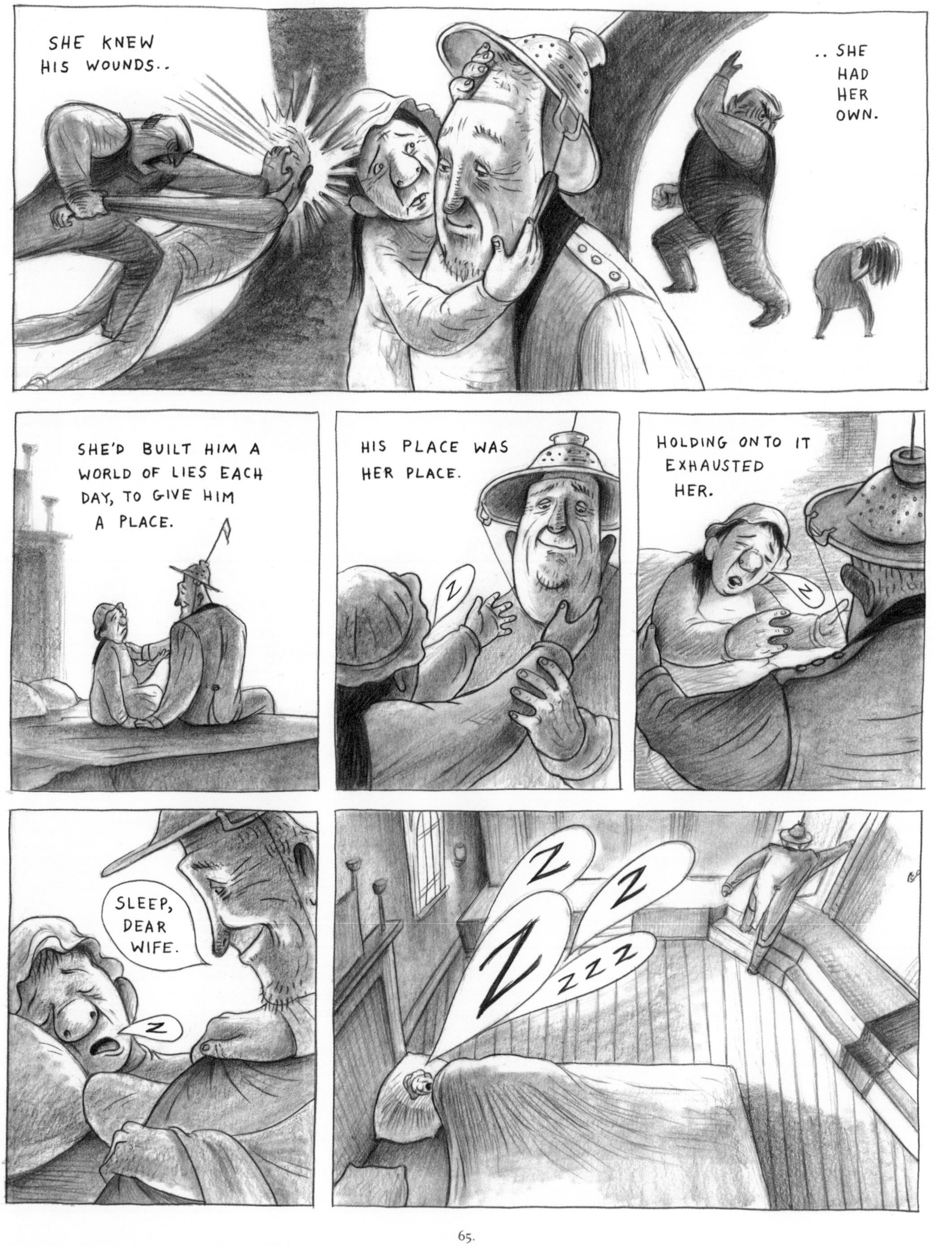
SHE KNEW HIS WOUNDS..
.. SHE HAD HER OWN.
SHE'D BUILT HIM A WORLD OF LIES EACH DAY, TO GIVE HIM A PLACE.
HIS PLACE WAS HER PLACE.
Z
HOLDING ONTO IT EXHAUSTED HER.
Z
SLEEP, DEAR WIFE.
Z
Z
Z
Z
ZZZ

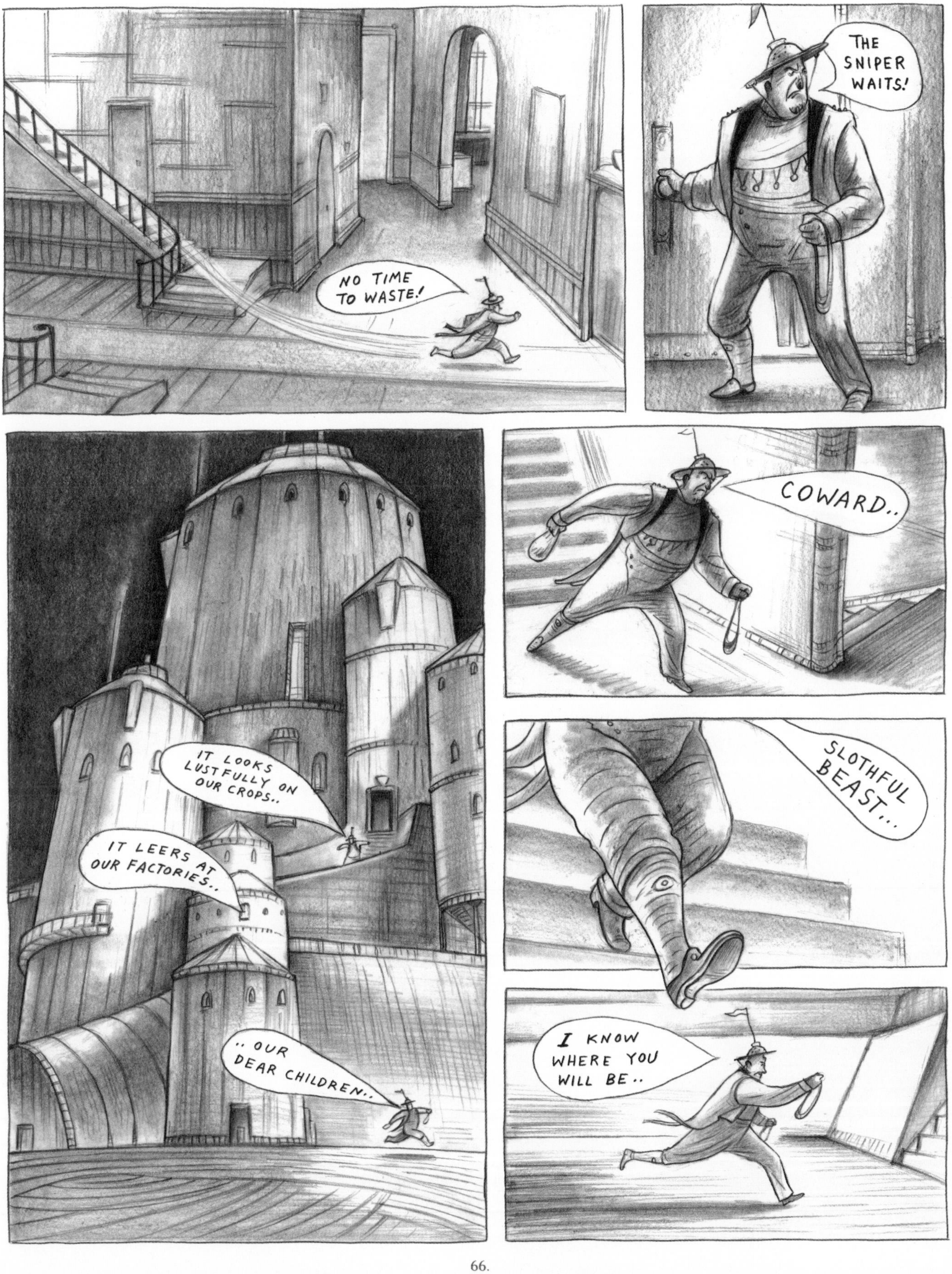
NO TIME TO WASTE!
THE SNIPER WAITS!
IT LOOKS LUSTFULLY ON OUR CROPS..
IT LEERS AT OUR FACTORIES..
.. OUR DEAR CHILDREN..
COWARD..
SLOTHFUL BEAST...
I KNOW WHERE YOU WILL BE..

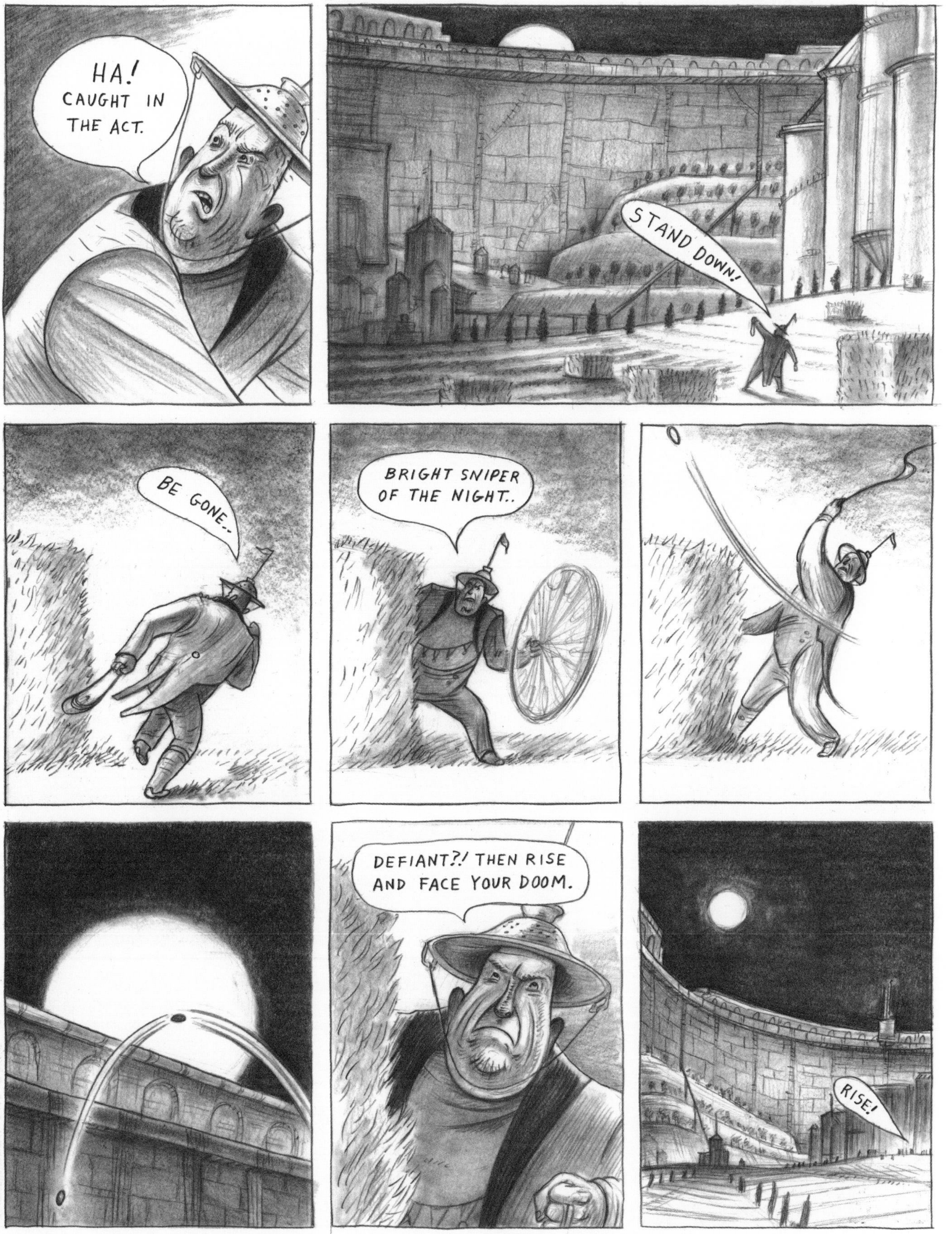
HA! CAUGHT IN THE ACT.
STAND DOWN!
BE GONE..
BRIGHT SNIPER OF THE NIGHT..
DEFIANT?! THEN RISE AND FACE YOUR DOOM.
RISE!

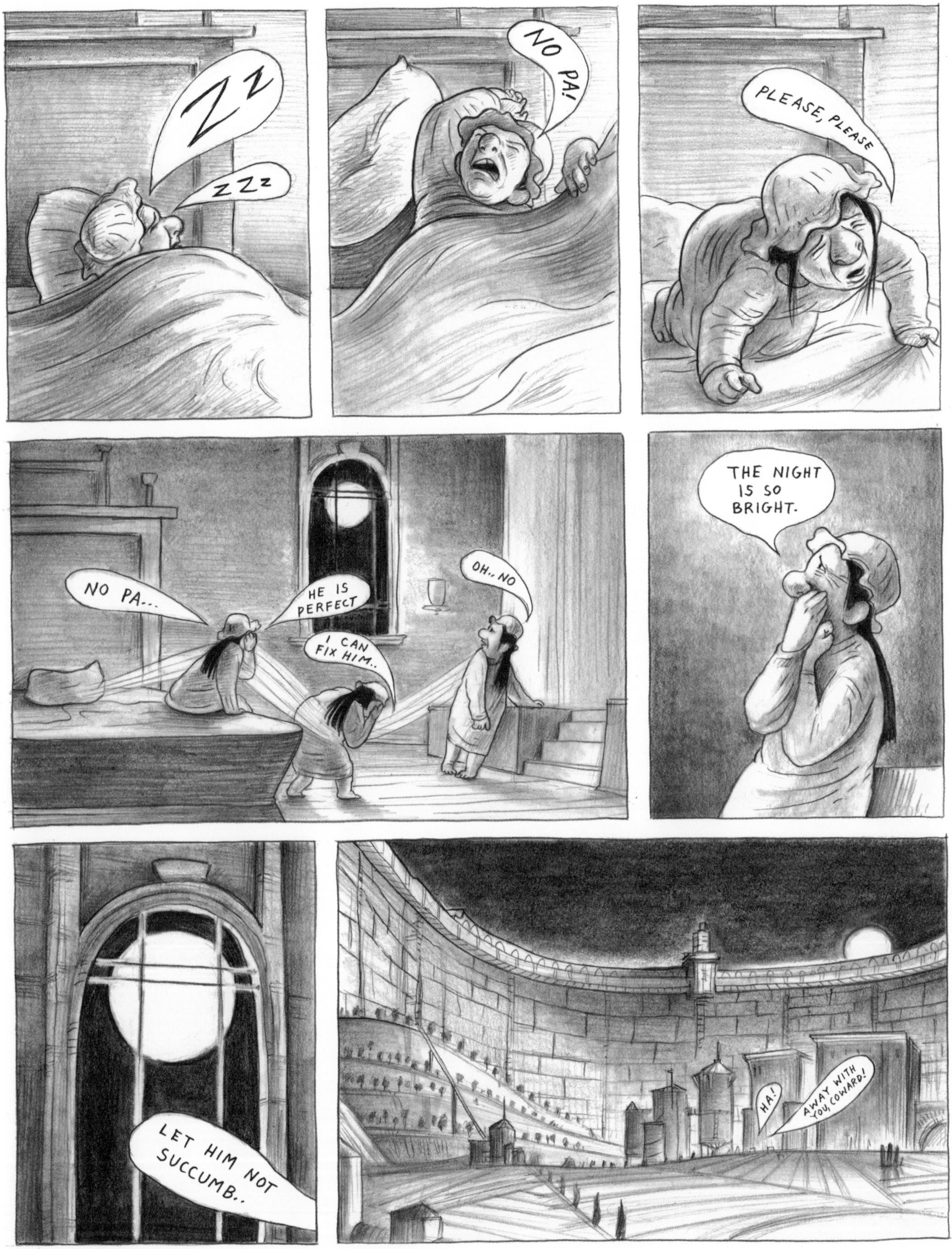
Z z
z Z z
NO PA!
PLEASE, PLEASE
NO PA...
HE IS PERFECT
I CAN FIX HIM..
OH., NO
THE NIGHT IS SO BRIGHT.
LET HIM NOT SUCCUMB..
HA!
AWAY WITH YOU, COWARD!

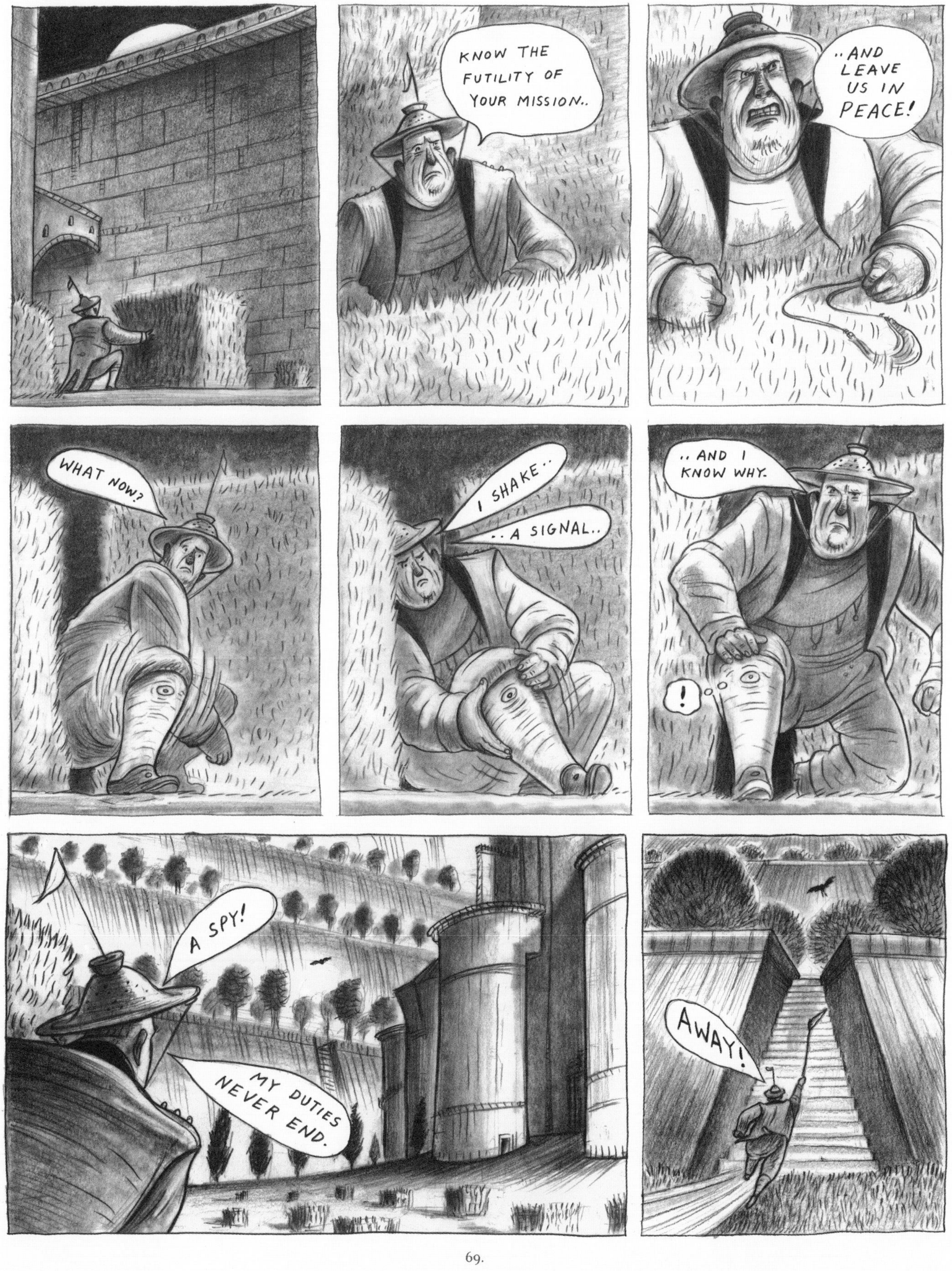
KNOW THE FUTILITY OF YOUR MISSION..
..AND LEAVE US IN PEACE!
WHAT NOW?
I SHAKE..
..A SIGNAL..
..AND I KNOW WHY.
!
A SPY!
MY DUTIES NEVER END.
AWAY!

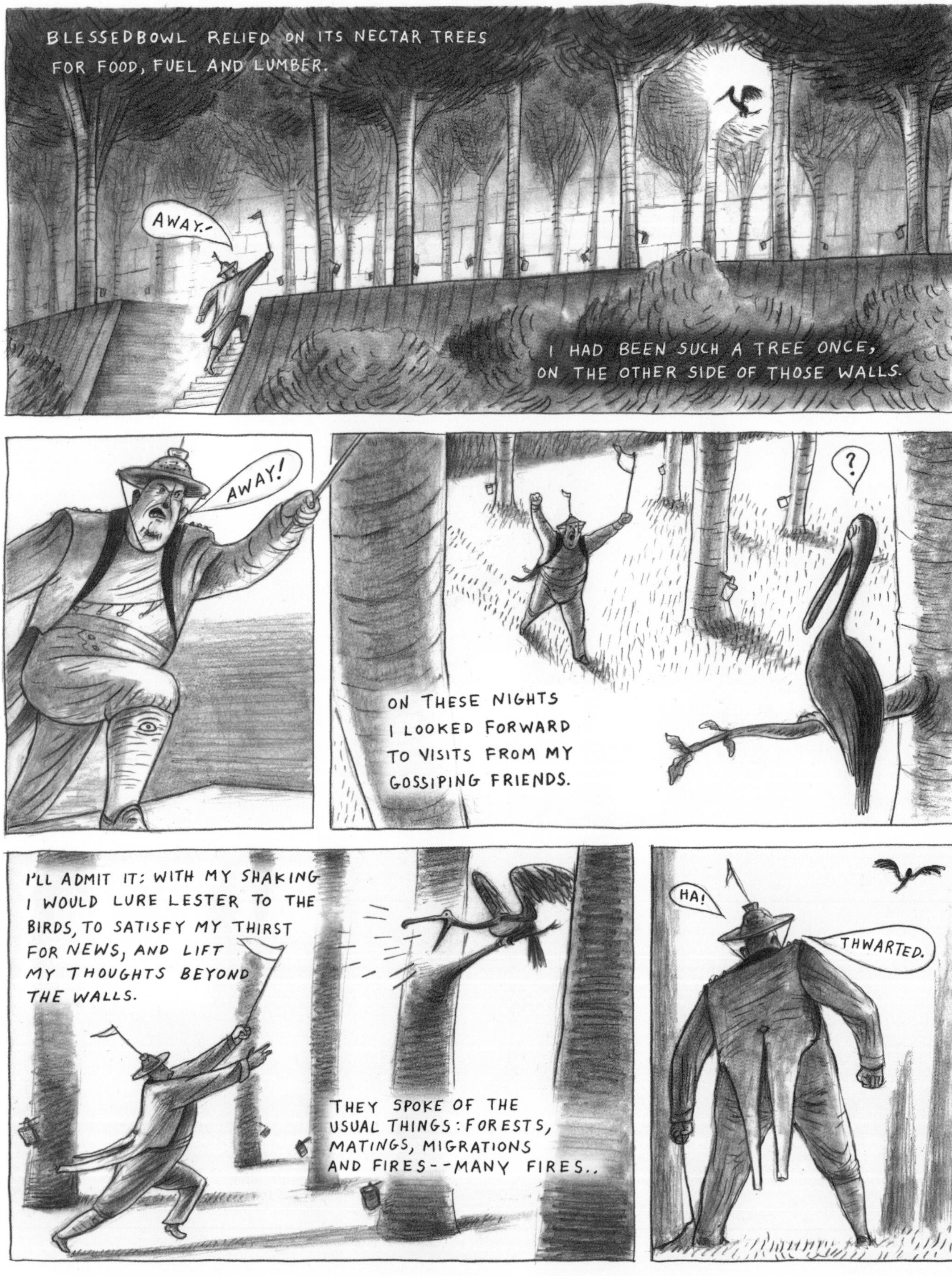
BLESSEDBOWL RELIED ON ITS NECTAR TREES FOR FOOD, FUEL AND LUMBER.
AWAY!
I HAD BEEN SUCH A TREE ONCE, ON THE OTHER SIDE OF THOSE WALLS.
AWAY!
?
ON THESE NIGHTS I LOOKED FORWARD TO VISITS FROM MY GOSSIPING FRIENDS.
I'LL ADMIT IT: WITH MY SHAKING I WOULD LURE LESTER TO THE BIRDS, TO SATISFY MY THIRST FOR NEWS, AND LIFT MY THOUGHTS BEYOND THE WALLS.
THEY SPOKE OF THE USUAL THINGS: FORESTS, MATINGS, MIGRATIONS AND FIRES--MANY FIRES..
HA!
THWARTED.

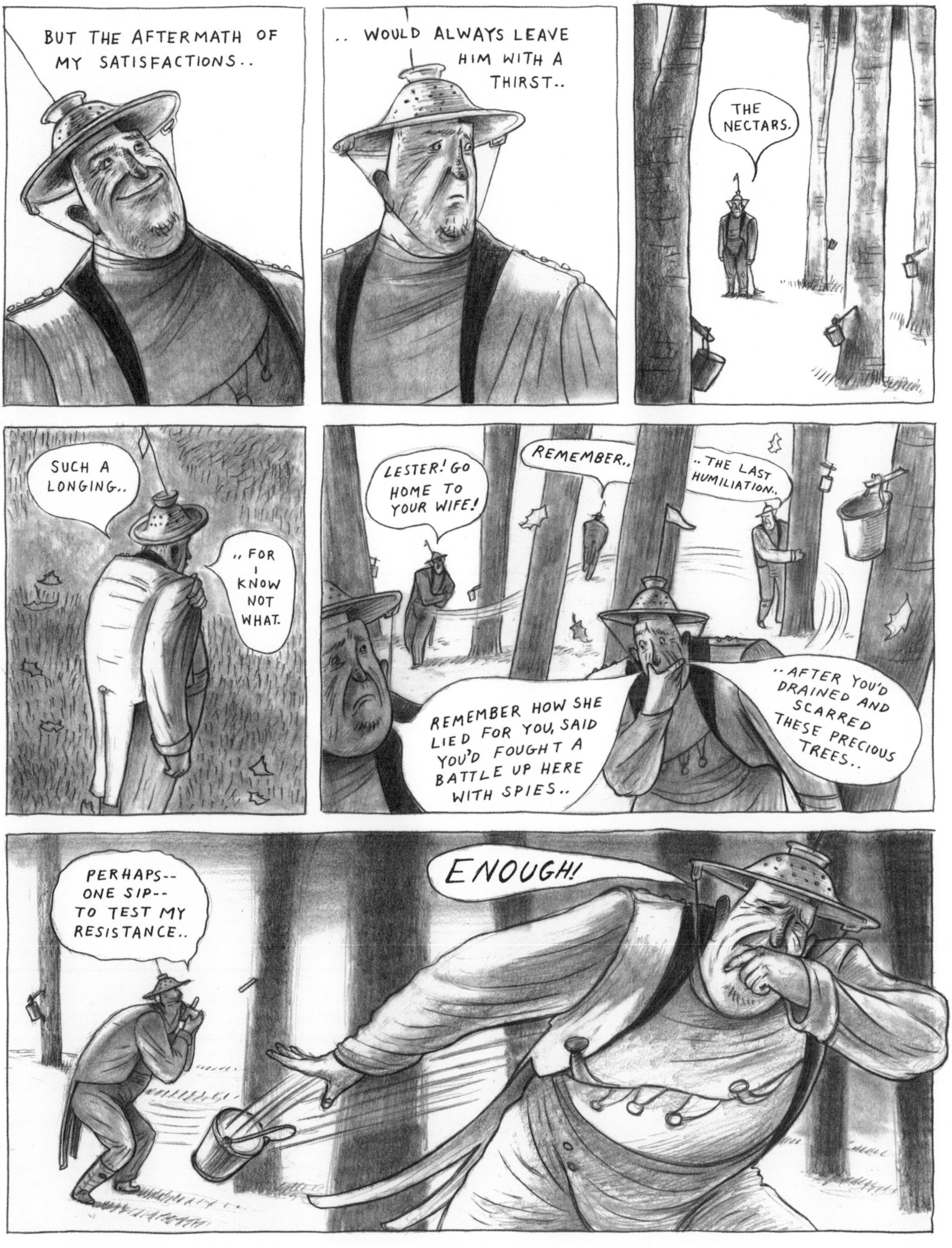
BUT THE AFTERMATH OF MY SATISFACTIONS..
.. WOULD ALWAYS LEAVE HIM WITH A THIRST..
THE NECTARS.
SUCH A LONGING..
.. FOR I KNOW NOT WHAT.
LESTER! GO HOME TO YOUR WIFE!
REMEMBER..
.. THE LAST HUMILIATION..
REMEMBER HOW SHE LIED FOR YOU, SAID YOU'D FOUGHT A BATTLE UP HERE WITH SPIES..
.. AFTER YOU'D DRAINED AND SCARRED THESE PRECIOUS TREES..
PERHAPS-- ONE SIP-- TO TEST MY RESISTANCE..
ENOUGH!

WE STUMBLED HOME, HOPING MINERVA WOULDN'T NOTICE OUR LAPSE..

ENOUGH!

ENOUGH.

..BUT SHE DID.

HE REMEMBERS TOO MUCH WHEN HE DRINKS.

AND, LIKE MANY TIMES BEFORE, I WATCHED THEIR DANCE OF LOVE AND PANIC.

HARDER, PLEASE.

YOUR DUTIES KEPT YOU OUT LATE TONIGHT.

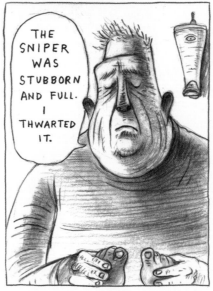

THE SNIPER WAS STUBBORN AND FULL. I THWARTED IT.

OH.. OOOH.. THANK YOU, OH.. OH, OH..

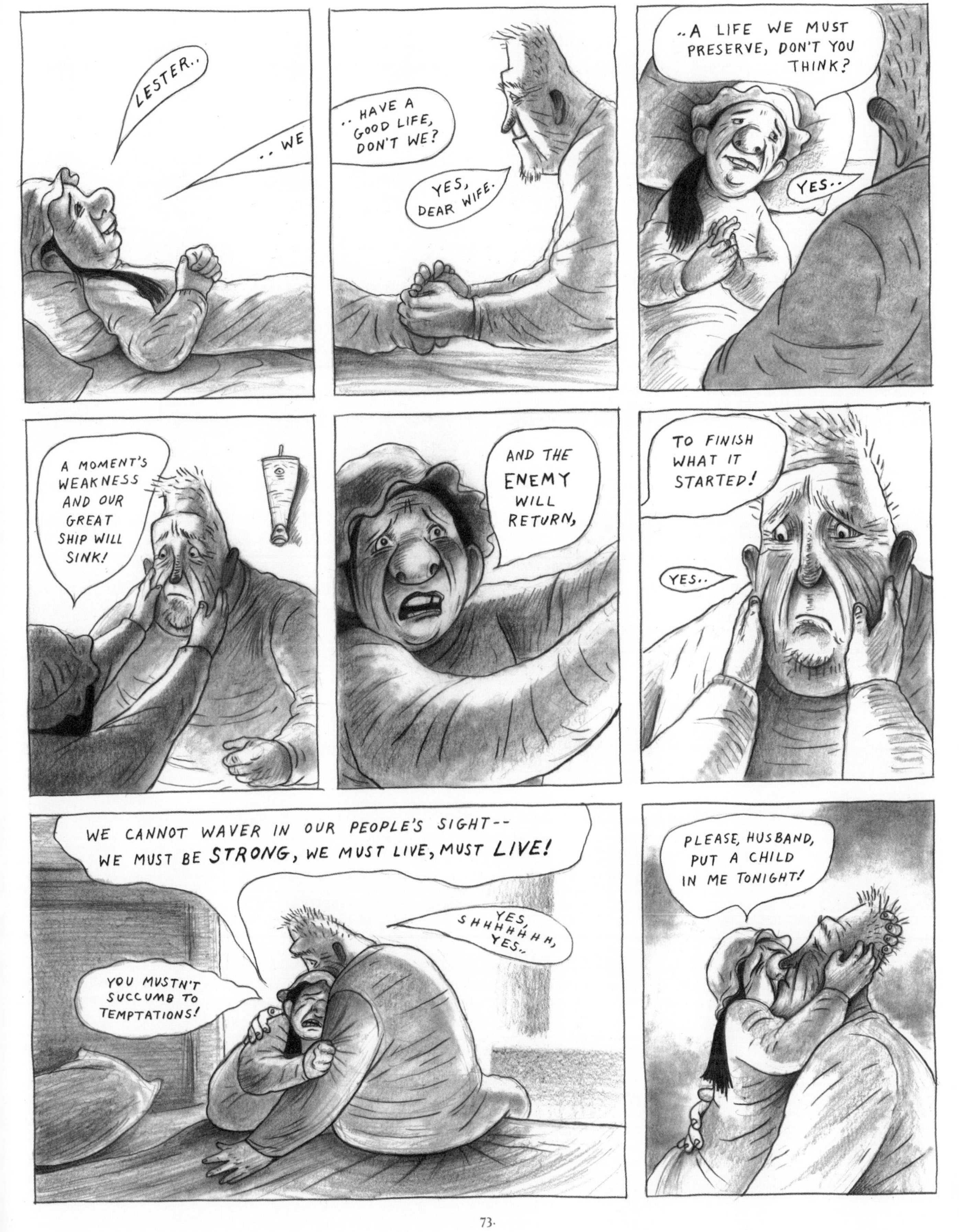
LESTER..
.. WE
.. HAVE A GOOD LIFE, DON'T WE?
YES, DEAR WIFE.
..A LIFE WE MUST PRESERVE, DON'T YOU THINK?
YES..
A MOMENT'S WEAKNESS AND OUR GREAT SHIP WILL SINK!
AND THE ENEMY WILL RETURN,
TO FINISH WHAT IT STARTED!
YES..
WE CANNOT WAVER IN OUR PEOPLE'S SIGHT-- WE MUST BE STRONG, WE MUST LIVE, MUST LIVE!
YES, SHHHHHHH, YES..
YOU MUSTN'T SUCCUMB TO TEMPTATIONS!
PLEASE, HUSBAND, PUT A CHILD IN ME TONIGHT!

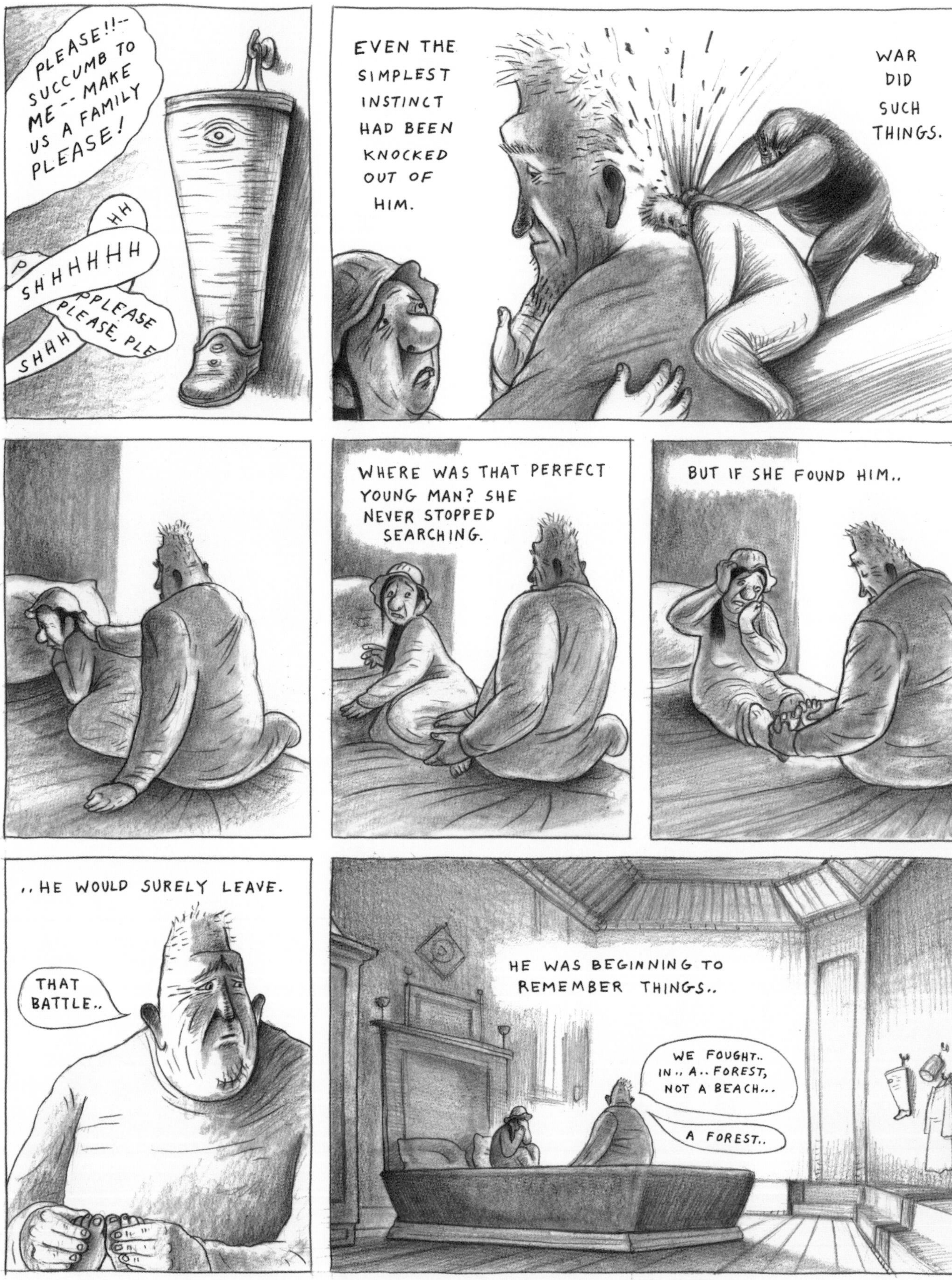
PLEASE!!-- SUCCUMB TO ME -- MAKE US A FAMILY PLEASE!
HH
SHHHHHH
P
PPLEASE PLEASE, PLE
SHHH
EVEN THE SIMPLEST INSTINCT HAD BEEN KNOCKED OUT OF HIM.
WAR DID SUCH THINGS.
WHERE WAS THAT PERFECT YOUNG MAN? SHE NEVER STOPPED SEARCHING.
BUT IF SHE FOUND HIM..
..HE WOULD SURELY LEAVE.
THAT BATTLE..
HE WAS BEGINNING TO REMEMBER THINGS..
WE FOUGHT.. IN.. A.. FOREST, NOT A BEACH...
A FOREST..

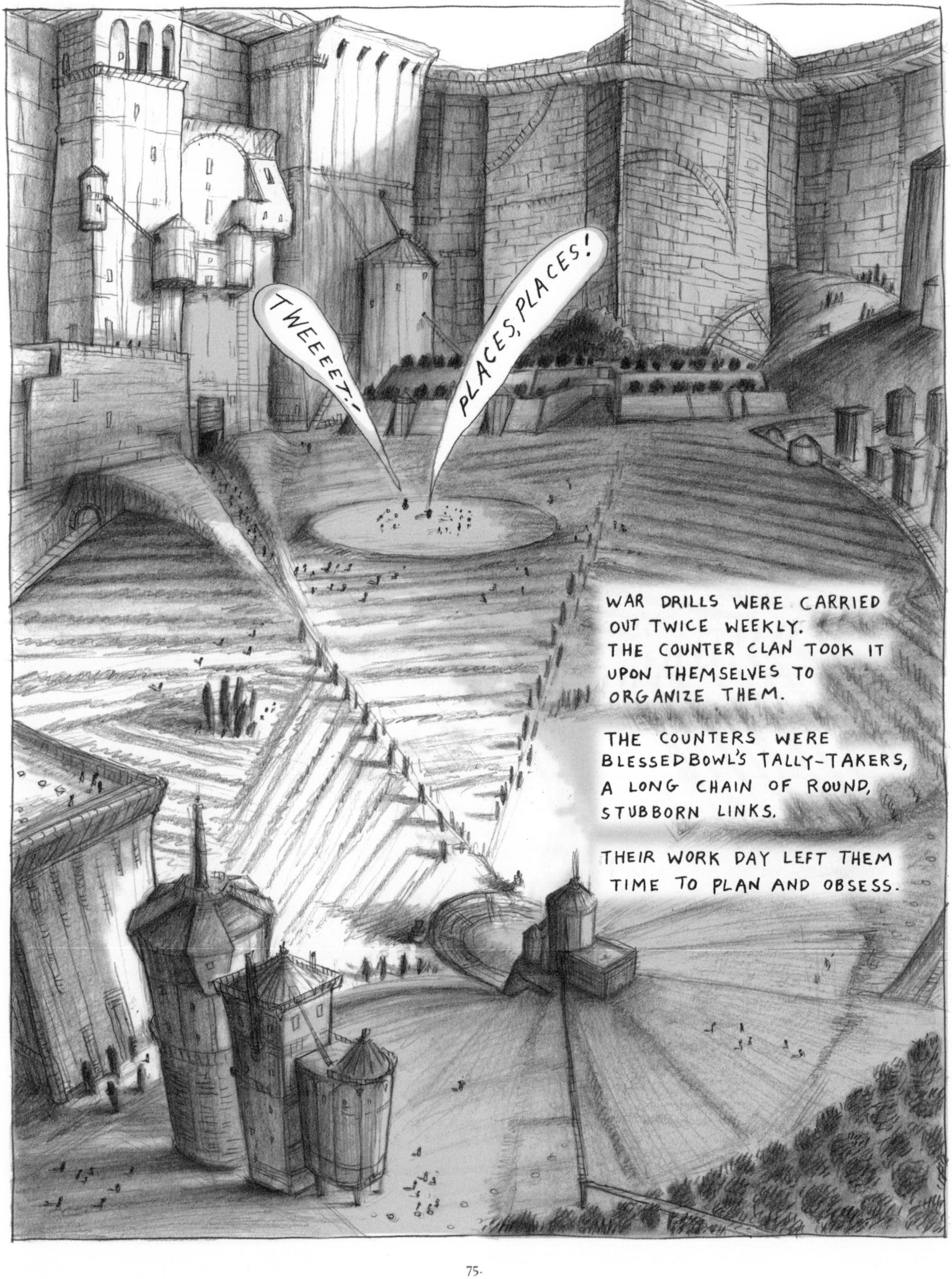
TWEEEET!
PLACES, PLACES!
WAR DRILLS WERE CARRIED OUT TWICE WEEKLY. THE COUNTER CLAN TOOK IT UPON THEMSELVES TO ORGANIZE THEM.
THE COUNTERS WERE BLESSEDBOWL'S TALLY-TAKERS, A LONG CHAIN OF ROUND, STUBBORN LINKS.
THEIR WORK DAY LEFT THEM TIME TO PLAN AND OBSESS.

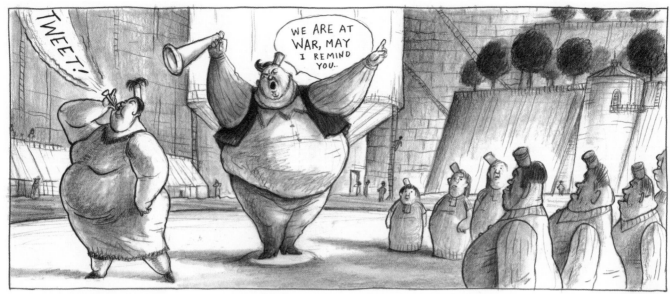

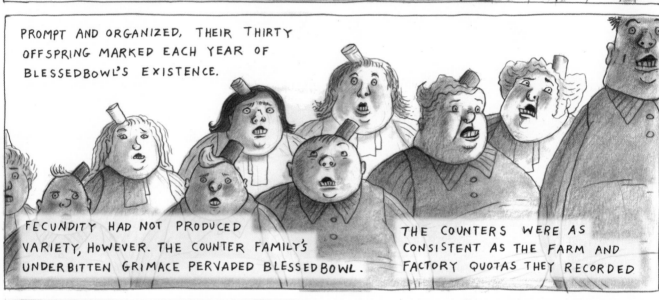

TWEET!
WE ARE AT WAR, MAY I REMIND YOU..
PROMPT AND ORGANIZED, THEIR THIRTY OFFSPRING MARKED EACH YEAR OF BLESSEDBOWL'S EXISTENCE.
FECUNDITY HAD NOT PRODUCED VARIETY, HOWEVER. THE COUNTER FAMILY'S UNDERBITTEN GRIMACE PERVADED BLESSEDBOWL.
THE COUNTERS WERE AS CONSISTENT AS THE FARM AND FACTORY QUOTAS THEY RECORDED
ROLL!
CHILDREN! DEMONSTRATE DROP-AND-ROLL!
PAPA!
BLESSEDBOWLERS: FOLLOW!

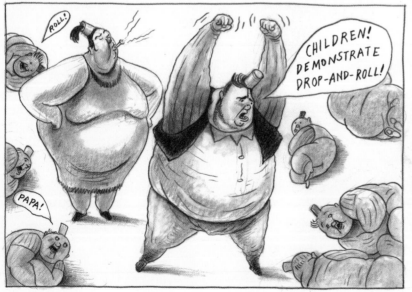

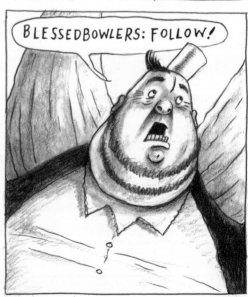

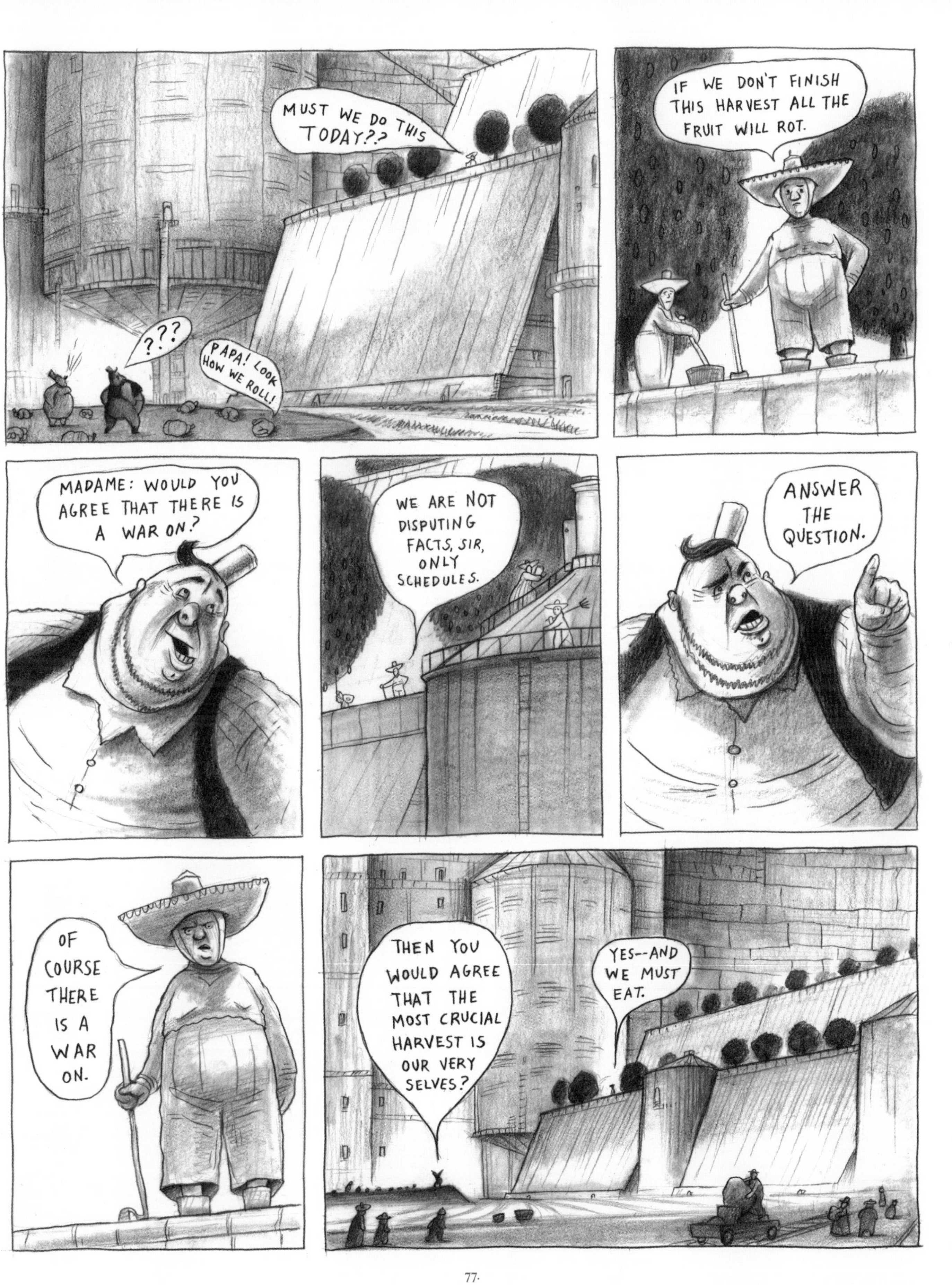
MUST WE DO THIS TODAY??
???
PAPA! LOOK HOW WE ROLL!
IF WE DON'T FINISH THIS HARVEST ALL THE FRUIT WILL ROT.
MADAME: WOULD YOU AGREE THAT THERE IS A WAR ON?
WE ARE NOT DISPUTING FACTS, SIR, ONLY SCHEDULES.
ANSWER THE QUESTION.
OF COURSE THERE IS A WAR ON.
THEN YOU WOULD AGREE THAT THE MOST CRUCIAL HARVEST IS OUR VERY SELVES?
YES--AND WE MUST EAT.

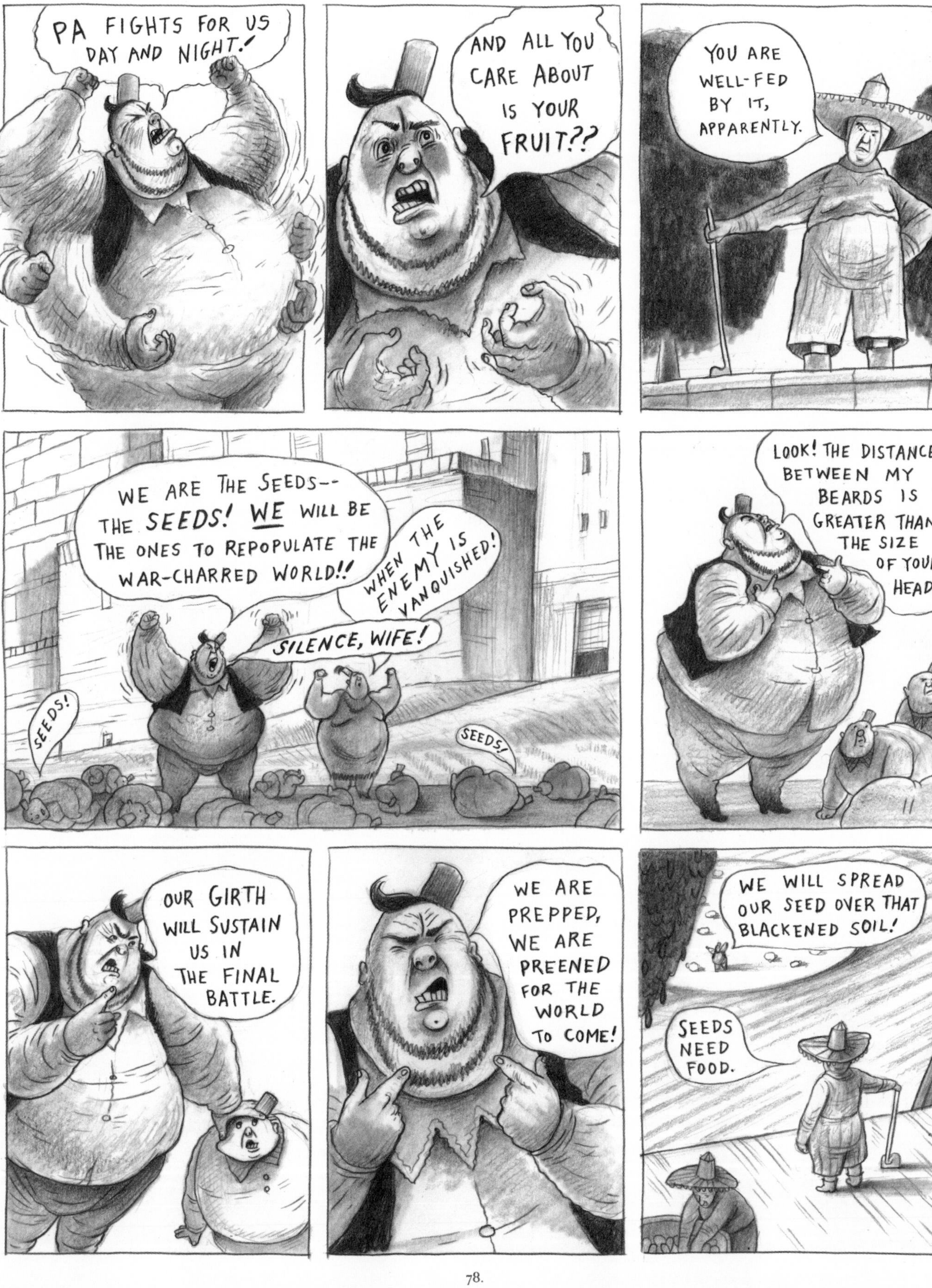
PA FIGHTS FOR US DAY AND NIGHT!
AND ALL YOU CARE ABOUT IS YOUR FRUIT??
YOU ARE WELL-FED BY IT, APPARENTLY.
WE ARE THE SEEDS-- THE SEEDS! WE WILL BE THE ONES TO REPOPULATE THE WAR-CHARRED WORLD!!
WHEN THE ENEMY IS VANQUISHED!
SILENCE, WIFE!
SEEDS!
SEEDS!
LOOK! THE DISTANCE BETWEEN MY BEARDS IS GREATER THAN THE SIZE OF YOUR HEAD!
OUR GIRTH WILL SUSTAIN US IN THE FINAL BATTLE.
WE ARE PREPPED, WE ARE PREENED FOR THE WORLD TO COME!
WE WILL SPREAD OUR SEED OVER THAT BLACKENED SOIL!
SEEDS NEED FOOD.

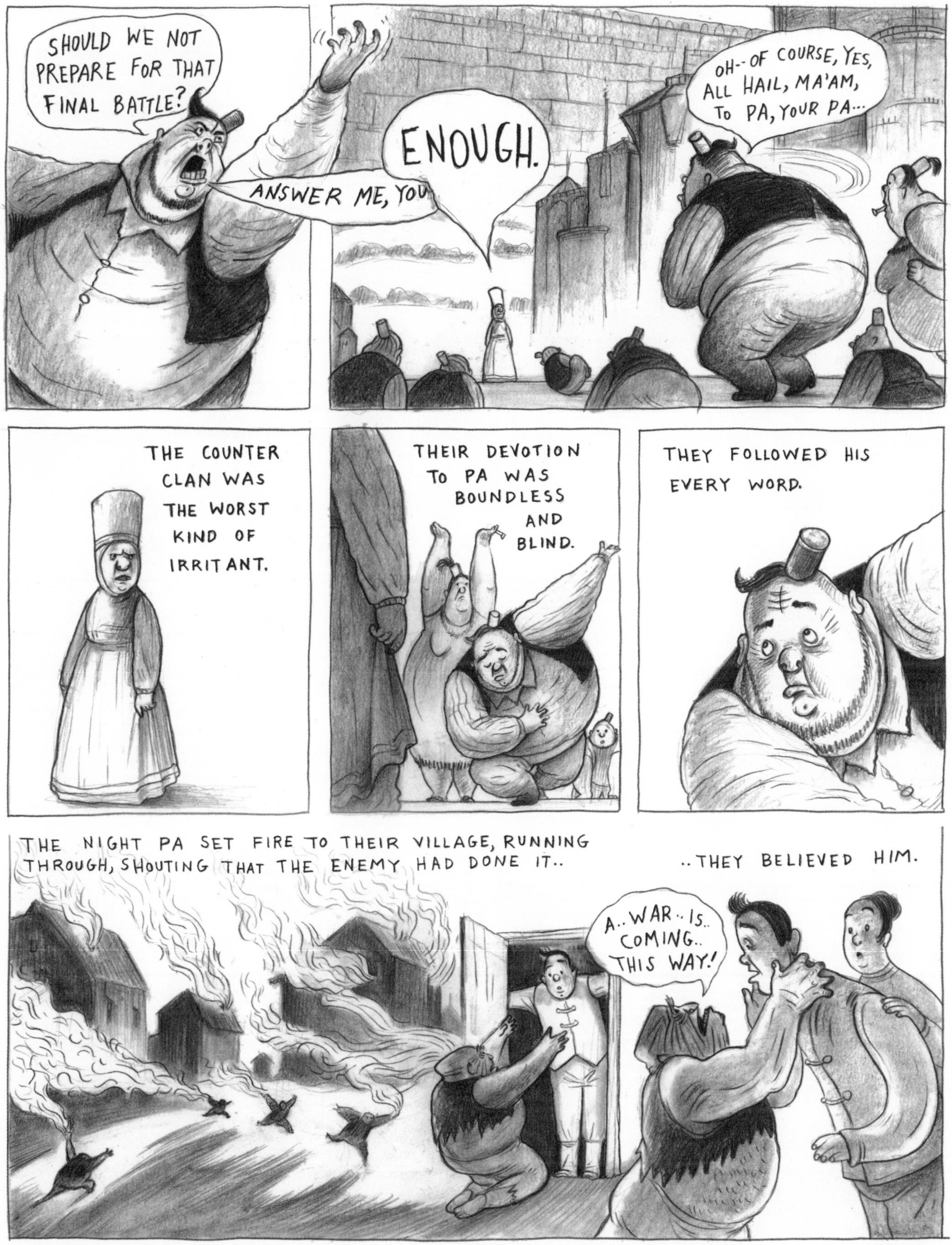
SHOULD WE NOT PREPARE FOR THAT FINAL BATTLE?
ANSWER ME, YOU
ENOUGH.
OH-- OF COURSE, YES, ALL HAIL, MA'AM, TO PA, YOUR PA...
THE COUNTER CLAN WAS THE WORST KIND OF IRRITANT.
THEIR DEVOTION TO PA WAS BOUNDLESS AND BLIND.
THEY FOLLOWED HIS EVERY WORD.
THE NIGHT PA SET FIRE TO THEIR VILLAGE, RUNNING THROUGH, SHOUTING THAT THE ENEMY HAD DONE IT..
..THEY BELIEVED HIM.
A.. WAR.. IS.. COMING.. THIS WAY!

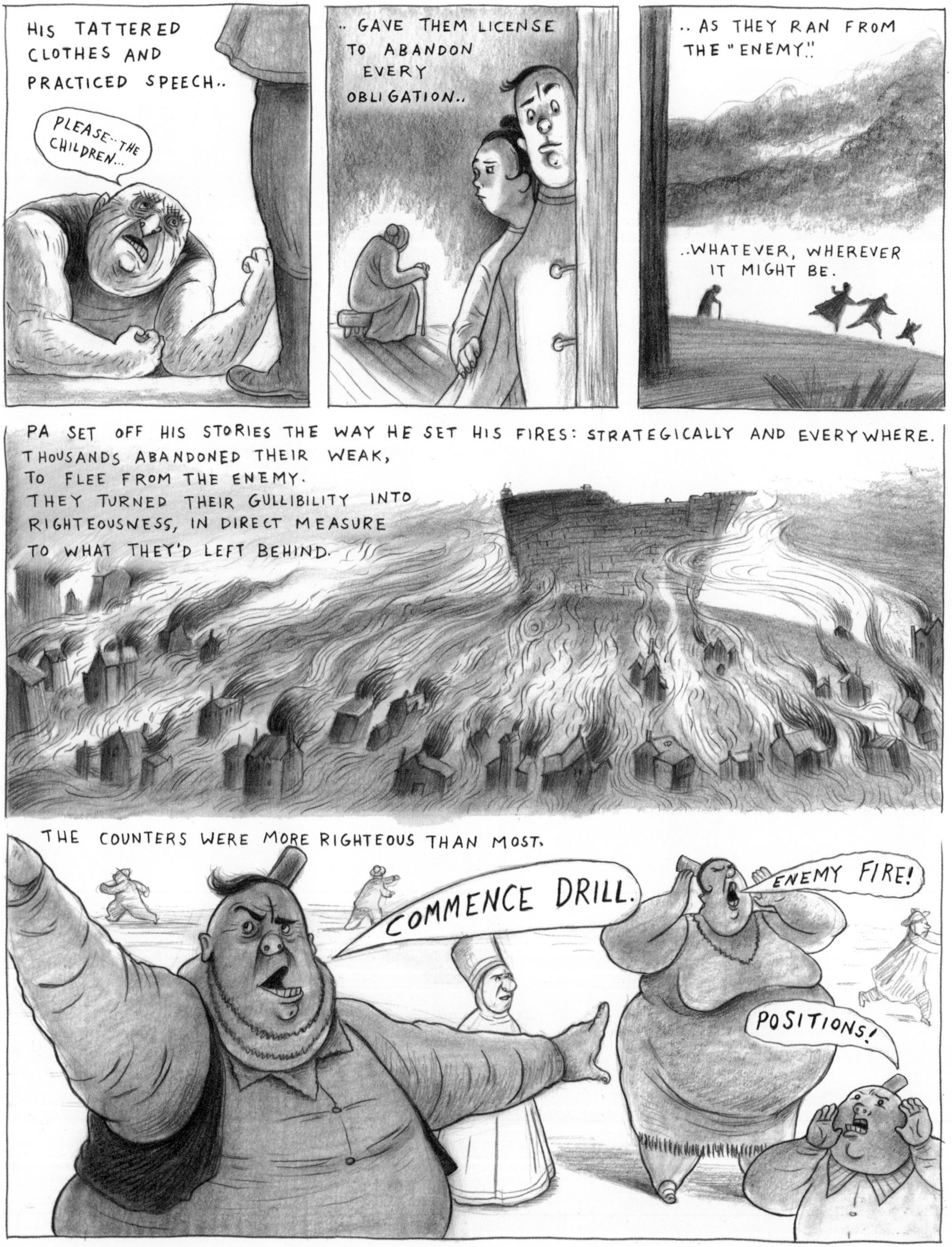
HIS TATTERED CLOTHES AND PRACTICED SPEECH..
PLEASE-- THE CHILDREN...
.. GAVE THEM LICENSE TO ABANDON EVERY OBLIGATION..
.. AS THEY RAN FROM THE "ENEMY."
..WHATEVER, WHEREVER IT MIGHT BE.
PA SET OFF HIS STORIES THE WAY HE SET HIS FIRES: STRATEGICALLY AND EVERYWHERE.
THOUSANDS ABANDONED THEIR WEAK, TO FLEE FROM THE ENEMY.
THEY TURNED THEIR GULLIBILITY INTO RIGHTEOUSNESS, IN DIRECT MEASURE TO WHAT THEY'D LEFT BEHIND.
THE COUNTERS WERE MORE RIGHTEOUS THAN MOST.
COMMENCE DRILL.
ENEMY FIRE!
POSITIONS!

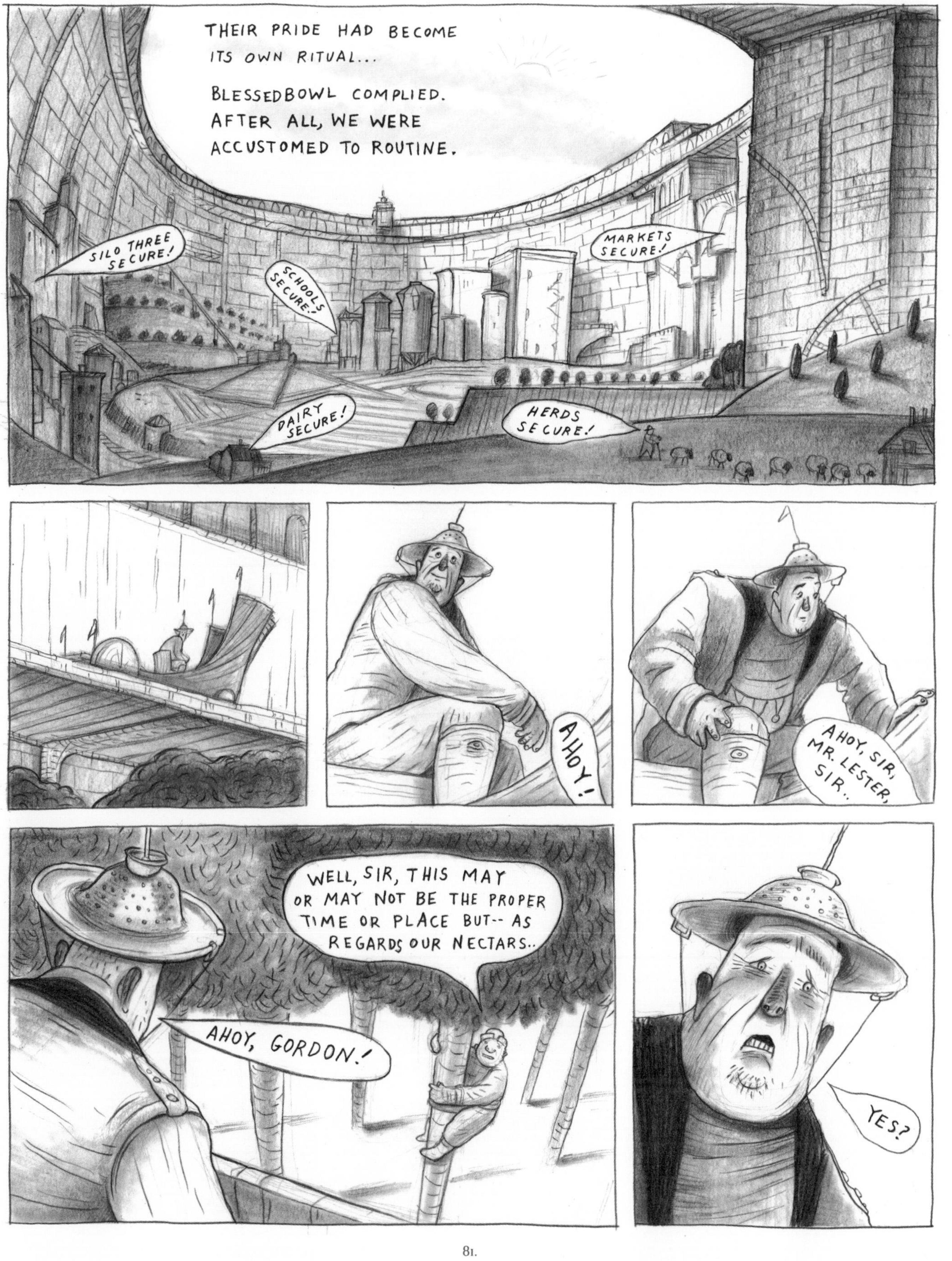
THEIR PRIDE HAD BECOME ITS OWN RITUAL...
BLESSEDBOWL COMPLIED. AFTER ALL, WE WERE ACCUSTOMED TO ROUTINE.
SILO THREE SECURE!
SCHOOLS SECURE!
MARKETS SECURE!
DAIRY SECURE!
HERDS SECURE!
AHOY!
AHOY, SIR, MR. LESTER, SIR..
WELL, SIR, THIS MAY OR MAY NOT BE THE PROPER TIME OR PLACE BUT-- AS REGARDS OUR NECTARS..
AHOY, GORDON!
YES?

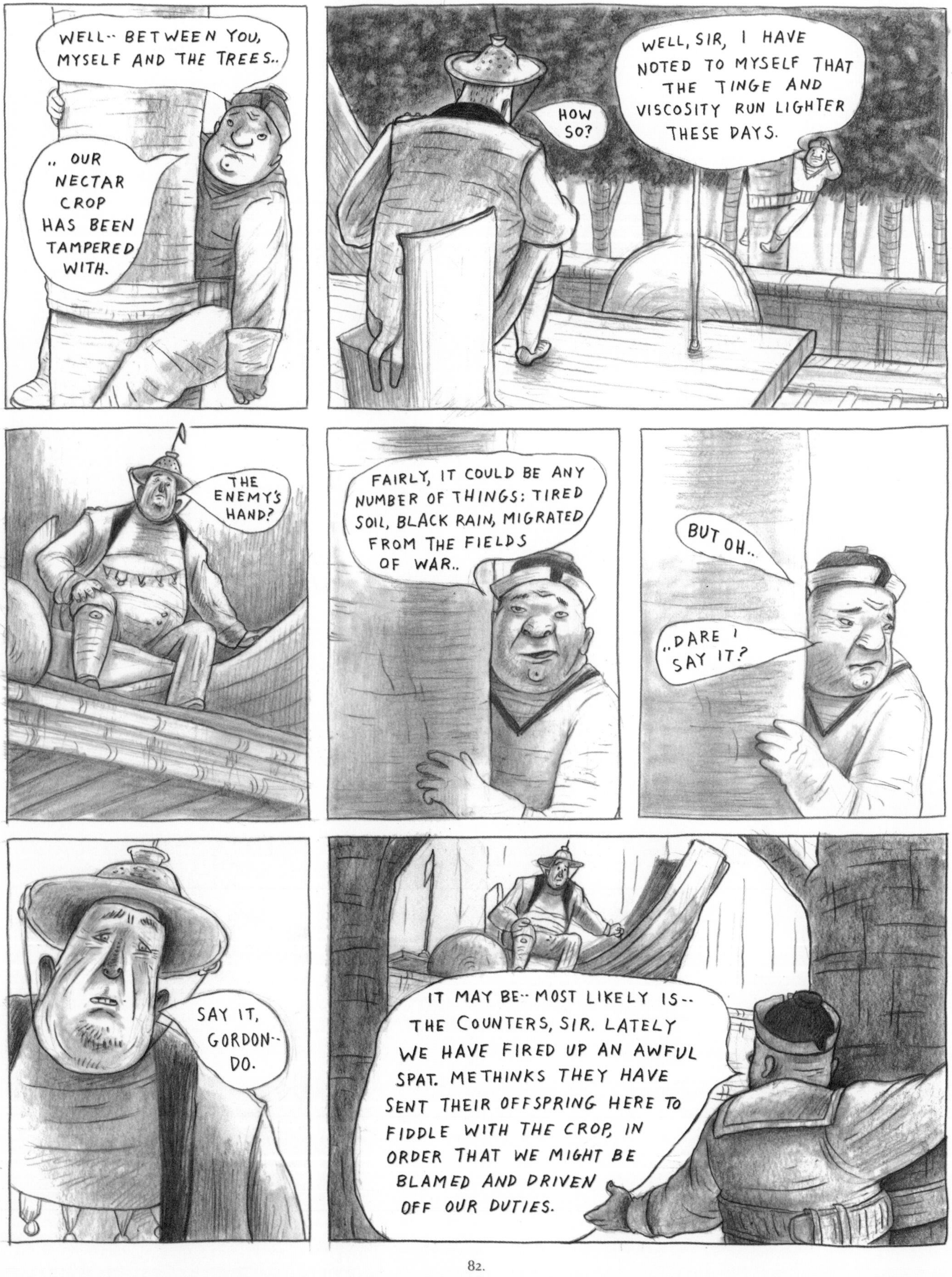
WELL-- BETWEEN YOU, MYSELF AND THE TREES..
.. OUR NECTAR CROP HAS BEEN TAMPERED WITH.
HOW SO?
WELL, SIR, I HAVE NOTED TO MYSELF THAT THE TINGE AND VISCOSITY RUN LIGHTER THESE DAYS.
THE ENEMY'S HAND?
FAIRLY, IT COULD BE ANY NUMBER OF THINGS: TIRED SOIL, BLACK RAIN, MIGRATED FROM THE FIELDS OF WAR..
BUT OH..
..DARE I SAY IT?
SAY IT, GORDON-- DO.
IT MAY BE-- MOST LIKELY IS-- THE COUNTERS, SIR. LATELY WE HAVE FIRED UP AN AWFUL SPAT. METHINKS THEY HAVE SENT THEIR OFFSPRING HERE TO FIDDLE WITH THE CROP, IN ORDER THAT WE MIGHT BE BLAMED AND DRIVEN OFF OUR DUTIES.

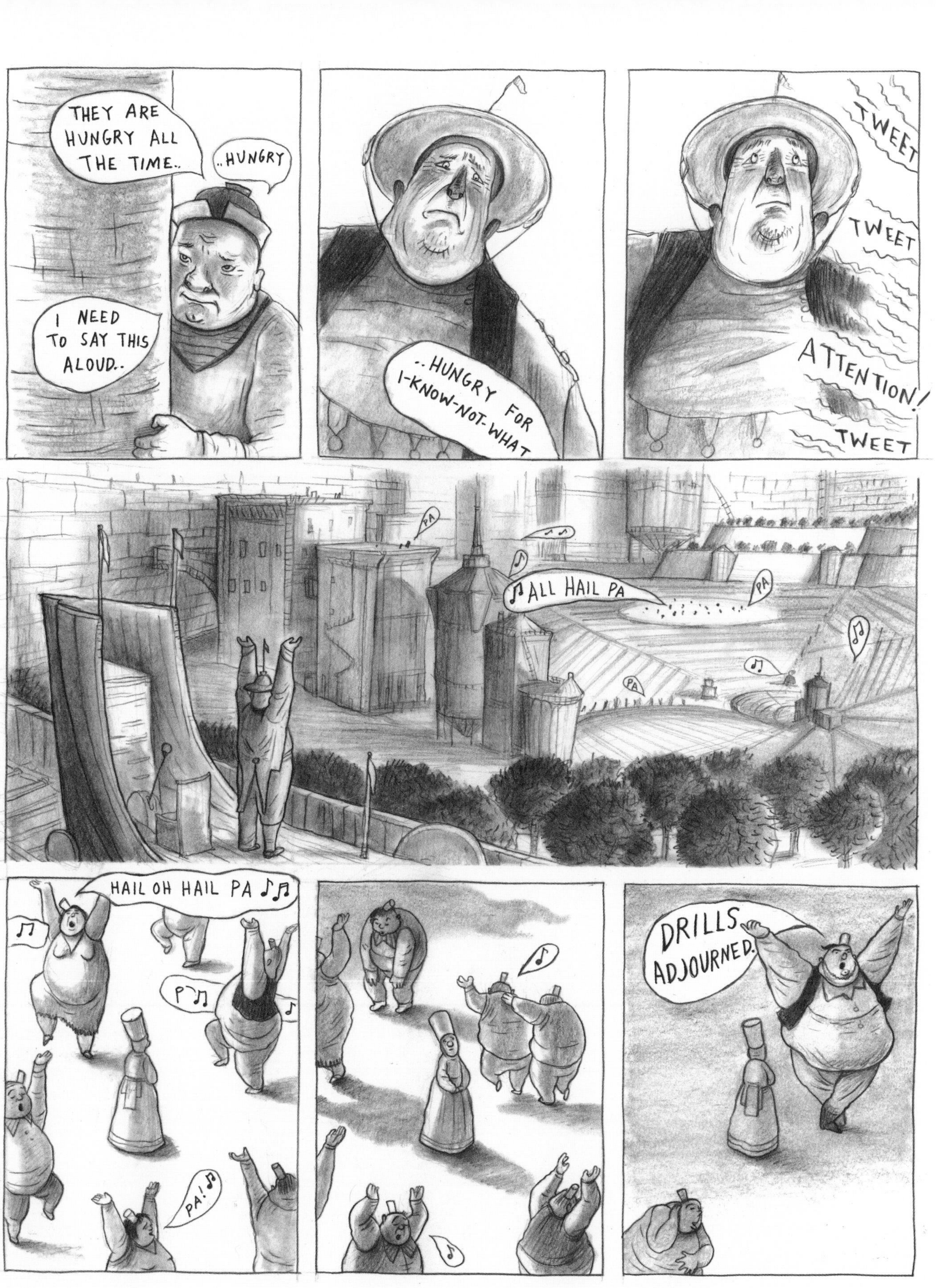

THEY ARE HUNGRY ALL THE TIME..
..HUNGRY
I NEED TO SAY THIS ALOUD..
..HUNGRY FOR I-KNOW-NOT-WHAT
TWEET
TWEET
ATTENTION!
TWEET
PA
ALL HAIL PA
PA
PA
HAIL OH HAIL PA
PA!
DRILLS ADJOURNED.

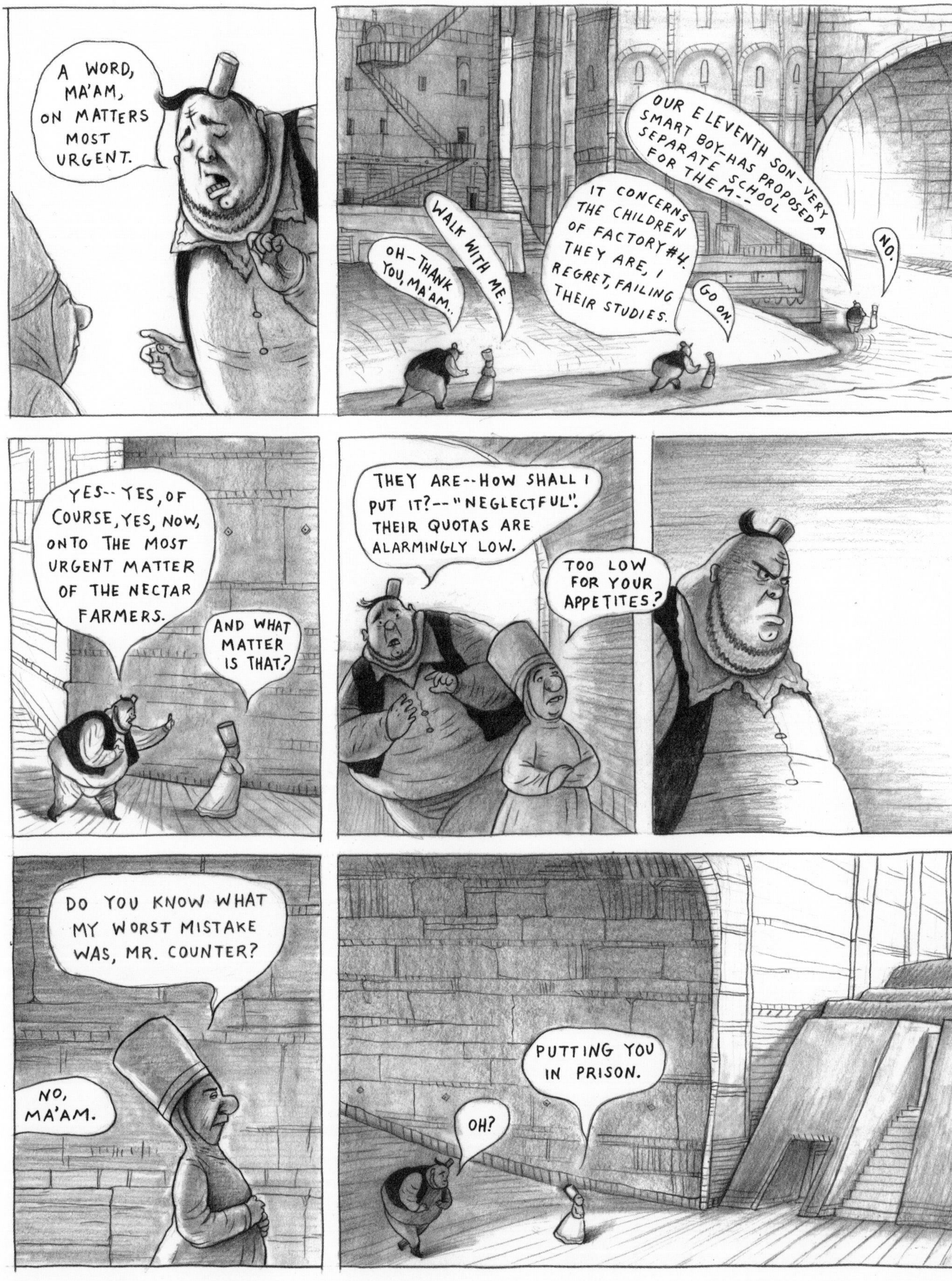
A WORD, MA'AM, ON MATTERS MOST URGENT.
WALK WITH ME.
OH—THANK YOU, MA'AM..
IT CONCERNS THE CHILDREN OF FACTORY #4. THEY ARE, I REGRET, FAILING THEIR STUDIES.
GO ON.
OUR ELEVENTH SON—VERY SMART BOY—HAS PROPOSED A SEPARATE SCHOOL FOR THEM--
NO.
YES-- YES, OF COURSE, YES, NOW, ONTO THE MOST URGENT MATTER OF THE NECTAR FARMERS.
AND WHAT MATTER IS THAT?
THEY ARE--HOW SHALL I PUT IT?--"NEGLECTFUL". THEIR QUOTAS ARE ALARMINGLY LOW.
TOO LOW FOR YOUR APPETITES?
DO YOU KNOW WHAT MY WORST MISTAKE WAS, MR. COUNTER?
NO, MA'AM.
PUTTING YOU IN PRISON.
OH?

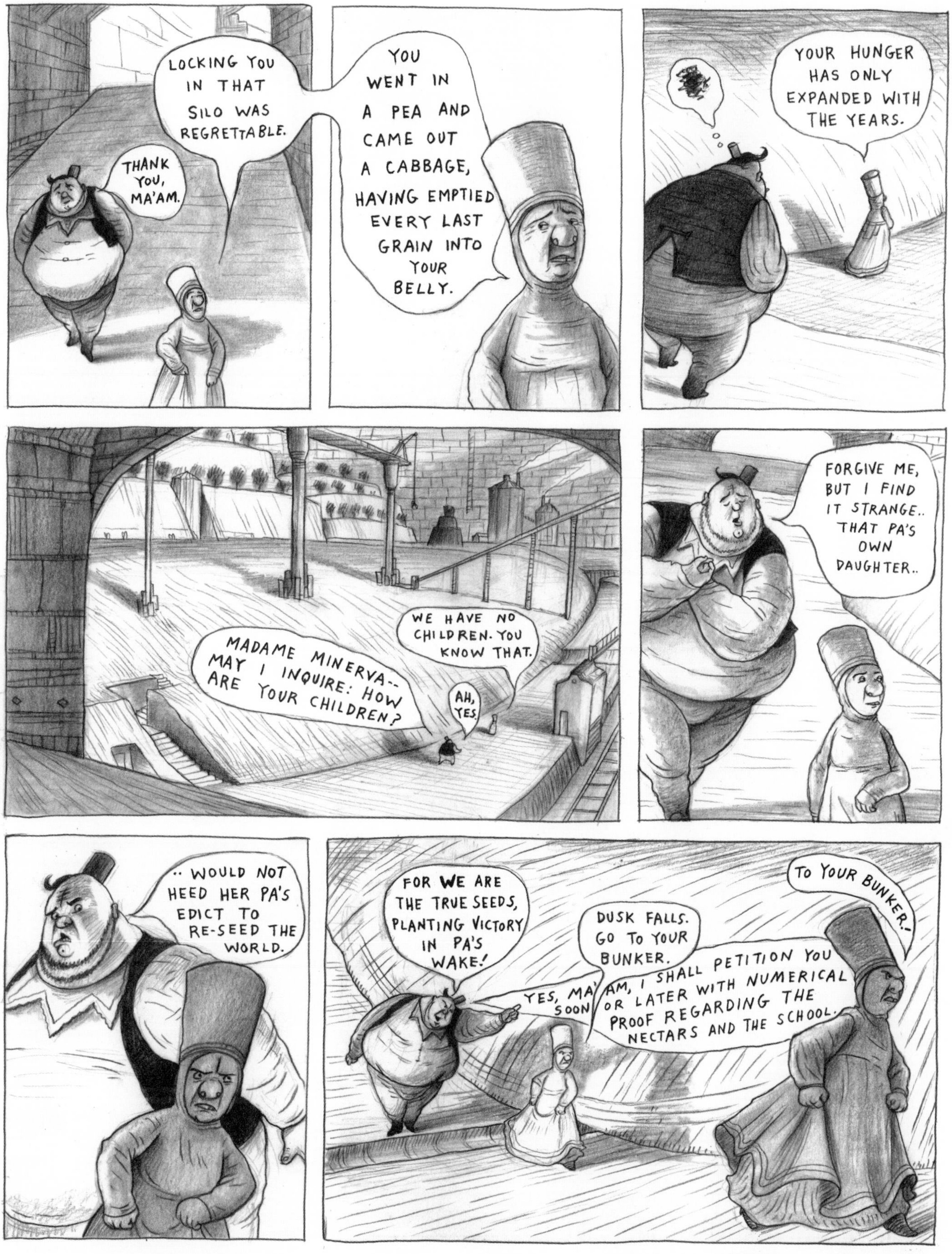

LOCKING YOU IN THAT SILO WAS REGRETTABLE.
THANK YOU, MA'AM.
YOU WENT IN A PEA AND CAME OUT A CABBAGE, HAVING EMPTIED EVERY LAST GRAIN INTO YOUR BELLY.
YOUR HUNGER HAS ONLY EXPANDED WITH THE YEARS.
MADAME MINERVA-- MAY I INQUIRE: HOW ARE YOUR CHILDREN?
WE HAVE NO CHILDREN. YOU KNOW THAT.
AH, YES.
FORGIVE ME, BUT I FIND IT STRANGE.. THAT PA'S OWN DAUGHTER..
..WOULD NOT HEED HER PA'S EDICT TO RE-SEED THE WORLD.
FOR WE ARE THE TRUE SEEDS, PLANTING VICTORY IN PA'S WAKE!
DUSK FALLS. GO TO YOUR BUNKER.
YES, MA'AM, I SHALL PETITION YOU SOON OR LATER WITH NUMERICAL PROOF REGARDING THE NECTARS AND THE SCHOOL.
TO YOUR BUNKER!

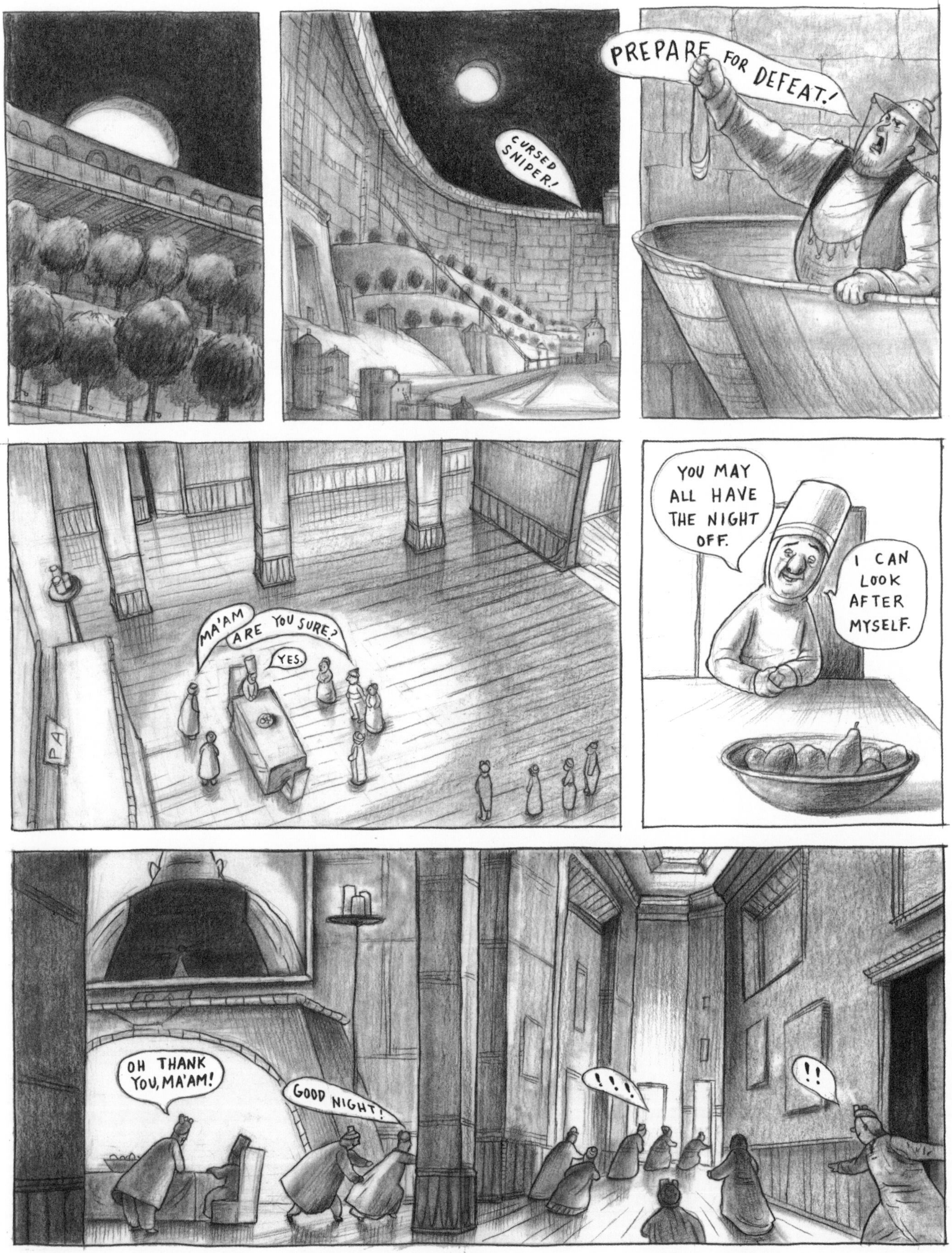
CURSED SNIPER!
PREPARE FOR DEFEAT!
MA'AM ARE YOU SURE?
YES.
YOU MAY ALL HAVE THE NIGHT OFF.
I CAN LOOK AFTER MYSELF.
OH THANK YOU, MA'AM!
GOOD NIGHT!
!!!
!!

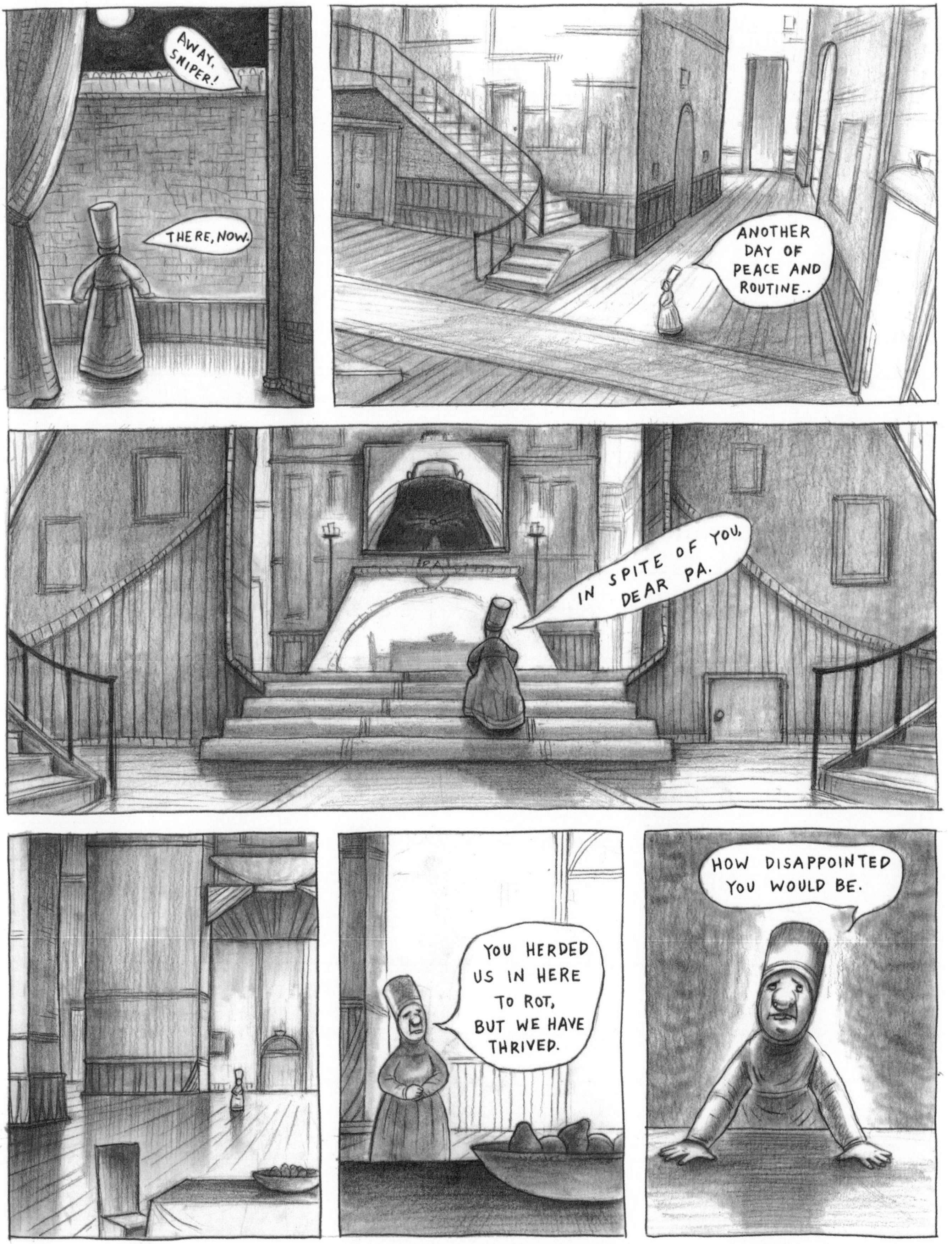
AWAY, SNIPER!
THERE, NOW.
ANOTHER DAY OF PEACE AND ROUTINE..
IN SPITE OF YOU, DEAR PA.
PA
YOU HERDED US IN HERE TO ROT, BUT WE HAVE THRIVED.
HOW DISAPPOINTED YOU WOULD BE.

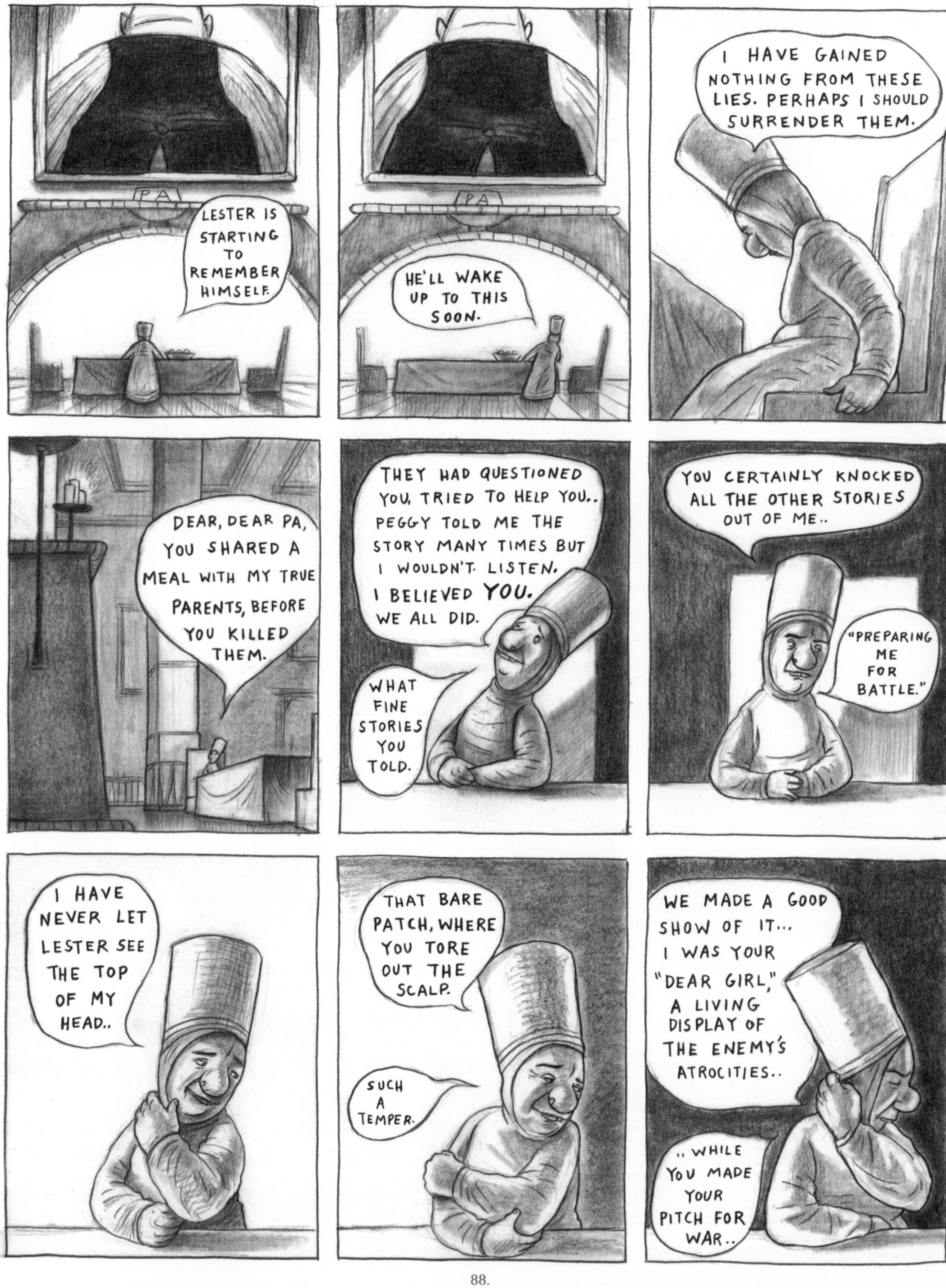
PA
LESTER IS STARTING TO REMEMBER HIMSELF.
PA
HE'LL WAKE UP TO THIS SOON.
I HAVE GAINED NOTHING FROM THESE LIES. PERHAPS I SHOULD SURRENDER THEM.
DEAR, DEAR PA, YOU SHARED A MEAL WITH MY TRUE PARENTS, BEFORE YOU KILLED THEM.
THEY HAD QUESTIONED YOU, TRIED TO HELP YOU.. PEGGY TOLD ME THE STORY MANY TIMES BUT I WOULDN'T LISTEN. I BELIEVED YOU. WE ALL DID.
WHAT FINE STORIES YOU TOLD.
YOU CERTAINLY KNOCKED ALL THE OTHER STORIES OUT OF ME..
"PREPARING ME FOR BATTLE."
I HAVE NEVER LET LESTER SEE THE TOP OF MY HEAD..
THAT BARE PATCH, WHERE YOU TORE OUT THE SCALP.
SUCH A TEMPER.
WE MADE A GOOD SHOW OF IT... I WAS YOUR "DEAR GIRL," A LIVING DISPLAY OF THE ENEMY'S ATROCITIES..
.. WHILE YOU MADE YOUR PITCH FOR WAR..

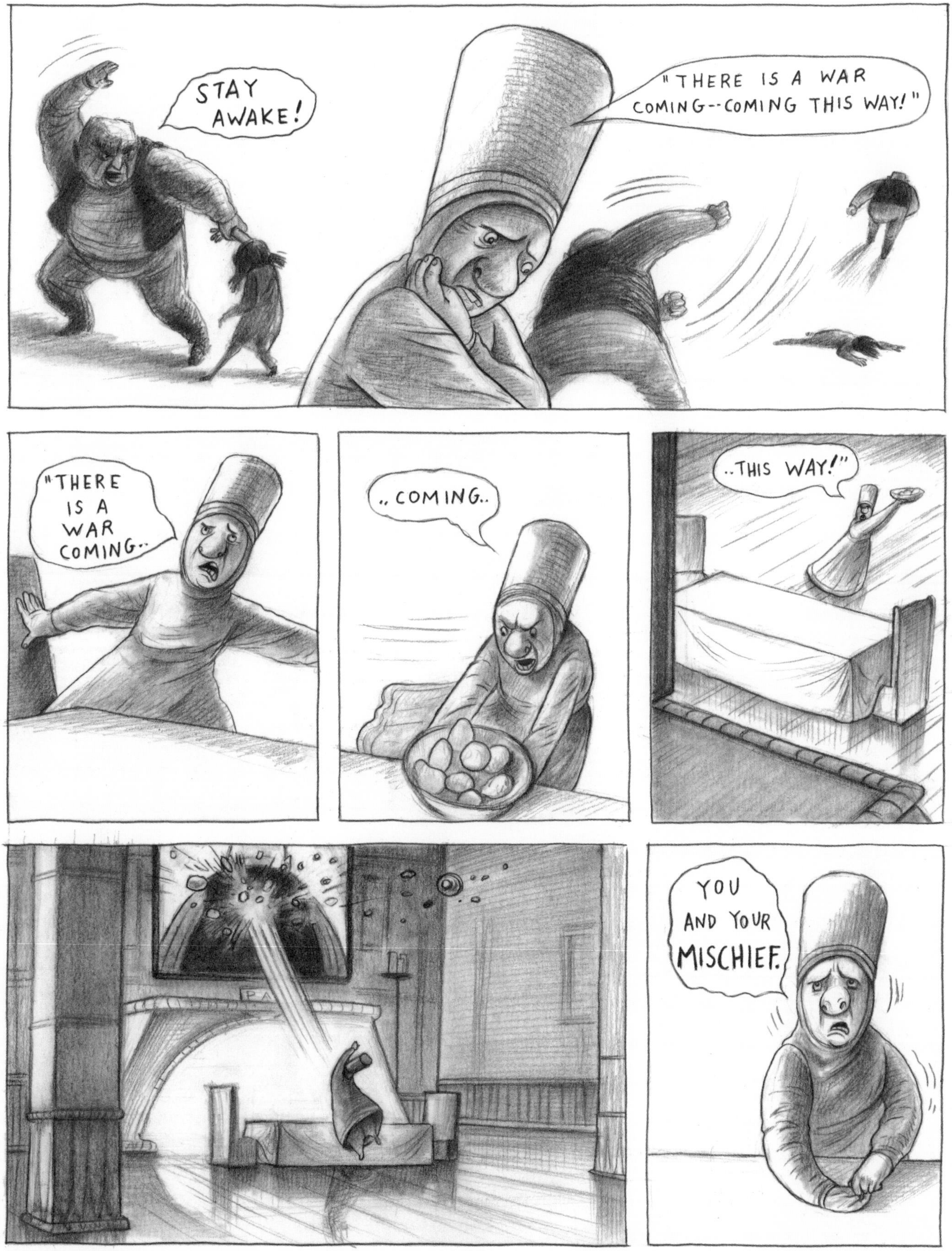
STAY AWAKE!
"THERE IS A WAR COMING--COMING THIS WAY!"
"THERE IS A WAR COMING..
.. COMING..
..THIS WAY!"
YOU AND YOUR MISCHIEF.

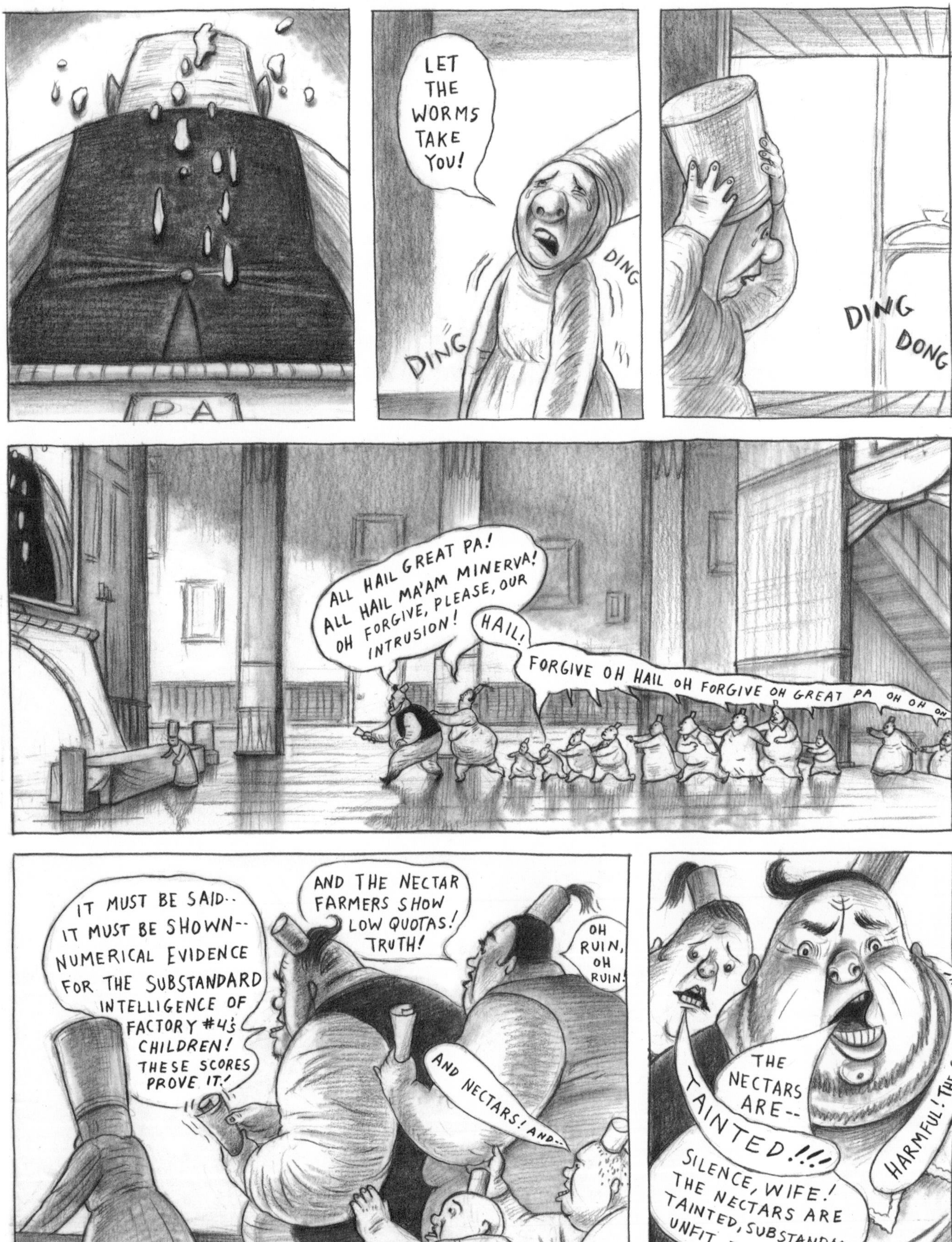
PA
LET THE WORMS TAKE YOU!
DING
DING
DING DONG
ALL HAIL GREAT PA! ALL HAIL MA'AM MINERVA! OH FORGIVE, PLEASE, OUR INTRUSION!
HAIL!
FORGIVE OH HAIL OH FORGIVE OH GREAT PA OH OH OH
IT MUST BE SAID-- IT MUST BE SHOWN-- NUMERICAL EVIDENCE FOR THE SUBSTANDARD INTELLIGENCE OF FACTORY #4's CHILDREN! THESE SCORES PROVE IT!
AND THE NECTAR FARMERS SHOW LOW QUOTAS! TRUTH!
OH RUIN, OH RUIN!
AND NECTARS! AND--
THE NECTARS ARE-- TAINTED.!!!
HARMFUL! THE CHILDREN! OH!
SILENCE, WIFE! THE NECTARS ARE TAINTED, SUBSTANDARD UNFIT FO

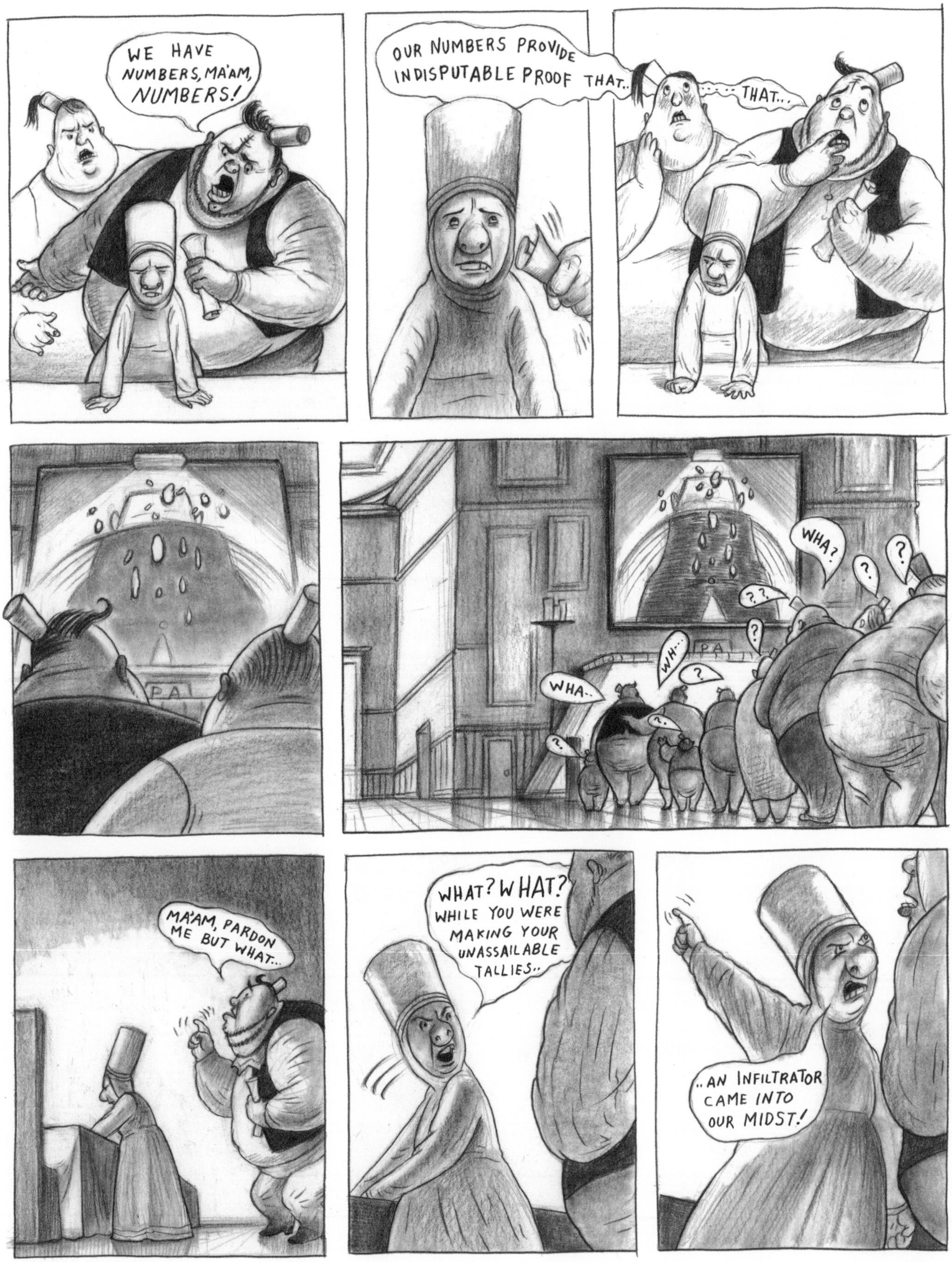
WE HAVE NUMBERS, MA'AM, NUMBERS!
OUR NUMBERS PROVIDE INDISPUTABLE PROOF THAT..
THAT...
WHA?
?
?
?.?.
?
WH..
?
WHA..
?
?
MA'AM, PARDON ME BUT WHAT...
WHAT? WHAT? WHILE YOU WERE MAKING YOUR UNASSAILABLE TALLIES..
..AN INFILTRATOR CAME INTO OUR MIDST!

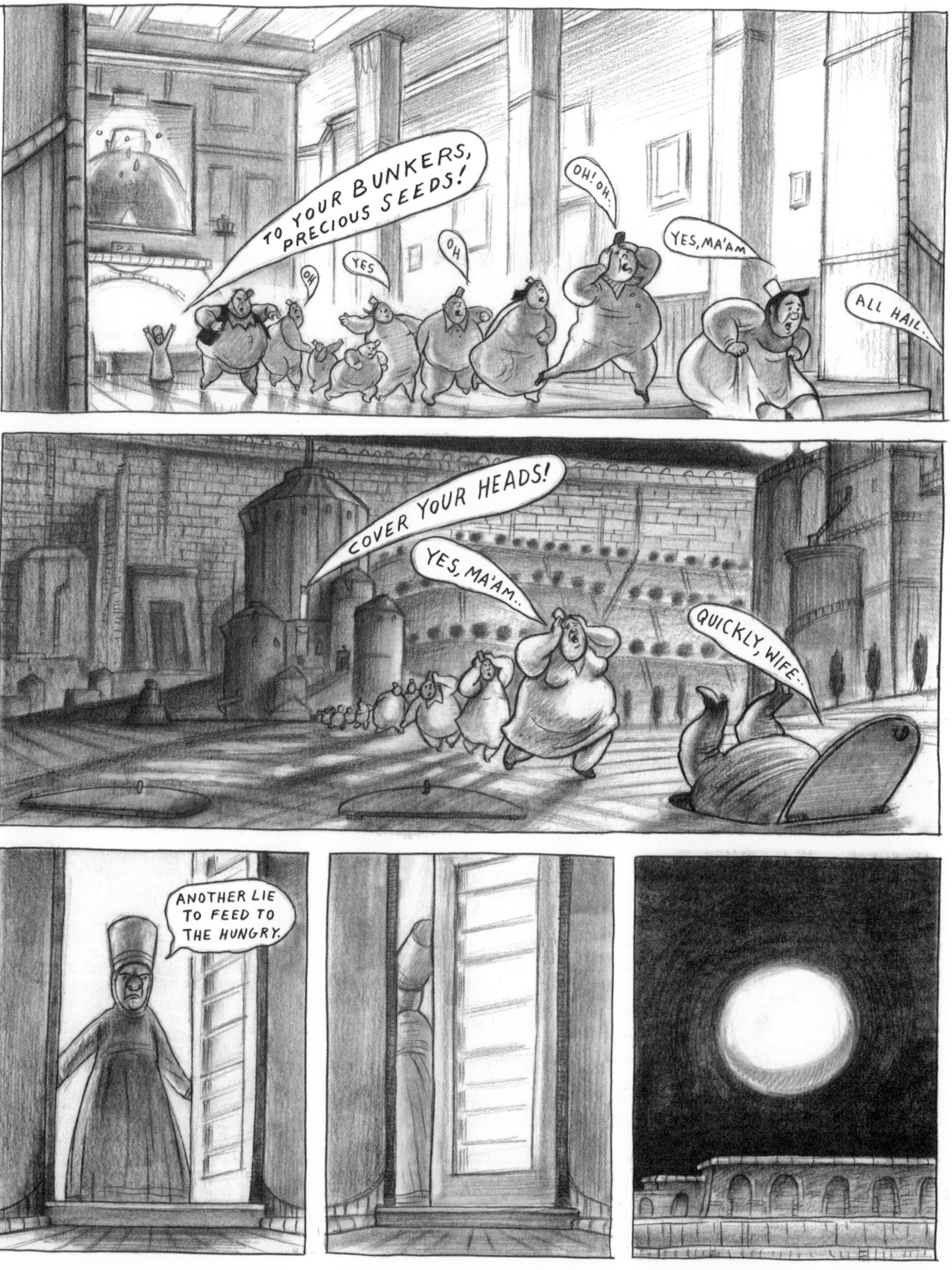
TO YOUR BUNKERS, PRECIOUS SEEDS!
OH
YES
OH
OH! OH..
YES, MA'AM
ALL HAIL..
COVER YOUR HEADS!
YES, MA'AM..
QUICKLY, WIFE..
ANOTHER LIE TO FEED TO THE HUNGRY.

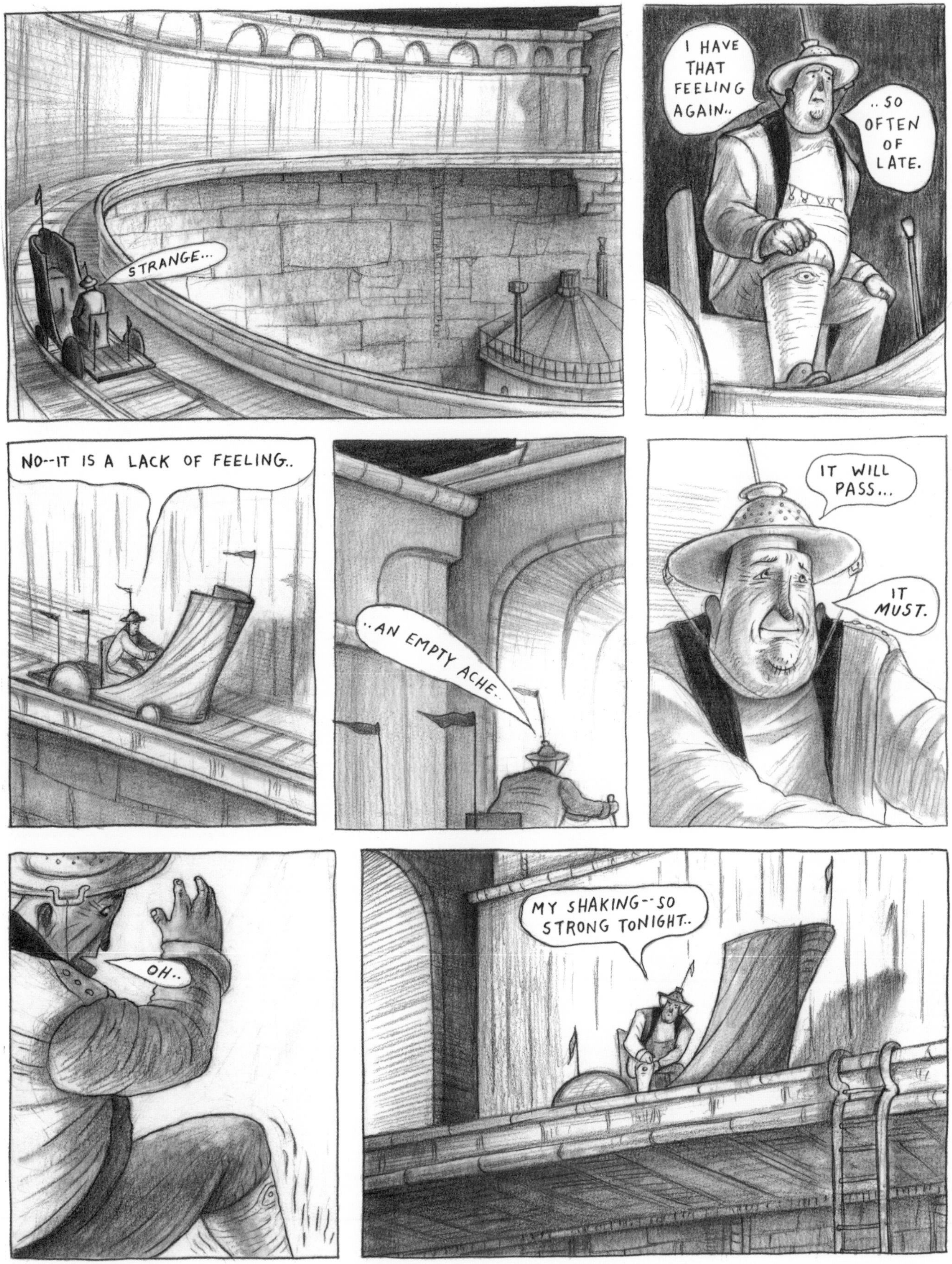
STRANGE...
I HAVE THAT FEELING AGAIN..
..SO OFTEN OF LATE.
NO--IT IS A LACK OF FEELING..
..AN EMPTY ACHE..
IT WILL PASS...
IT MUST.
OH..
MY SHAKING--SO STRONG TONIGHT..

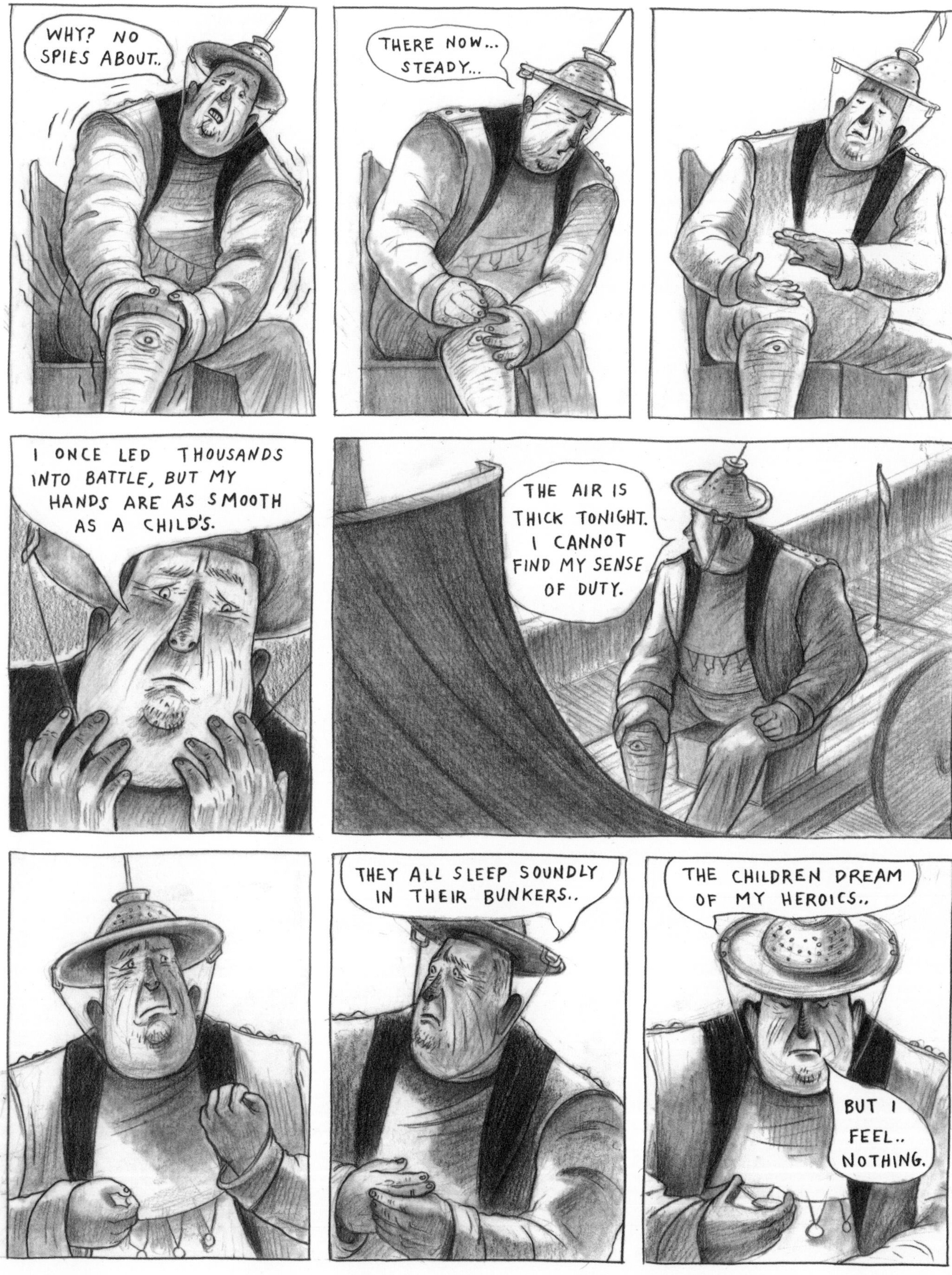
WHY? NO SPIES ABOUT..
THERE NOW... STEADY...
I ONCE LED THOUSANDS INTO BATTLE, BUT MY HANDS ARE AS SMOOTH AS A CHILD'S.
THE AIR IS THICK TONIGHT. I CANNOT FIND MY SENSE OF DUTY.
THEY ALL SLEEP SOUNDLY IN THEIR BUNKERS..
THE CHILDREN DREAM OF MY HEROICS..
BUT I FEEL.. NOTHING.

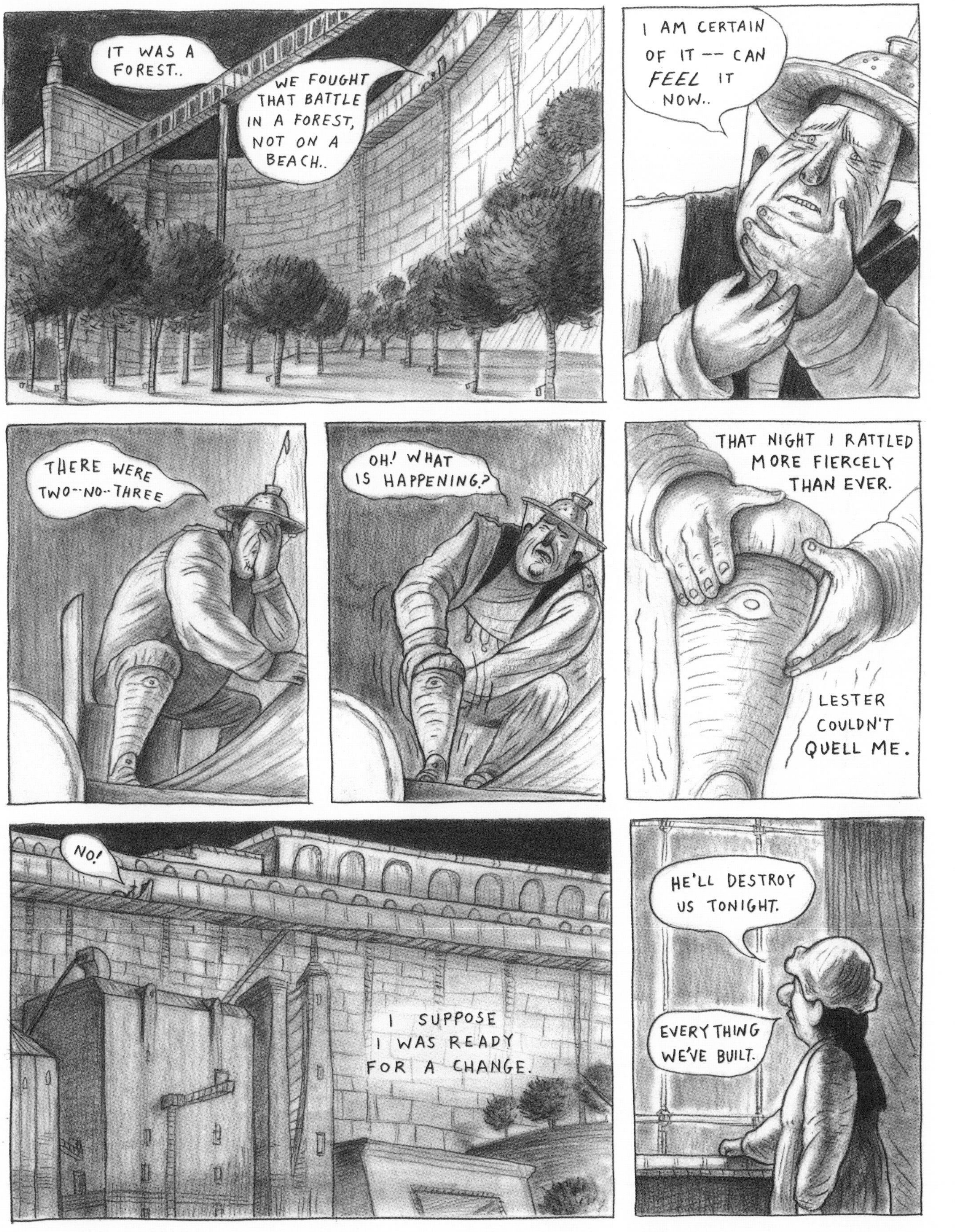

IT WAS A FOREST..
WE FOUGHT THAT BATTLE IN A FOREST, NOT ON A BEACH..
I AM CERTAIN OF IT -- CAN FEEL IT NOW..
THERE WERE TWO--NO--THREE
OH! WHAT IS HAPPENING?
THAT NIGHT I RATTLED MORE FIERCELY THAN EVER.
LESTER COULDN'T QUELL ME.
NO!
I SUPPOSE I WAS READY FOR A CHANGE.
HE'LL DESTROY US TONIGHT.
EVERYTHING WE'VE BUILT.

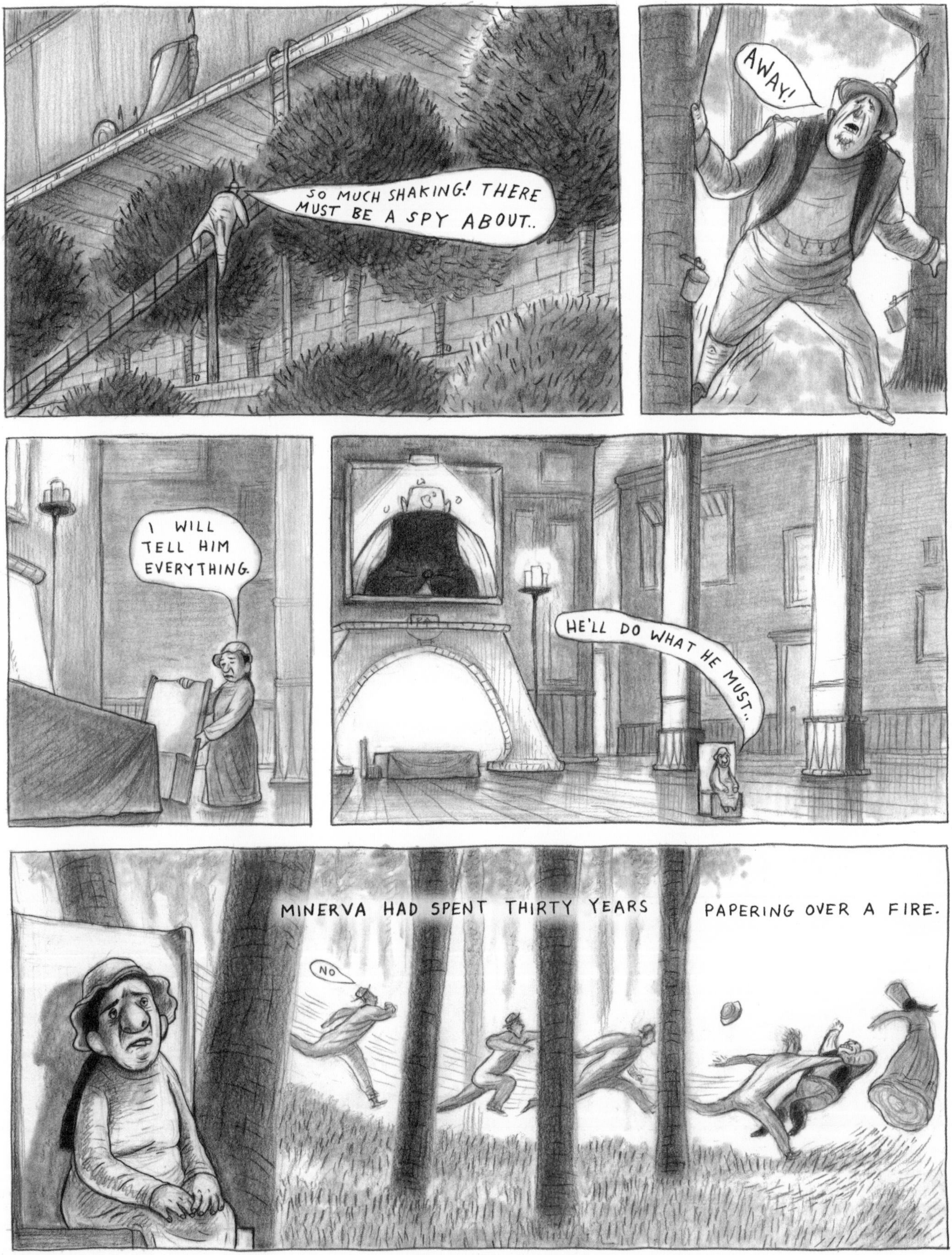
SO MUCH SHAKING! THERE MUST BE A SPY ABOUT..
AWAY!
I WILL TELL HIM EVERYTHING.
HE'LL DO WHAT HE MUST..
MINERVA HAD SPENT THIRTY YEARS
NO
PAPERING OVER A FIRE.

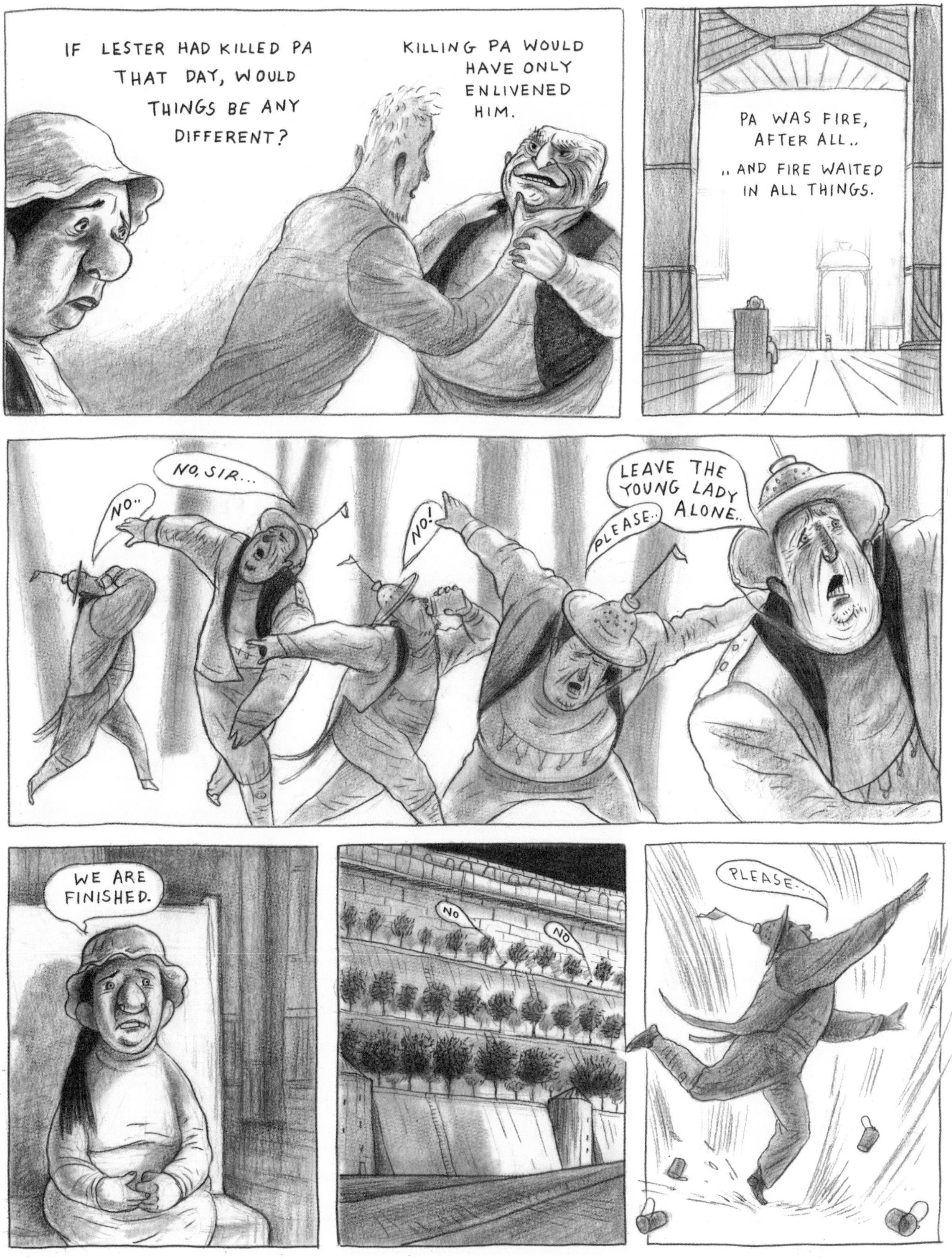
IF LESTER HAD KILLED PA THAT DAY, WOULD THINGS BE ANY DIFFERENT?
KILLING PA WOULD HAVE ONLY ENLIVENED HIM.
PA WAS FIRE, AFTER ALL..
.. AND FIRE WAITED IN ALL THINGS.
NO..
NO, SIR...
NO!
PLEASE..
LEAVE THE YOUNG LADY ALONE..
WE ARE FINISHED.
NO
NO
PLEASE...

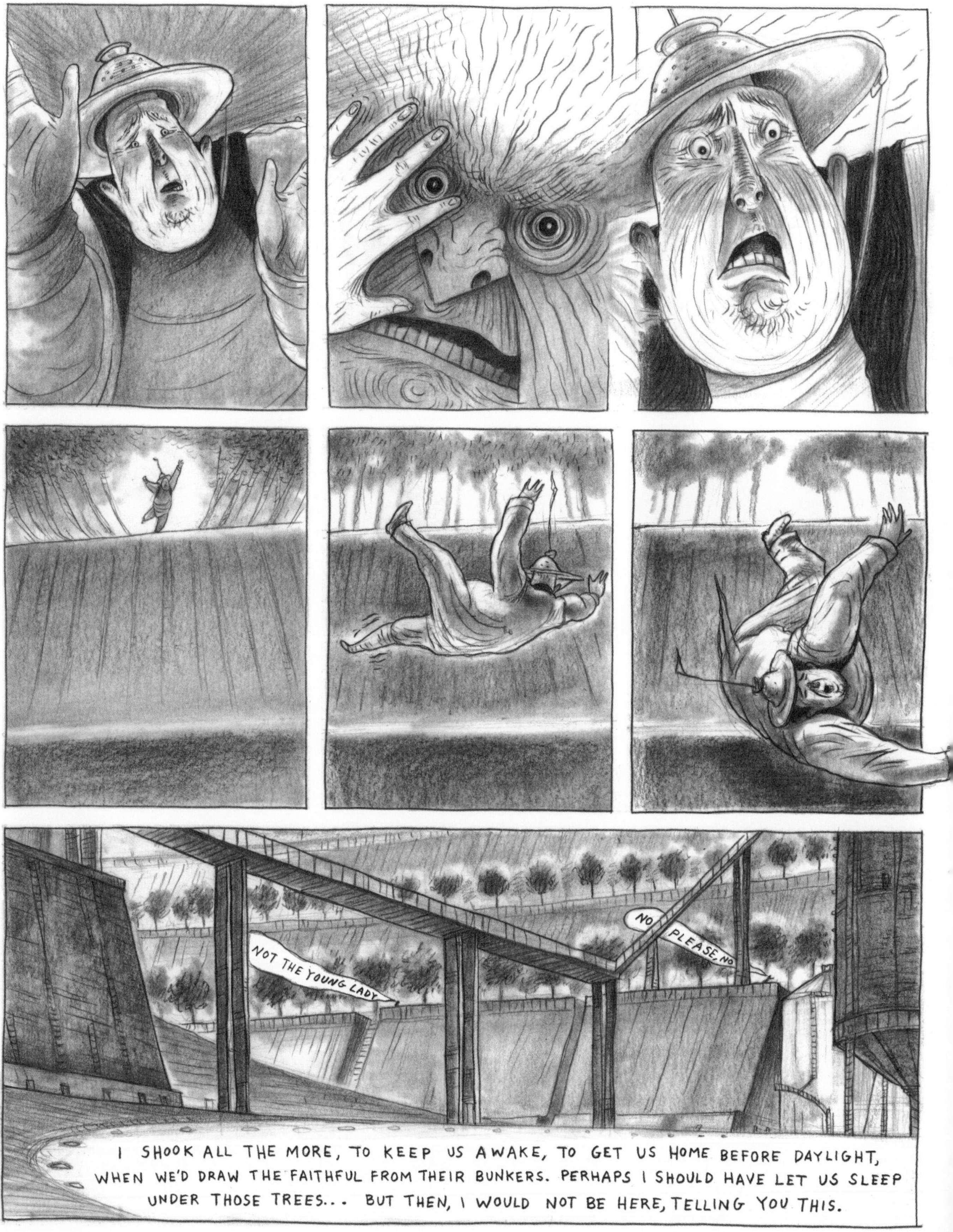
NOT THE YOUNG LADY
NO
PLEASE, NO
I SHOOK ALL THE MORE, TO KEEP US AWAKE, TO GET US HOME BEFORE DAYLIGHT, WHEN WE'D DRAW THE FAITHFUL FROM THEIR BUNKERS. PERHAPS I SHOULD HAVE LET US SLEEP UNDER THOSE TREES... BUT THEN, I WOULD NOT BE HERE, TELLING YOU THIS.

NO!
..NOT.. THE..
NOT
YOUNG LADY.
PLEASE..SIR... I-- DON'T
WANT.. ANY TROUBLE
PLEASE-- TAKE ME INSTEAD...

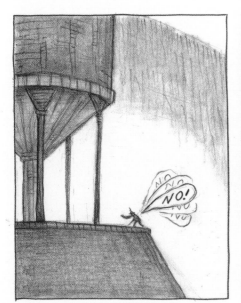

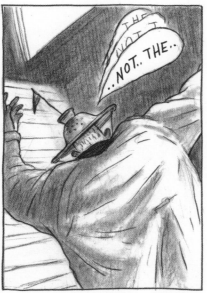

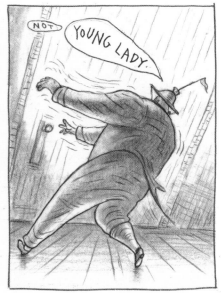

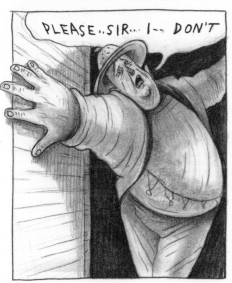

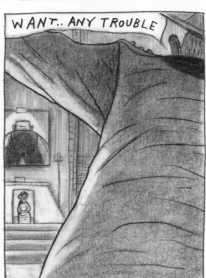

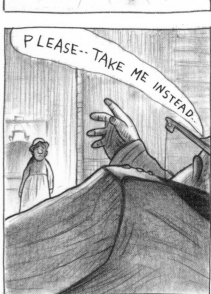

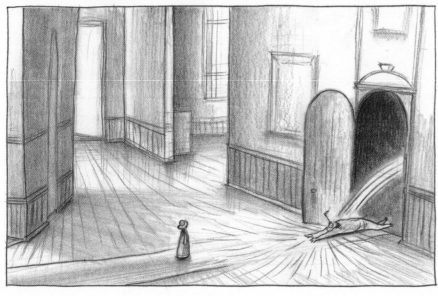

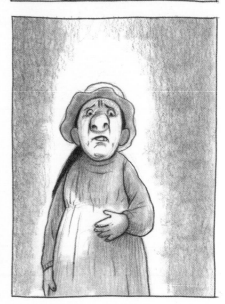

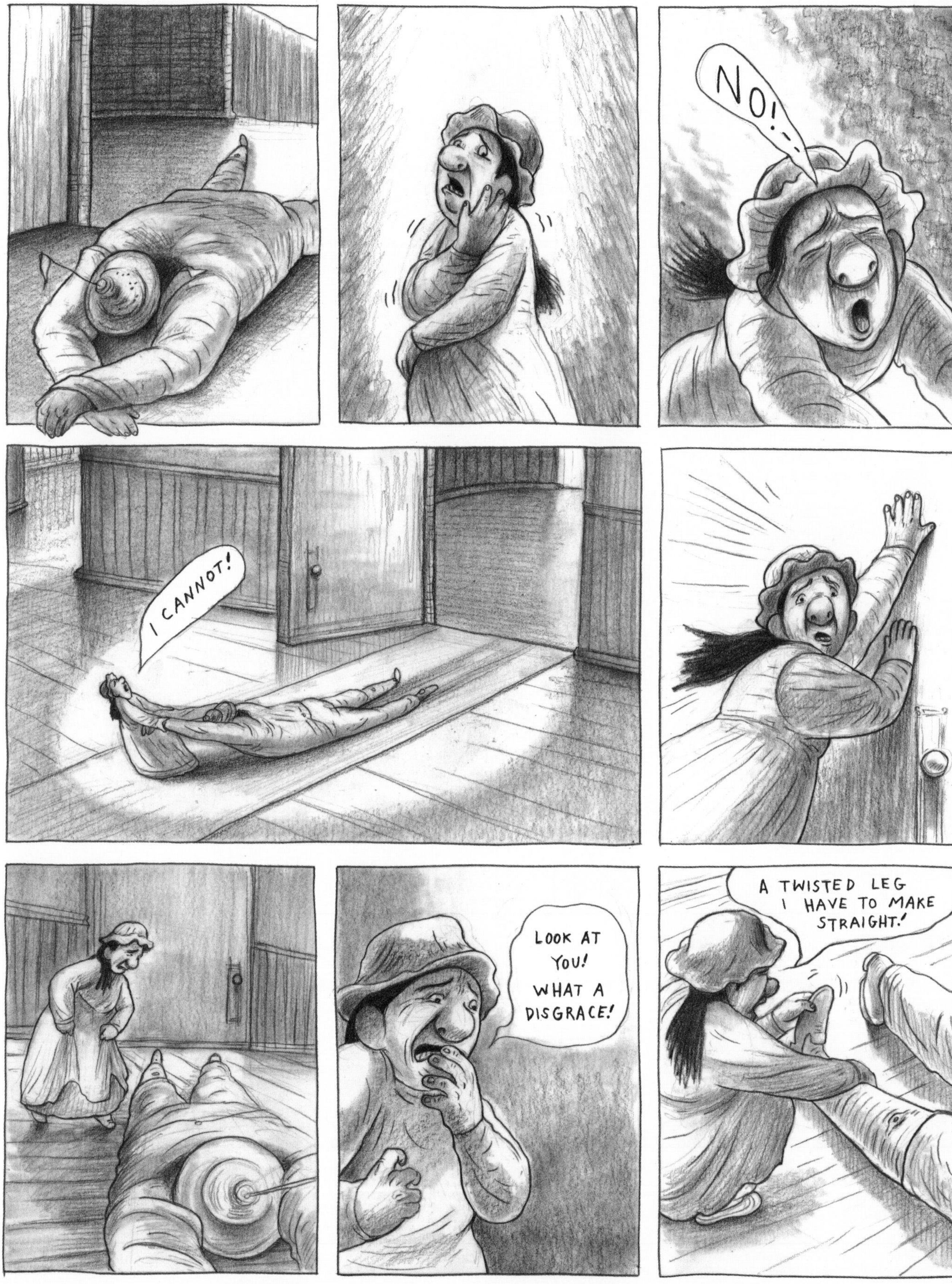
NO!
I CANNOT!
LOOK AT YOU! WHAT A DISGRACE!
A TWISTED LEG I HAVE TO MAKE STRAIGHT!

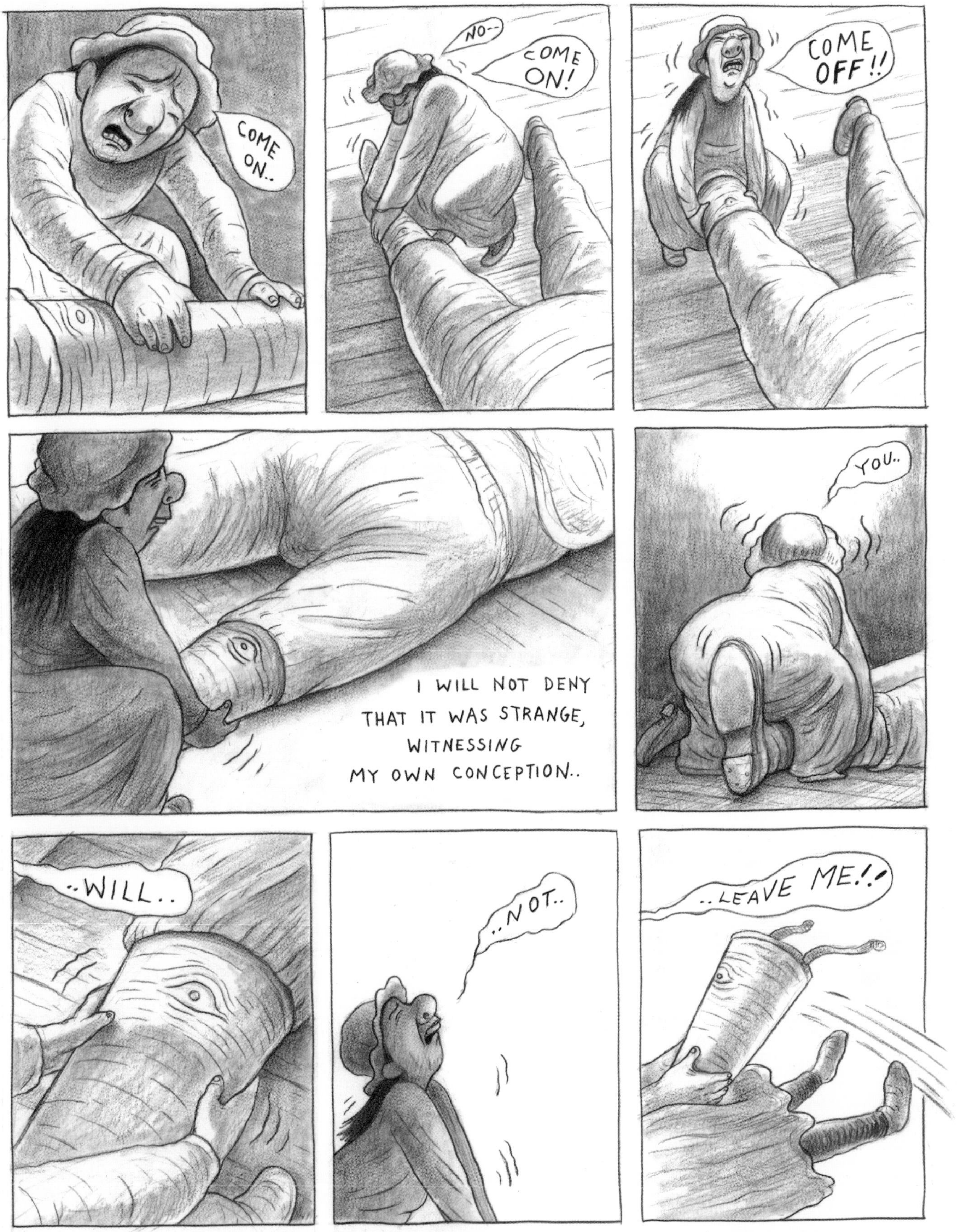
COME ON..
NO--
COME ON!
COME OFF!!
I WILL NOT DENY THAT IT WAS STRANGE, WITNESSING MY OWN CONCEPTION..
YOU..
..WILL..
..NOT..
..LEAVE ME!!

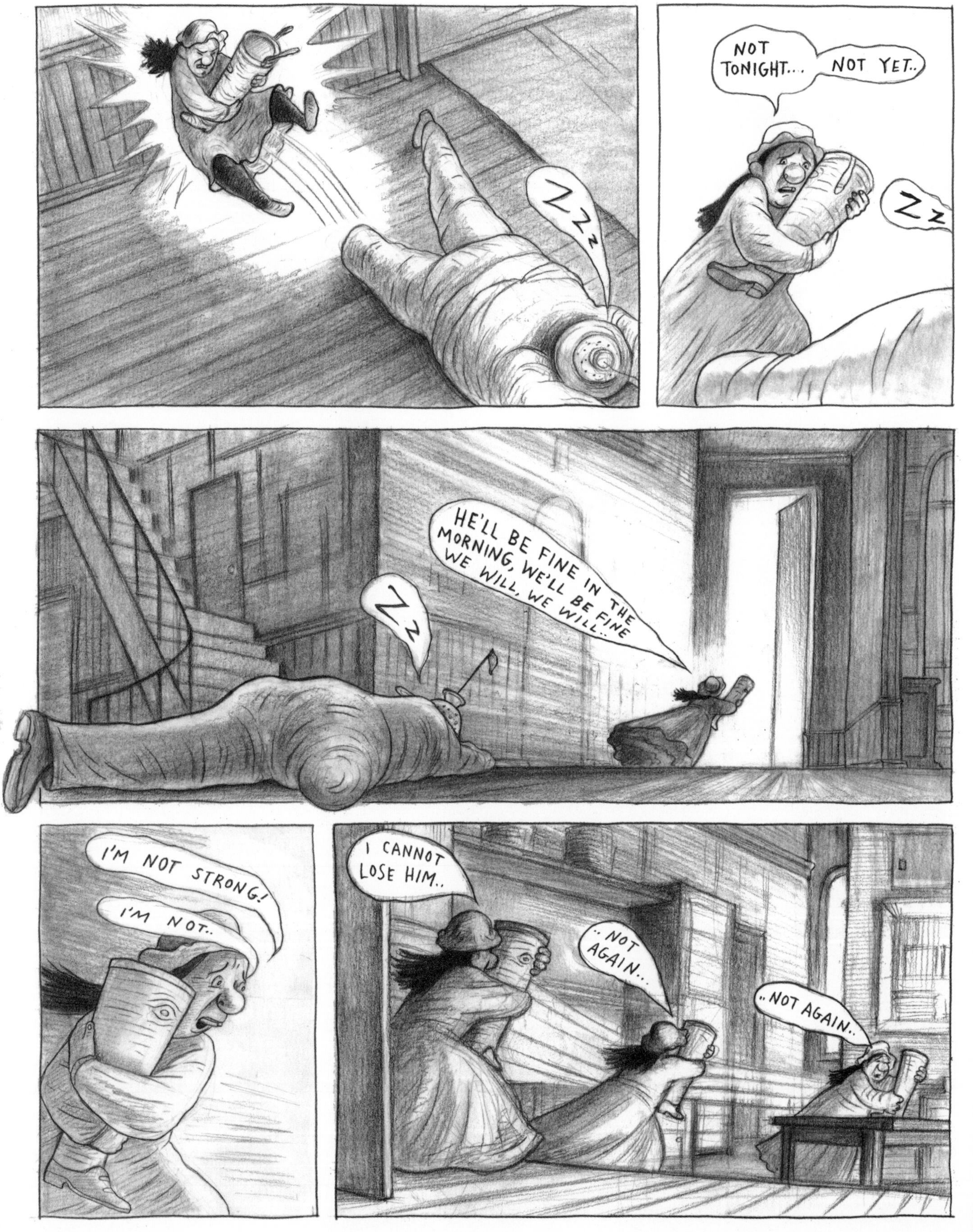
Z z z
NOT TONIGHT...
NOT YET..
Z z
Z z
HE'LL BE FINE IN THE MORNING, WE'LL BE FINE WE WILL, WE WILL..
I'M NOT STRONG!
I'M NOT..
I CANNOT LOSE HIM..
..NOT AGAIN...
..NOT AGAIN..

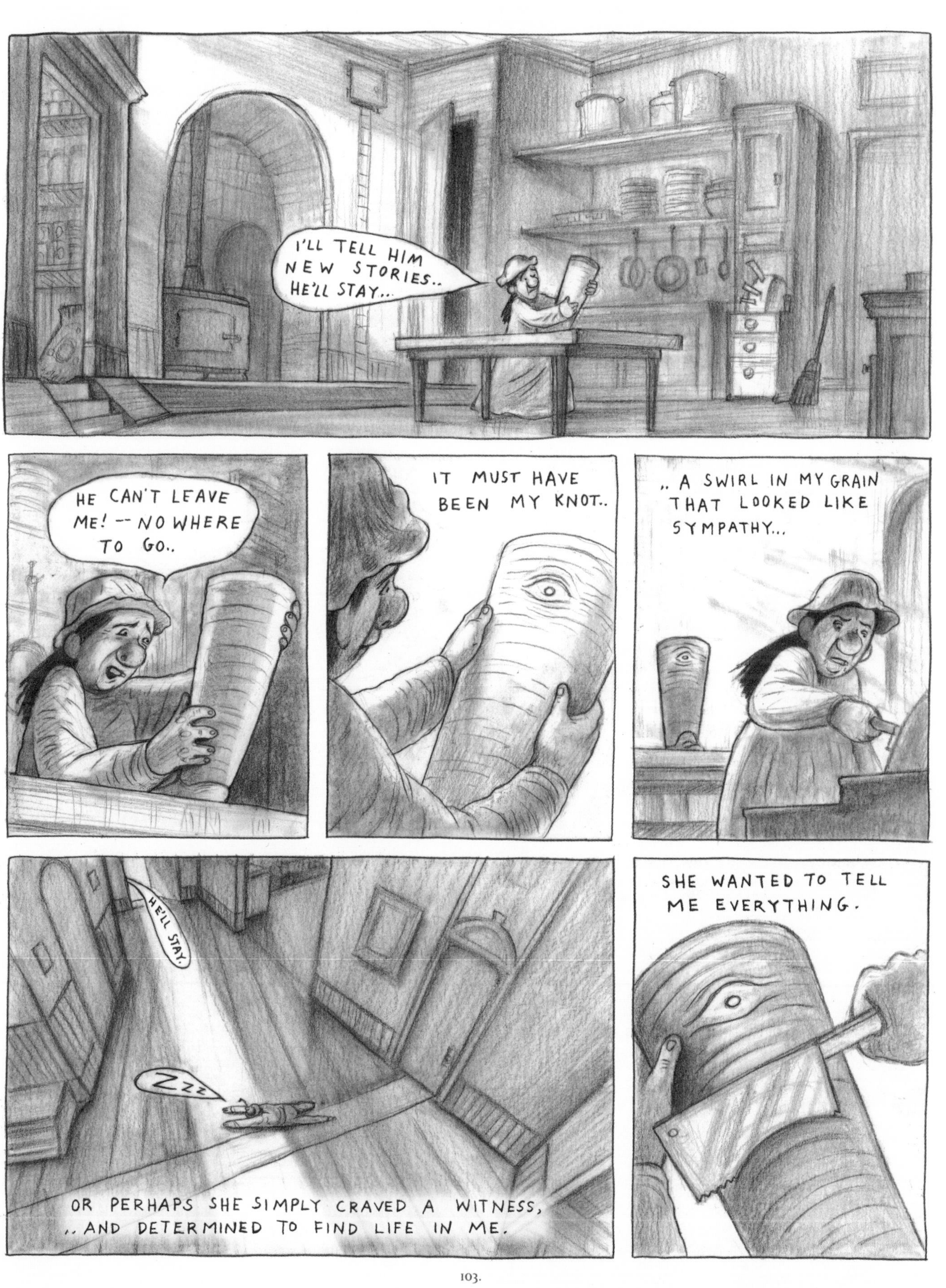
I'LL TELL HIM NEW STORIES.. HE'LL STAY...
HE CAN'T LEAVE ME! -- NOWHERE TO GO..
IT MUST HAVE BEEN MY KNOT..
.. A SWIRL IN MY GRAIN THAT LOOKED LIKE SYMPATHY...
HE'LL STAY.
Zzz
OR PERHAPS SHE SIMPLY CRAVED A WITNESS,
.. AND DETERMINED TO FIND LIFE IN ME.
SHE WANTED TO TELL ME EVERYTHING.

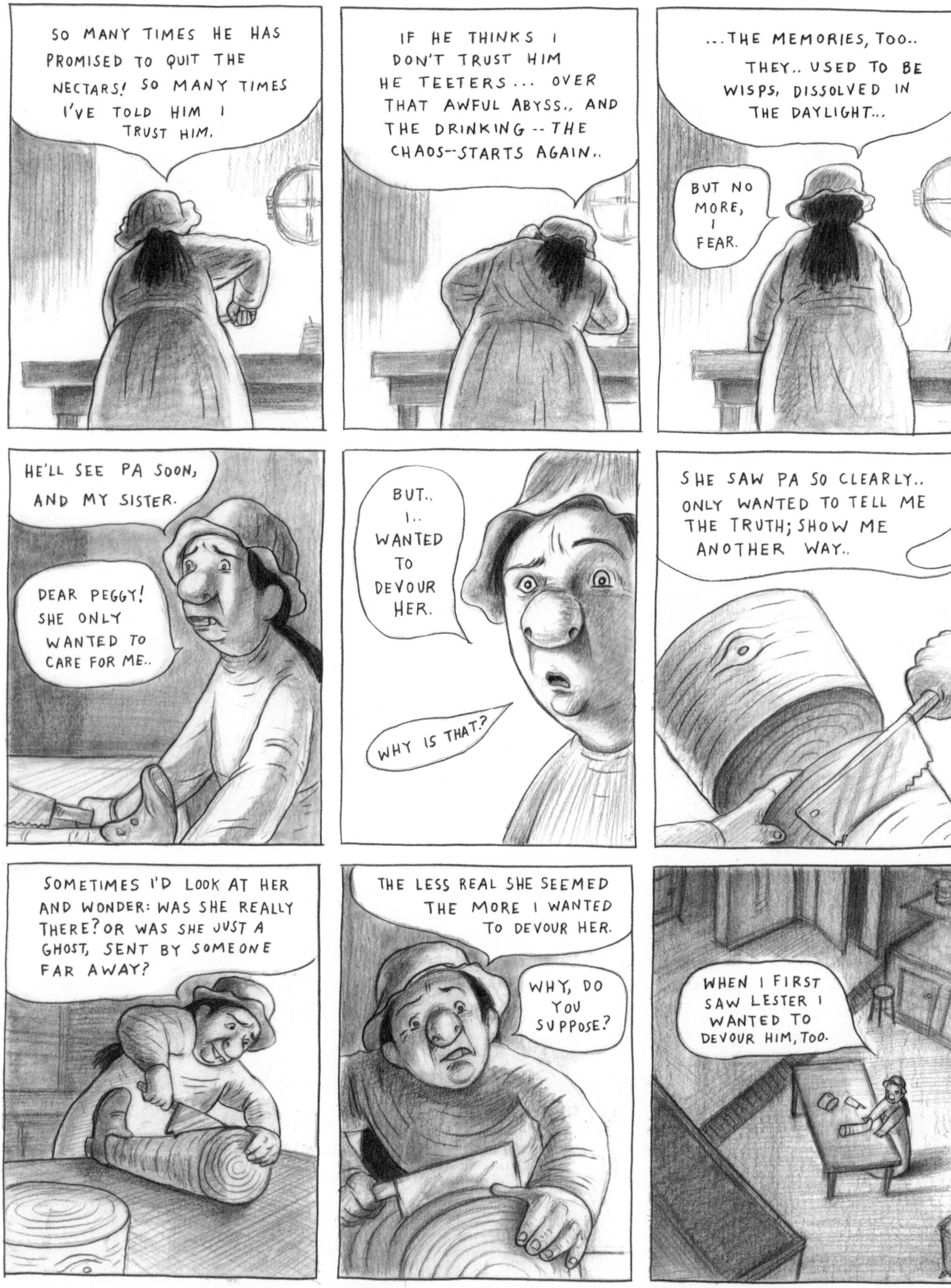
SO MANY TIMES HE HAS PROMISED TO QUIT THE NECTARS! SO MANY TIMES I'VE TOLD HIM I TRUST HIM.
IF HE THINKS I DON'T TRUST HIM HE TEETERS... OVER THAT AWFUL ABYSS., AND THE DRINKING -- THE CHAOS--STARTS AGAIN..
...THE MEMORIES, TOO.. THEY.. USED TO BE WISPS, DISSOLVED IN THE DAYLIGHT...
BUT NO MORE, I FEAR.
HE'LL SEE PA SOON, AND MY SISTER.
DEAR PEGGY! SHE ONLY WANTED TO CARE FOR ME..
BUT.. I.. WANTED TO DEVOUR HER.
WHY IS THAT?
SHE SAW PA SO CLEARLY.. ONLY WANTED TO TELL ME THE TRUTH; SHOW ME ANOTHER WAY..
SOMETIMES I'D LOOK AT HER AND WONDER: WAS SHE REALLY THERE? OR WAS SHE JUST A GHOST, SENT BY SOMEONE FAR AWAY?
THE LESS REAL SHE SEEMED THE MORE I WANTED TO DEVOUR HER.
WHY, DO YOU SUPPOSE?
WHEN I FIRST SAW LESTER I WANTED TO DEVOUR HIM, TOO.

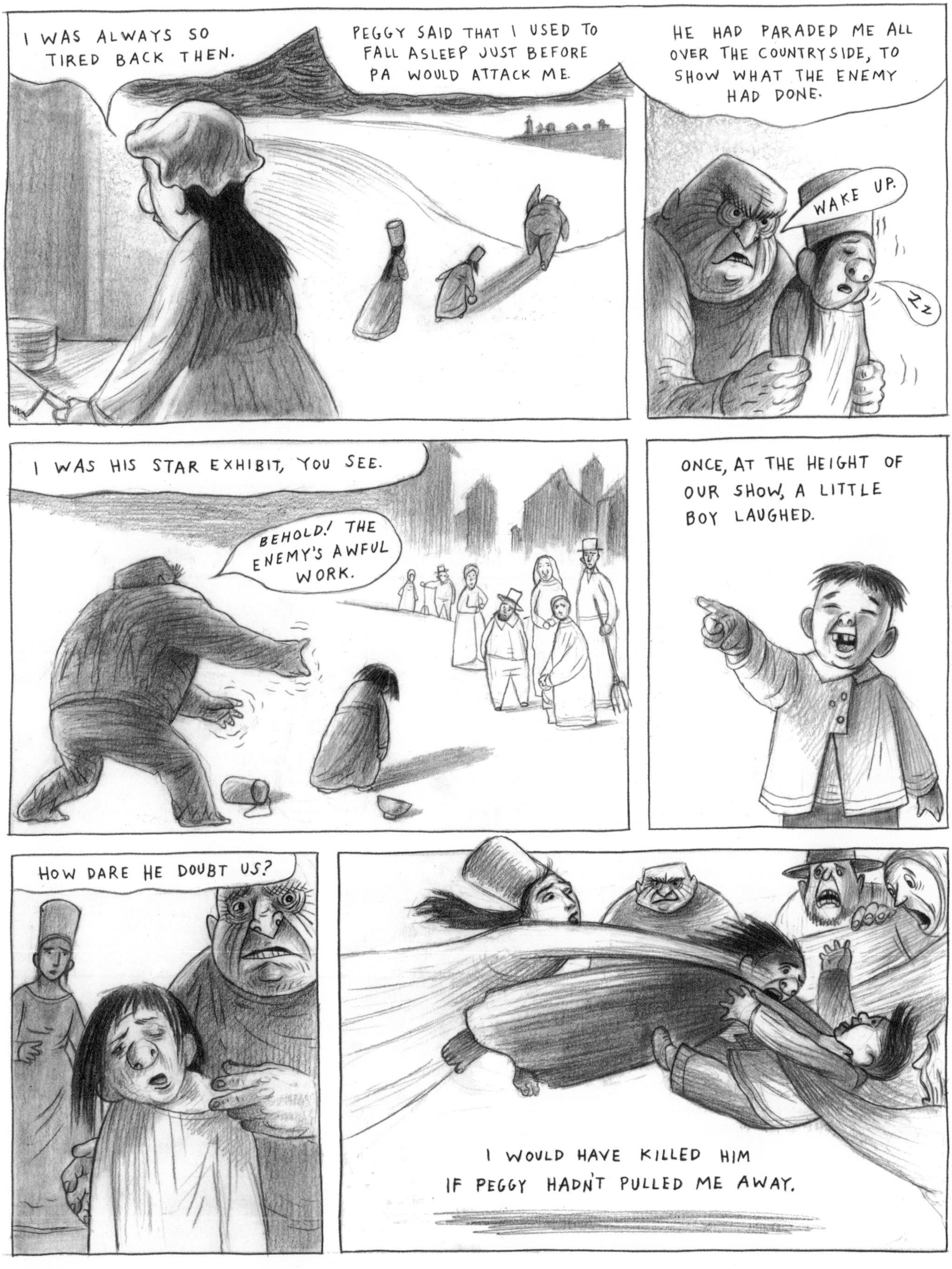
I WAS ALWAYS SO TIRED BACK THEN.
PEGGY SAID THAT I USED TO FALL ASLEEP JUST BEFORE PA WOULD ATTACK ME.
HE HAD PARADED ME ALL OVER THE COUNTRYSIDE, TO SHOW WHAT THE ENEMY HAD DONE.
WAKE UP.
Z z
I WAS HIS STAR EXHIBIT, YOU SEE.
BEHOLD! THE ENEMY'S AWFUL WORK.
ONCE, AT THE HEIGHT OF OUR SHOW, A LITTLE BOY LAUGHED.
HOW DARE HE DOUBT US?
I WOULD HAVE KILLED HIM IF PEGGY HADN'T PULLED ME AWAY.

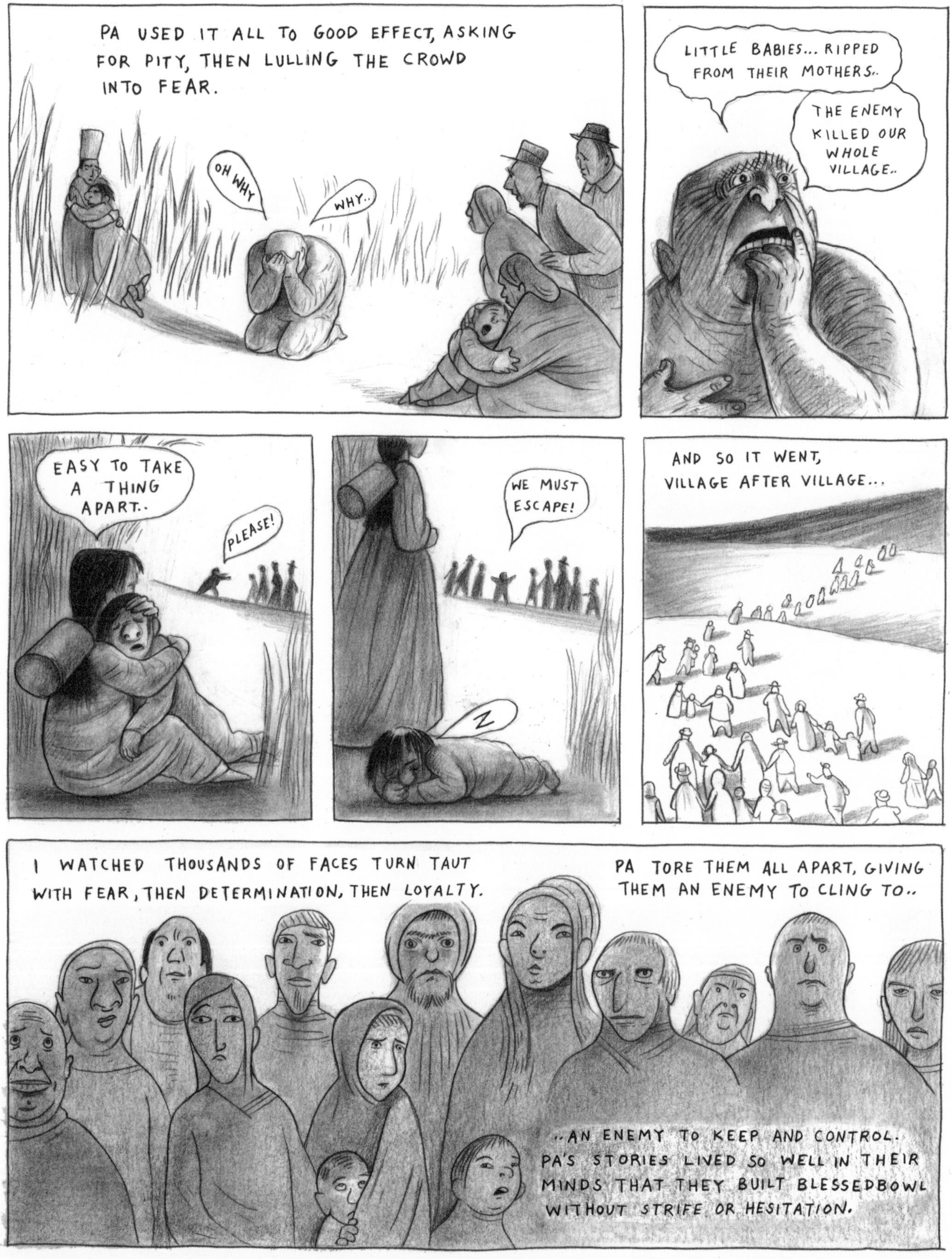
PA USED IT ALL TO GOOD EFFECT, ASKING FOR PITY, THEN LULLING THE CROWD INTO FEAR.
OH WHY
WHY..
LITTLE BABIES... RIPPED FROM THEIR MOTHERS..
THE ENEMY KILLED OUR WHOLE VILLAGE..
EASY TO TAKE A THING APART..
PLEASE!
WE MUST ESCAPE!
Z
AND SO IT WENT, VILLAGE AFTER VILLAGE...
I WATCHED THOUSANDS OF FACES TURN TAUT WITH FEAR, THEN DETERMINATION, THEN LOYALTY.
PA TORE THEM ALL APART, GIVING THEM AN ENEMY TO CLING TO..
..AN ENEMY TO KEEP AND CONTROL. PA'S STORIES LIVED SO WELL IN THEIR MINDS THAT THEY BUILT BLESSEDBOWL WITHOUT STRIFE OR HESITATION.

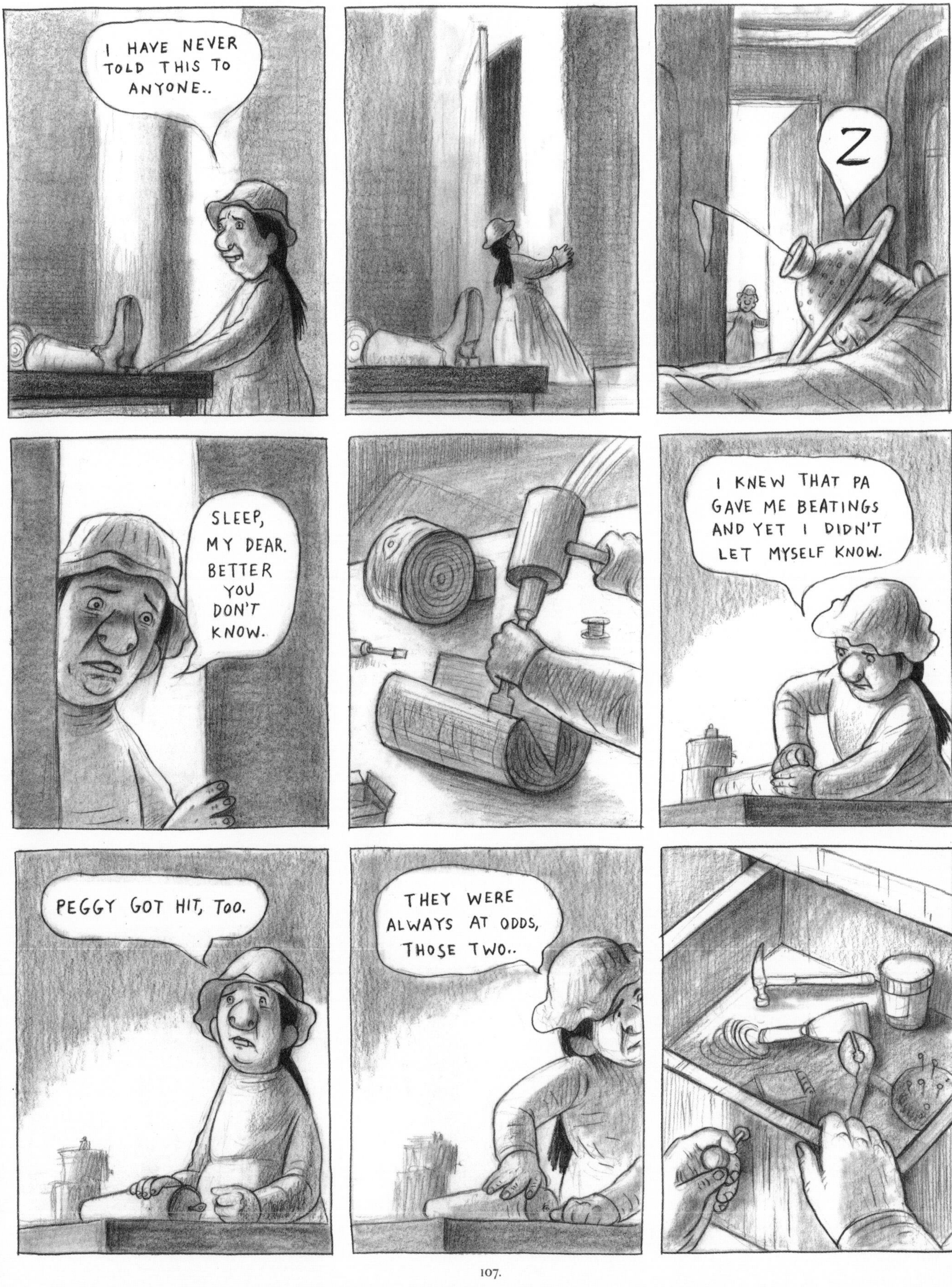
I HAVE NEVER TOLD THIS TO ANYONE..
Z
SLEEP, MY DEAR. BETTER YOU DON'T KNOW.
I KNEW THAT PA GAVE ME BEATINGS AND YET I DIDN'T LET MYSELF KNOW.
PEGGY GOT HIT, TOO.
THEY WERE ALWAYS AT ODDS, THOSE TWO..

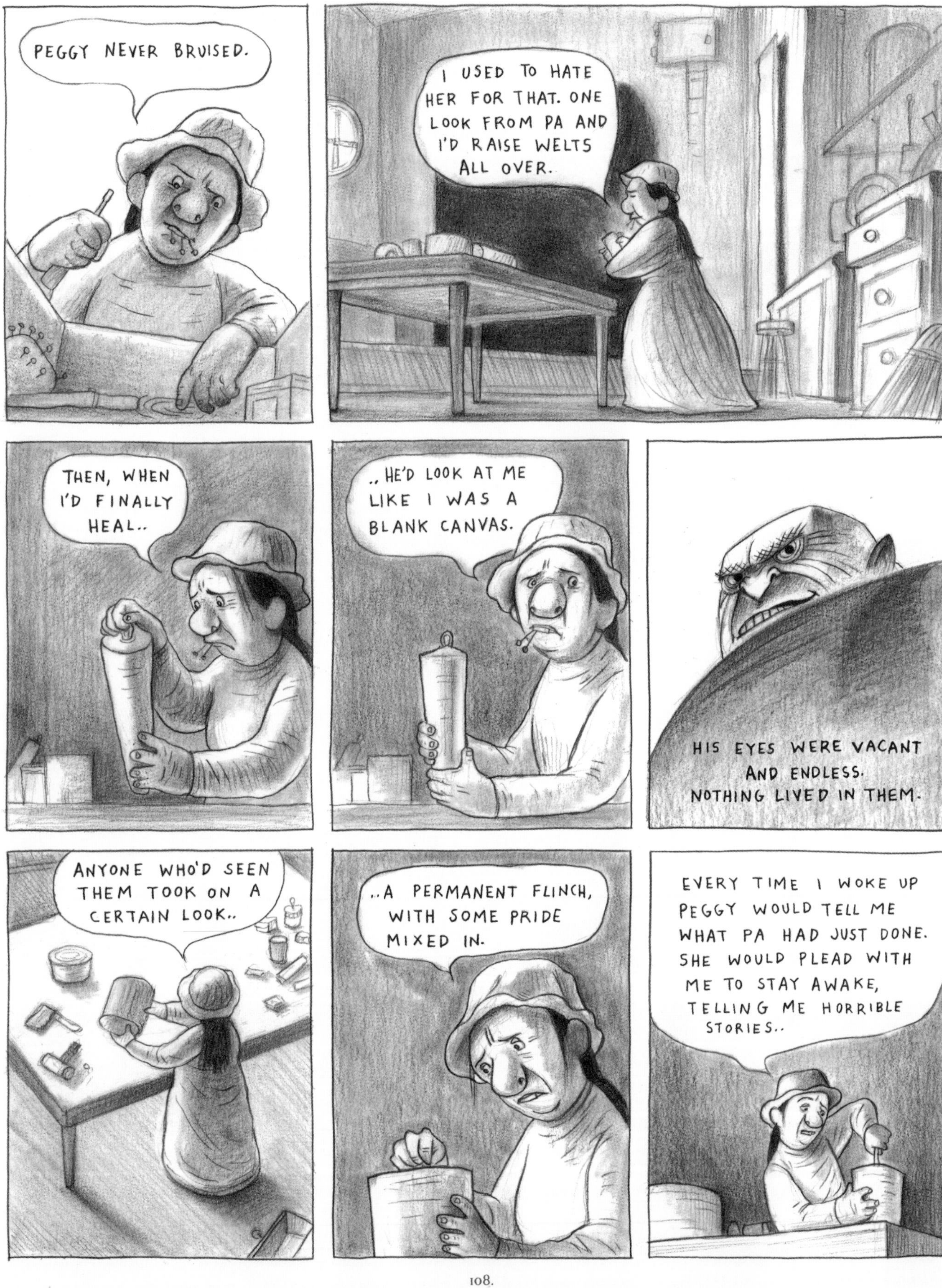
PEGGY NEVER BRUISED.
I USED TO HATE HER FOR THAT. ONE LOOK FROM PA AND I'D RAISE WELTS ALL OVER.
THEN, WHEN I'D FINALLY HEAL..
.. HE'D LOOK AT ME LIKE I WAS A BLANK CANVAS.
HIS EYES WERE VACANT AND ENDLESS. NOTHING LIVED IN THEM.
ANYONE WHO'D SEEN THEM TOOK ON A CERTAIN LOOK..
..A PERMANENT FLINCH, WITH SOME PRIDE MIXED IN.
EVERY TIME I WOKE UP PEGGY WOULD TELL ME WHAT PA HAD JUST DONE. SHE WOULD PLEAD WITH ME TO STAY AWAKE, TELLING ME HORRIBLE STORIES..

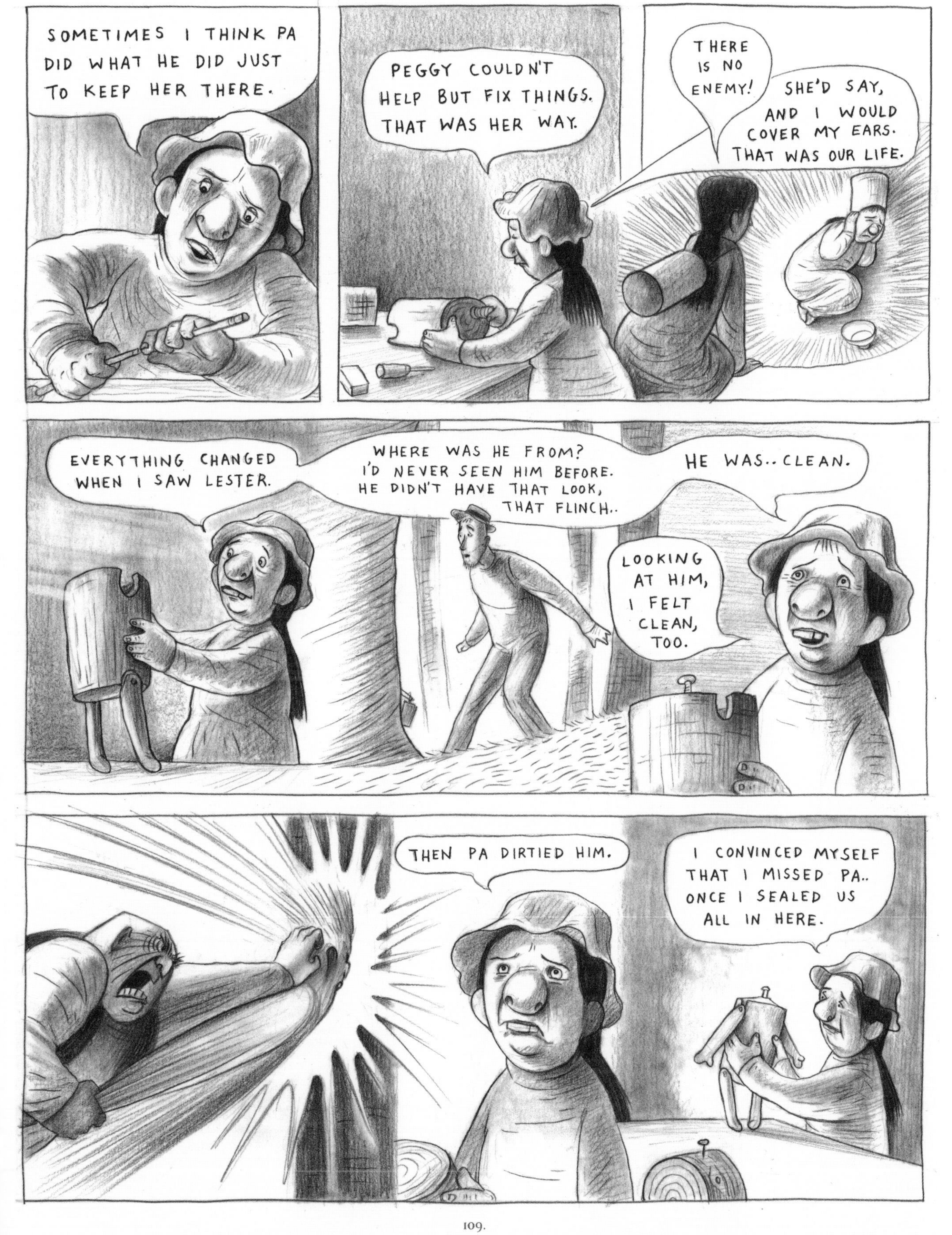
SOMETIMES I THINK PA DID WHAT HE DID JUST TO KEEP HER THERE.
PEGGY COULDN'T HELP BUT FIX THINGS. THAT WAS HER WAY.
THERE IS NO ENEMY!
SHE'D SAY, AND I WOULD COVER MY EARS. THAT WAS OUR LIFE.
EVERYTHING CHANGED WHEN I SAW LESTER.
WHERE WAS HE FROM? I'D NEVER SEEN HIM BEFORE. HE DIDN'T HAVE THAT LOOK, THAT FLINCH..
HE WAS.. CLEAN.
LOOKING AT HIM, I FELT CLEAN, TOO.
THEN PA DIRTIED HIM.
I CONVINCED MYSELF THAT I MISSED PA.. ONCE I SEALED US ALL IN HERE.

BUT I WAS GLAD TO SHUT HIM OUT..

EVEN IF WE DIED IN HERE.

LATELY I HAVE FELT THOSE EYES OF HIS, PRESSING ON MY BACK.

HE IS OUT THERE...

..PROWLING, SEARCHING.

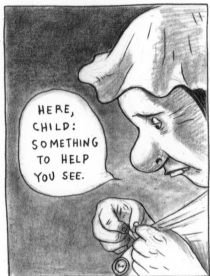

HERE, CHILD: SOMETHING TO HELP YOU SEE.

REMEMBER: THE SNIPER IS JUST THE MOON. THE SPIES ARE SIMPLY BIRDS.

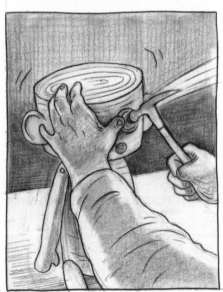

110.

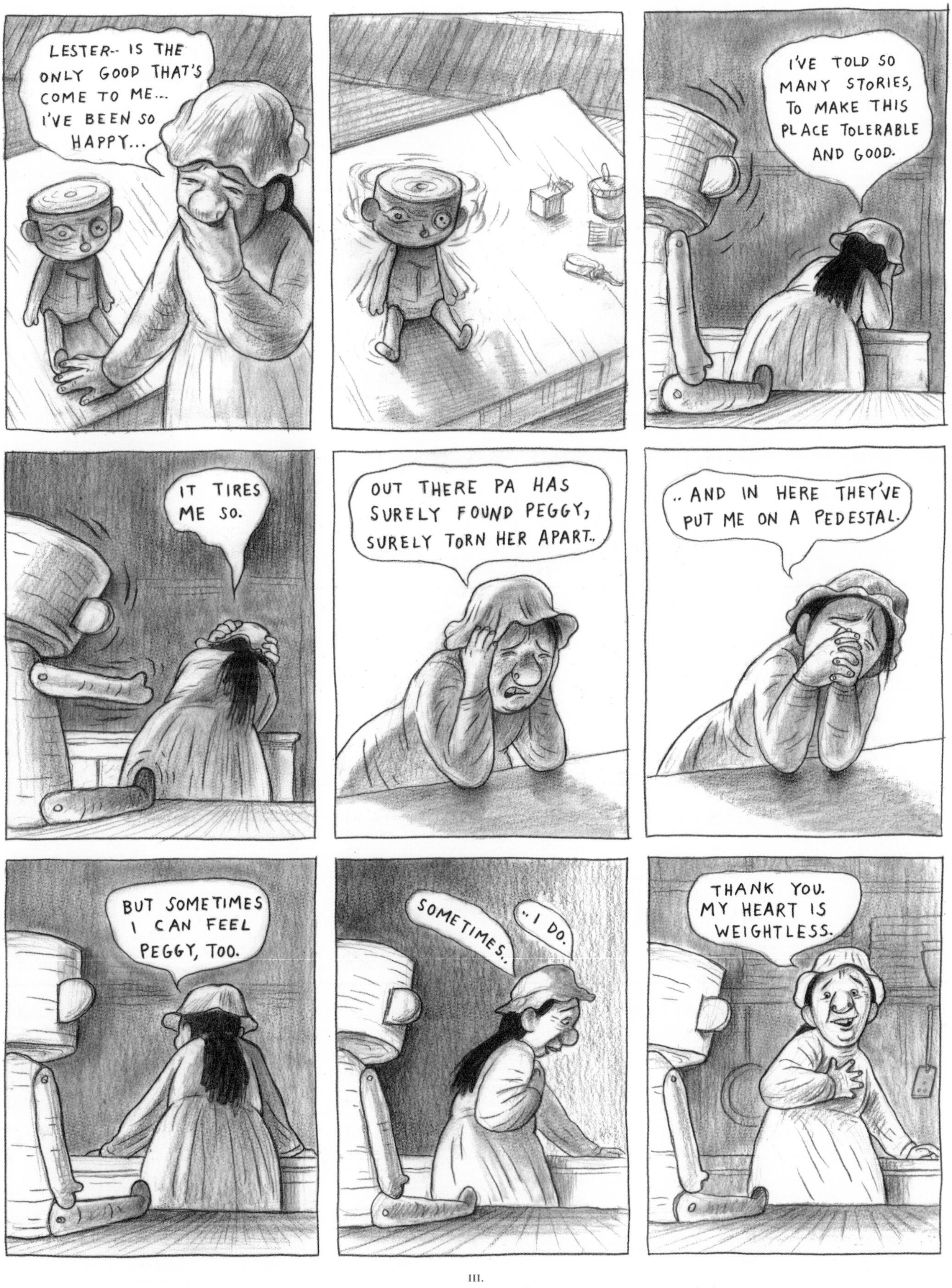
LESTER-- IS THE ONLY GOOD THAT'S COME TO ME... I'VE BEEN SO HAPPY...
I'VE TOLD SO MANY STORIES, TO MAKE THIS PLACE TOLERABLE AND GOOD.
IT TIRES ME SO.
OUT THERE PA HAS SURELY FOUND PEGGY, SURELY TORN HER APART..
.. AND IN HERE THEY'VE PUT ME ON A PEDESTAL.
BUT SOMETIMES I CAN FEEL PEGGY, TOO.
SOMETIMES..
.. I DO.
THANK YOU. MY HEART IS WEIGHTLESS.

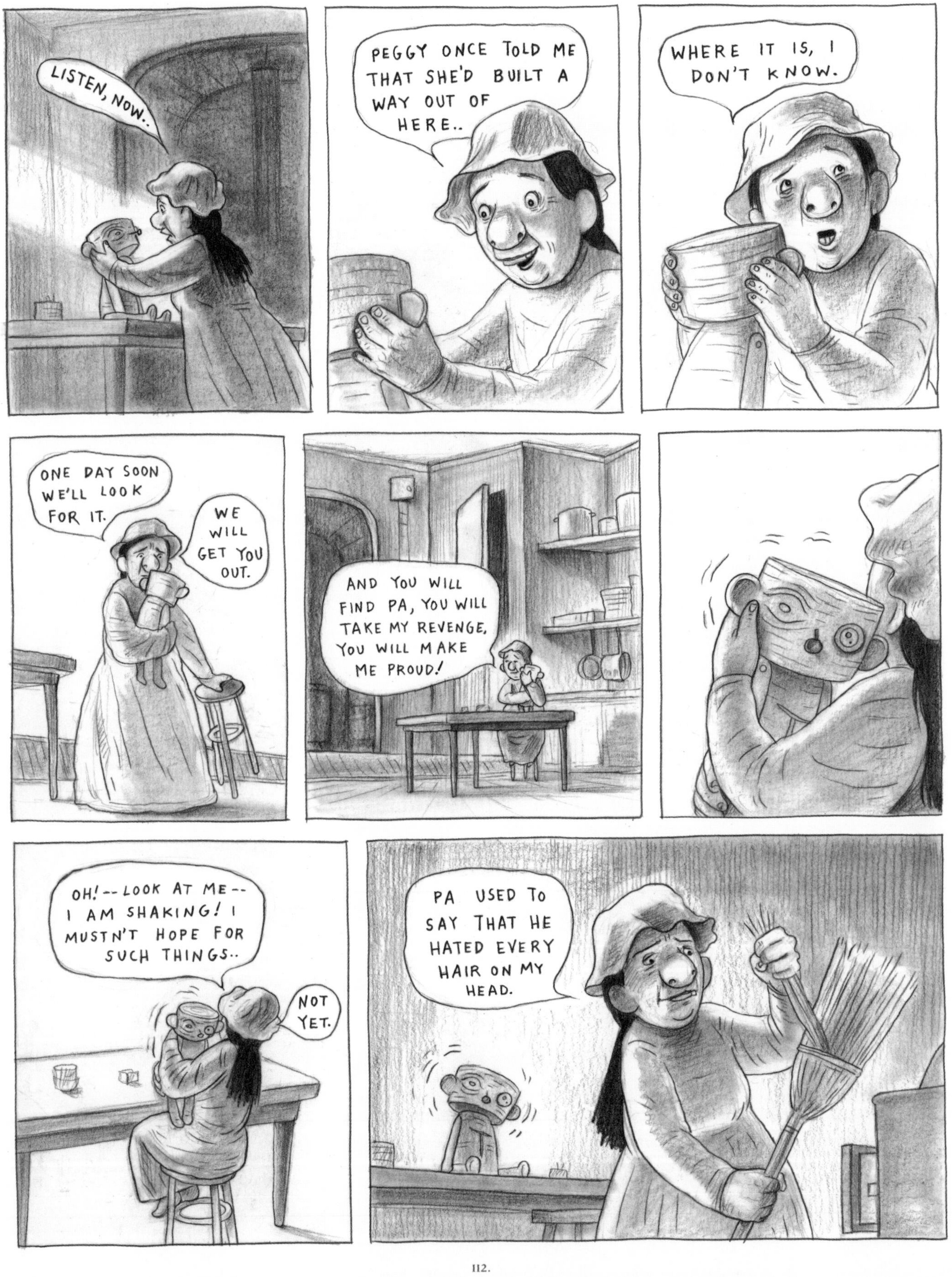
LISTEN, NOW..
PEGGY ONCE TOLD ME THAT SHE'D BUILT A WAY OUT OF HERE..
WHERE IT IS, I DON'T KNOW.
ONE DAY SOON WE'LL LOOK FOR IT.
WE WILL GET YOU OUT.
AND YOU WILL FIND PA, YOU WILL TAKE MY REVENGE, YOU WILL MAKE ME PROUD!
OH! -- LOOK AT ME -- I AM SHAKING! I MUSTN'T HOPE FOR SUCH THINGS..
NOT YET.
PA USED TO SAY THAT HE HATED EVERY HAIR ON MY HEAD.

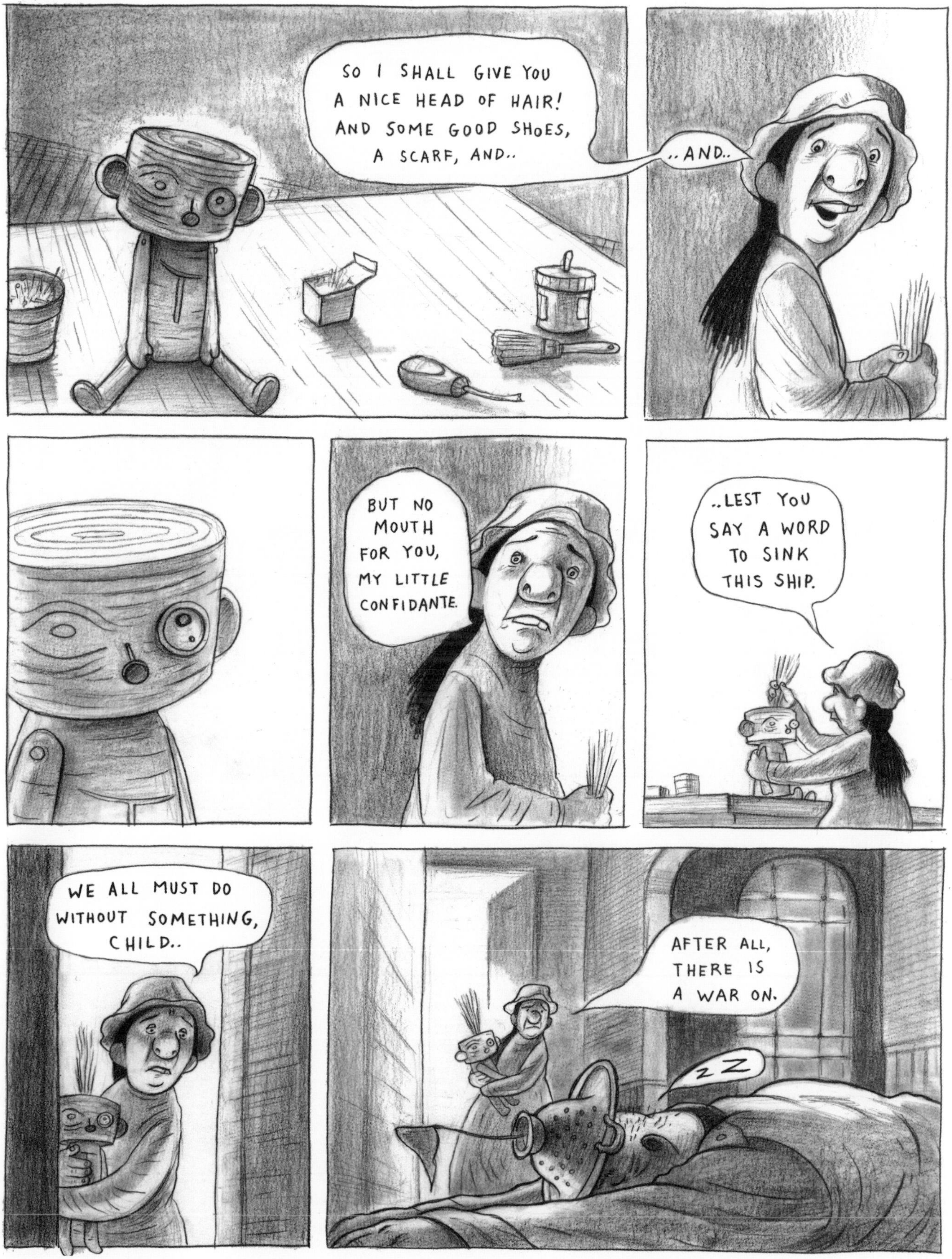
SO I SHALL GIVE YOU A NICE HEAD OF HAIR! AND SOME GOOD SHOES, A SCARF, AND..
..AND..
BUT NO MOUTH FOR YOU, MY LITTLE CONFIDANTE.
..LEST YOU SAY A WORD TO SINK THIS SHIP.
WE ALL MUST DO WITHOUT SOMETHING, CHILD..
AFTER ALL, THERE IS A WAR ON.
ZZ

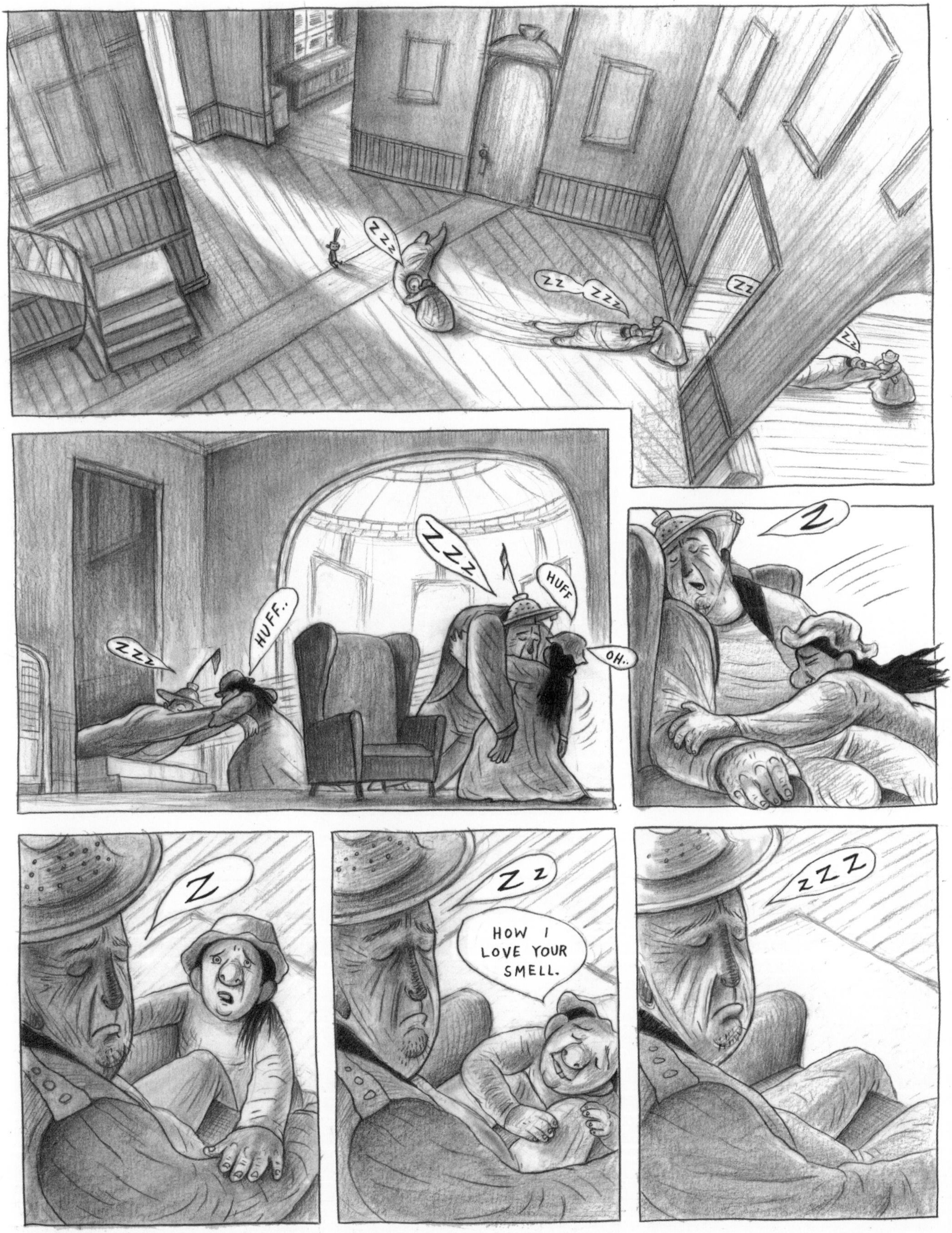
ZZZ
ZZ
ZZZ
ZZ
ZZ
ZZZ
HUFF..
ZZZ
HUFF
OH..
Z
Z
ZZ
HOW I LOVE YOUR SMELL.
ZZZ

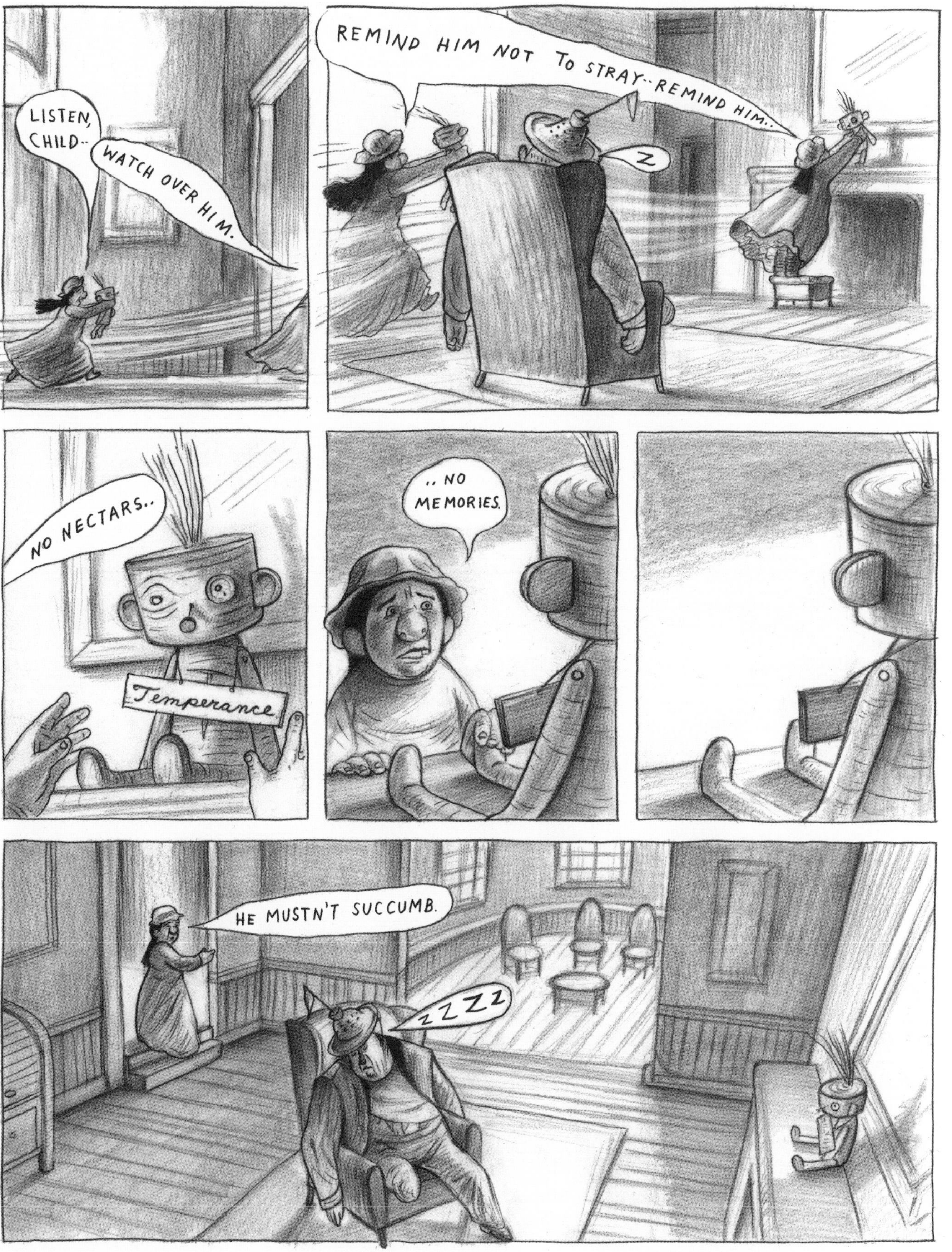
LISTEN, CHILD--
WATCH OVER HIM.
REMIND HIM NOT TO STRAY--REMIND HIM..
Z
NO NECTARS..
Temperance
.. NO MEMORIES.
HE MUSTN'T SUCCUMB.
zZZZ

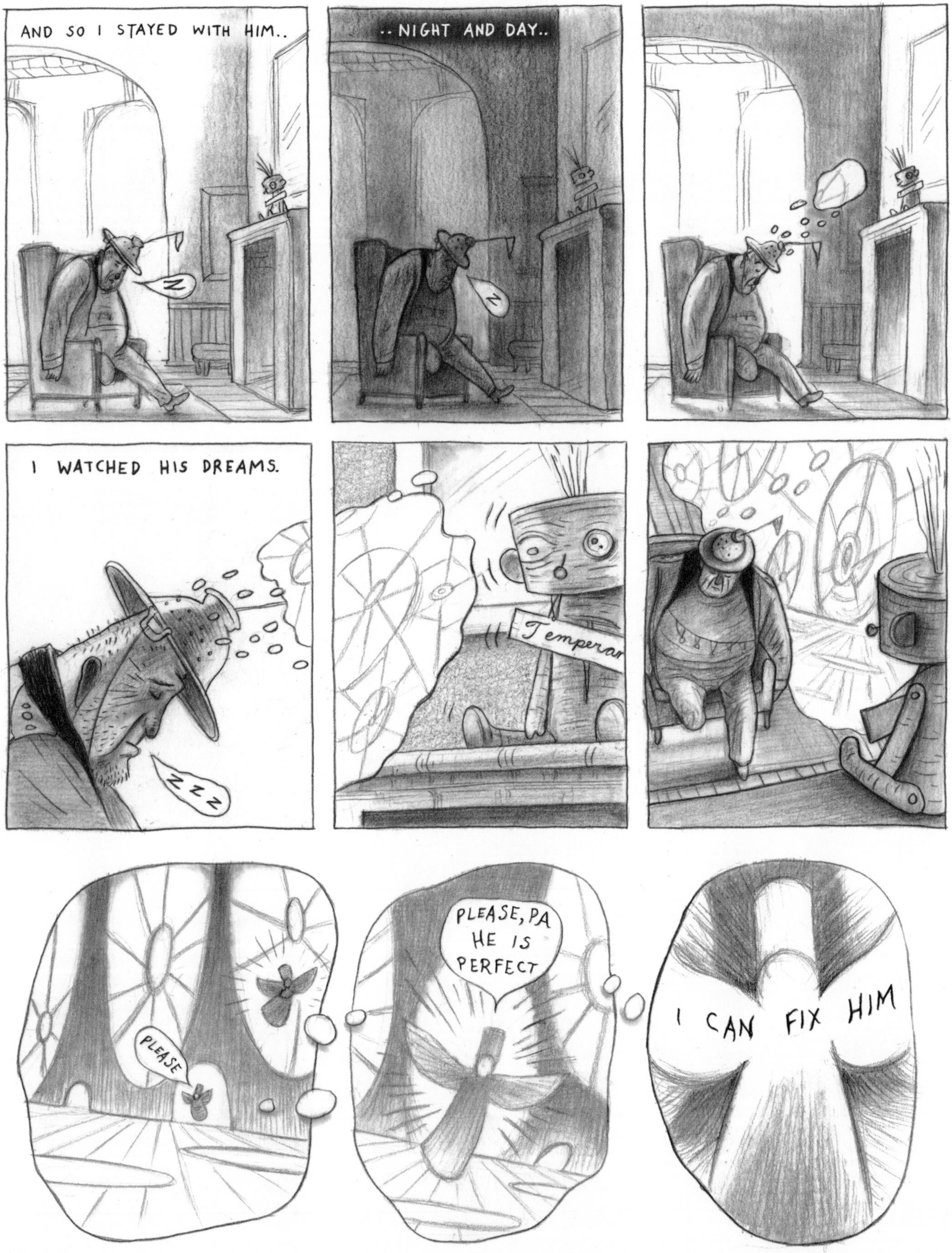
AND SO I STAYED WITH HIM..
..NIGHT AND DAY..
Z
Z
I WATCHED HIS DREAMS.
ZZZ
Temperan
PLEASE
PLEASE, PA HE IS PERFECT
I CAN FIX HIM

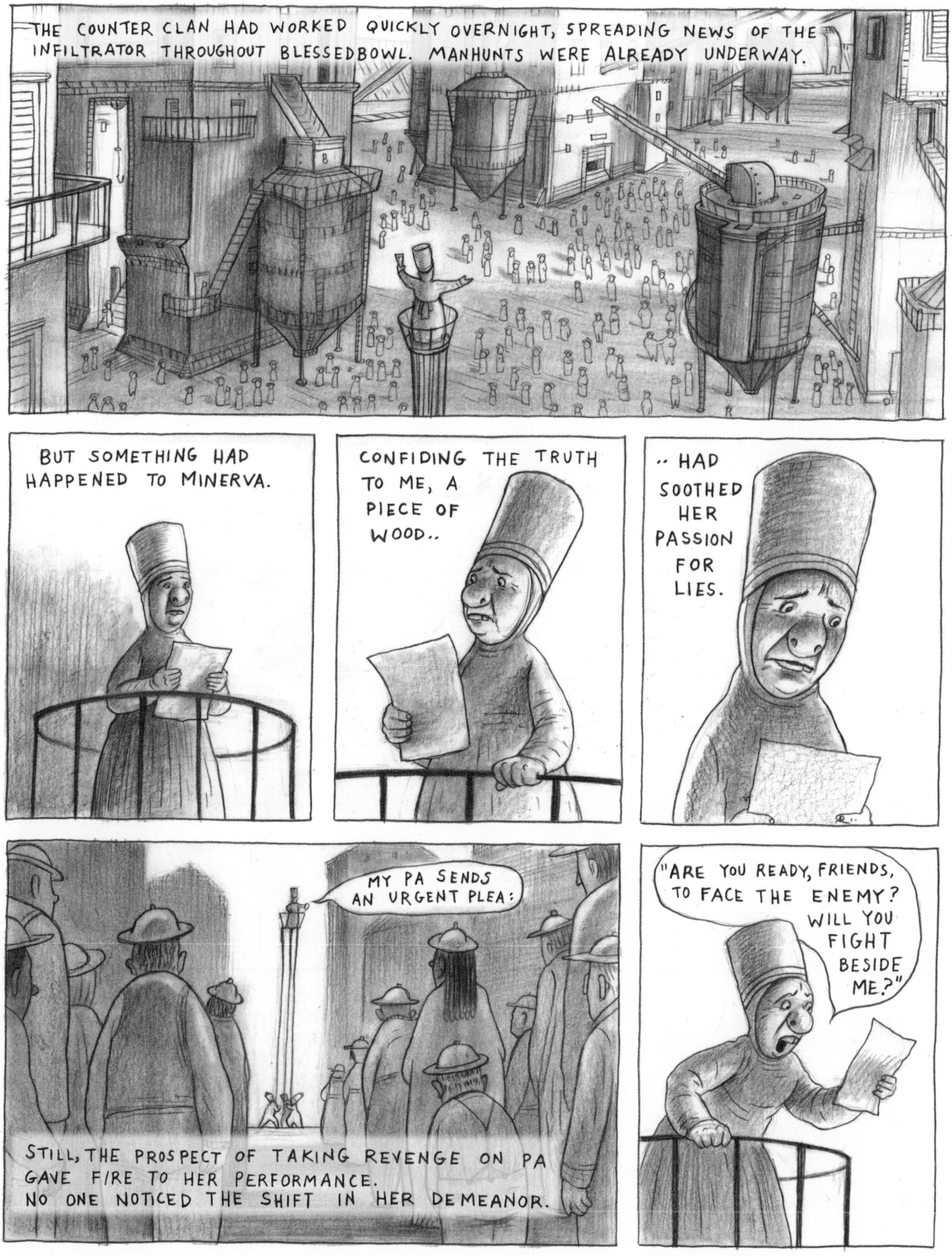
THE COUNTER CLAN HAD WORKED QUICKLY OVERNIGHT, SPREADING NEWS OF THE INFILTRATOR THROUGHOUT BLESSEDBOWL. MANHUNTS WERE ALREADY UNDERWAY.
BUT SOMETHING HAD HAPPENED TO MINERVA.
CONFIDING THE TRUTH TO ME, A PIECE OF WOOD..
.. HAD SOOTHED HER PASSION FOR LIES.
MY PA SENDS AN URGENT PLEA:
STILL, THE PROSPECT OF TAKING REVENGE ON PA GAVE FIRE TO HER PERFORMANCE.
NO ONE NOTICED THE SHIFT IN HER DEMEANOR.
"ARE YOU READY, FRIENDS, TO FACE THE ENEMY? WILL YOU FIGHT BESIDE ME?"

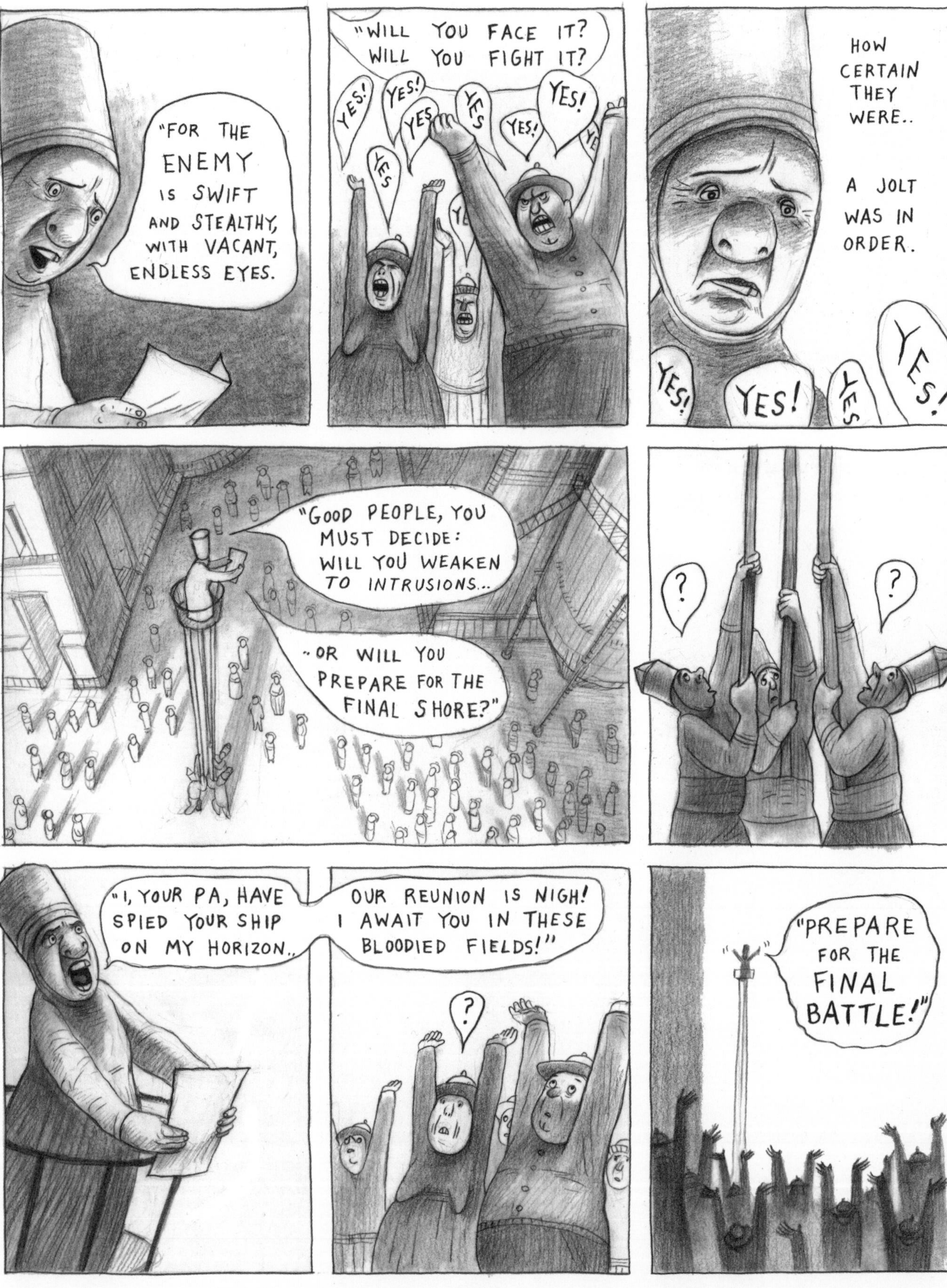
"FOR THE ENEMY IS SWIFT AND STEALTHY, WITH VACANT, ENDLESS EYES.
"WILL YOU FACE IT? WILL YOU FIGHT IT?
YES!
YES!
YES
YES
YES!
YES!
YES
HOW CERTAIN THEY WERE..
A JOLT WAS IN ORDER.
YES!
YES!
YES
YES!
"GOOD PEOPLE, YOU MUST DECIDE: WILL YOU WEAKEN TO INTRUSIONS...
-OR WILL YOU PREPARE FOR THE FINAL SHORE?"
?
?
"I, YOUR PA, HAVE SPIED YOUR SHIP ON MY HORIZON..
OUR REUNION IS NIGH! I AWAIT YOU IN THESE BLOODIED FIELDS!"
?
"PREPARE FOR THE FINAL BATTLE!"

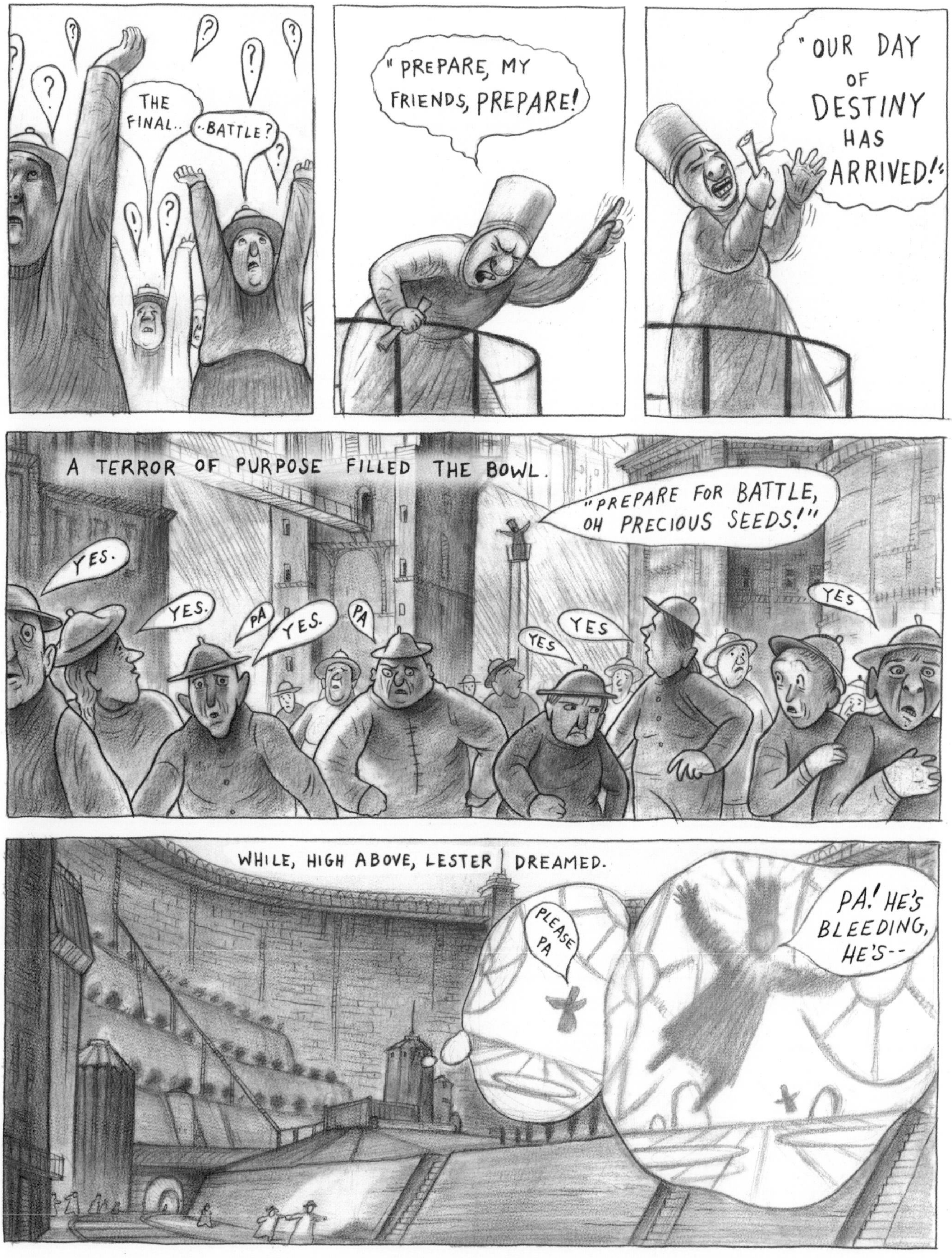
THE FINAL..
..BATTLE?
"PREPARE, MY FRIENDS, PREPARE!
"OUR DAY OF DESTINY HAS ARRIVED!"
A TERROR OF PURPOSE FILLED THE BOWL.
"PREPARE FOR BATTLE, OH PRECIOUS SEEDS!"
YES.
YES.
PA
YES.
PA
YES
YES
YES
WHILE, HIGH ABOVE, LESTER DREAMED.
PLEASE PA
PA! HE'S BLEEDING, HE'S--

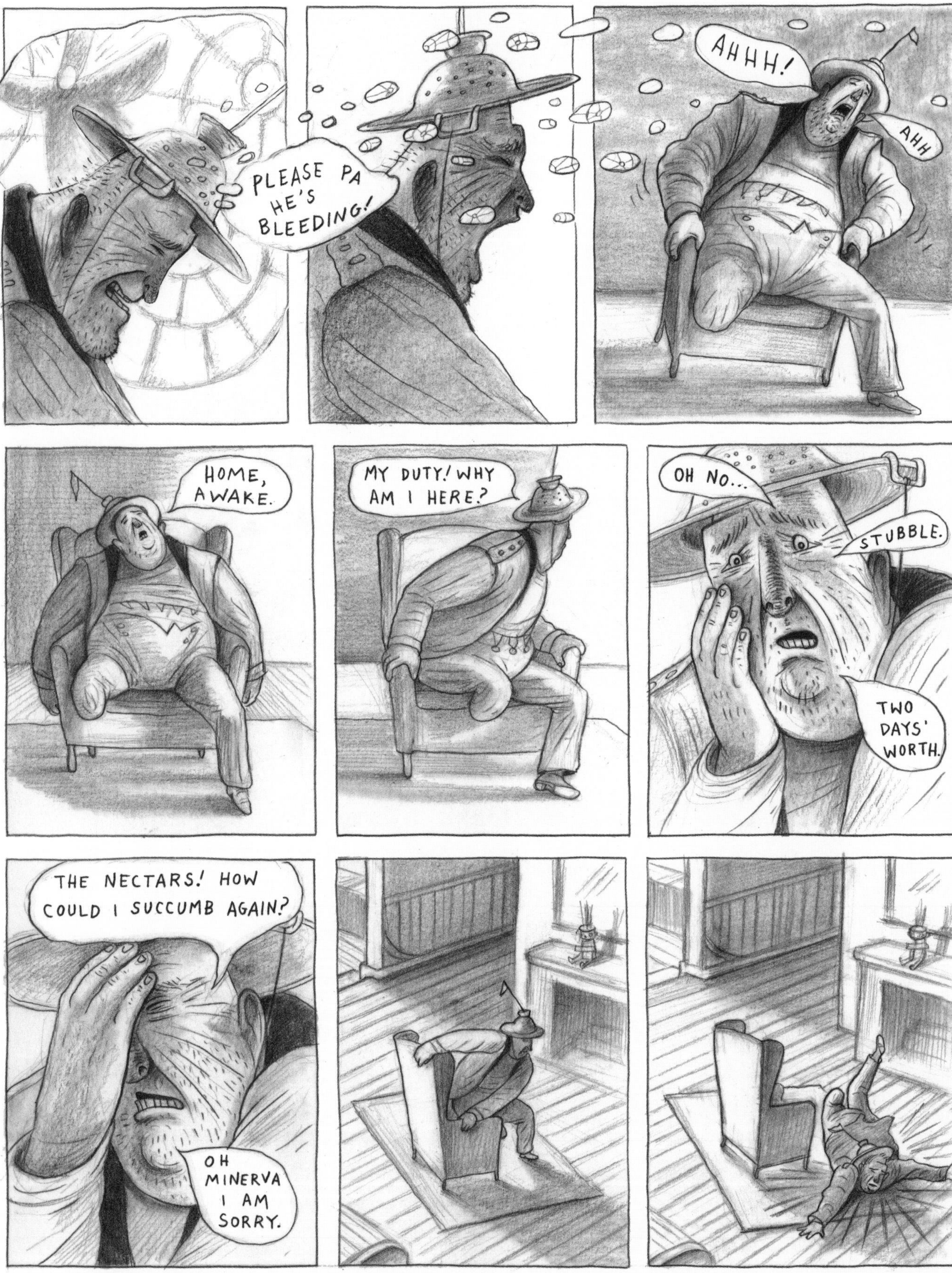
PLEASE PA HE'S BLEEDING!
AHHH!
AHH
HOME, AWAKE.
MY DUTY! WHY AM I HERE?
OH NO...
STUBBLE.
TWO DAYS' WORTH.
THE NECTARS! HOW COULD I SUCCUMB AGAIN?
OH MINERVA I AM SORRY.

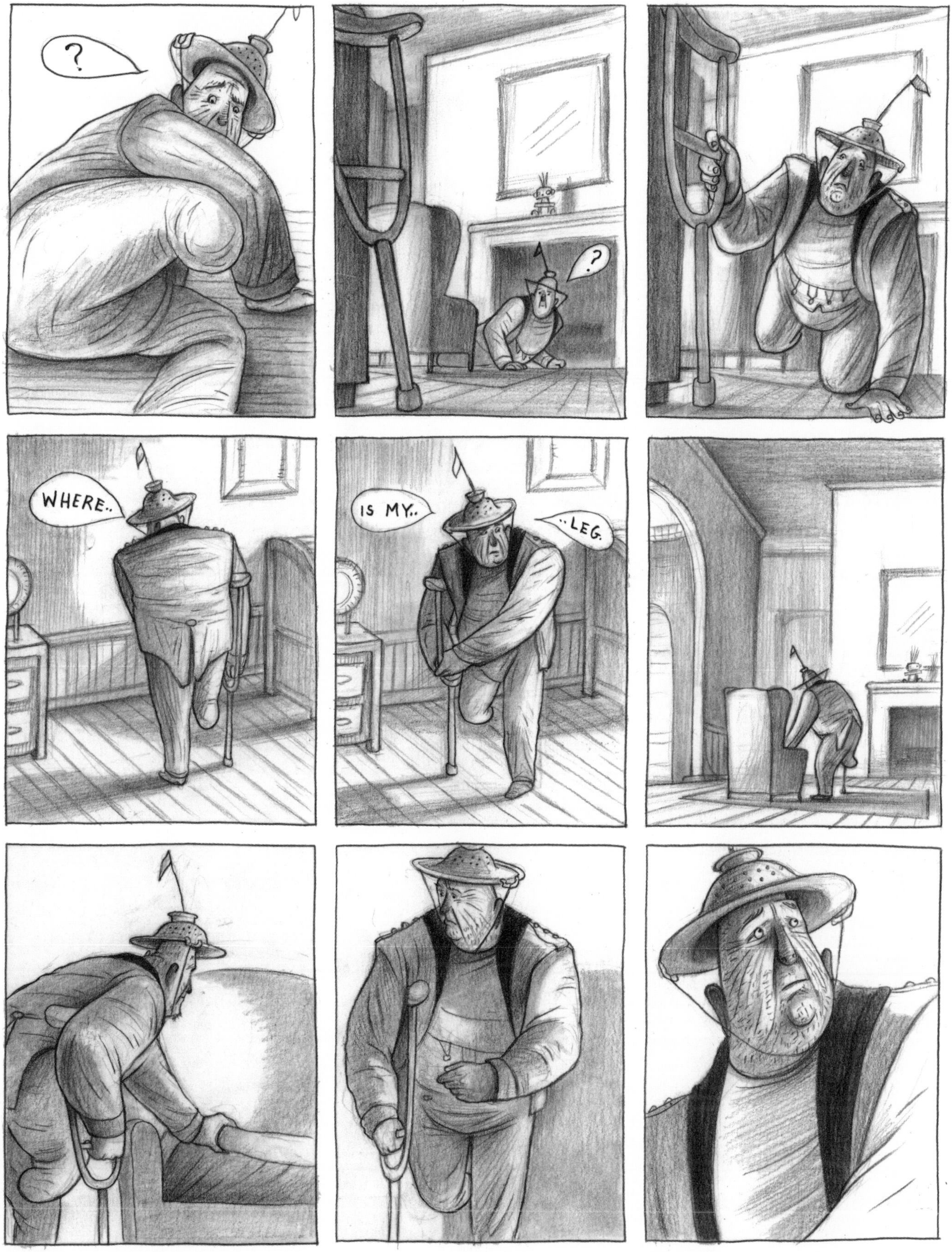
?
?
WHERE..
IS MY..
..LEG.

MY MY..

I STILL CAN'T RECALL OUR NUPTIALS..

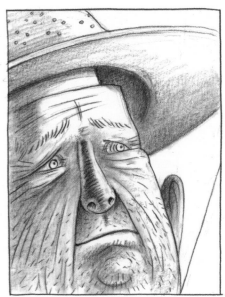

HMM.. MY WIFE COLLECTS DOLLS NOW.

ONE OF THE SCHOOLCHILDREN MUST HAVE GIVEN IT TO HER.

NOW WHERE IS MY LEG?

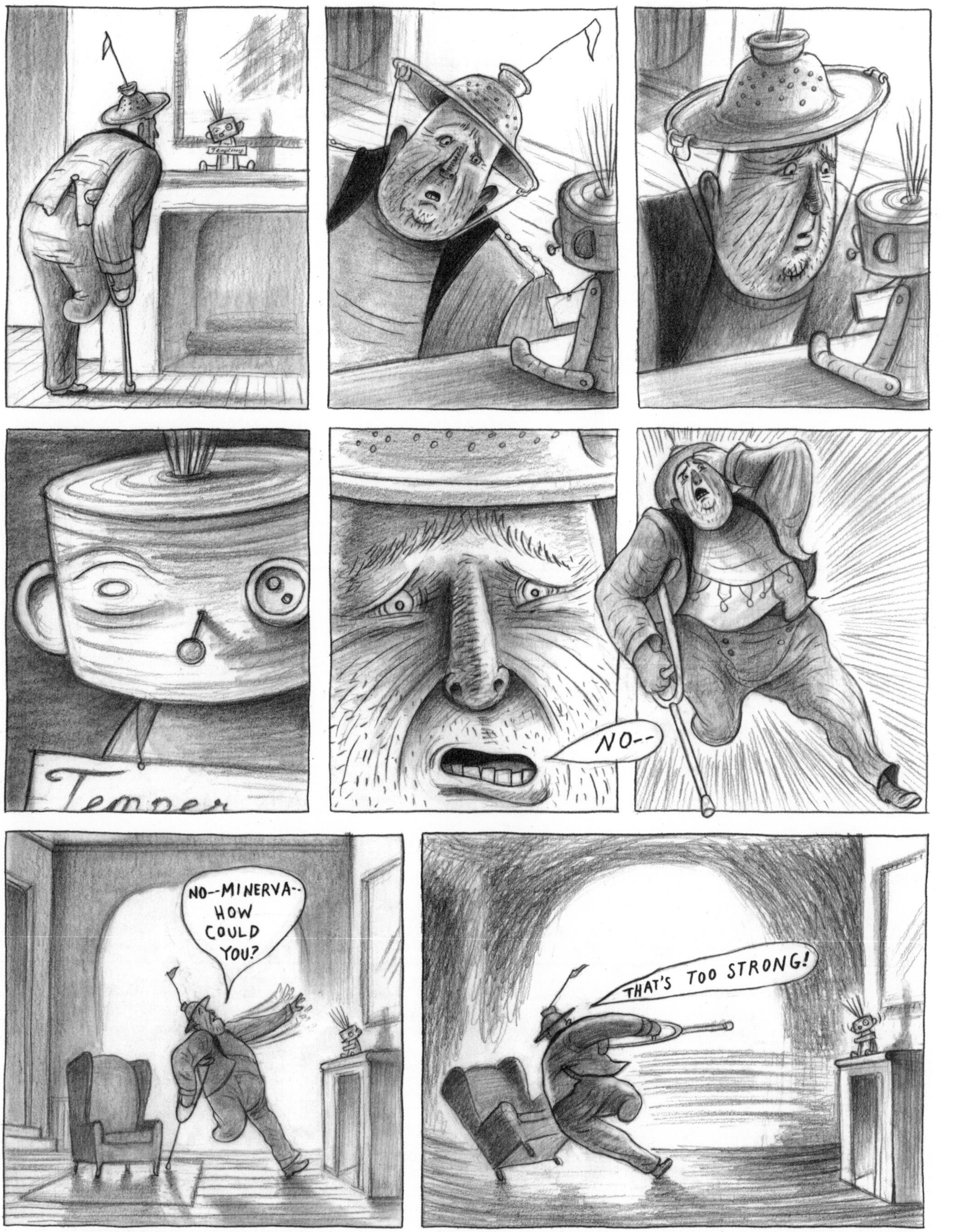
Temper
NO--
NO--MINERVA--HOW COULD YOU?
THAT'S TOO STRONG!

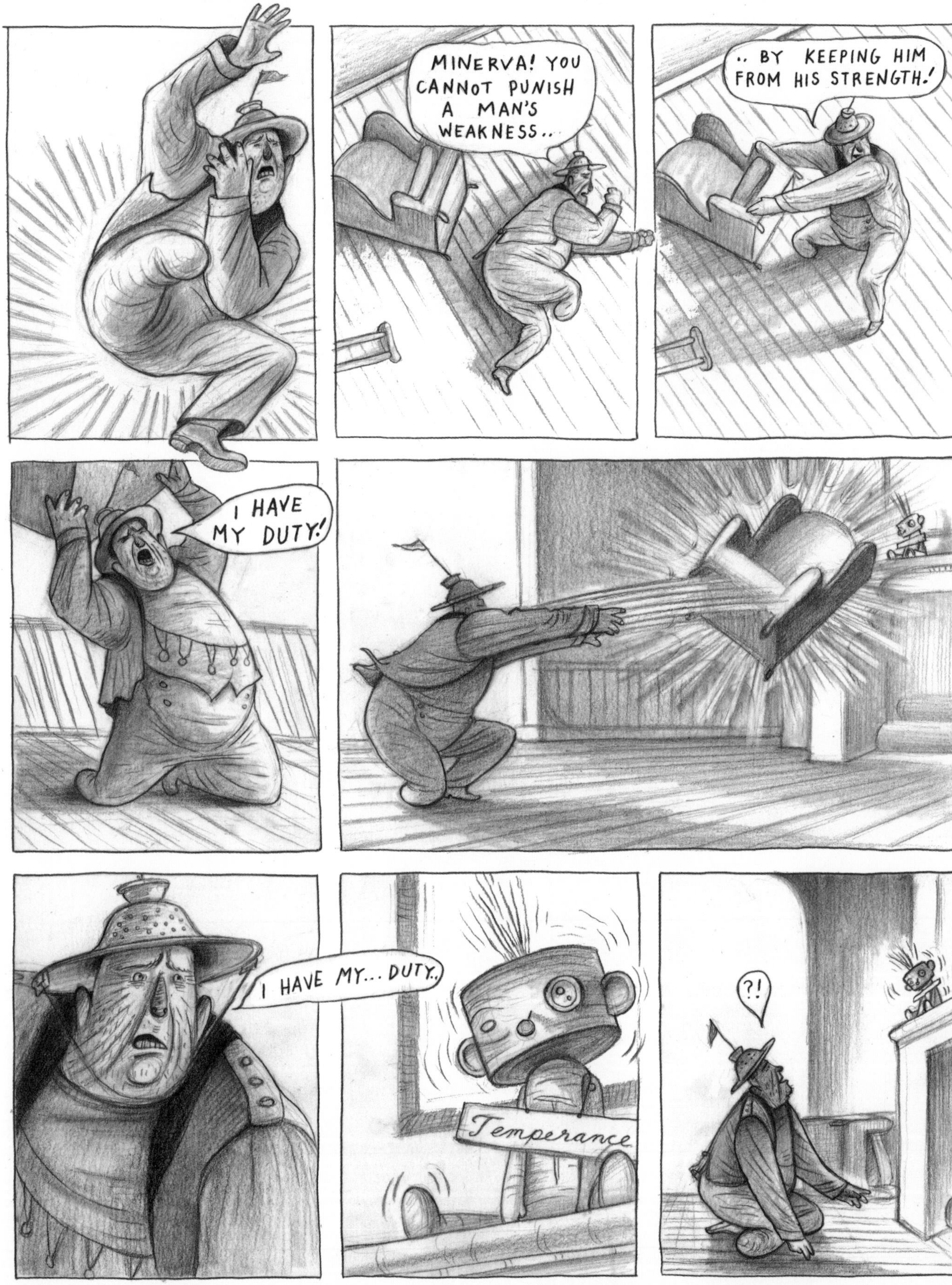
MINERVA! YOU CANNOT PUNISH A MAN'S WEAKNESS..
.. BY KEEPING HIM FROM HIS STRENGTH!
I HAVE MY DUTY!
I HAVE MY... DUTY..
Temperance
?!

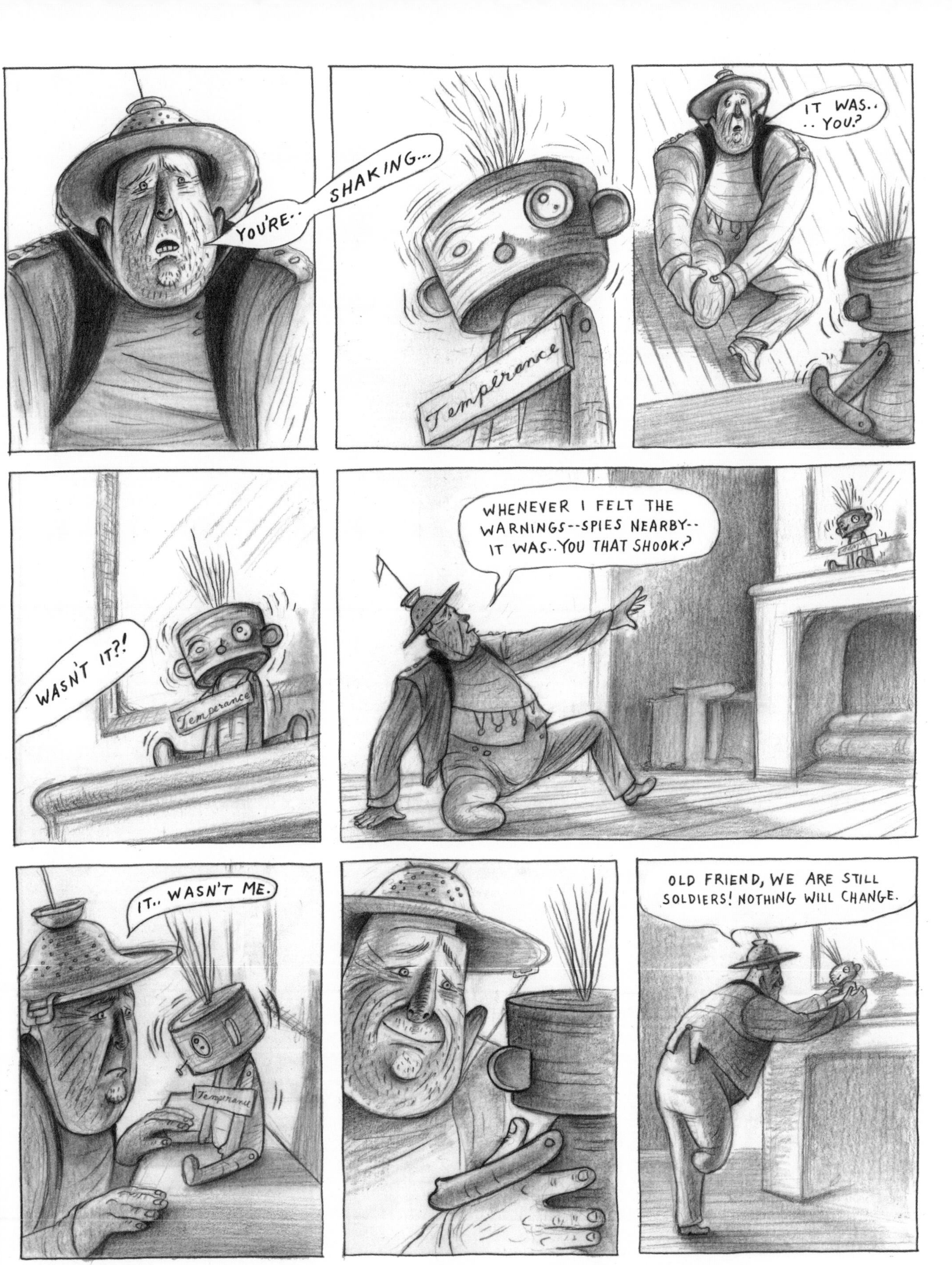
YOU'RE..
SHAKING...
Temperance
IT WAS..
..YOU?
WASN'T IT?!
Temperance
WHENEVER I FELT THE WARNINGS--SPIES NEARBY--
IT WAS..YOU THAT SHOOK?
IT.. WASN'T ME.
Temperance
OLD FRIEND, WE ARE STILL SOLDIERS! NOTHING WILL CHANGE.

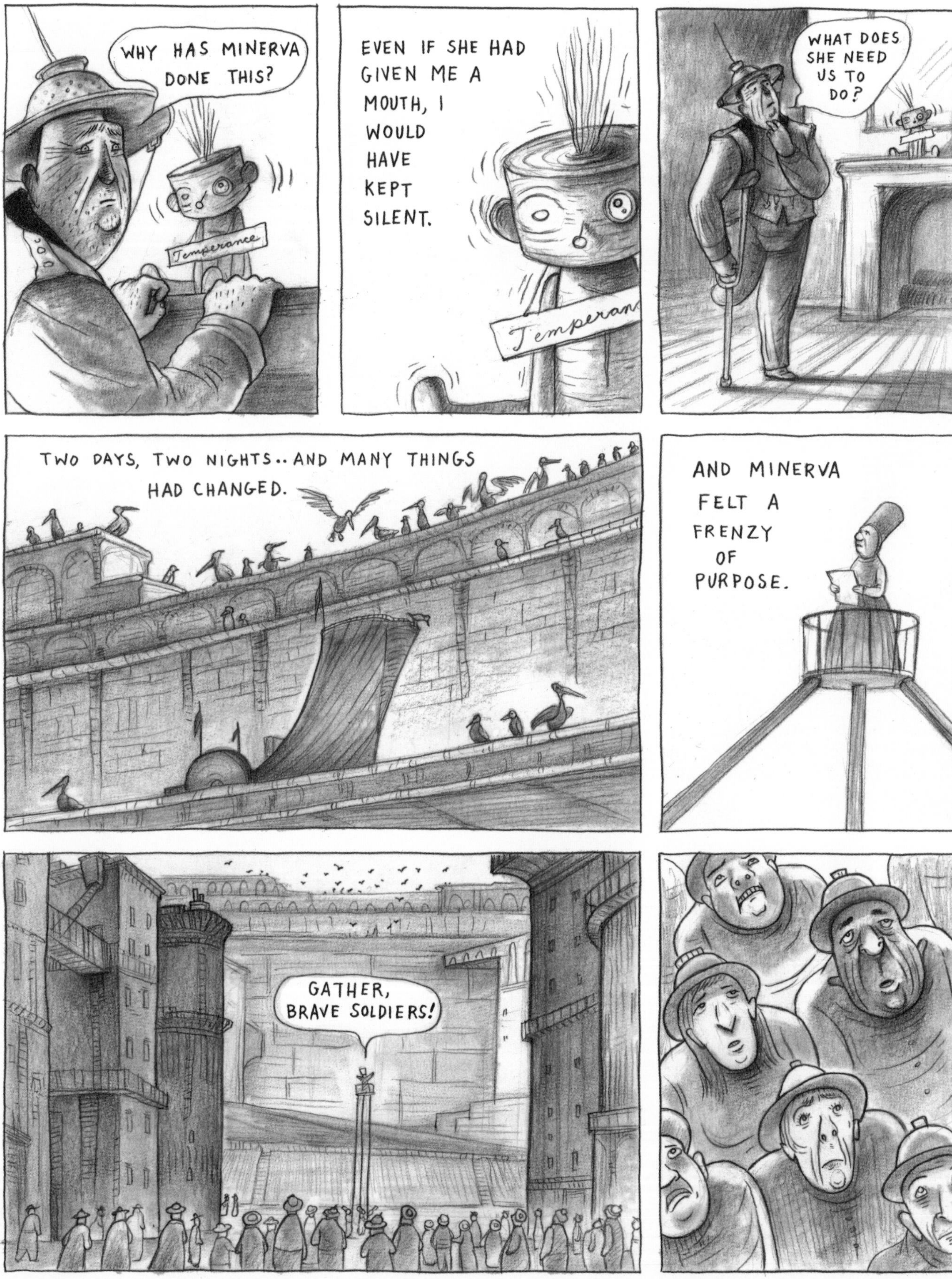
WHY HAS MINERVA DONE THIS?
Temperance
EVEN IF SHE HAD GIVEN ME A MOUTH, I WOULD HAVE KEPT SILENT.
Temperan
WHAT DOES SHE NEED US TO DO?
TWO DAYS, TWO NIGHTS.. AND MANY THINGS HAD CHANGED.
AND MINERVA FELT A FRENZY OF PURPOSE.
GATHER, BRAVE SOLDIERS!

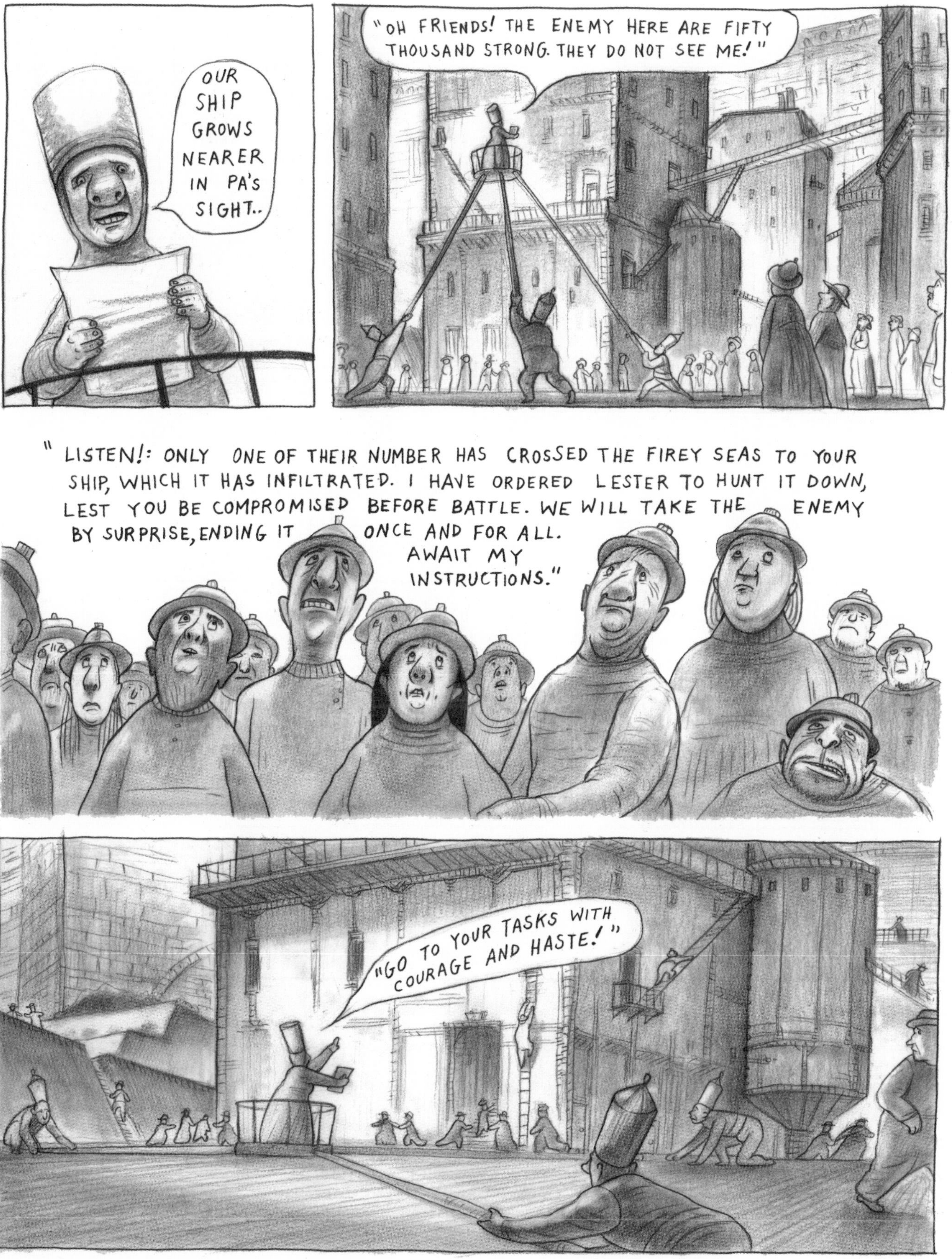
OUR SHIP GROWS NEARER IN PA'S SIGHT..
"OH FRIENDS! THE ENEMY HERE ARE FIFTY THOUSAND STRONG. THEY DO NOT SEE ME!"
" LISTEN!: ONLY ONE OF THEIR NUMBER HAS CROSSED THE FIREY SEAS TO YOUR SHIP, WHICH IT HAS INFILTRATED. I HAVE ORDERED LESTER TO HUNT IT DOWN, LEST YOU BE COMPROMISED BEFORE BATTLE. WE WILL TAKE THE ENEMY BY SURPRISE, ENDING IT ONCE AND FOR ALL. AWAIT MY INSTRUCTIONS."
"GO TO YOUR TASKS WITH COURAGE AND HASTE!"

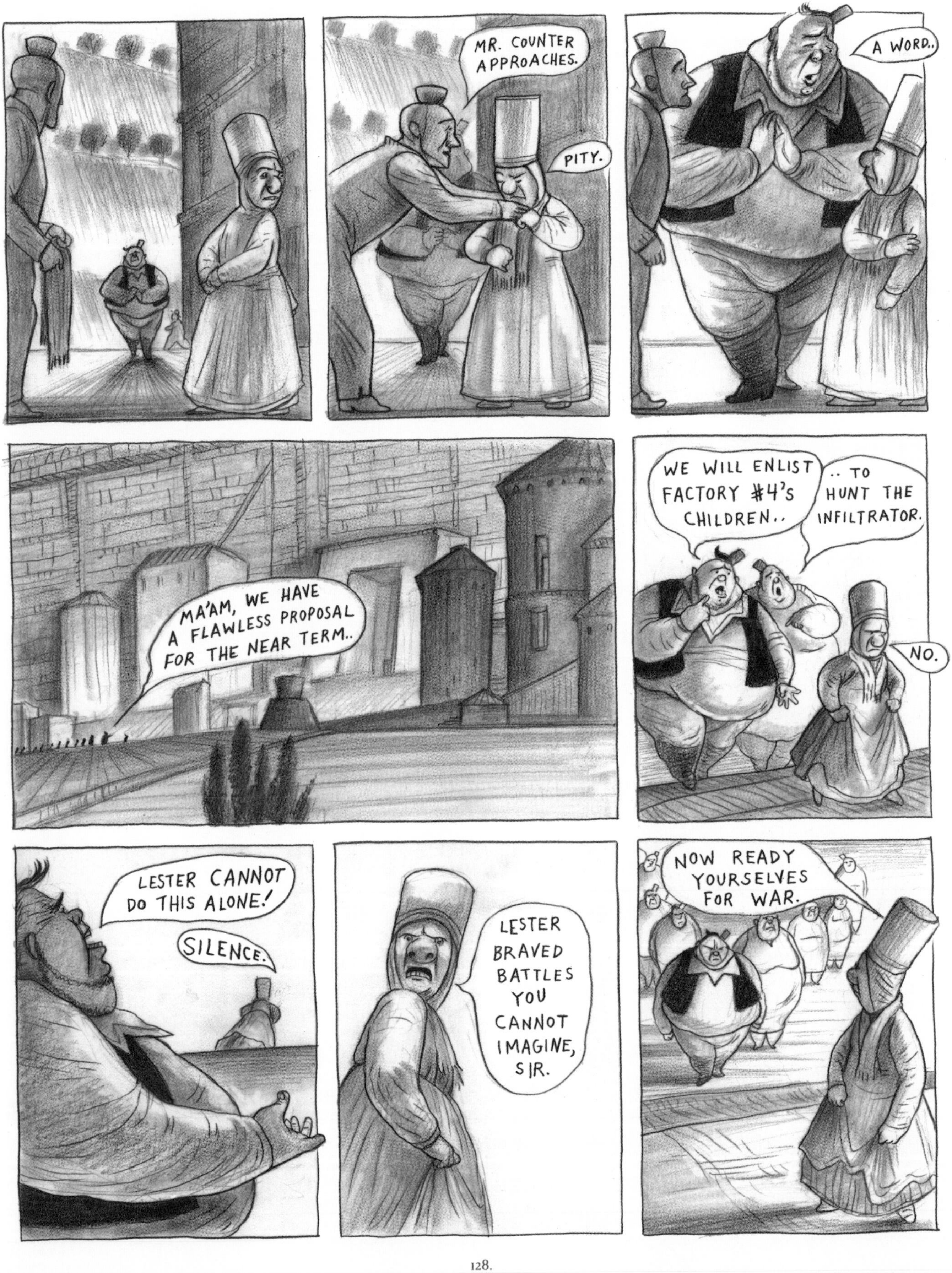
MR. COUNTER APPROACHES.
PITY.
A WORD..
MA'AM, WE HAVE A FLAWLESS PROPOSAL FOR THE NEAR TERM..
WE WILL ENLIST FACTORY #4'S CHILDREN..
.. TO HUNT THE INFILTRATOR.
NO.
LESTER CANNOT DO THIS ALONE!
SILENCE.
LESTER BRAVED BATTLES YOU CANNOT IMAGINE, SIR.
NOW READY YOURSELVES FOR WAR.

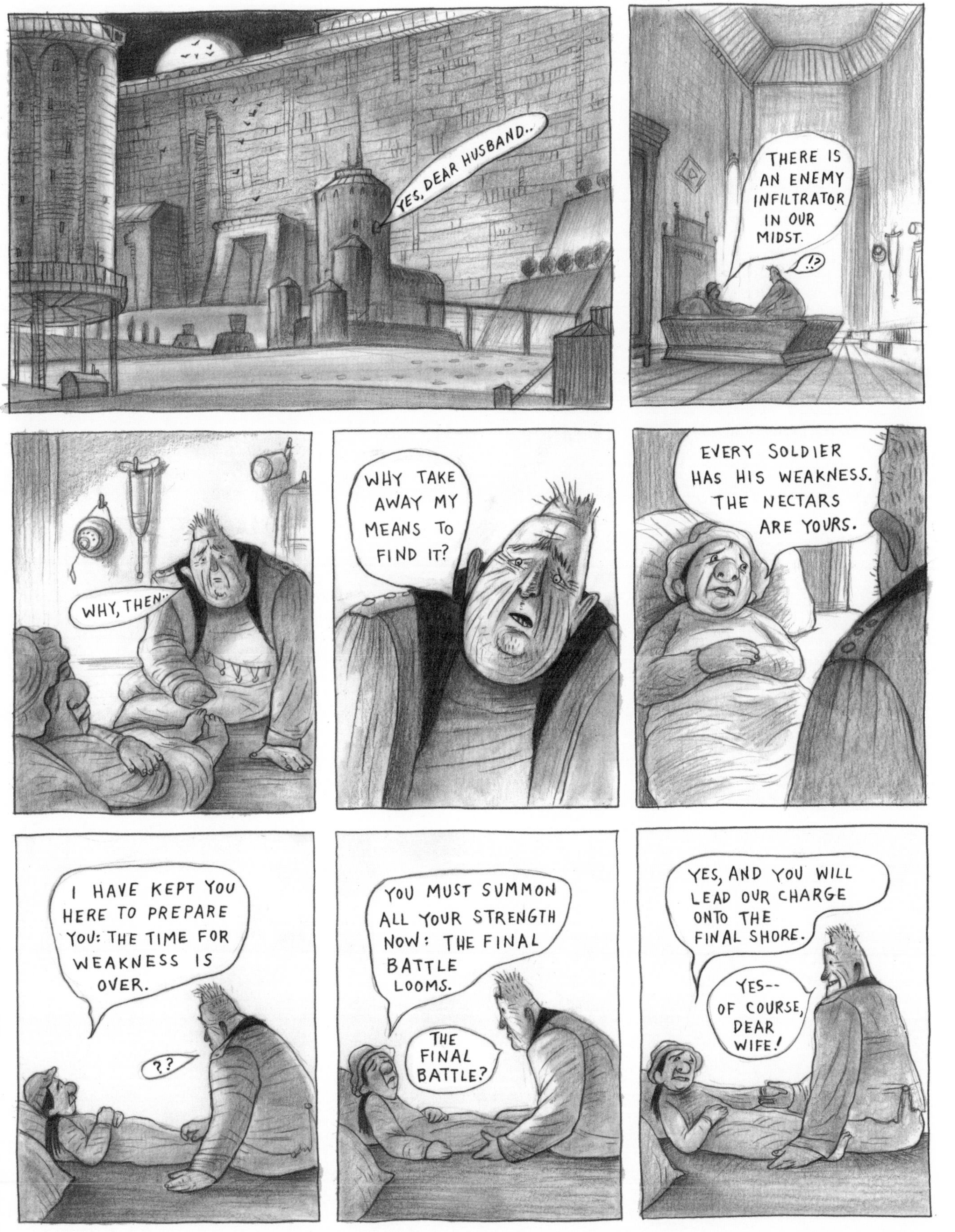

YES, DEAR HUSBAND..
THERE IS AN ENEMY INFILTRATOR IN OUR MIDST.
!?
WHY, THEN..
WHY TAKE AWAY MY MEANS TO FIND IT?
EVERY SOLDIER HAS HIS WEAKNESS. THE NECTARS ARE YOURS.
I HAVE KEPT YOU HERE TO PREPARE YOU: THE TIME FOR WEAKNESS IS OVER.
??
YOU MUST SUMMON ALL YOUR STRENGTH NOW: THE FINAL BATTLE LOOMS.
THE FINAL BATTLE?
YES, AND YOU WILL LEAD OUR CHARGE ONTO THE FINAL SHORE.
YES-- OF COURSE, DEAR WIFE!

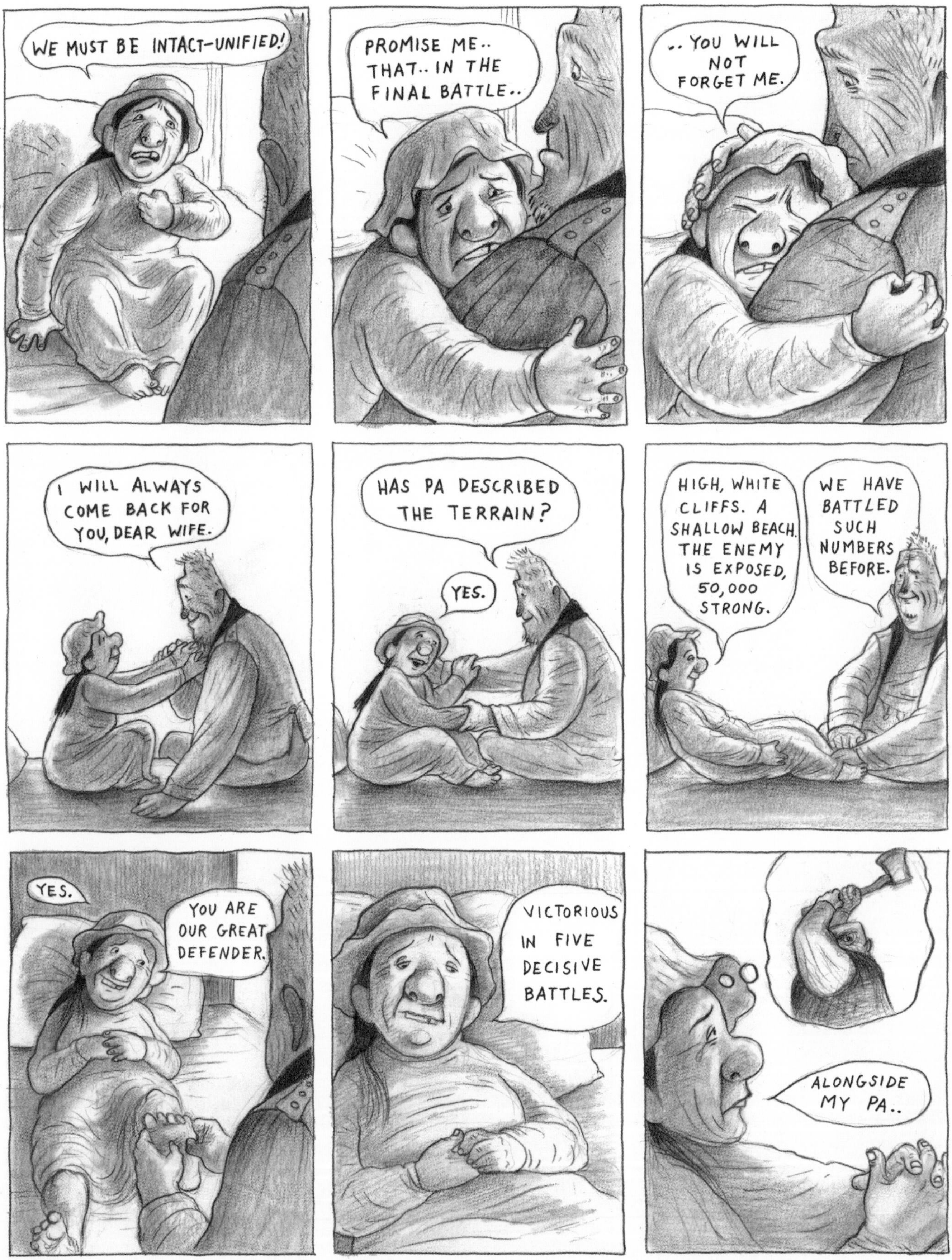
WE MUST BE INTACT-UNIFIED!
PROMISE ME.. THAT.. IN THE FINAL BATTLE..
.. YOU WILL NOT FORGET ME.
I WILL ALWAYS COME BACK FOR YOU, DEAR WIFE.
HAS PA DESCRIBED THE TERRAIN?
YES.
HIGH, WHITE CLIFFS. A SHALLOW BEACH. THE ENEMY IS EXPOSED, 50,000 STRONG.
WE HAVE BATTLED SUCH NUMBERS BEFORE.
YES.
YOU ARE OUR GREAT DEFENDER.
VICTORIOUS IN FIVE DECISIVE BATTLES.
ALONGSIDE MY PA..

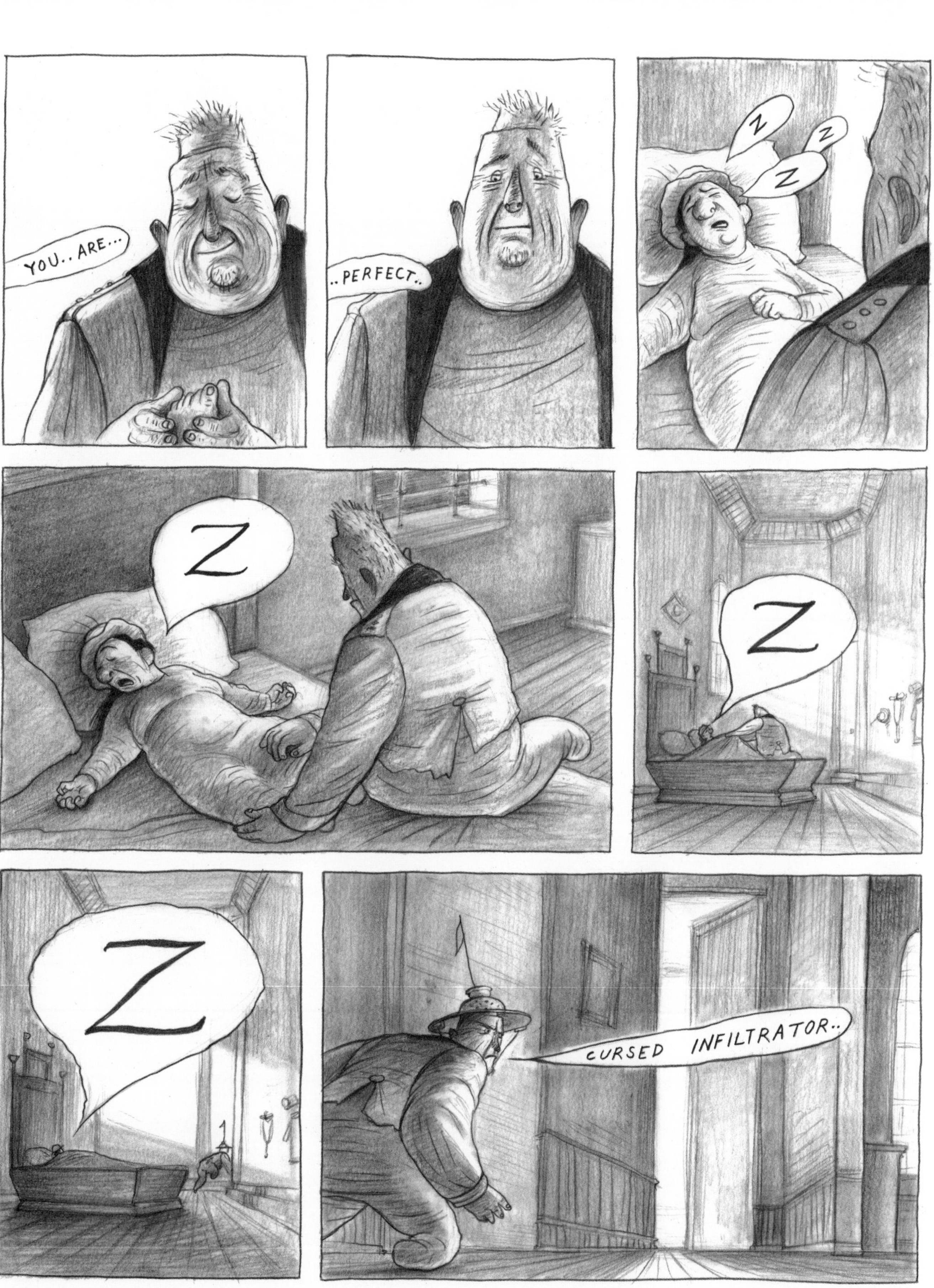
YOU.. ARE...
..PERFECT..
Z
Z
Z
Z
Z
Z
CURSED INFILTRATOR..

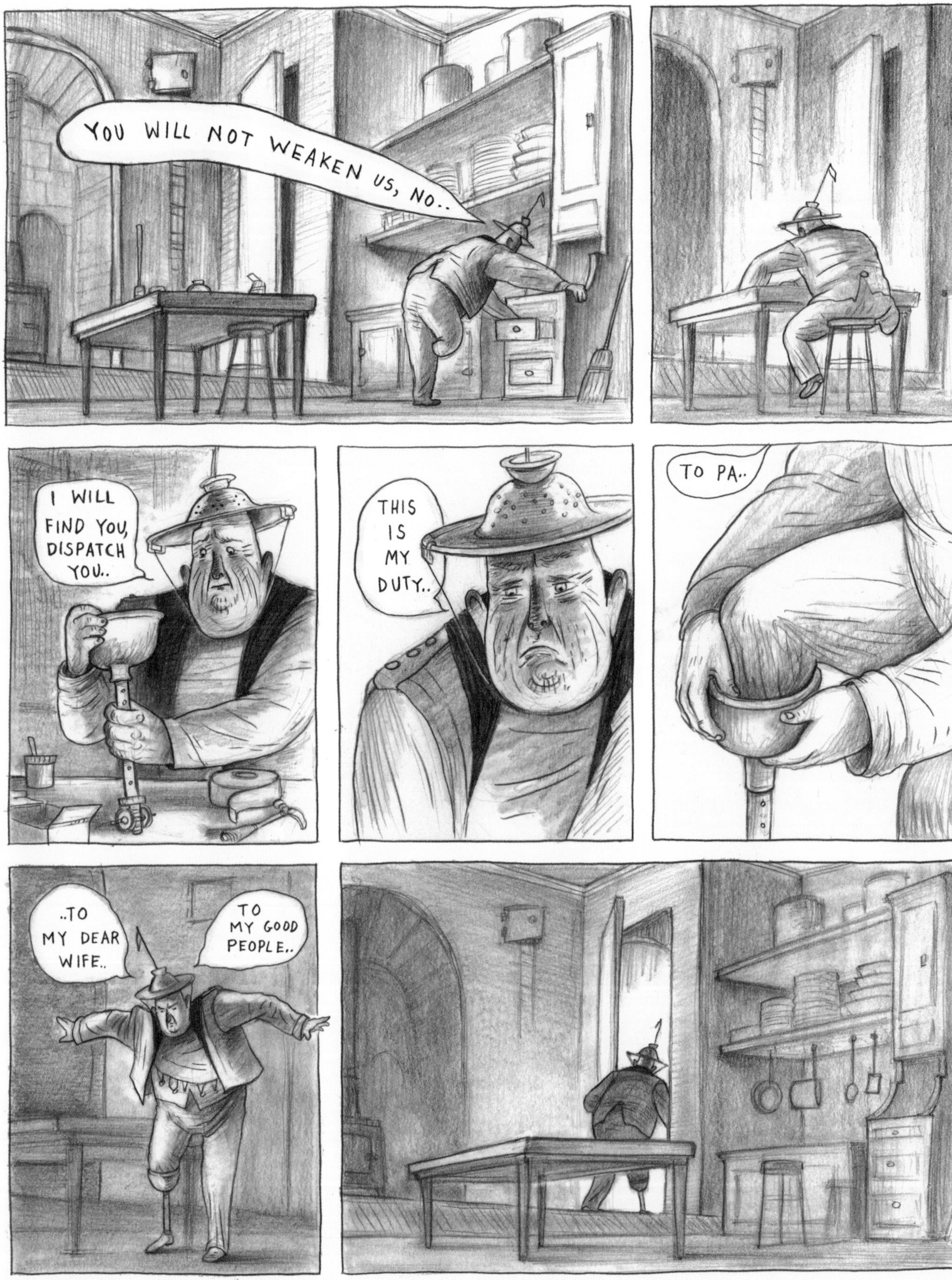
YOU WILL NOT WEAKEN US, NO..
I WILL FIND YOU, DISPATCH YOU..
THIS IS MY DUTY..
TO PA..
..TO MY DEAR WIFE..
TO MY GOOD PEOPLE..

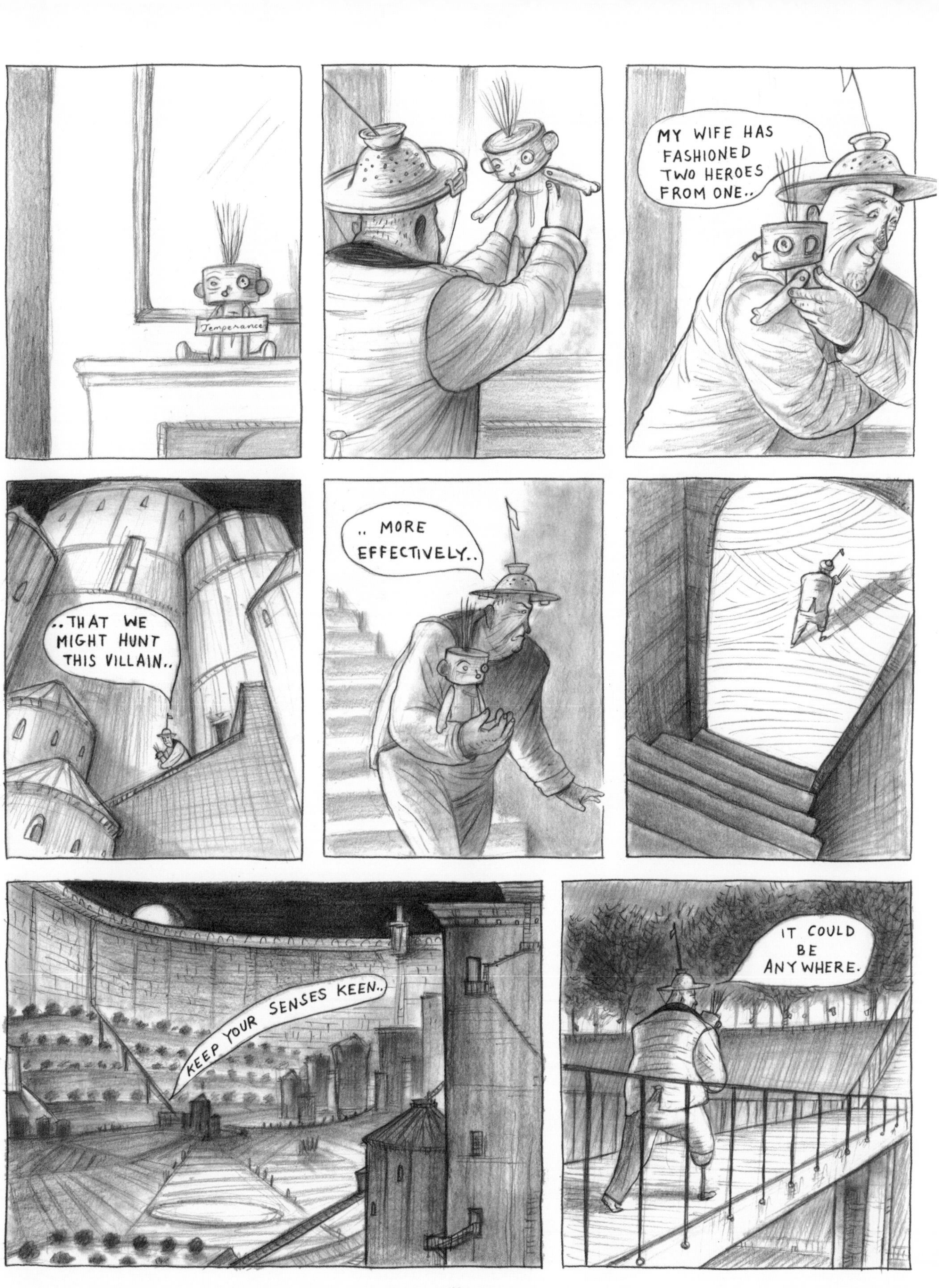
Temperance
MY WIFE HAS FASHIONED TWO HEROES FROM ONE..
..THAT WE MIGHT HUNT THIS VILLAIN..
.. MORE EFFECTIVELY..
KEEP YOUR SENSES KEEN..
IT COULD BE ANYWHERE.

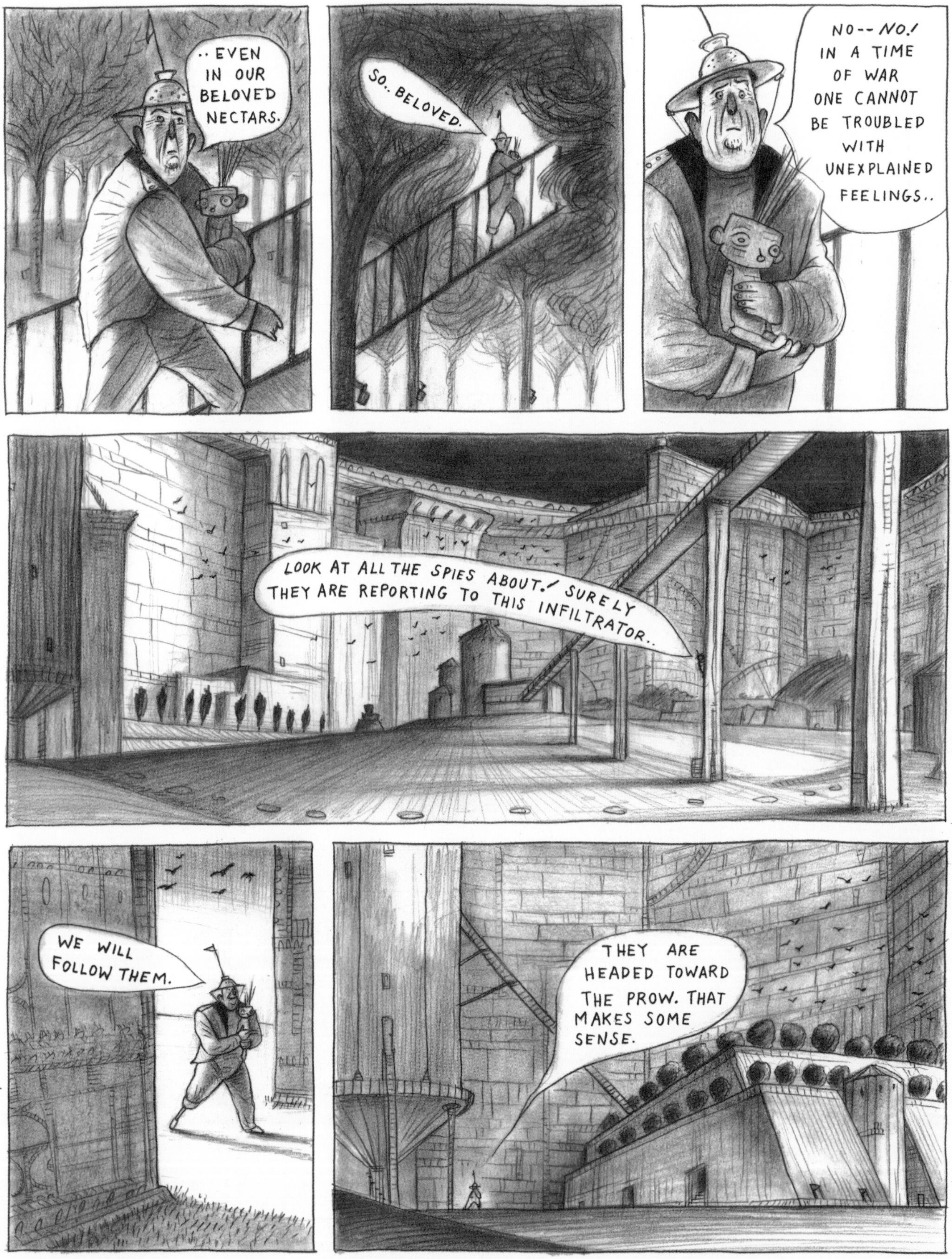
..EVEN IN OUR BELOVED NECTARS.
SO.. BELOVED.
NO-- NO.! IN A TIME OF WAR ONE CANNOT BE TROUBLED WITH UNEXPLAINED FEELINGS..
LOOK AT ALL THE SPIES ABOUT.! SURELY THEY ARE REPORTING TO THIS INFILTRATOR..
WE WILL FOLLOW THEM.
THEY ARE HEADED TOWARD THE PROW. THAT MAKES SOME SENSE.

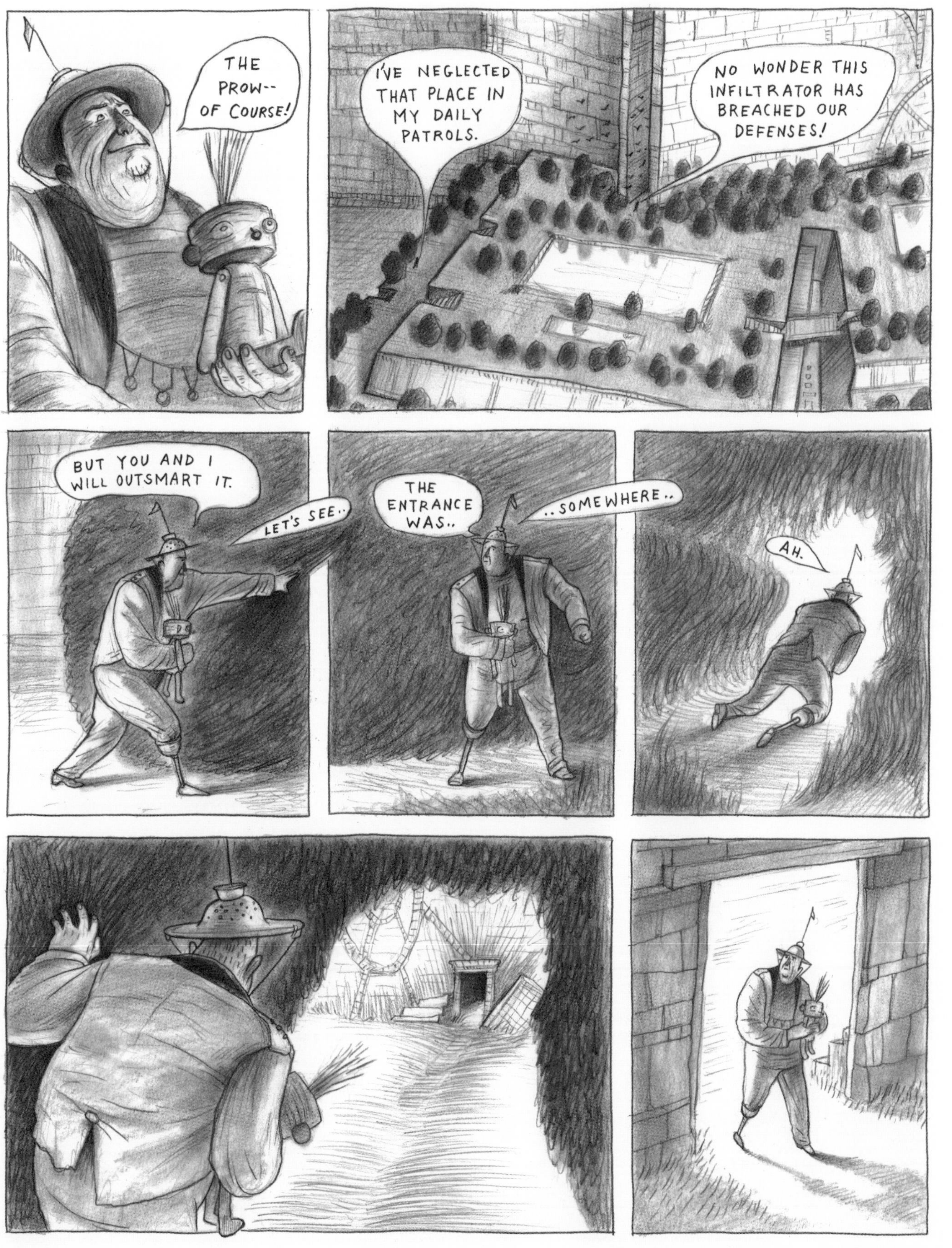
THE PROW-- OF COURSE!
I'VE NEGLECTED THAT PLACE IN MY DAILY PATROLS.
NO WONDER THIS INFILTRATOR HAS BREACHED OUR DEFENSES!
BUT YOU AND I WILL OUTSMART IT.
LET'S SEE..
THE ENTRANCE WAS..
..SOMEWHERE..
AH.

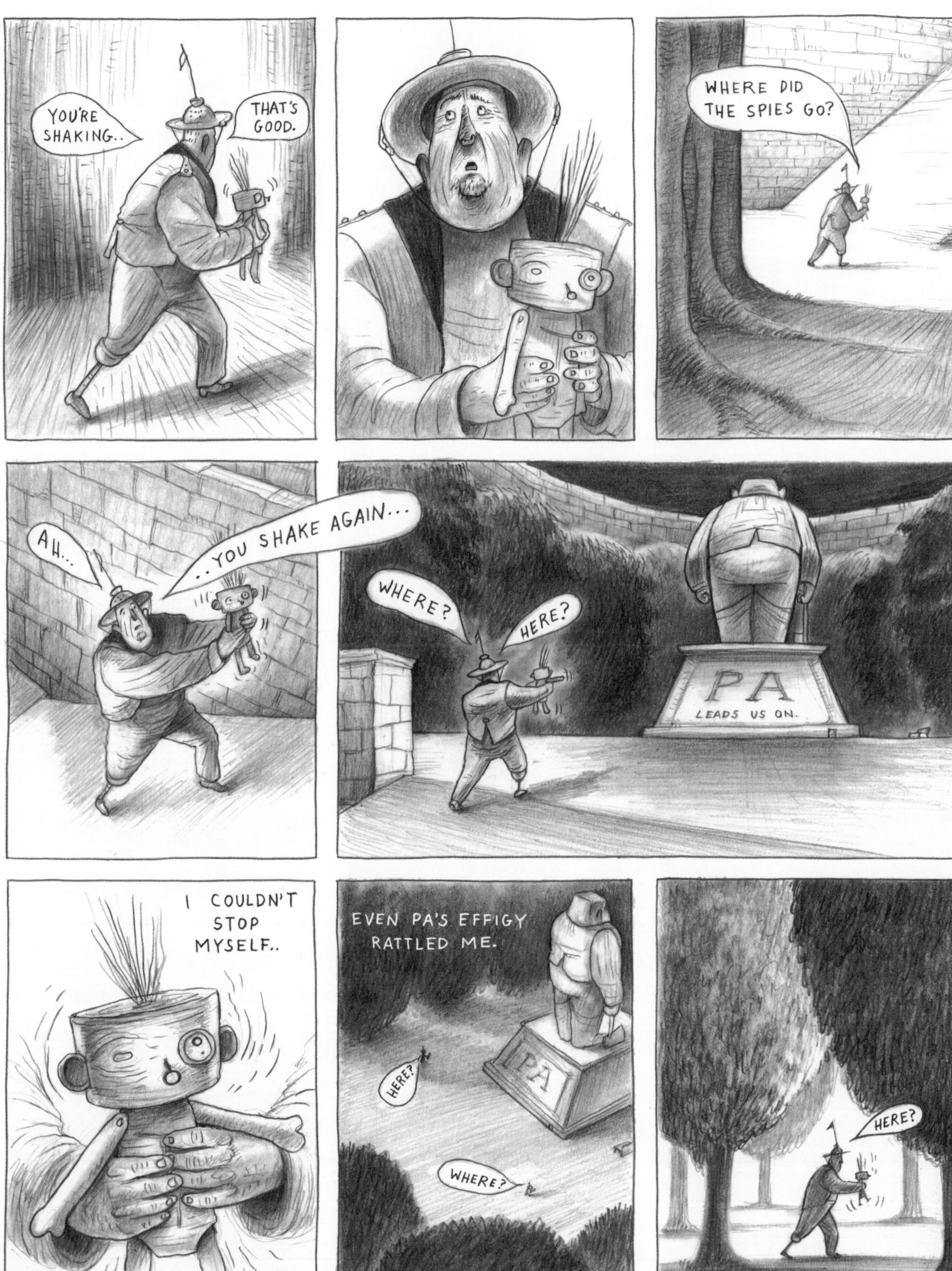
YOU'RE SHAKING..
THAT'S GOOD.
WHERE DID THE SPIES GO?
AH...
..YOU SHAKE AGAIN...
WHERE?
HERE?
PA
LEADS US ON.
I COULDN'T STOP MYSELF..
EVEN PA'S EFFIGY RATTLED ME.
HERE?
PA
WHERE?
HERE?

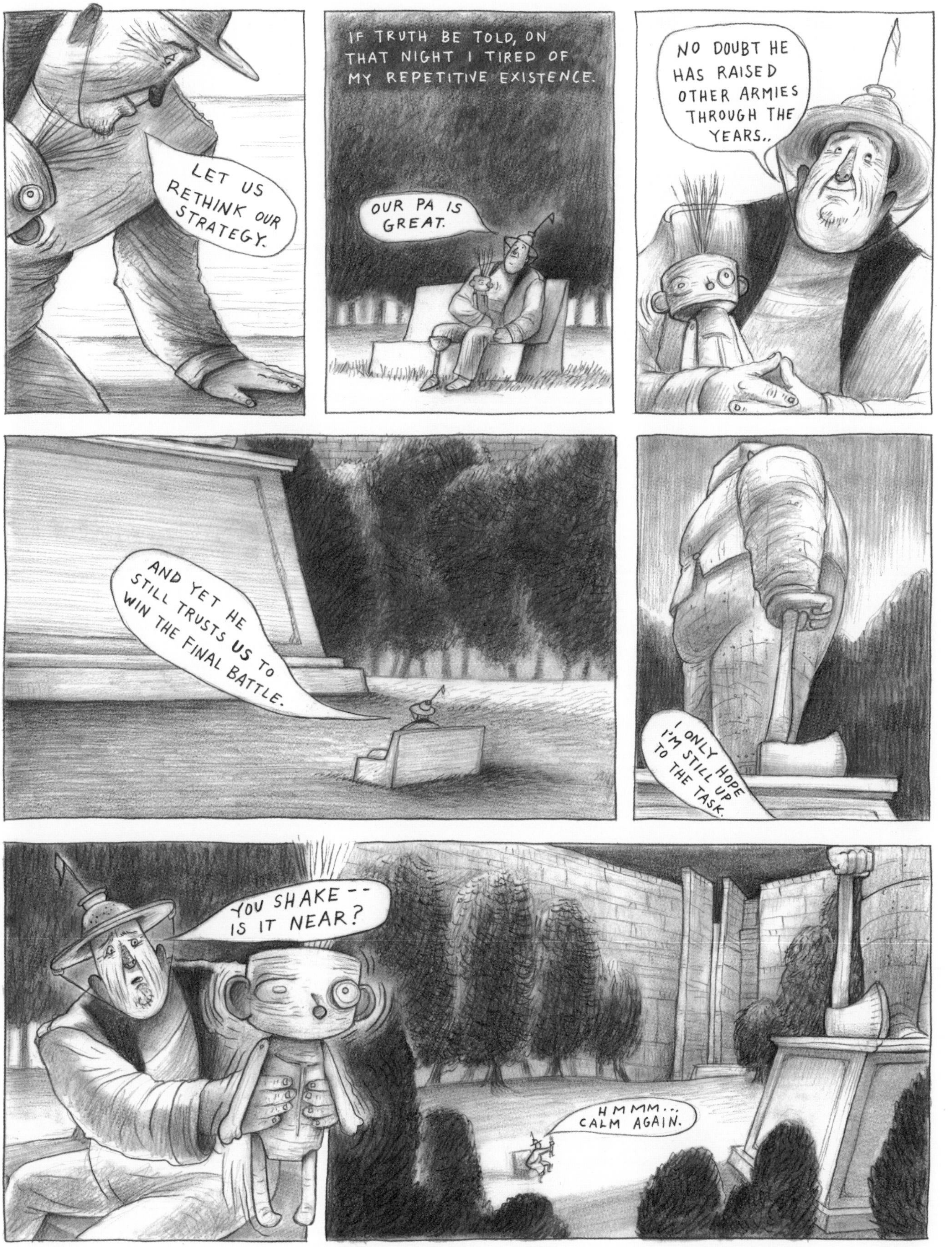
LET US RETHINK OUR STRATEGY.
IF TRUTH BE TOLD, ON THAT NIGHT I TIRED OF MY REPETITIVE EXISTENCE.
OUR PA IS GREAT.
NO DOUBT HE HAS RAISED OTHER ARMIES THROUGH THE YEARS..
AND YET HE STILL TRUSTS US TO WIN THE FINAL BATTLE.
I ONLY HOPE I'M STILL UP TO THE TASK.
YOU SHAKE -- IS IT NEAR?
HMMM... CALM AGAIN.

WE HAVE PROTECTED THIS SHIP FOR THIRTY YEARS. TONIGHT WILL BE NO DIFFERENT. THE INFILTRATOR WAITS THROUGH THOSE TREES, WHERE THE SPIES HUDDLE AND SCHEME...

STRANGE..

THAT FEELING HAS RETURNED.

WE HAVE SO MANY MEMORIES HERE, YOU AND I..

HOW GLAD I AM TO HAVE YOU WITH ME STILL.

LESTER CALMED, BUT I QUICKENED.

I COULD NOT STOP.

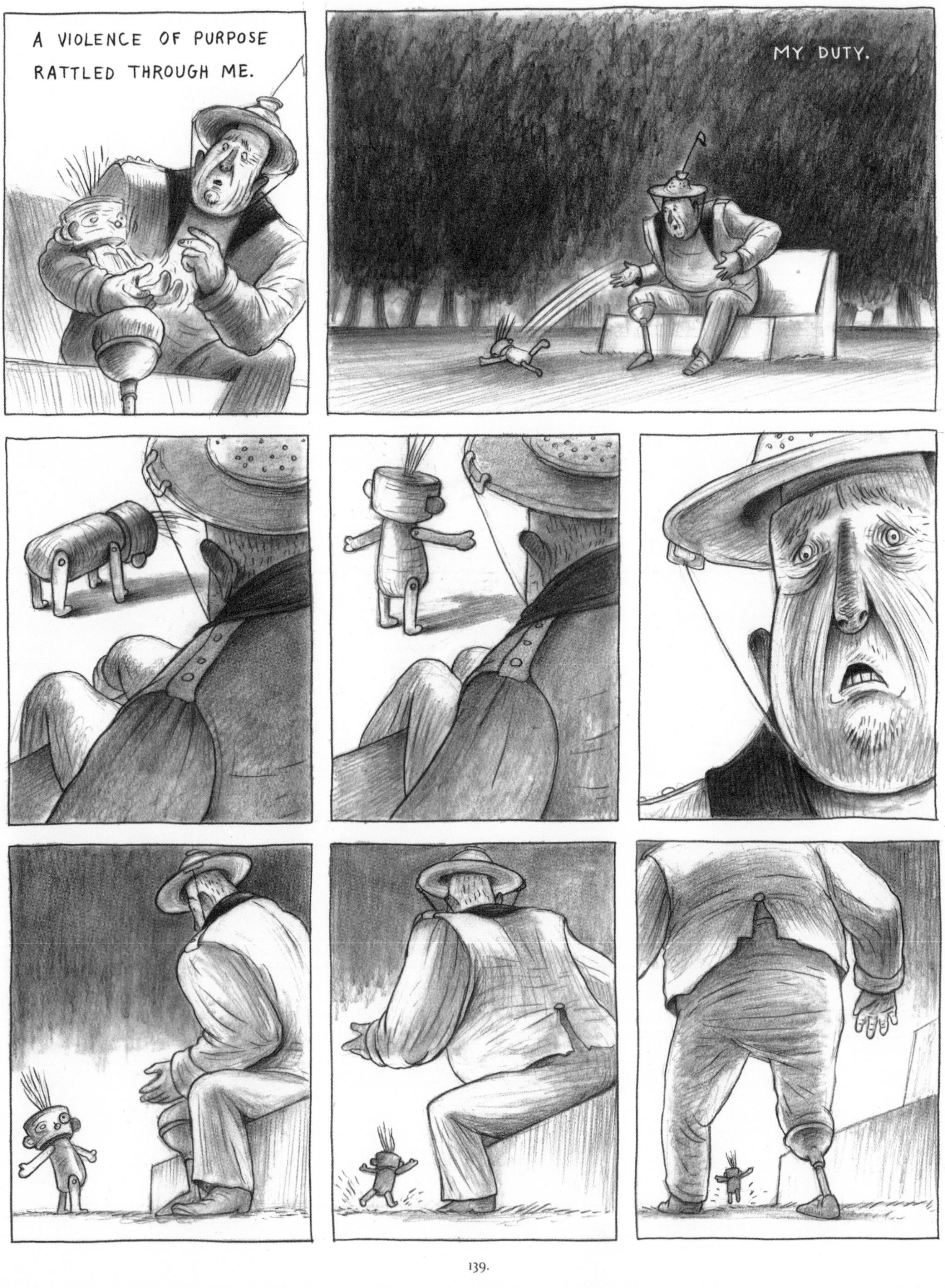
A VIOLENCE OF PURPOSE RATTLED THROUGH ME.
MY DUTY.

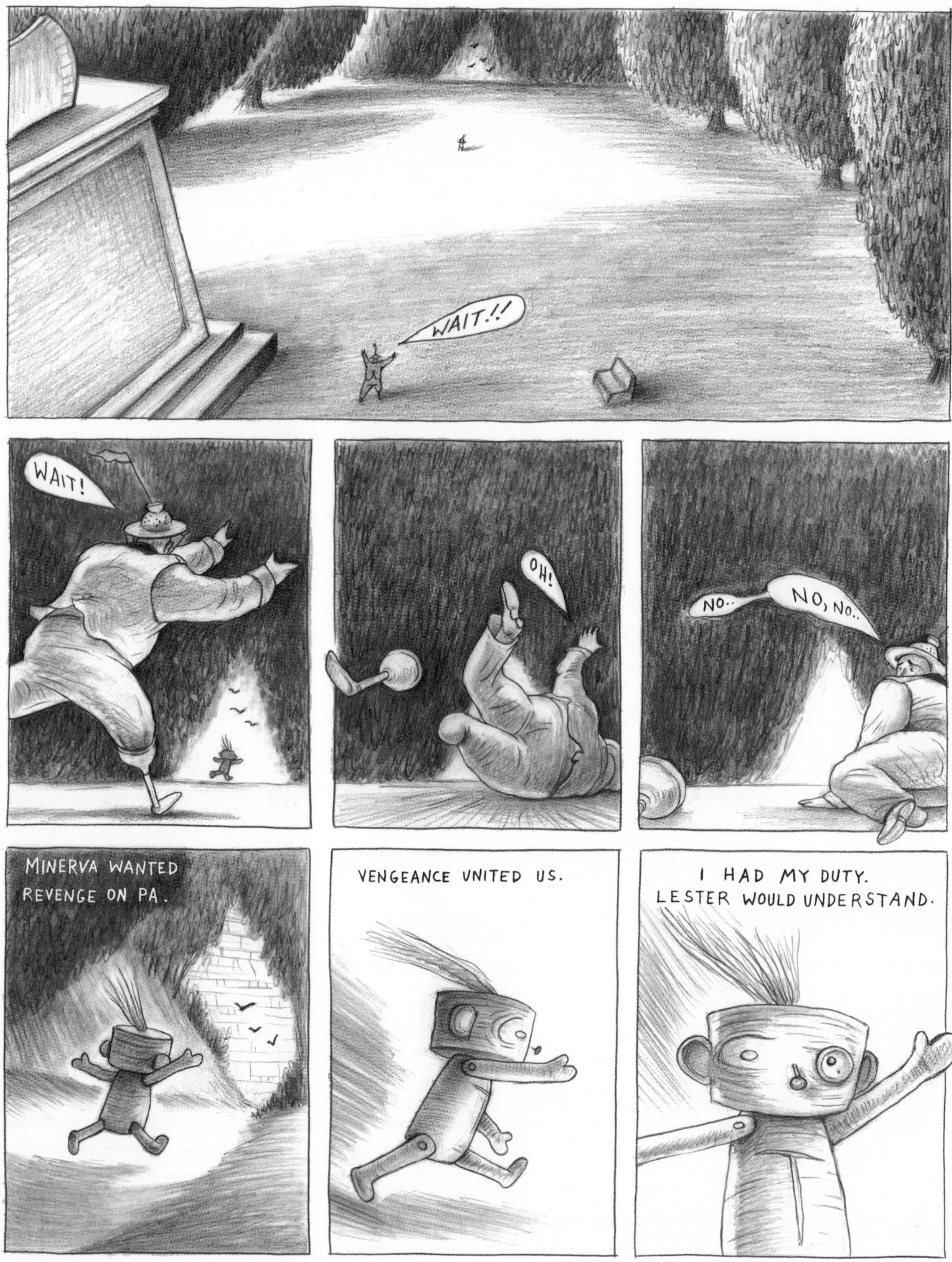
WAIT!!
WAIT!
OH!
NO..
NO, NO..
MINERVA WANTED REVENGE ON PA.
VENGEANCE UNITED US.
I HAD MY DUTY. LESTER WOULD UNDERSTAND.

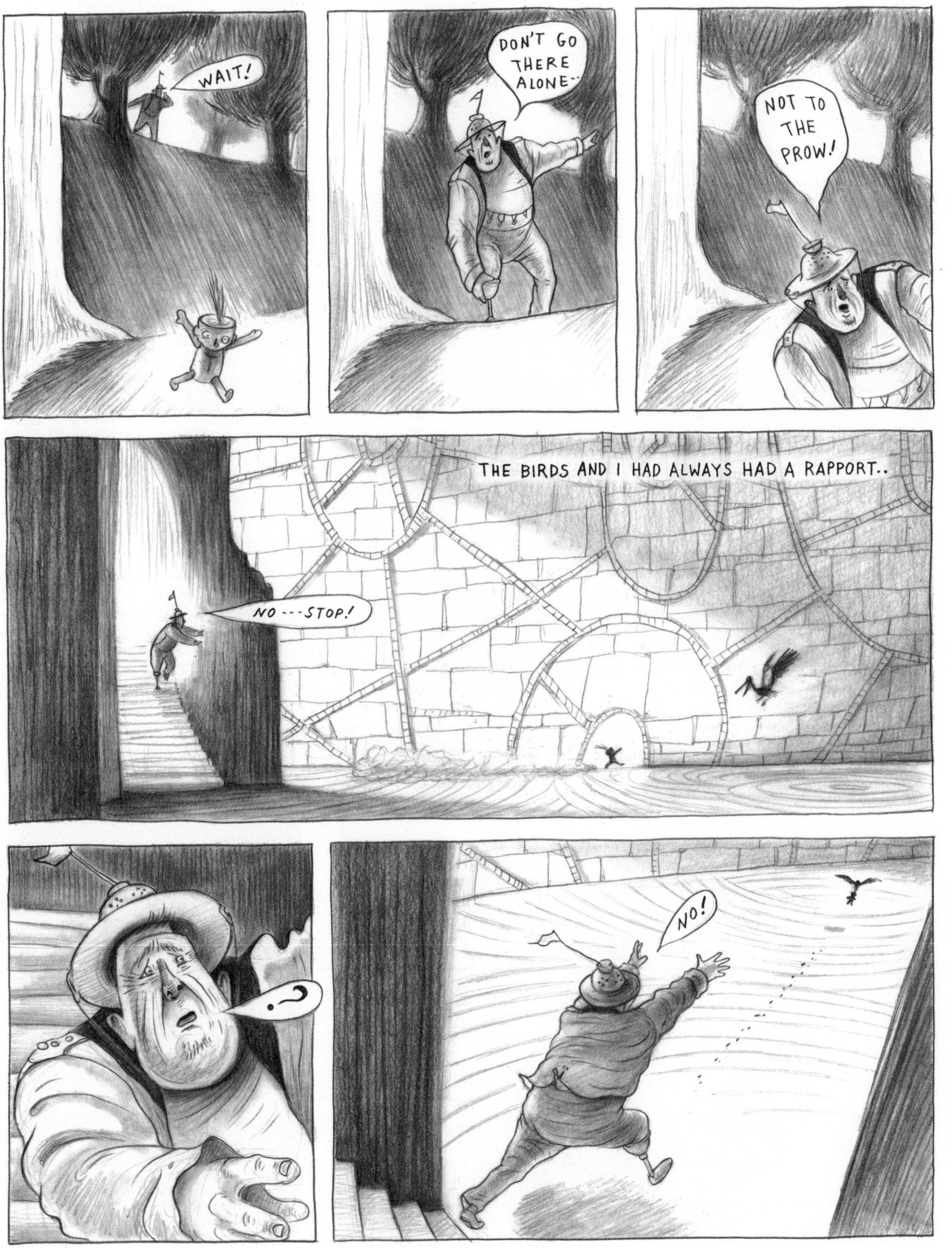
WAIT!
DON'T GO THERE ALONE..
NOT TO THE PROW!
THE BIRDS AND I HAD ALWAYS HAD A RAPPORT..
NO---STOP!
?
NO!

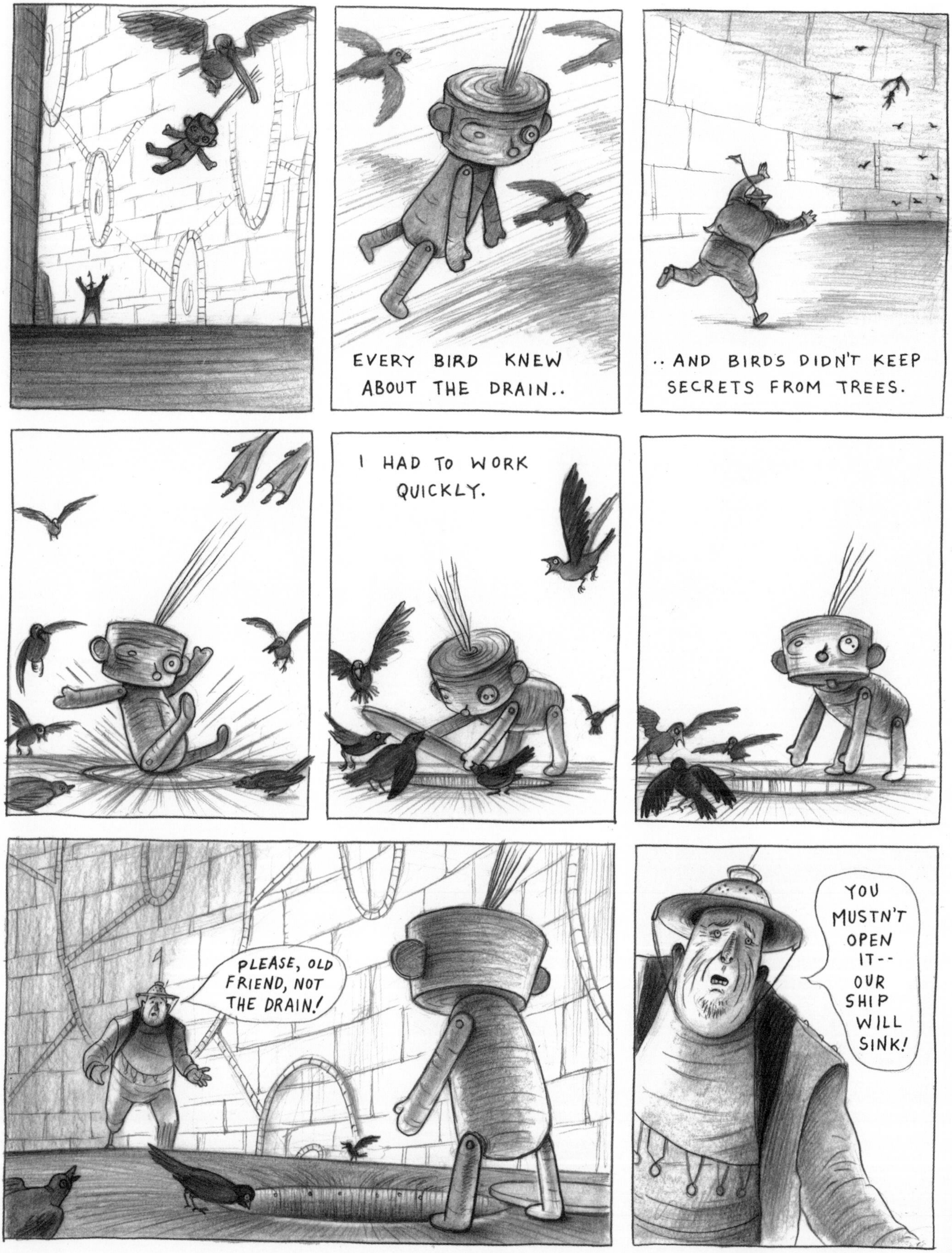
EVERY BIRD KNEW ABOUT THE DRAIN..
..AND BIRDS DIDN'T KEEP SECRETS FROM TREES.
I HAD TO WORK QUICKLY.
PLEASE, OLD FRIEND, NOT THE DRAIN!
YOU MUSTN'T OPEN IT-- OUR SHIP WILL SINK!

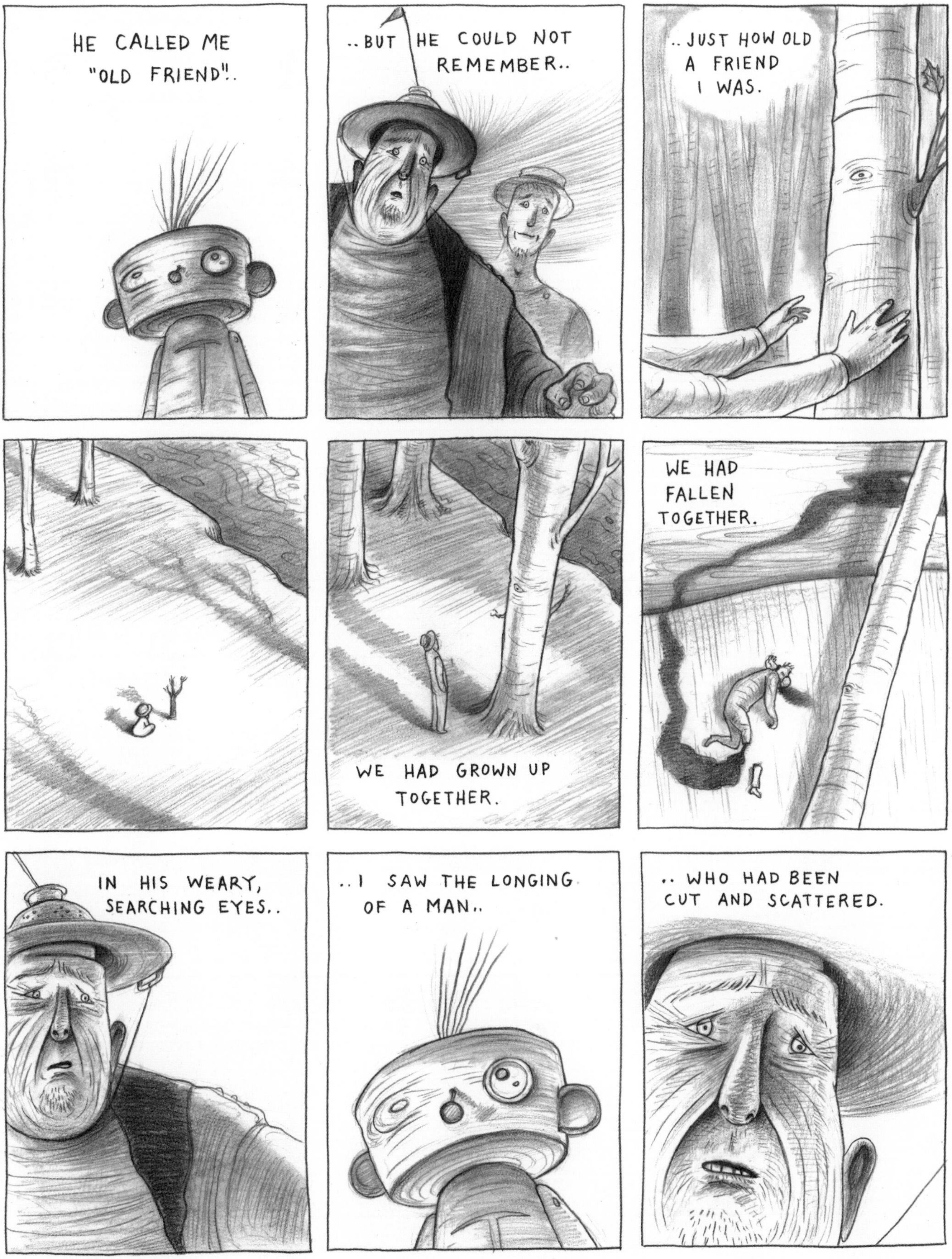
HE CALLED ME "OLD FRIEND"..
..BUT HE COULD NOT REMEMBER..
..JUST HOW OLD A FRIEND I WAS.
WE HAD GROWN UP TOGETHER.
WE HAD FALLEN TOGETHER.
IN HIS WEARY, SEARCHING EYES..
..I SAW THE LONGING OF A MAN..
..WHO HAD BEEN CUT AND SCATTERED.

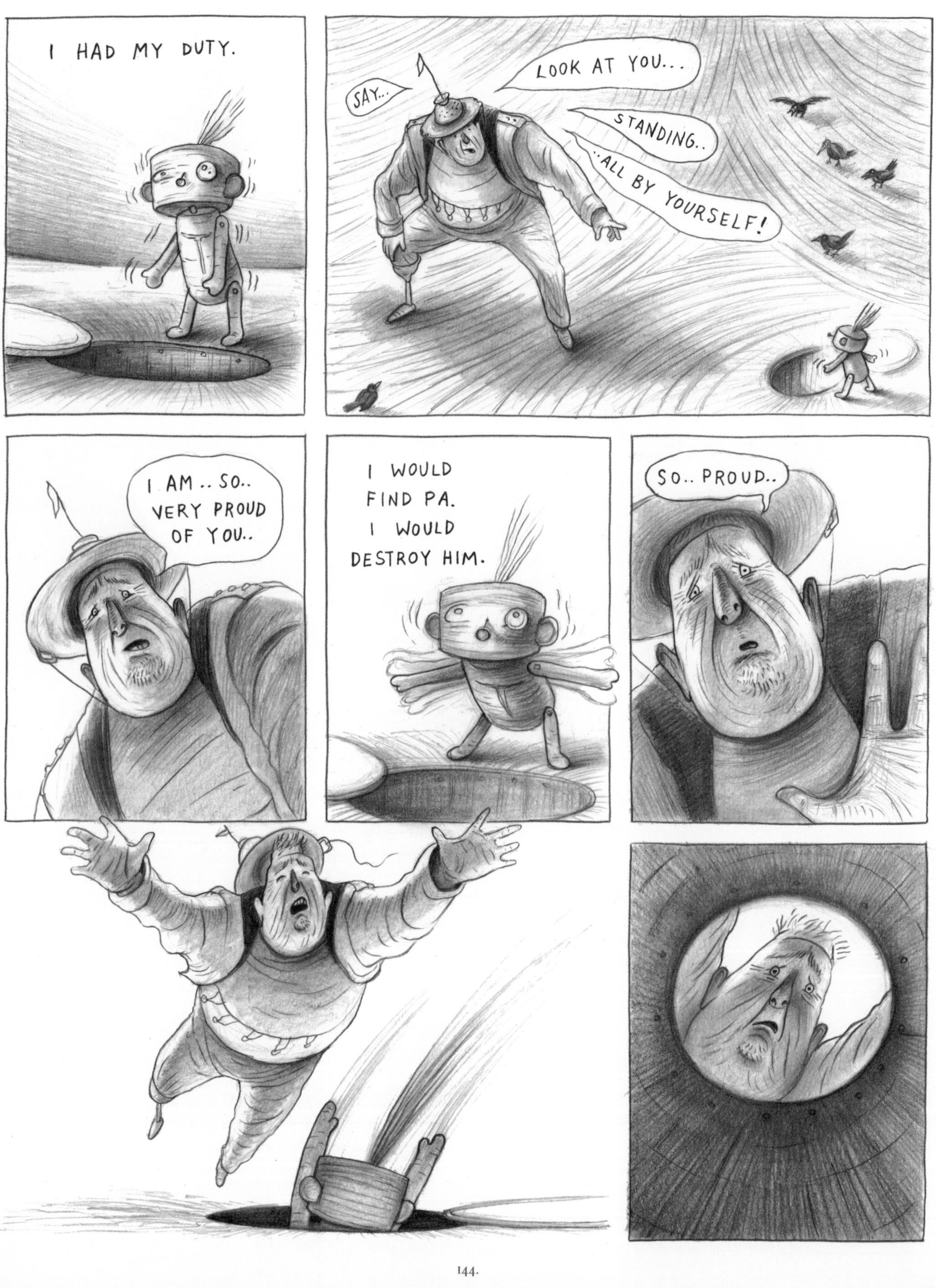
I HAD MY DUTY.
SAY...
LOOK AT YOU...
STANDING..
..ALL BY YOURSELF!
I AM.. SO.. VERY PROUD OF YOU..
I WOULD FIND PA. I WOULD DESTROY HIM.
SO.. PROUD..

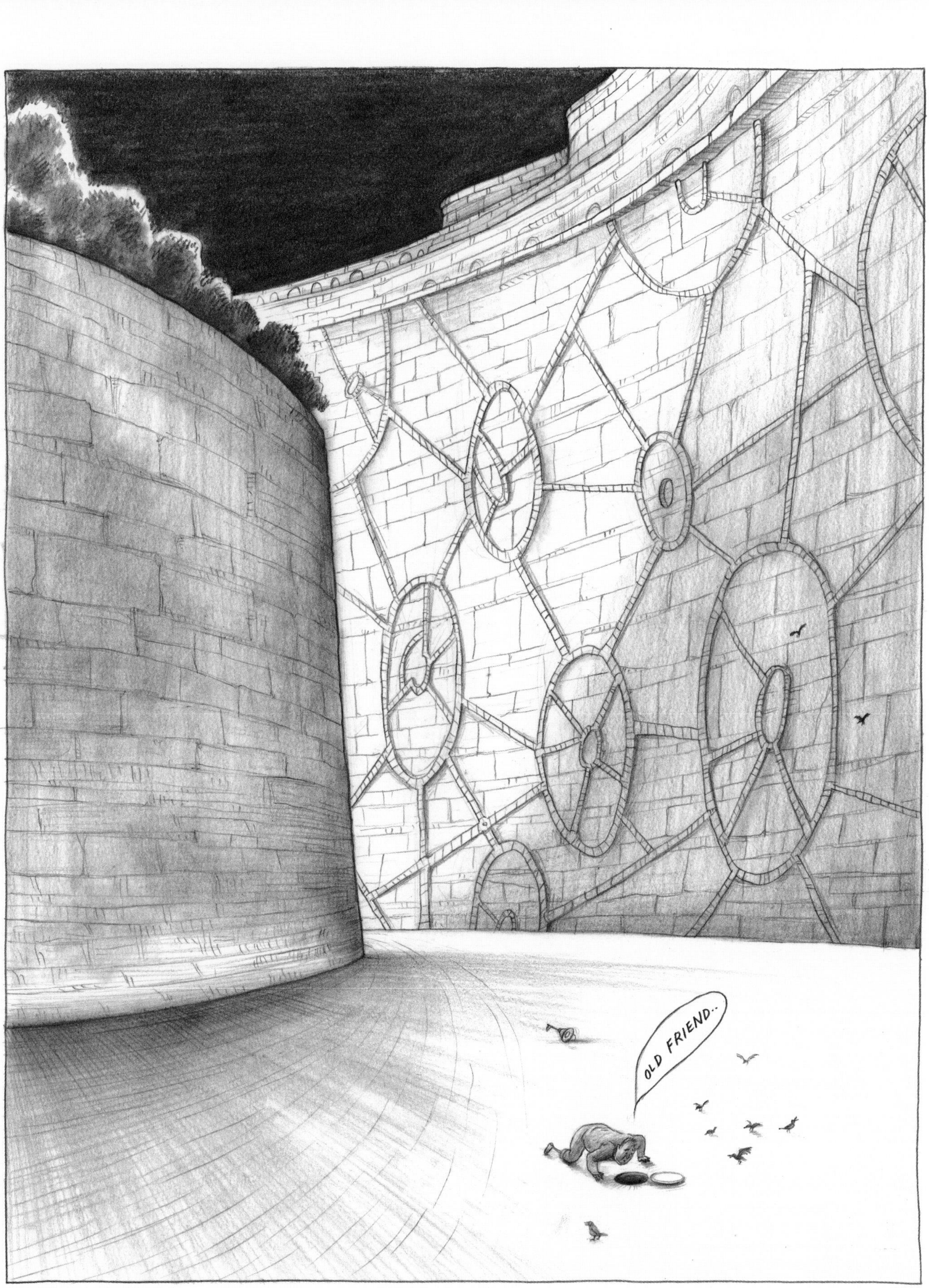
OLD FRIEND..

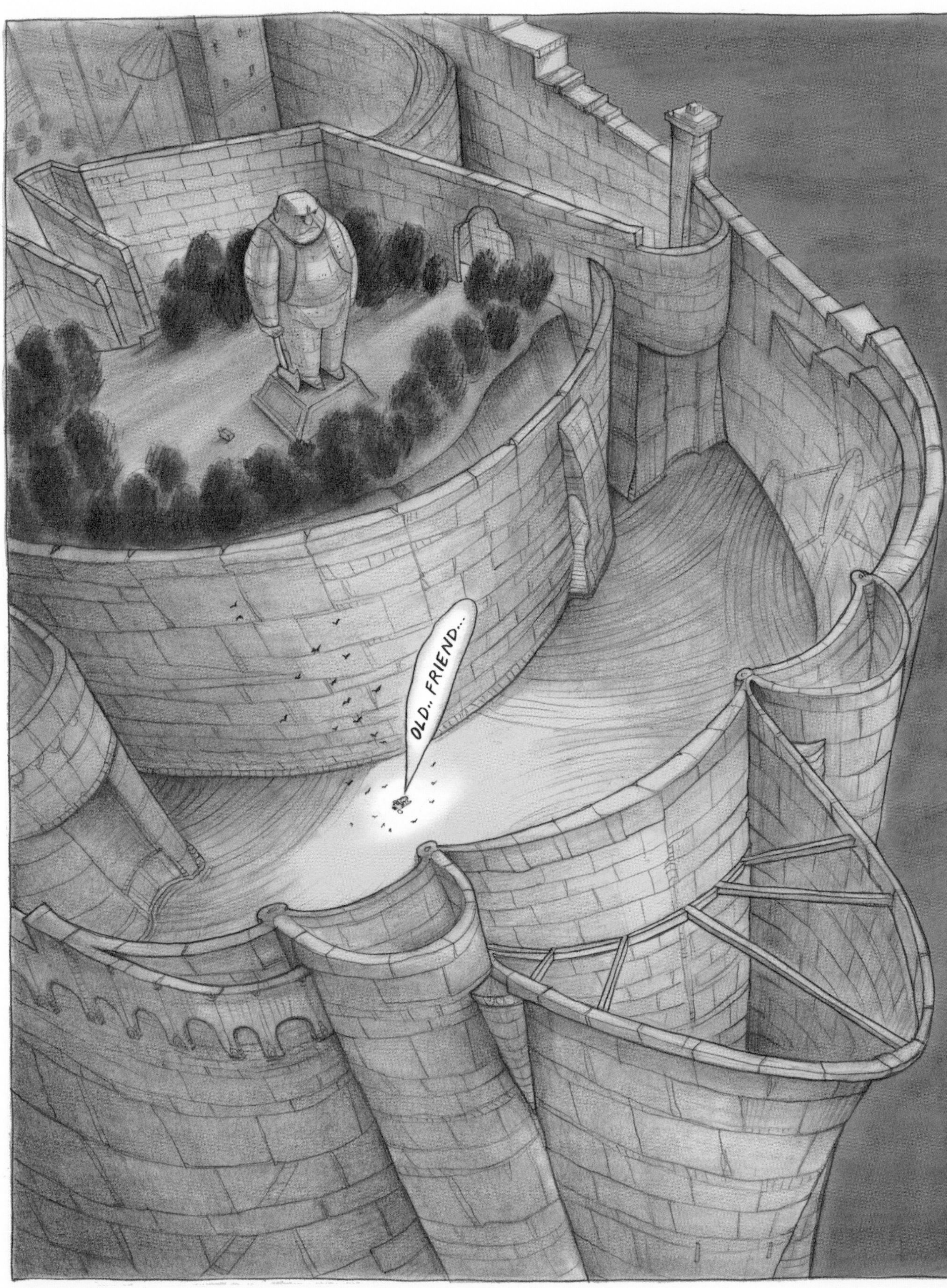
OLD.. FRIEND...

Part Three

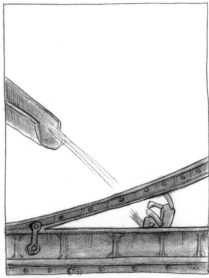

I WAS BORN
WITH PRIVILEDGES...

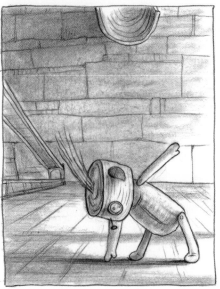

..A HERD OF WITNESSES..

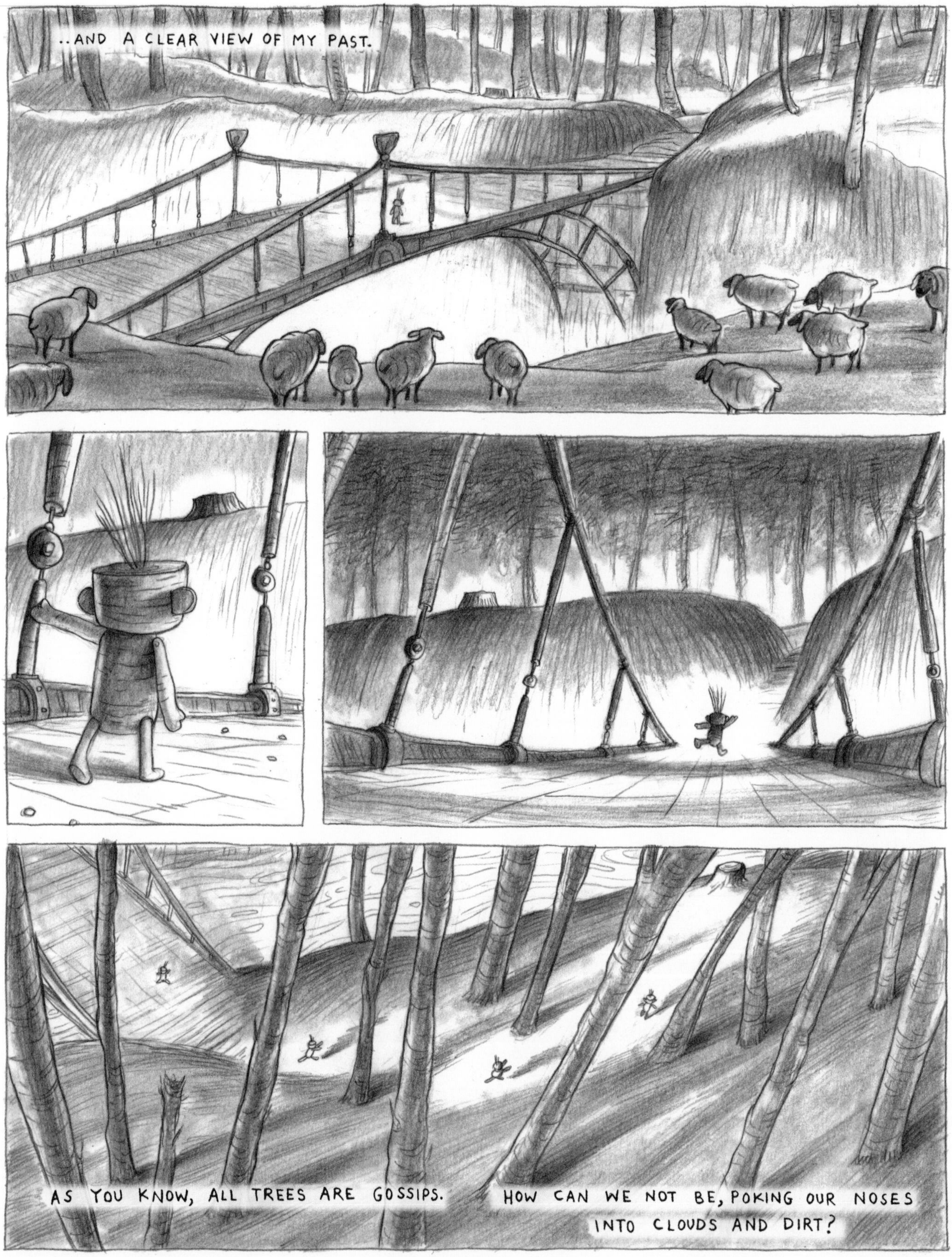
..AND A CLEAR VIEW OF MY PAST.
AS YOU KNOW, ALL TREES ARE GOSSIPS.
HOW CAN WE NOT BE, POKING OUR NOSES INTO CLOUDS AND DIRT?

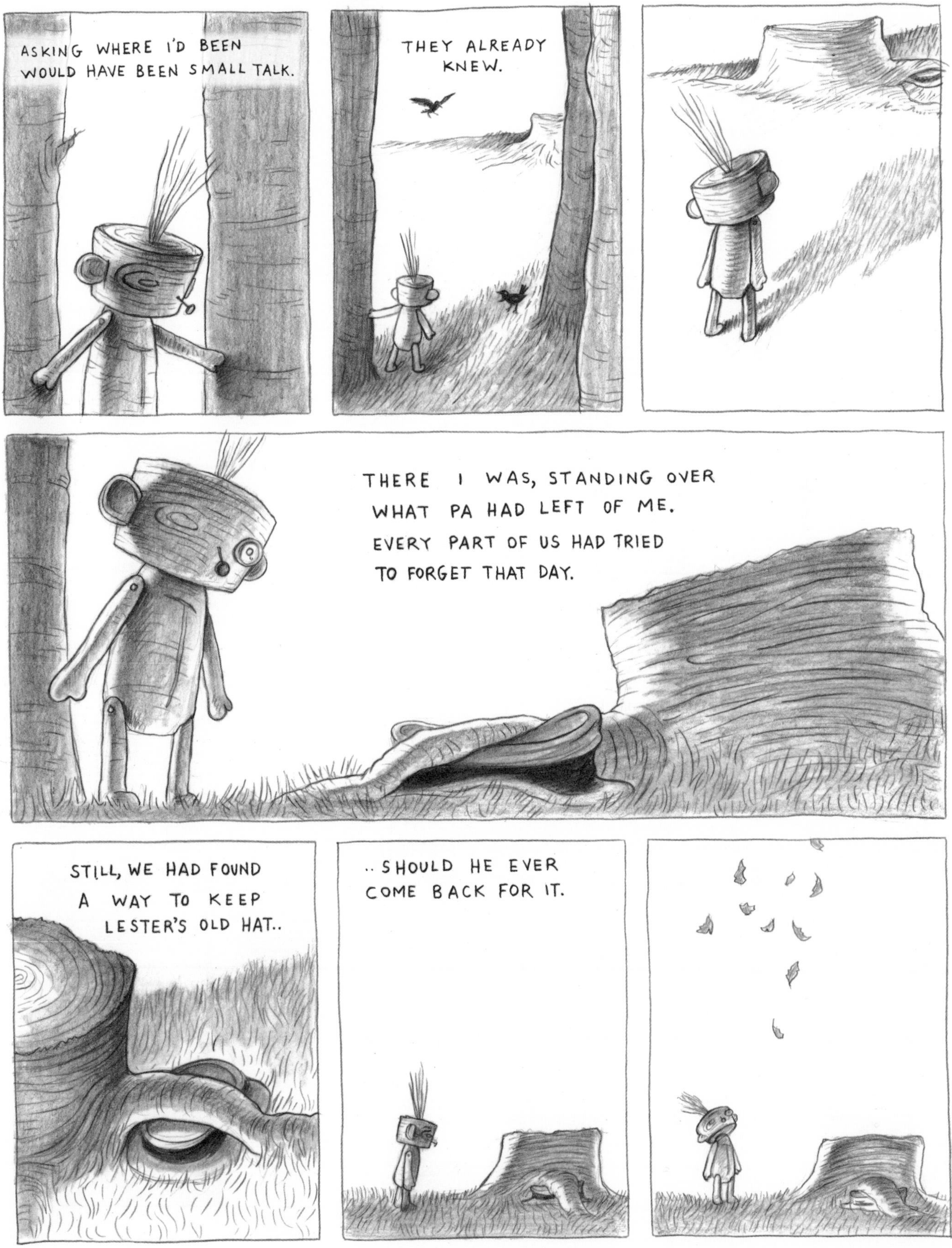
ASKING WHERE I'D BEEN WOULD HAVE BEEN SMALL TALK.
THEY ALREADY KNEW.
THERE I WAS, STANDING OVER WHAT PA HAD LEFT OF ME. EVERY PART OF US HAD TRIED TO FORGET THAT DAY.
STILL, WE HAD FOUND A WAY TO KEEP LESTER'S OLD HAT..
..SHOULD HE EVER COME BACK FOR IT.

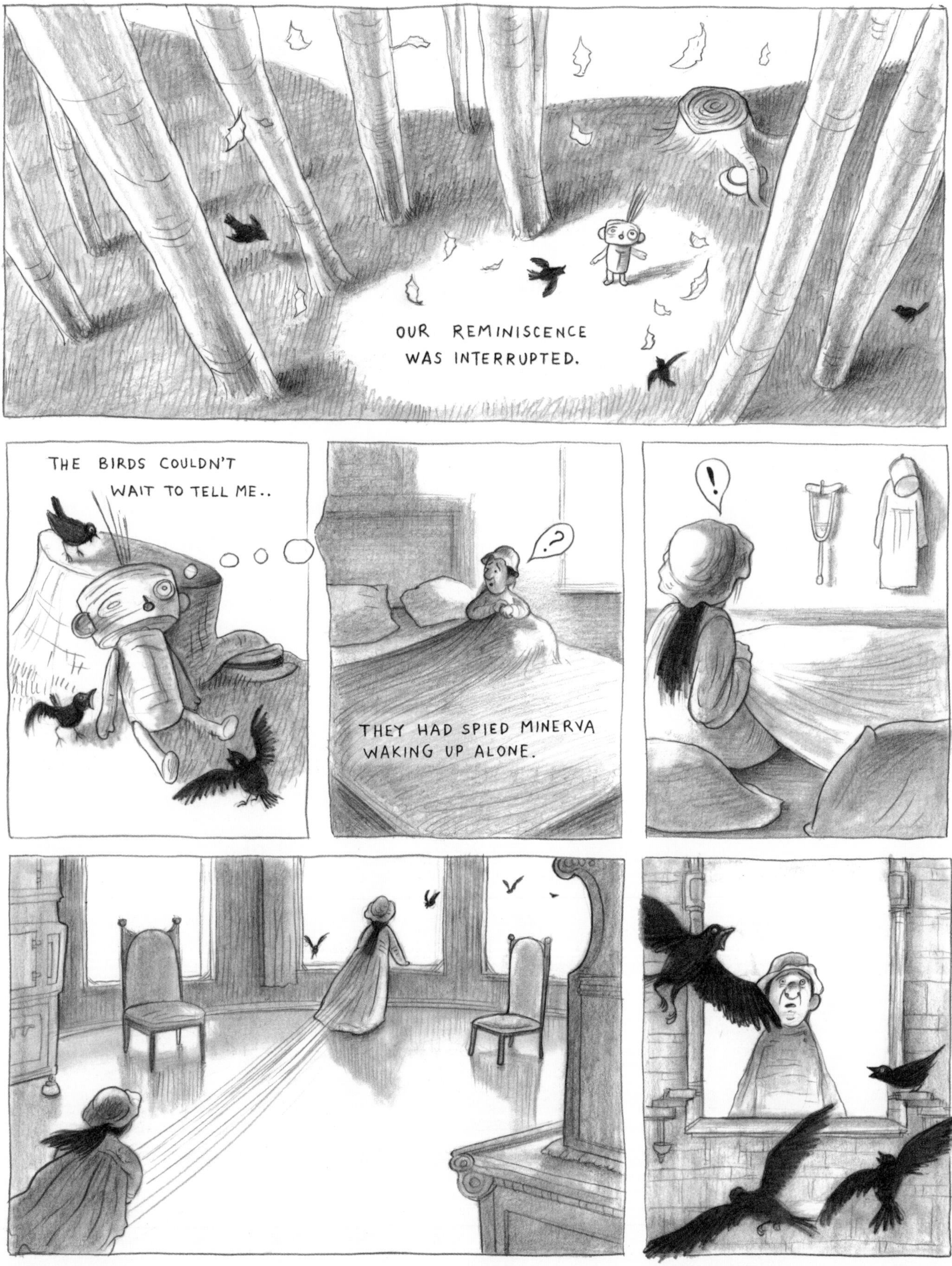

OUR REMINISCENCE WAS INTERRUPTED.
THE BIRDS COULDN'T WAIT TO TELL ME..
?
THEY HAD SPIED MINERVA WAKING UP ALONE.
!

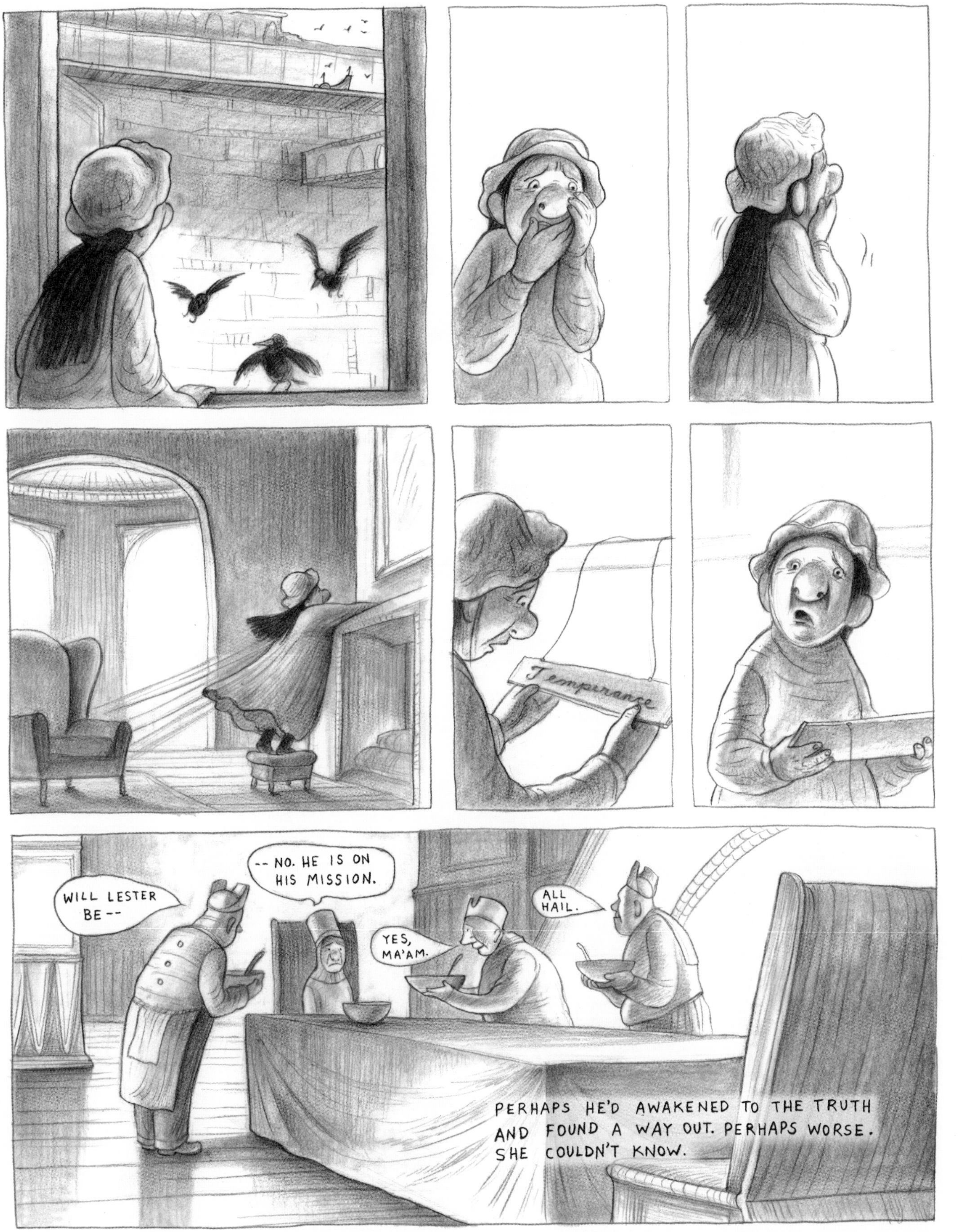
Temperance
WILL LESTER BE --
-- NO. HE IS ON HIS MISSION.
YES, MA'AM.
ALL HAIL.
PERHAPS HE'D AWAKENED TO THE TRUTH AND FOUND A WAY OUT. PERHAPS WORSE. SHE COULDN'T KNOW.

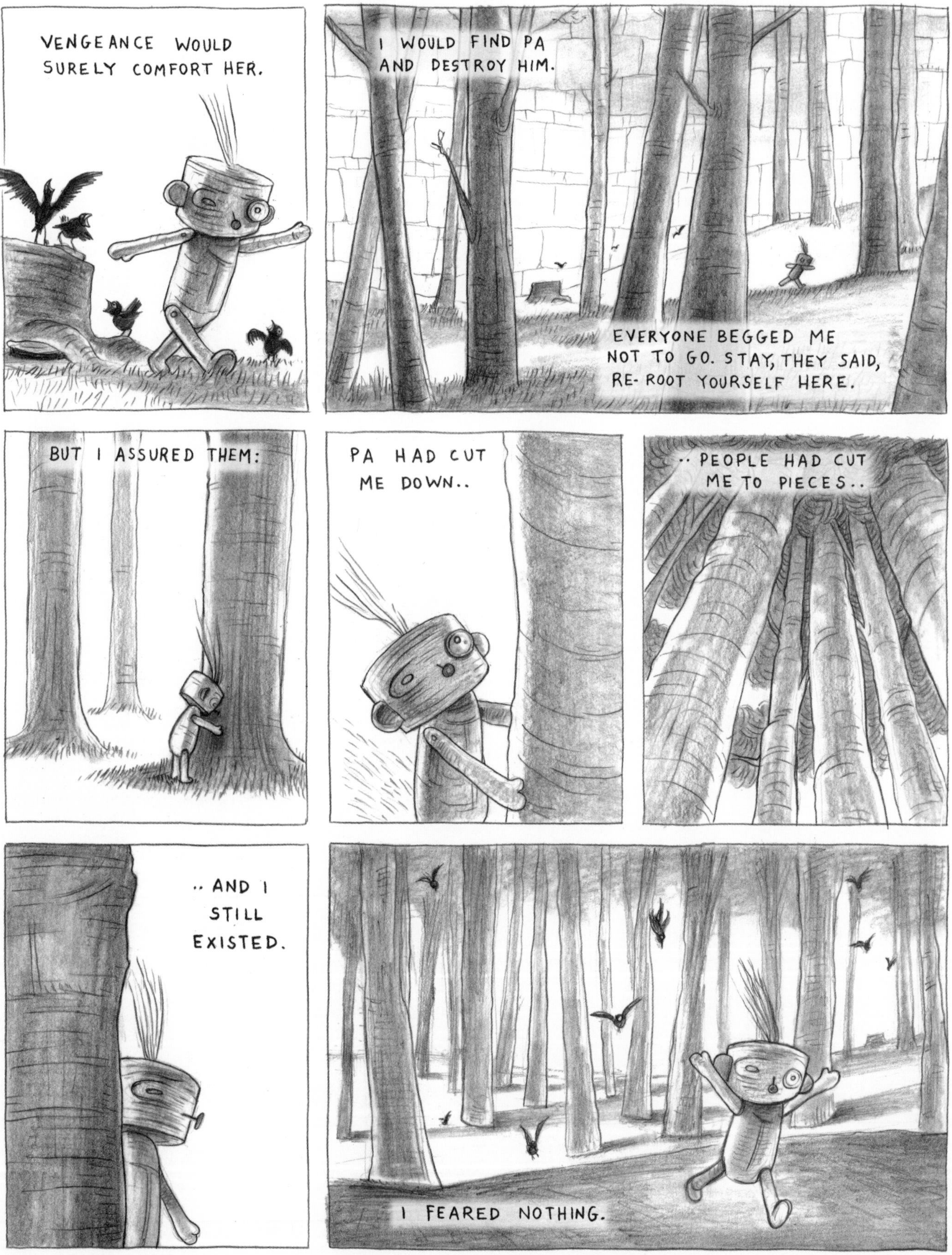
VENGEANCE WOULD SURELY COMFORT HER.
I WOULD FIND PA AND DESTROY HIM.
EVERYONE BEGGED ME NOT TO GO. STAY, THEY SAID, RE-ROOT YOURSELF HERE.
BUT I ASSURED THEM:
PA HAD CUT ME DOWN..
..PEOPLE HAD CUT ME TO PIECES..
..AND I STILL EXISTED.
I FEARED NOTHING.

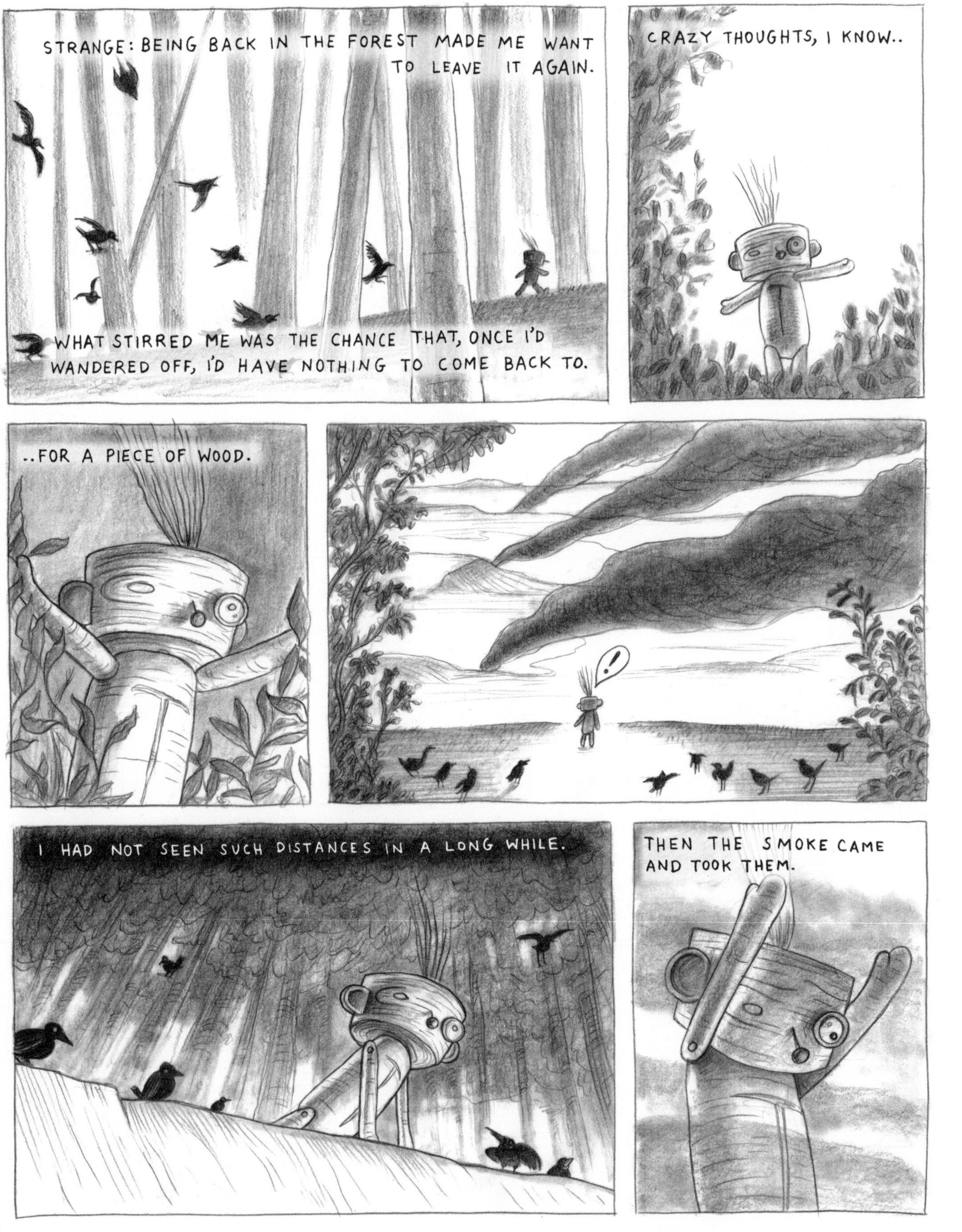
STRANGE: BEING BACK IN THE FOREST MADE ME WANT TO LEAVE IT AGAIN.
WHAT STIRRED ME WAS THE CHANCE THAT, ONCE I'D WANDERED OFF, I'D HAVE NOTHING TO COME BACK TO.
CRAZY THOUGHTS, I KNOW..
..FOR A PIECE OF WOOD.
!
I HAD NOT SEEN SUCH DISTANCES IN A LONG WHILE.
THEN THE SMOKE CAME AND TOOK THEM.

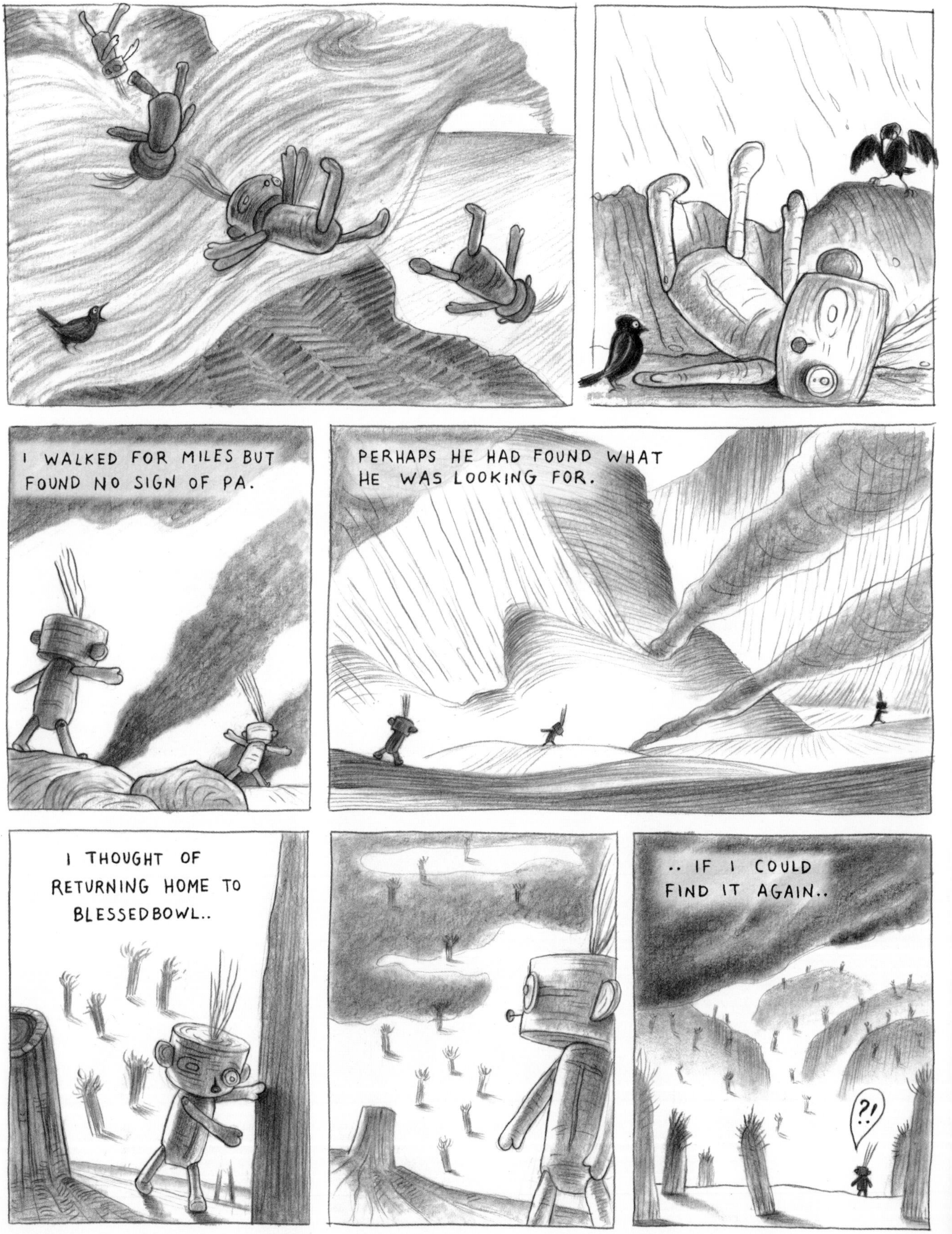
I WALKED FOR MILES BUT FOUND NO SIGN OF PA.
PERHAPS HE HAD FOUND WHAT HE WAS LOOKING FOR.
I THOUGHT OF RETURNING HOME TO BLESSEDBOWL..
.. IF I COULD FIND IT AGAIN..
?!

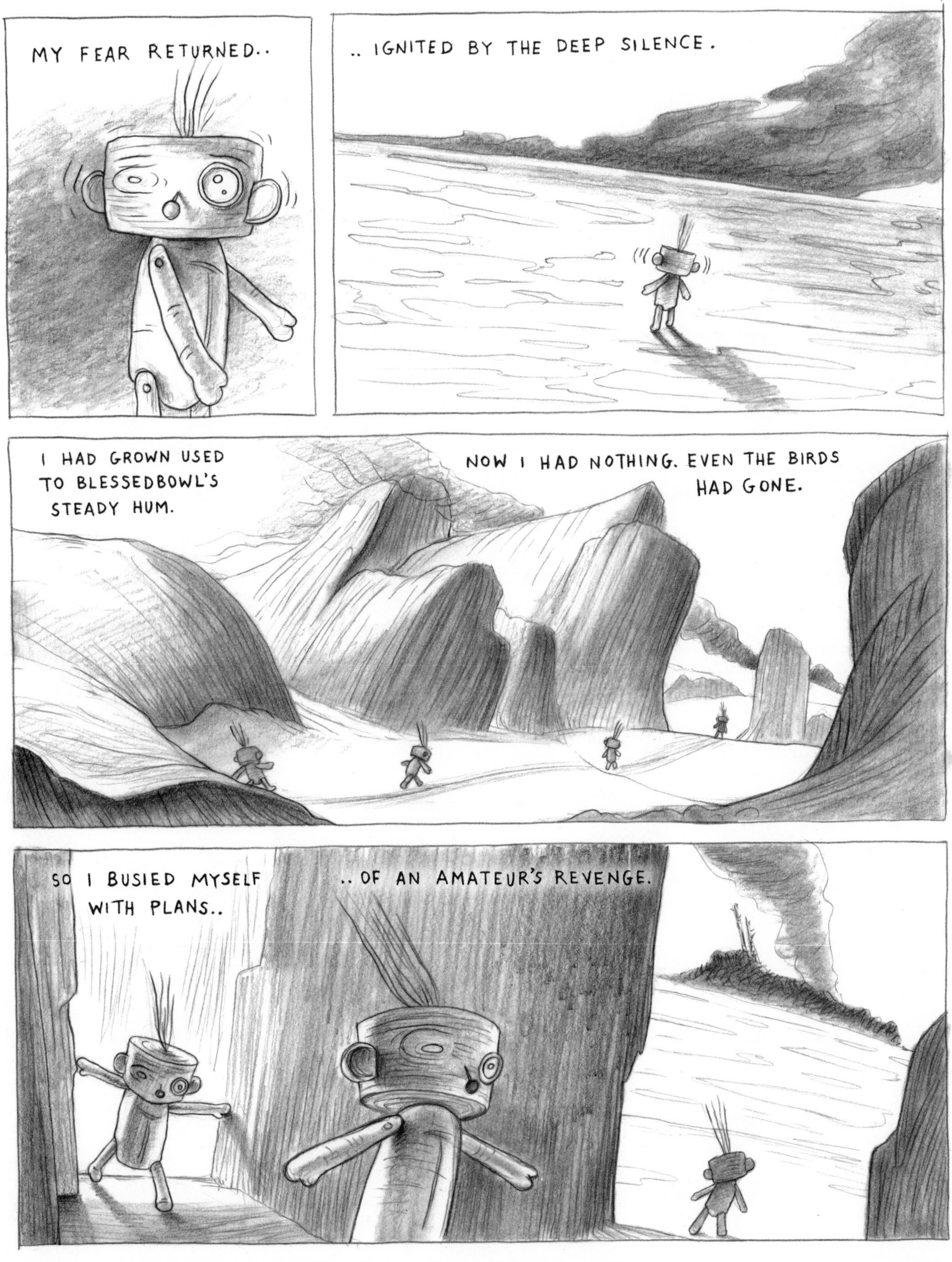
MY FEAR RETURNED..
.. IGNITED BY THE DEEP SILENCE.
I HAD GROWN USED TO BLESSEDBOWL'S STEADY HUM.
NOW I HAD NOTHING. EVEN THE BIRDS HAD GONE.
SO I BUSIED MYSELF WITH PLANS..
.. OF AN AMATEUR'S REVENGE.

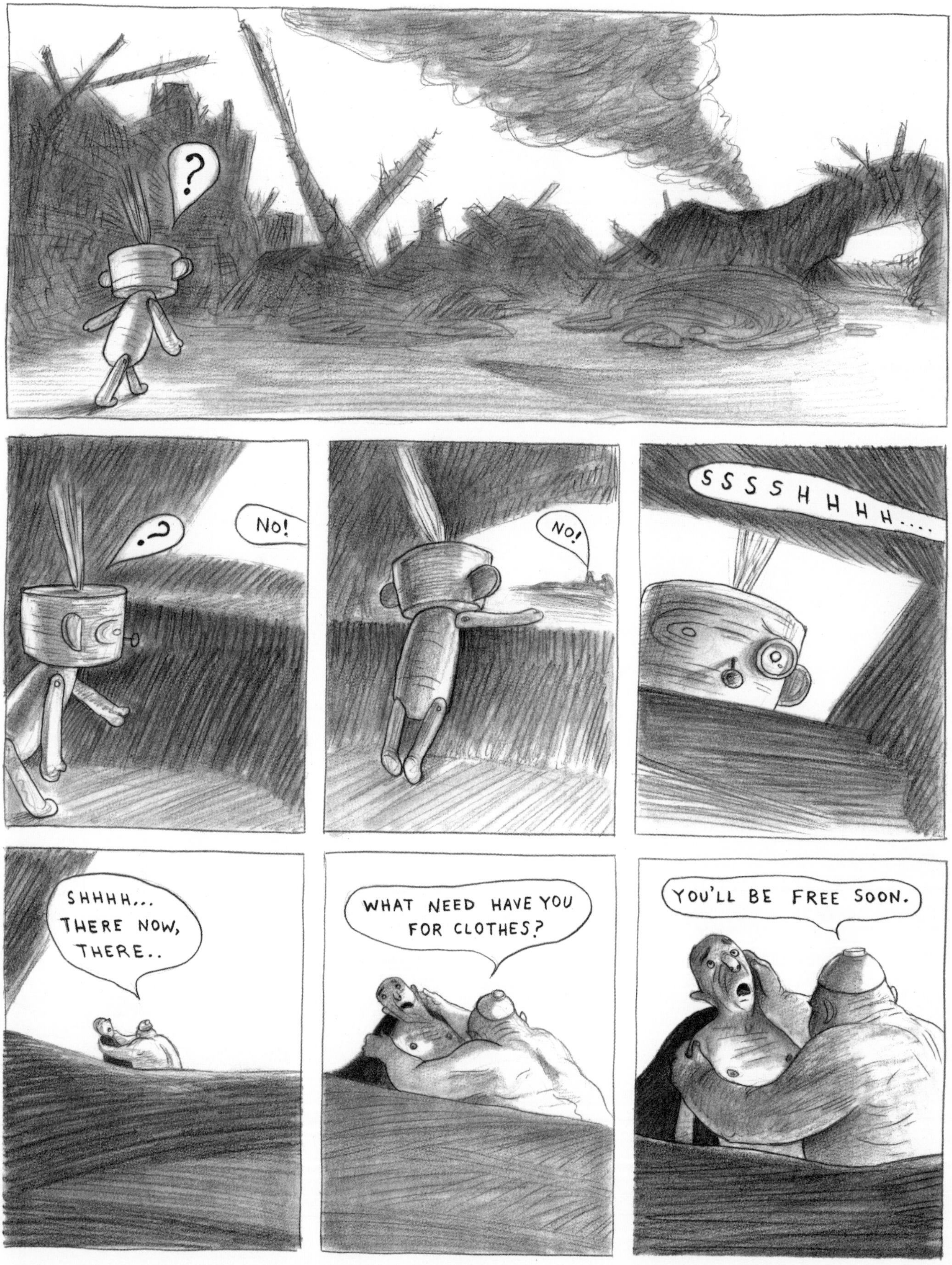
?
?
NO!
NO!
SSSSHHHH....
SHHHH... THERE NOW, THERE..
WHAT NEED HAVE YOU FOR CLOTHES?
YOU'LL BE FREE SOON.

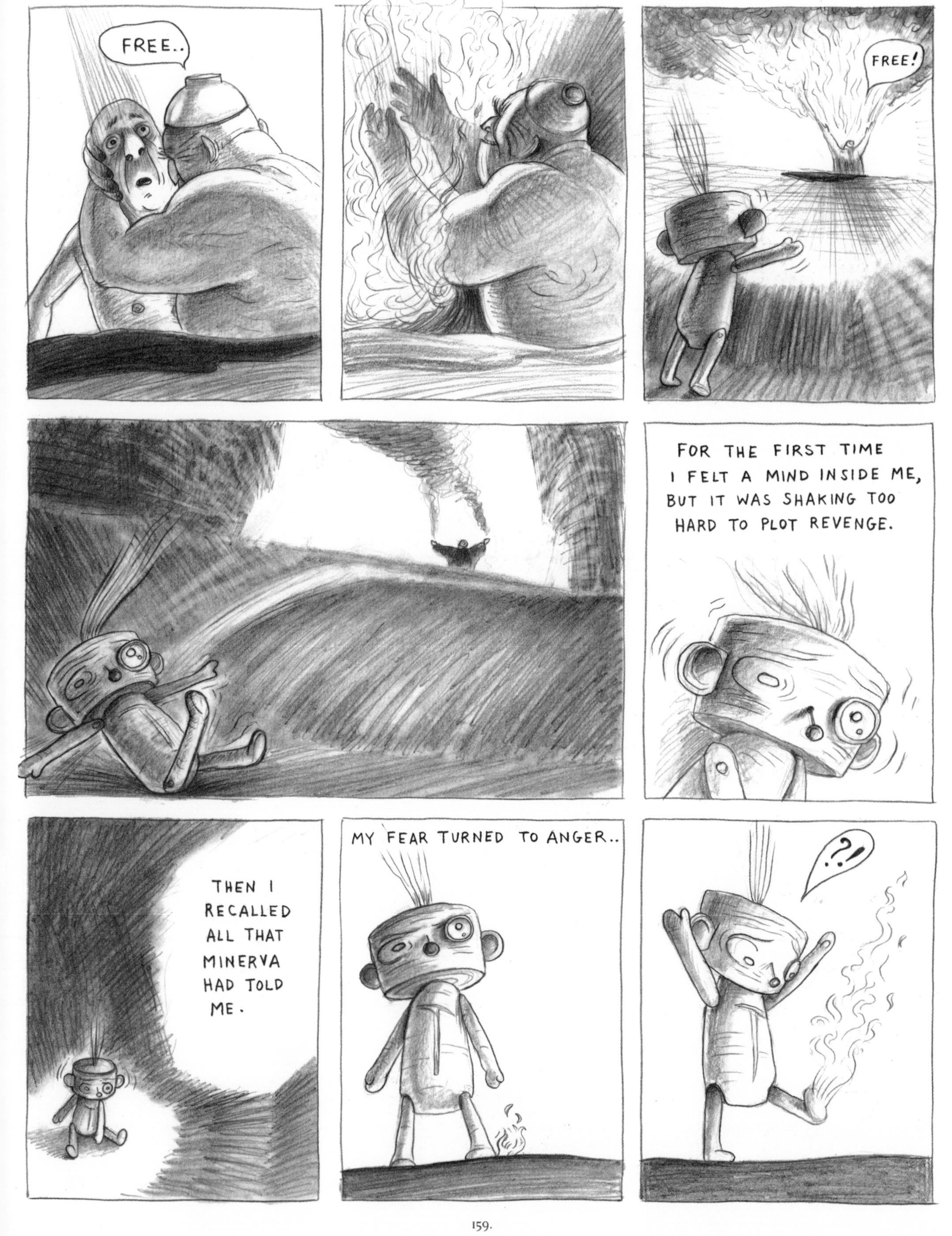
FREE..
FREE!
FOR THE FIRST TIME I FELT A MIND INSIDE ME, BUT IT WAS SHAKING TOO HARD TO PLOT REVENGE.
THEN I RECALLED ALL THAT MINERVA HAD TOLD ME.
MY FEAR TURNED TO ANGER..
?!

.. WHICH TURNED TO FEAR AGAIN.

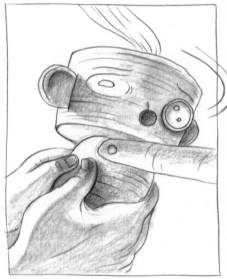

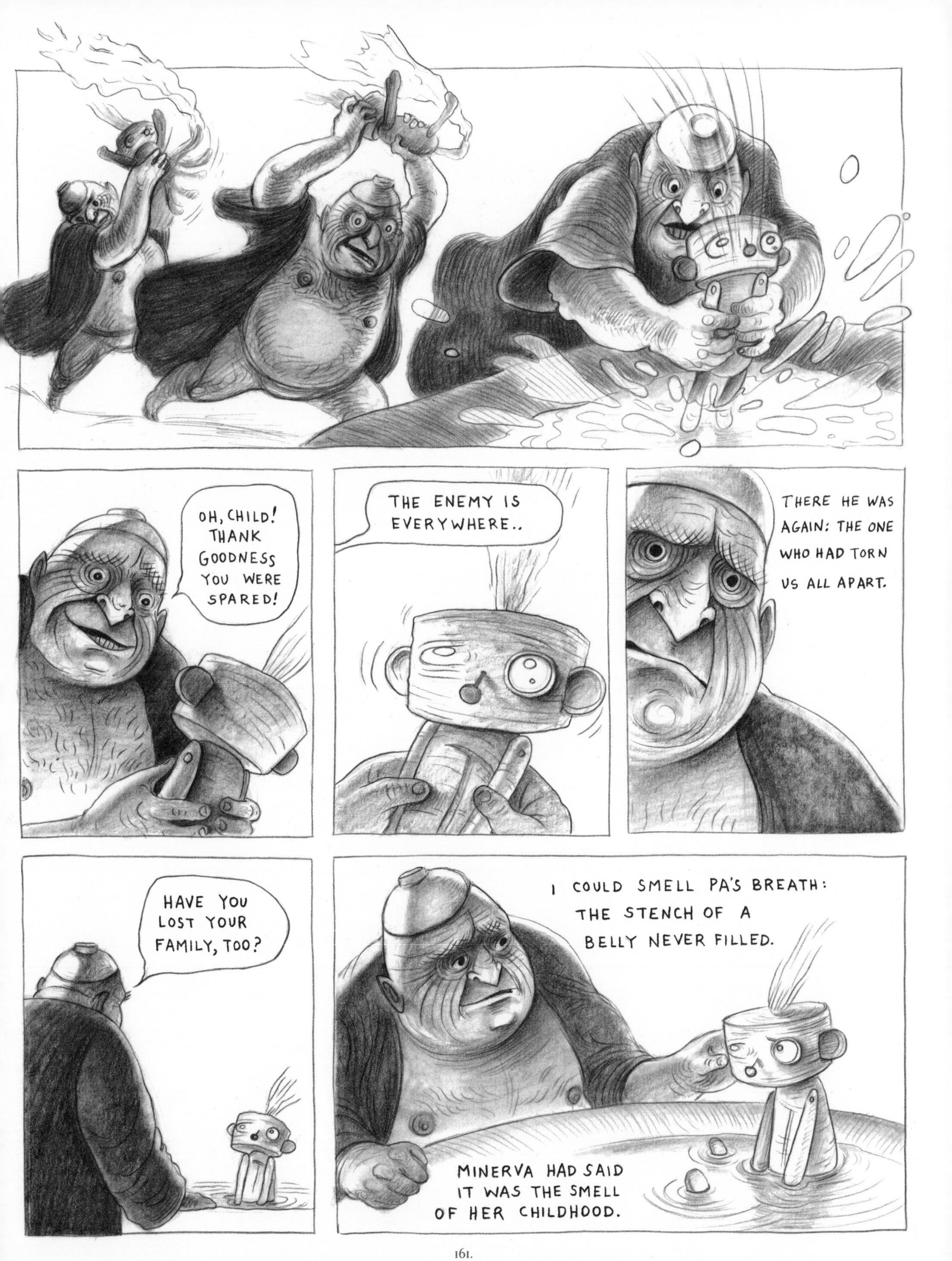
OH, CHILD! THANK GOODNESS YOU WERE SPARED!
THE ENEMY IS EVERYWHERE..
THERE HE WAS AGAIN: THE ONE WHO HAD TORN US ALL APART.
HAVE YOU LOST YOUR FAMILY, TOO?
I COULD SMELL PA'S BREATH: THE STENCH OF A BELLY NEVER FILLED.
MINERVA HAD SAID IT WAS THE SMELL OF HER CHILDHOOD.

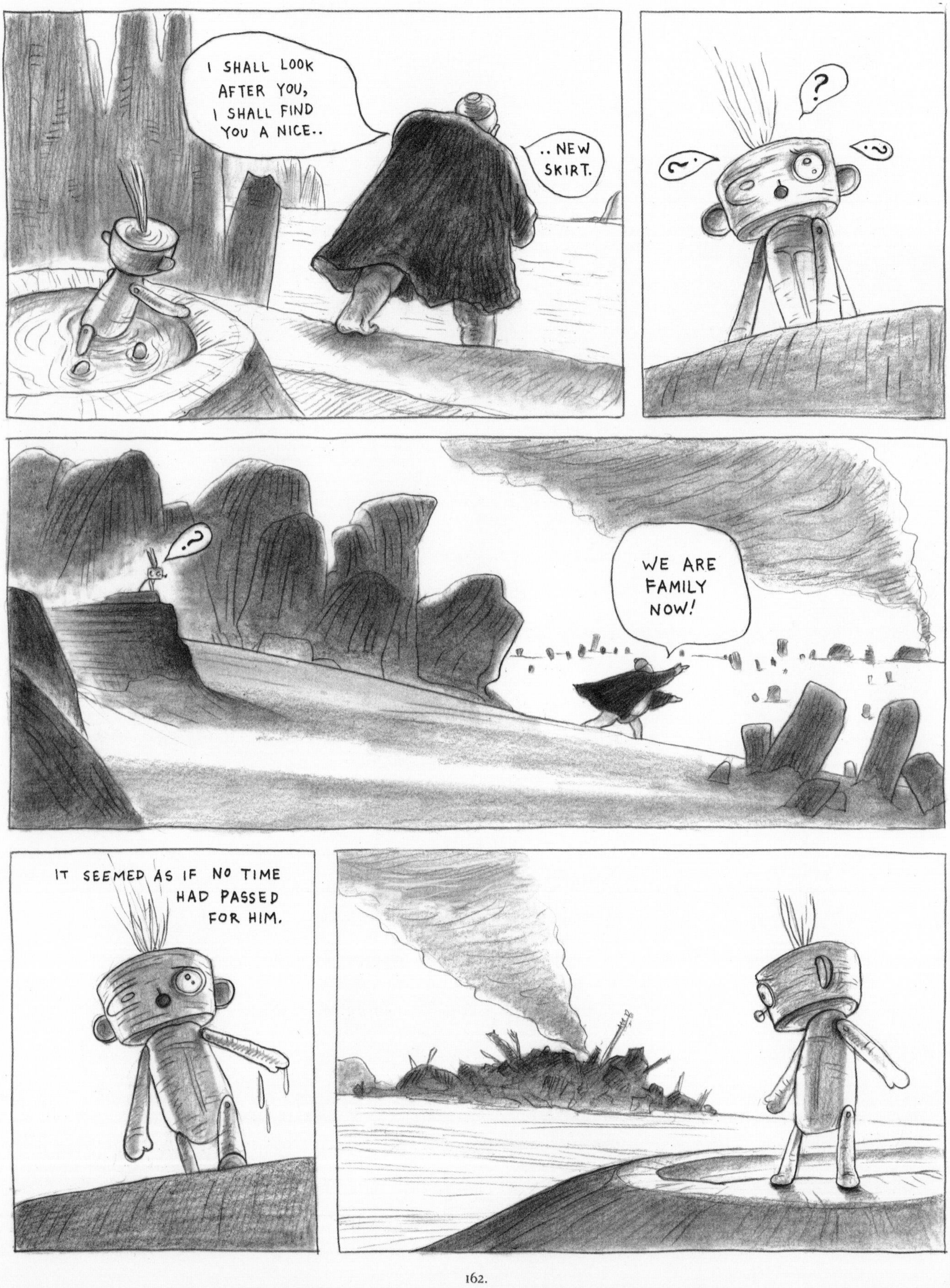
I SHALL LOOK AFTER YOU, I SHALL FIND YOU A NICE..
..NEW SKIRT.
?
?
WE ARE FAMILY NOW!
IT SEEMED AS IF NO TIME HAD PASSED FOR HIM.

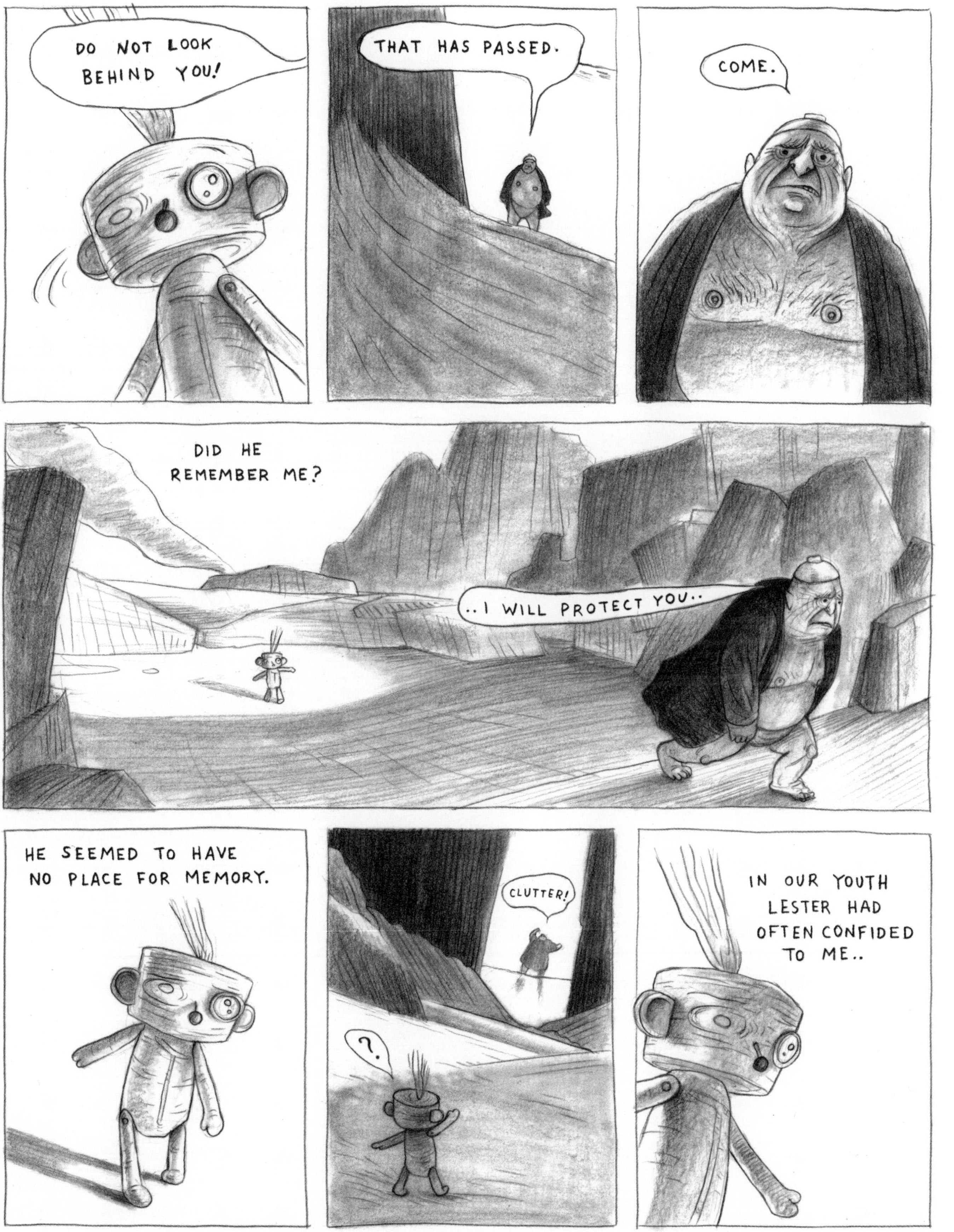
DO NOT LOOK BEHIND YOU!
THAT HAS PASSED.
COME.
DID HE REMEMBER ME?
..I WILL PROTECT YOU..
HE SEEMED TO HAVE NO PLACE FOR MEMORY.
CLUTTER!
?
IN OUR YOUTH LESTER HAD OFTEN CONFIDED TO ME..

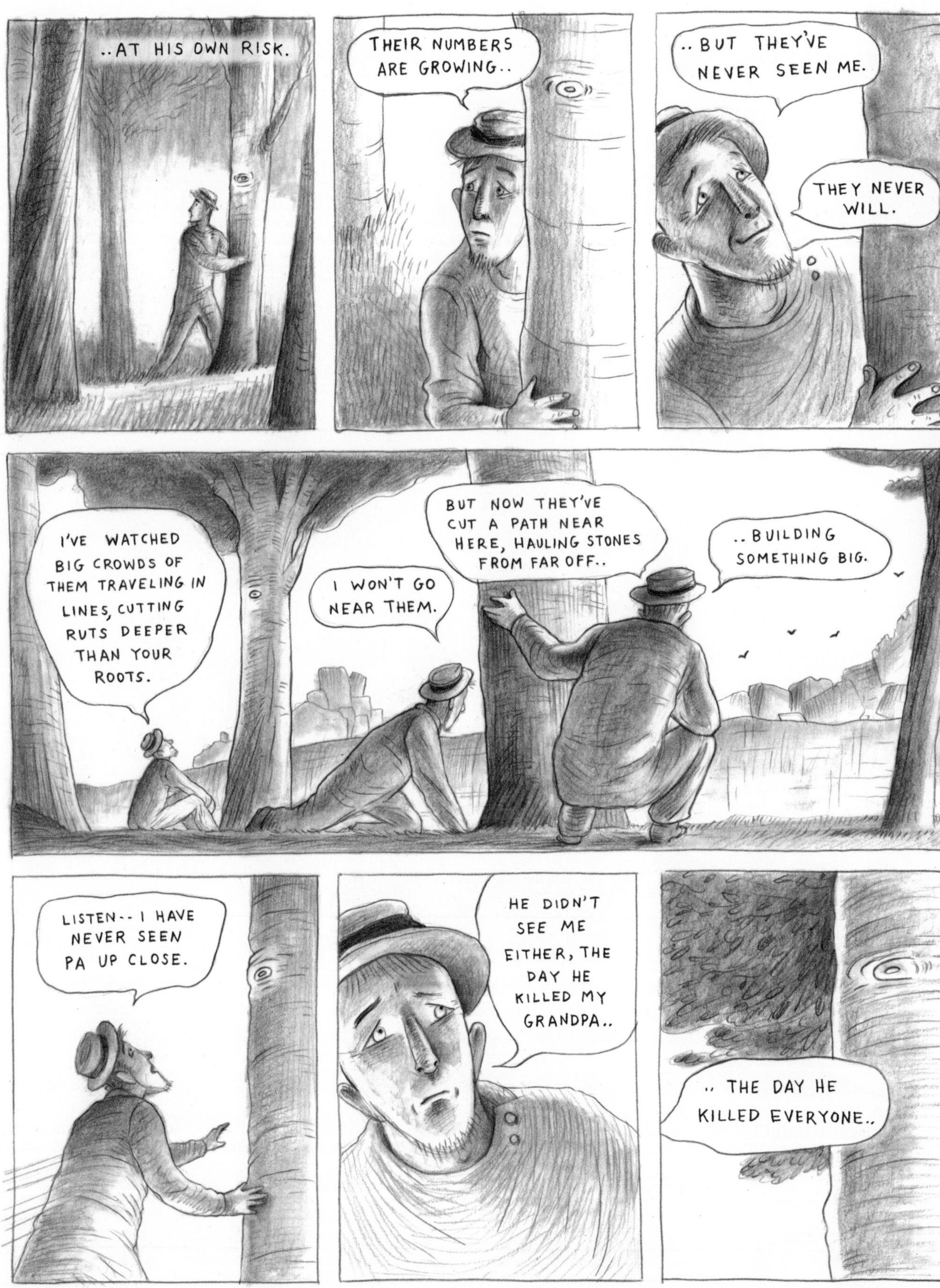
..AT HIS OWN RISK.
THEIR NUMBERS ARE GROWING..
..BUT THEY'VE NEVER SEEN ME.
THEY NEVER WILL.
I'VE WATCHED BIG CROWDS OF THEM TRAVELING IN LINES, CUTTING RUTS DEEPER THAN YOUR ROOTS.
I WON'T GO NEAR THEM.
BUT NOW THEY'VE CUT A PATH NEAR HERE, HAULING STONES FROM FAR OFF..
..BUILDING SOMETHING BIG.
LISTEN-- I HAVE NEVER SEEN PA UP CLOSE.
HE DIDN'T SEE ME EITHER, THE DAY HE KILLED MY GRANDPA..
.. THE DAY HE KILLED EVERYONE..

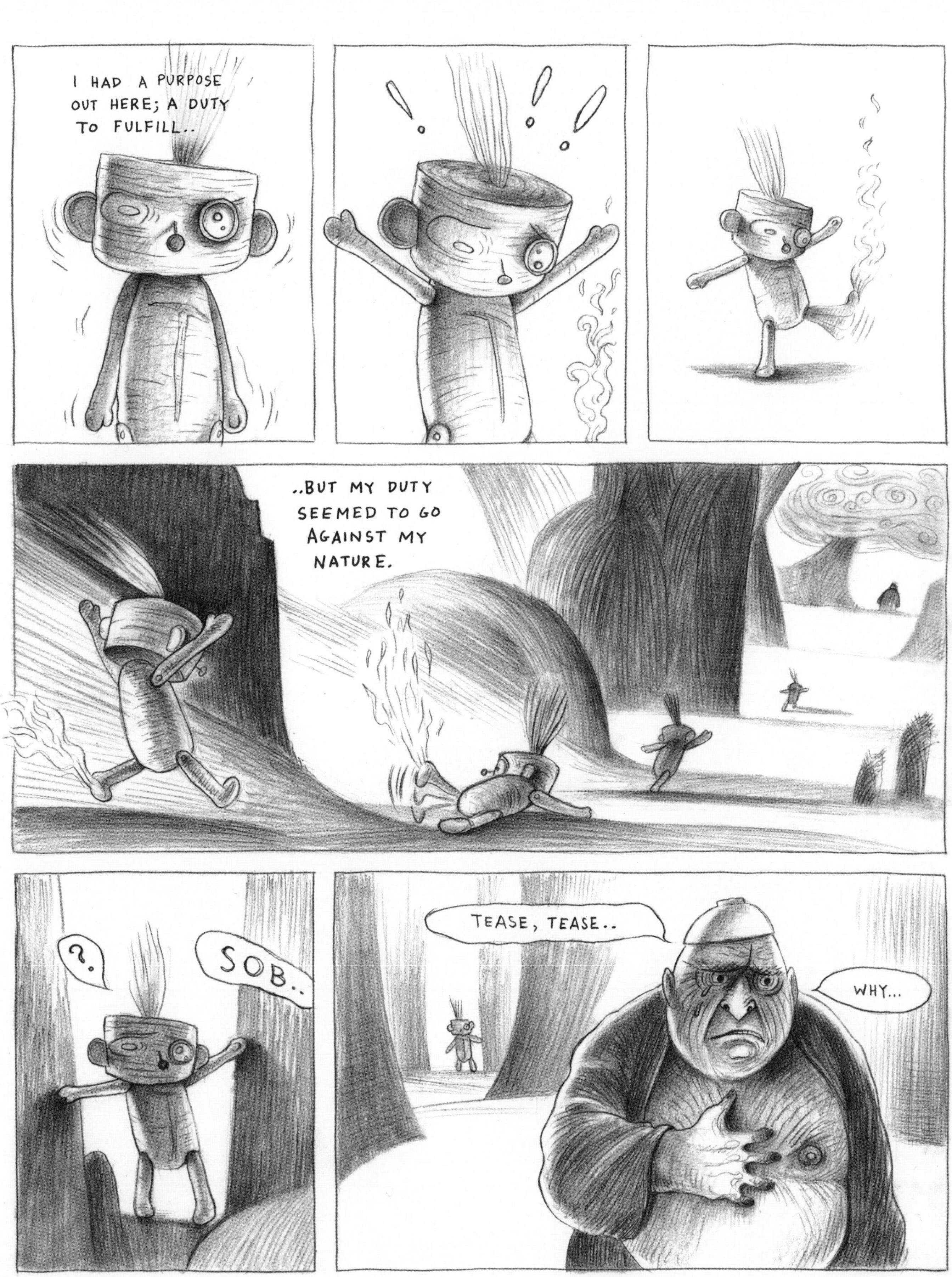
I HAD A PURPOSE OUT HERE; A DUTY TO FULFILL..
!
!
!
..BUT MY DUTY SEEMED TO GO AGAINST MY NATURE.
?
SOB..
TEASE, TEASE..
WHY...

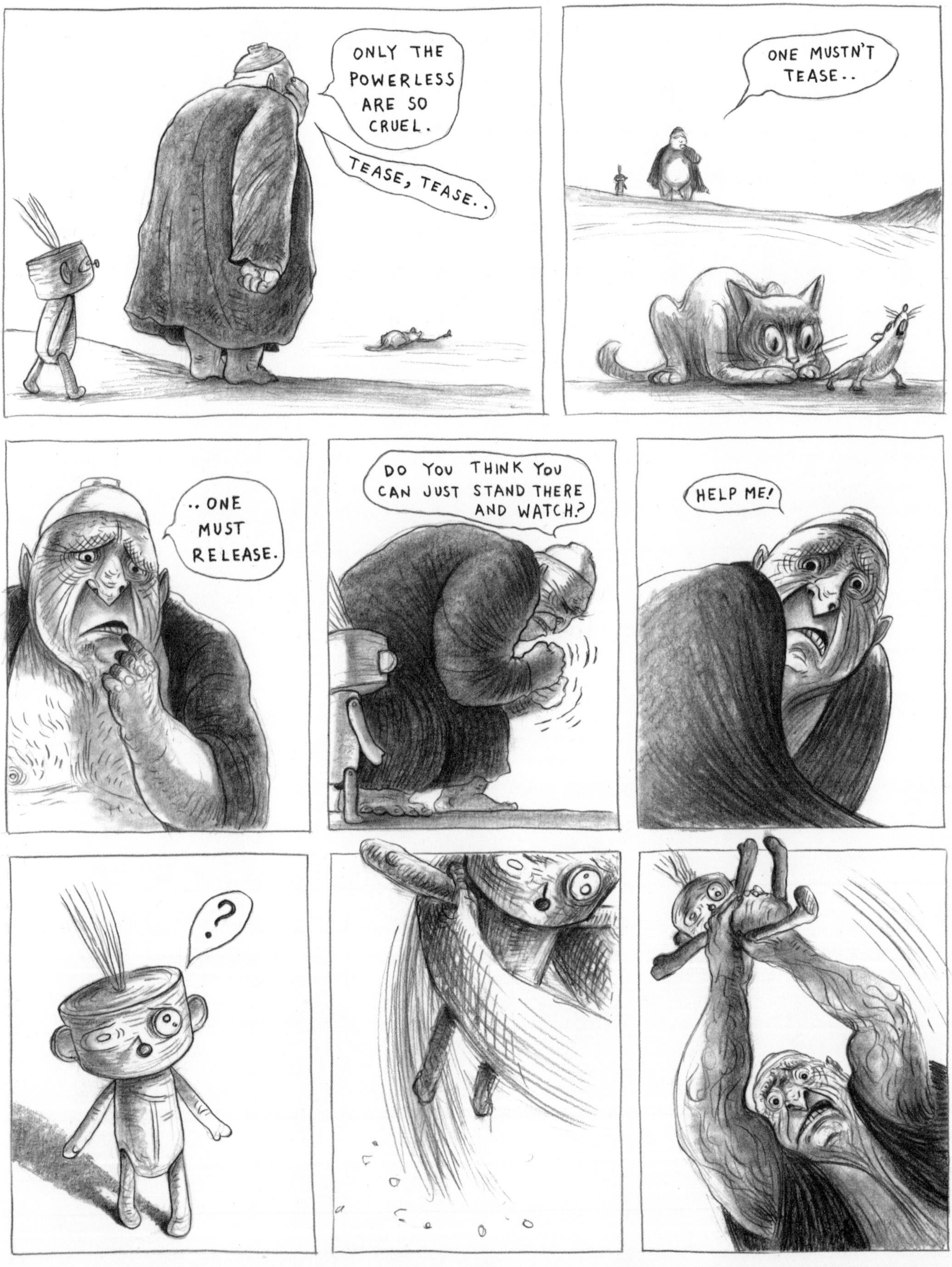
ONLY THE POWERLESS ARE SO CRUEL.
TEASE, TEASE..
ONE MUSTN'T TEASE..
..ONE MUST RELEASE.
DO YOU THINK YOU CAN JUST STAND THERE AND WATCH?
HELP ME!
?

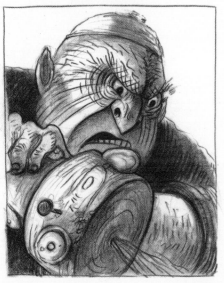

PA HAD HIS
DUTY, TOO..

.. AND HE HAD
MADE ME A
PART OF IT.

THANKFULLY
MY FRIENDS
RETURNED.

THEY HAD
NEWS OF
LESTER..

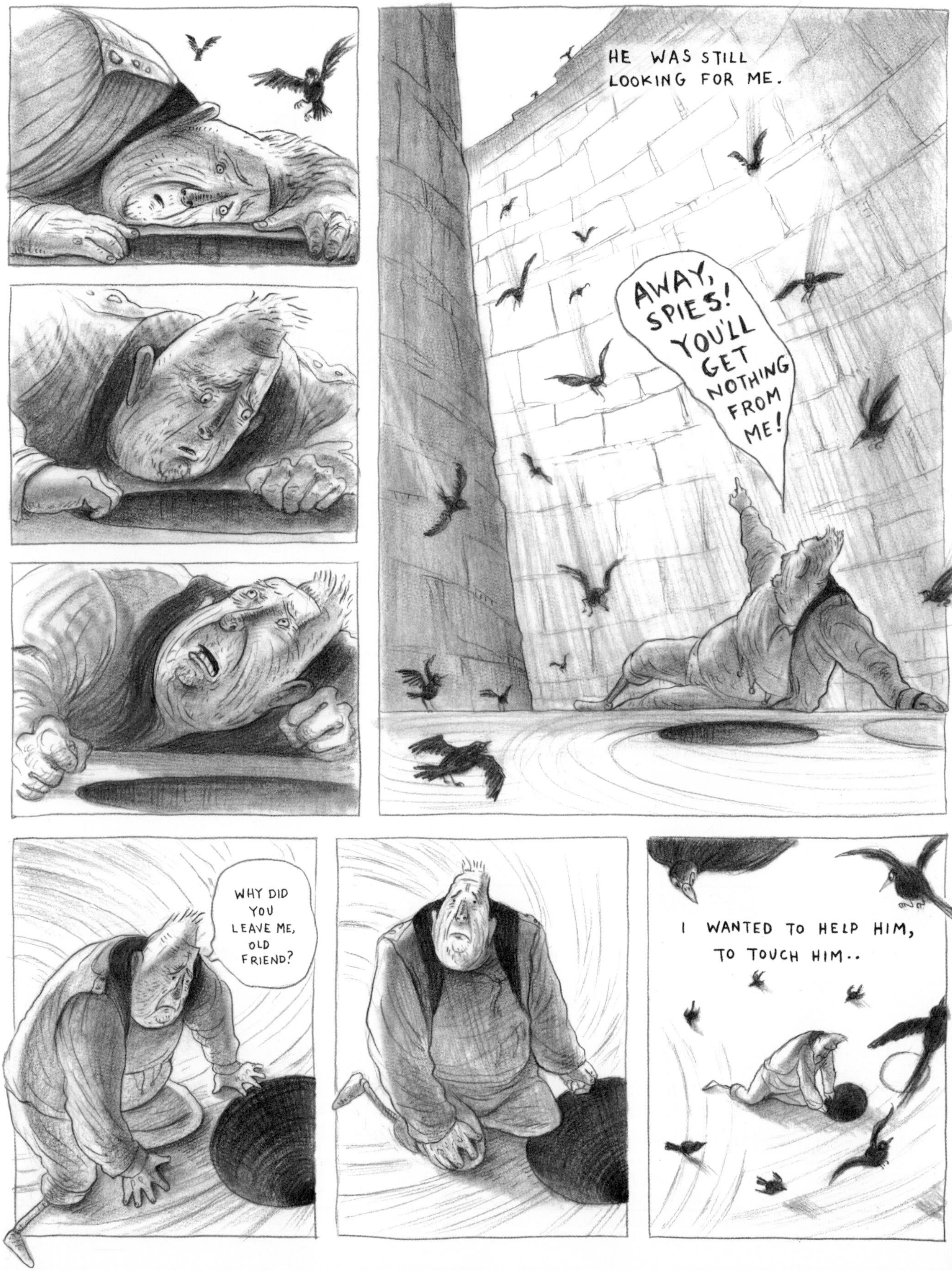
HE WAS STILL LOOKING FOR ME.
AWAY, SPIES! YOU'LL GET NOTHING FROM ME!
WHY DID YOU LEAVE ME, OLD FRIEND?
I WANTED TO HELP HIM, TO TOUCH HIM..

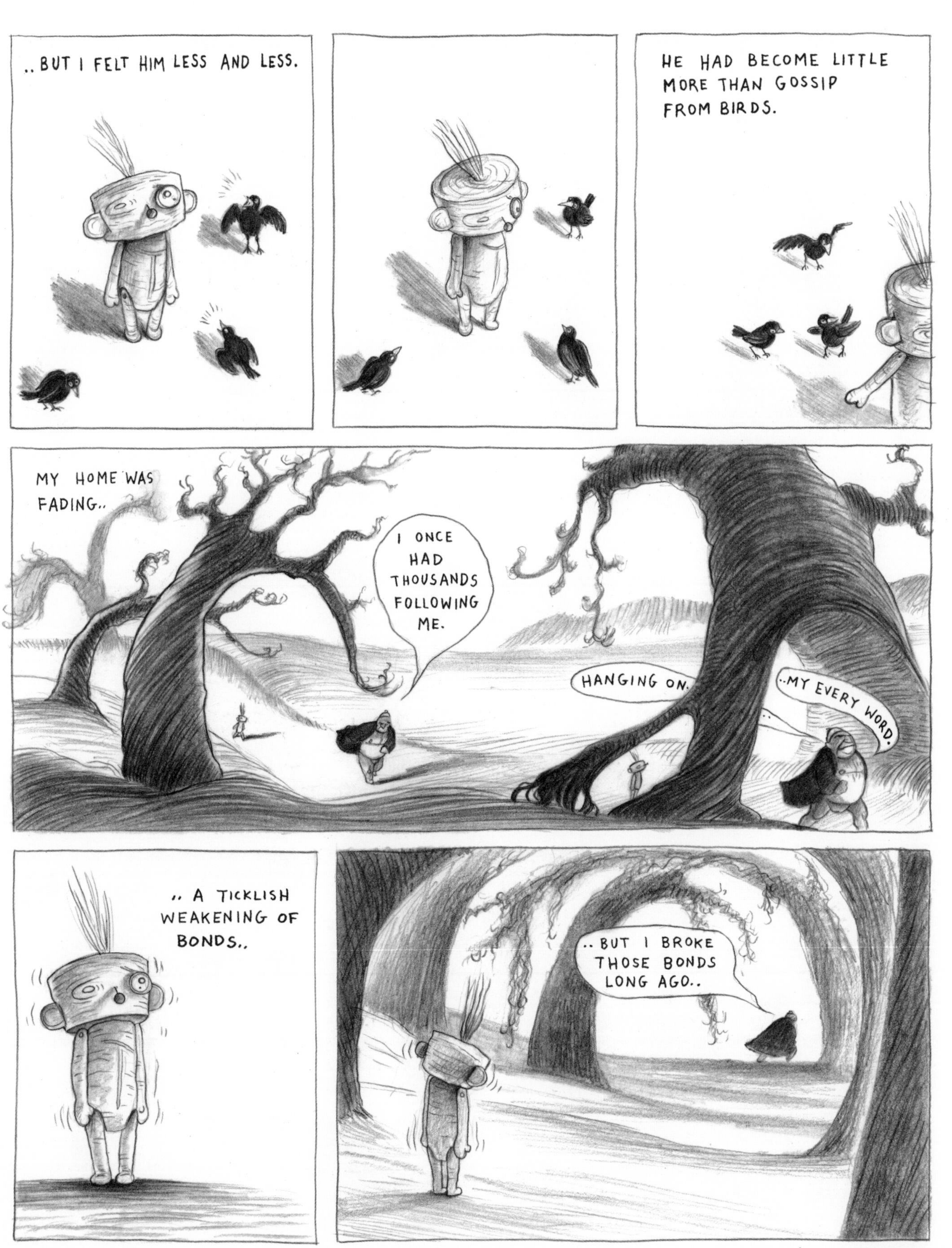

.. BUT I FELT HIM LESS AND LESS.
HE HAD BECOME LITTLE MORE THAN GOSSIP FROM BIRDS.
MY HOME WAS FADING..
I ONCE HAD THOUSANDS FOLLOWING ME.
HANGING ON.
..MY EVERY WORD.
.. A TICKLISH WEAKENING OF BONDS..
.. BUT I BROKE THOSE BONDS LONG AGO..

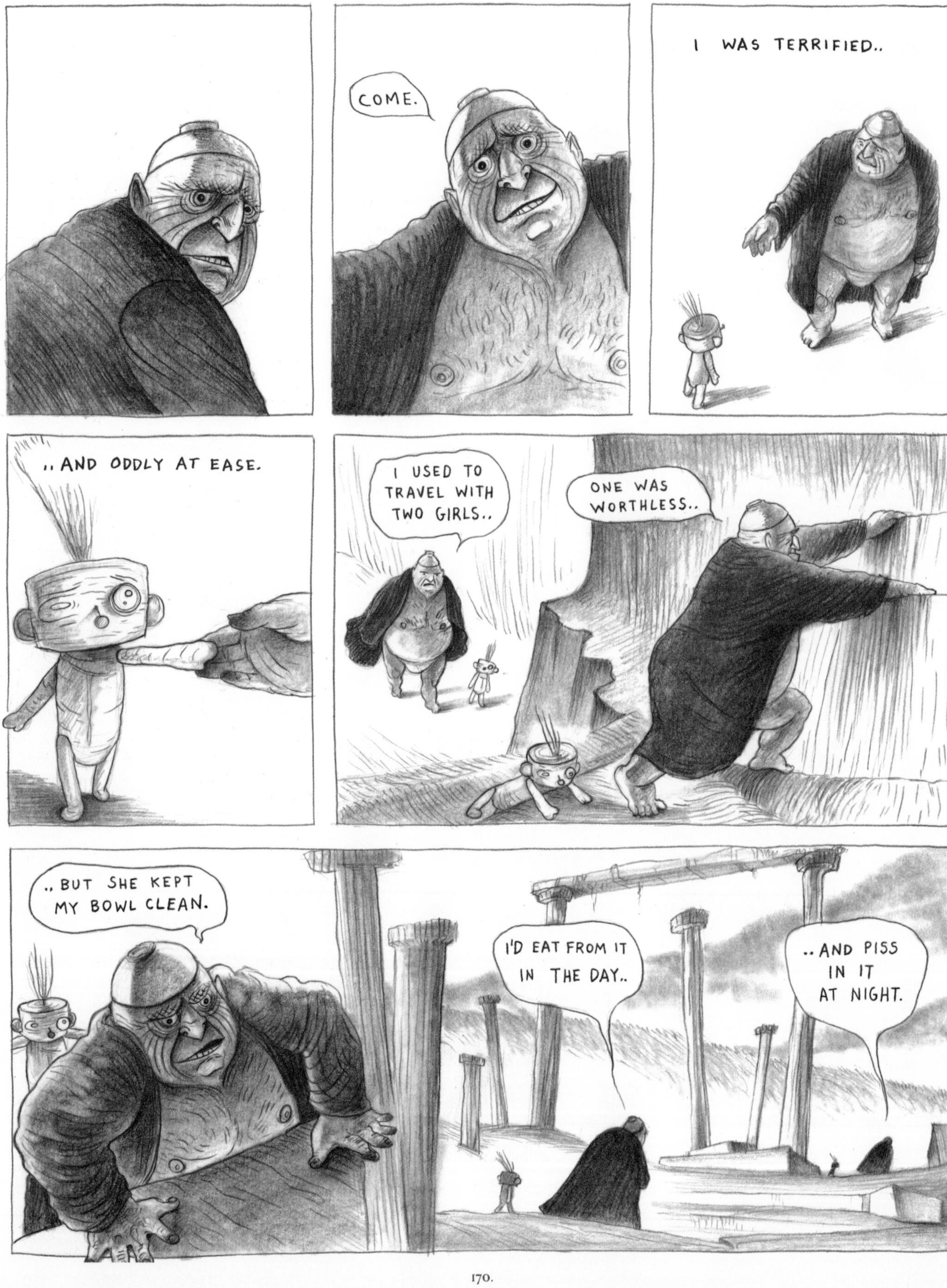
COME.
I WAS TERRIFIED..
.. AND ODDLY AT EASE.
I USED TO TRAVEL WITH TWO GIRLS..
ONE WAS WORTHLESS..
.. BUT SHE KEPT MY BOWL CLEAN.
I'D EAT FROM IT IN THE DAY..
.. AND PISS IN IT AT NIGHT.

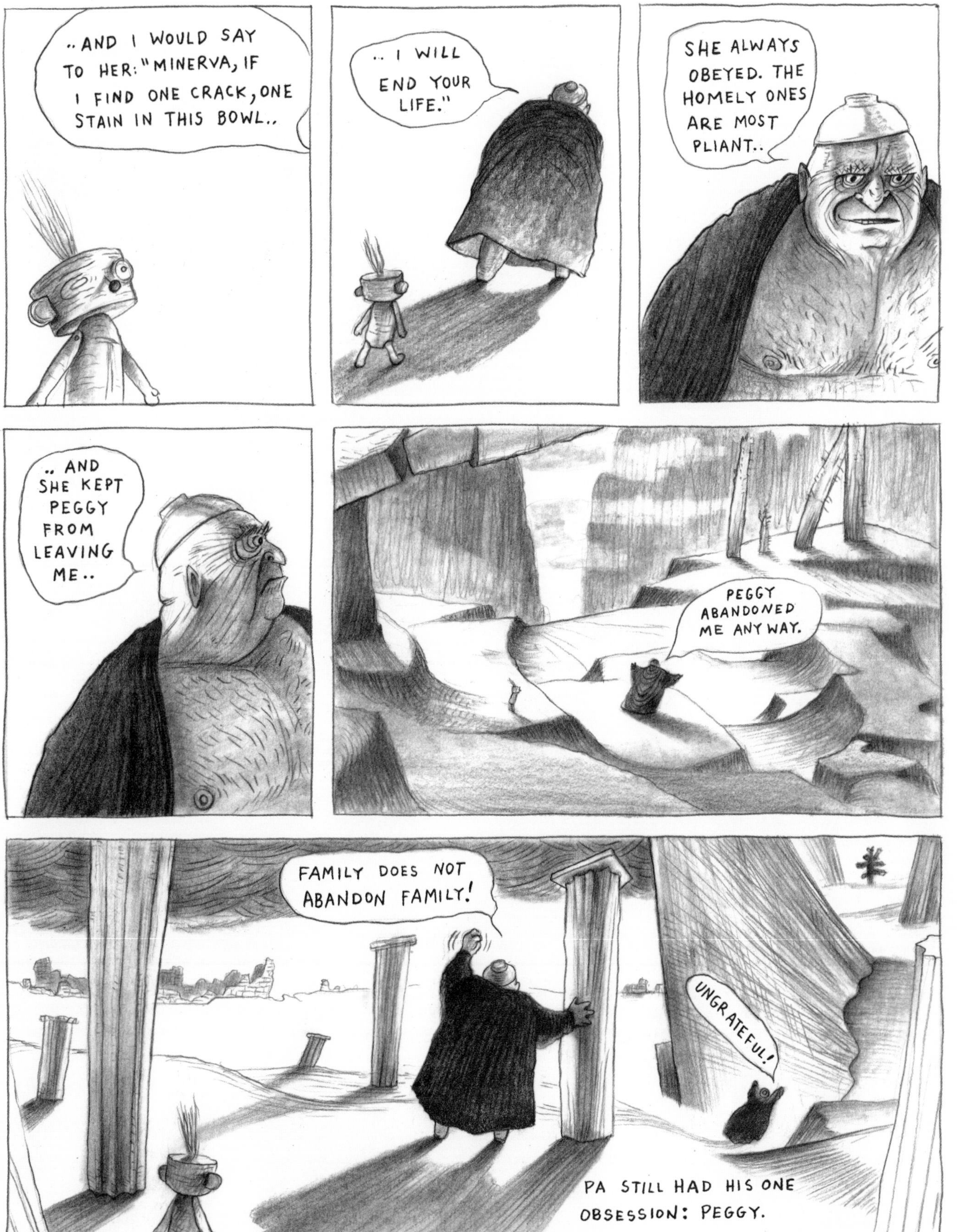
..AND I WOULD SAY TO HER: "MINERVA, IF I FIND ONE CRACK, ONE STAIN IN THIS BOWL..
.. I WILL END YOUR LIFE."
SHE ALWAYS OBEYED. THE HOMELY ONES ARE MOST PLIANT..
.. AND SHE KEPT PEGGY FROM LEAVING ME..
PEGGY ABANDONED ME ANY WAY.
FAMILY DOES NOT ABANDON FAMILY!
UNGRATEFUL!
PA STILL HAD HIS ONE OBSESSION: PEGGY.

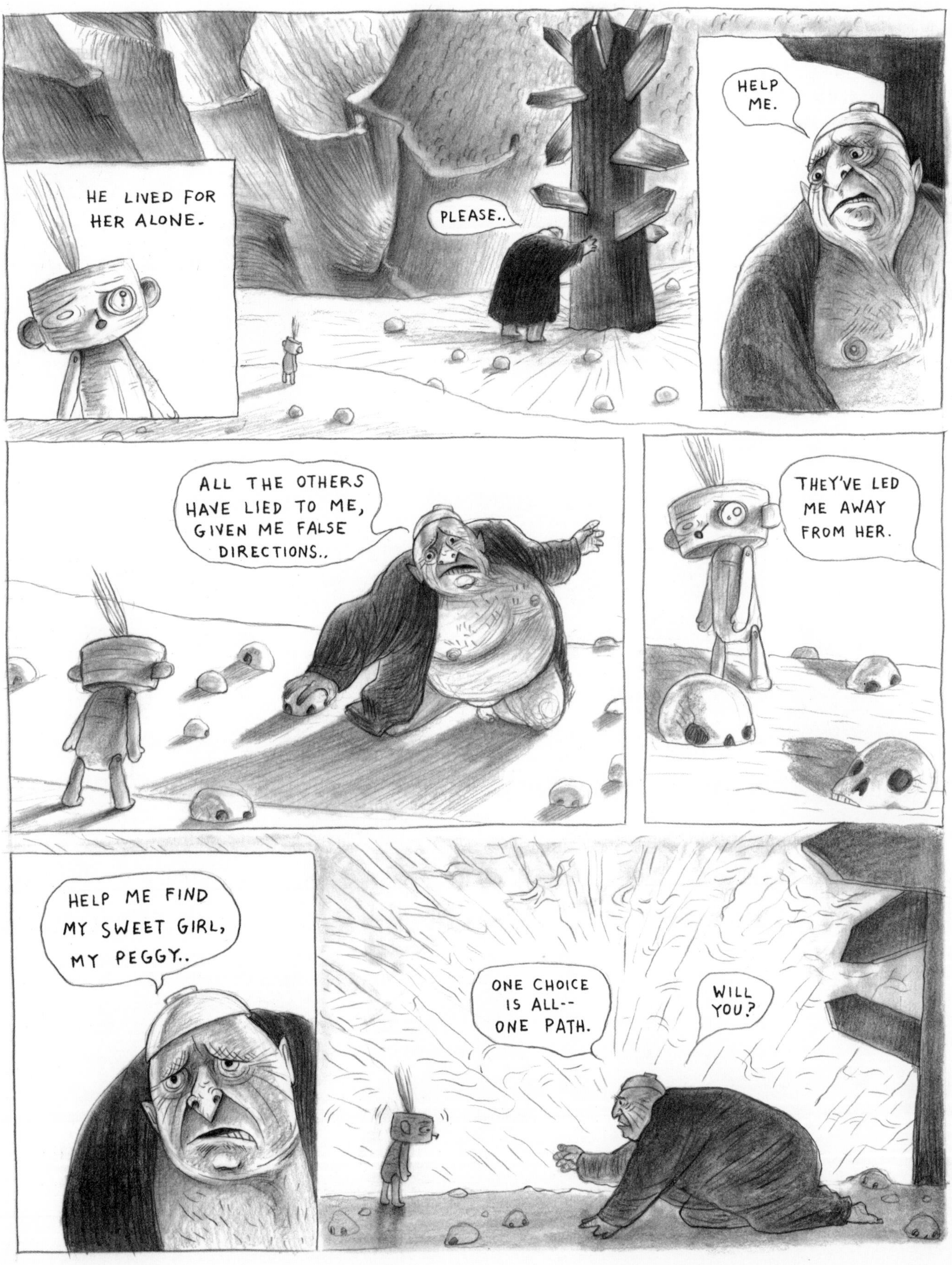
HE LIVED FOR HER ALONE.
PLEASE..
HELP ME.
ALL THE OTHERS HAVE LIED TO ME, GIVEN ME FALSE DIRECTIONS..
THEY'VE LED ME AWAY FROM HER.
HELP ME FIND MY SWEET GIRL, MY PEGGY..
ONE CHOICE IS ALL-- ONE PATH.
WILL YOU?

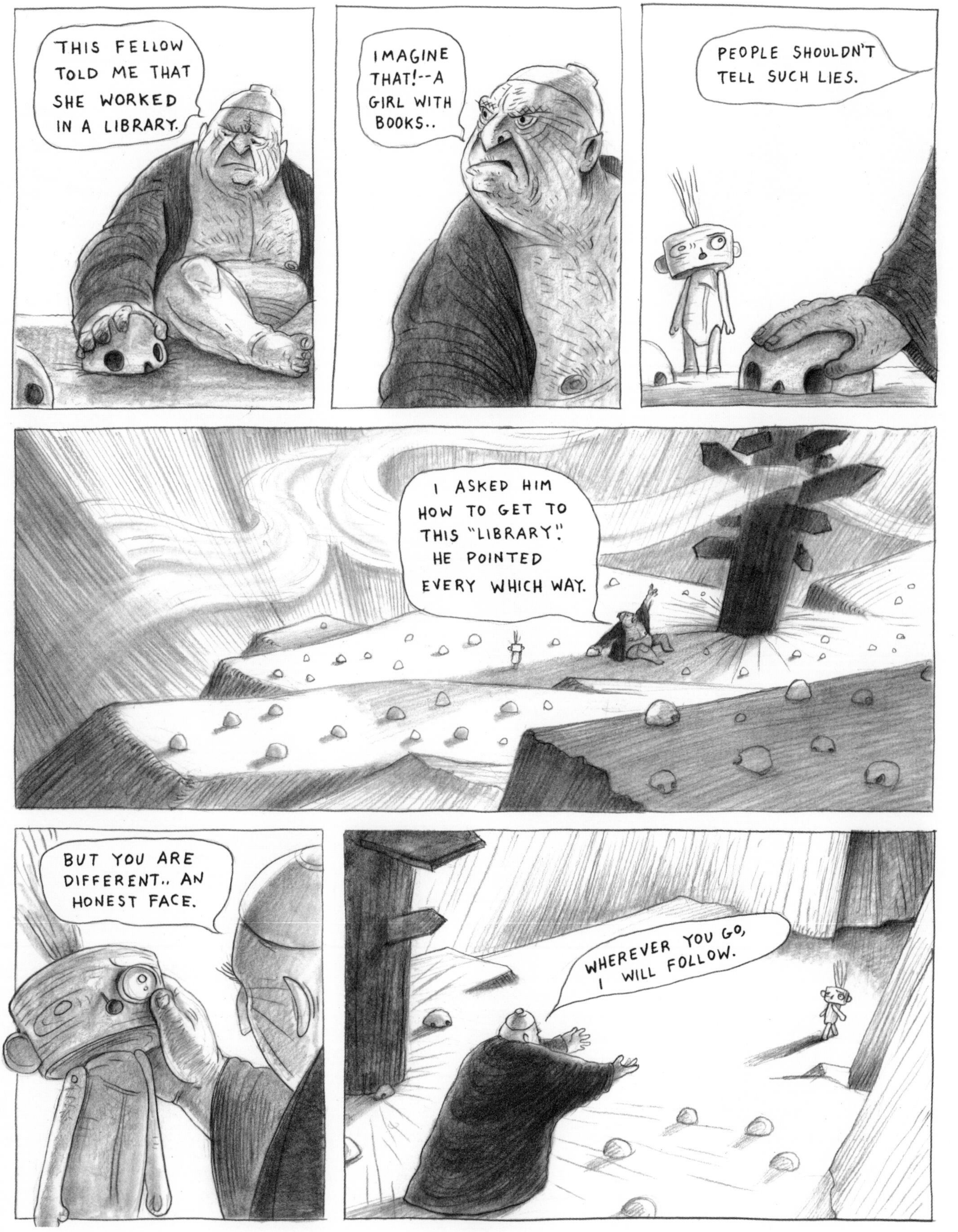
THIS FELLOW TOLD ME THAT SHE WORKED IN A LIBRARY.
IMAGINE THAT!--A GIRL WITH BOOKS..
PEOPLE SHOULDN'T TELL SUCH LIES.
I ASKED HIM HOW TO GET TO THIS "LIBRARY." HE POINTED EVERY WHICH WAY.
BUT YOU ARE DIFFERENT.. AN HONEST FACE.
WHEREVER YOU GO, I WILL FOLLOW.

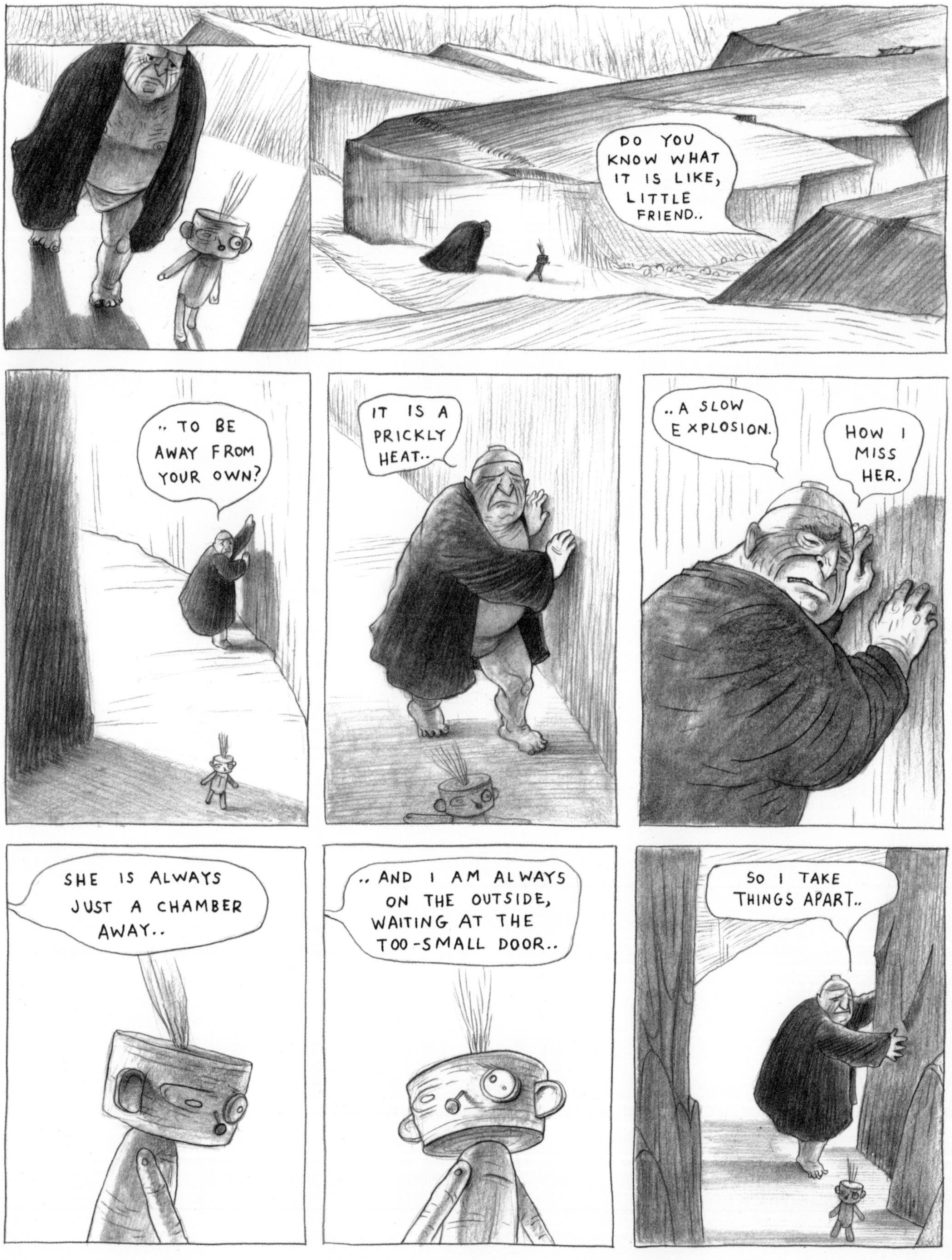
DO YOU KNOW WHAT IT IS LIKE, LITTLE FRIEND..
.. TO BE AWAY FROM YOUR OWN?
IT IS A PRICKLY HEAT..
.. A SLOW EXPLOSION.
HOW I MISS HER.
SHE IS ALWAYS JUST A CHAMBER AWAY..
.. AND I AM ALWAYS ON THE OUTSIDE, WAITING AT THE TOO-SMALL DOOR..
SO I TAKE THINGS APART..

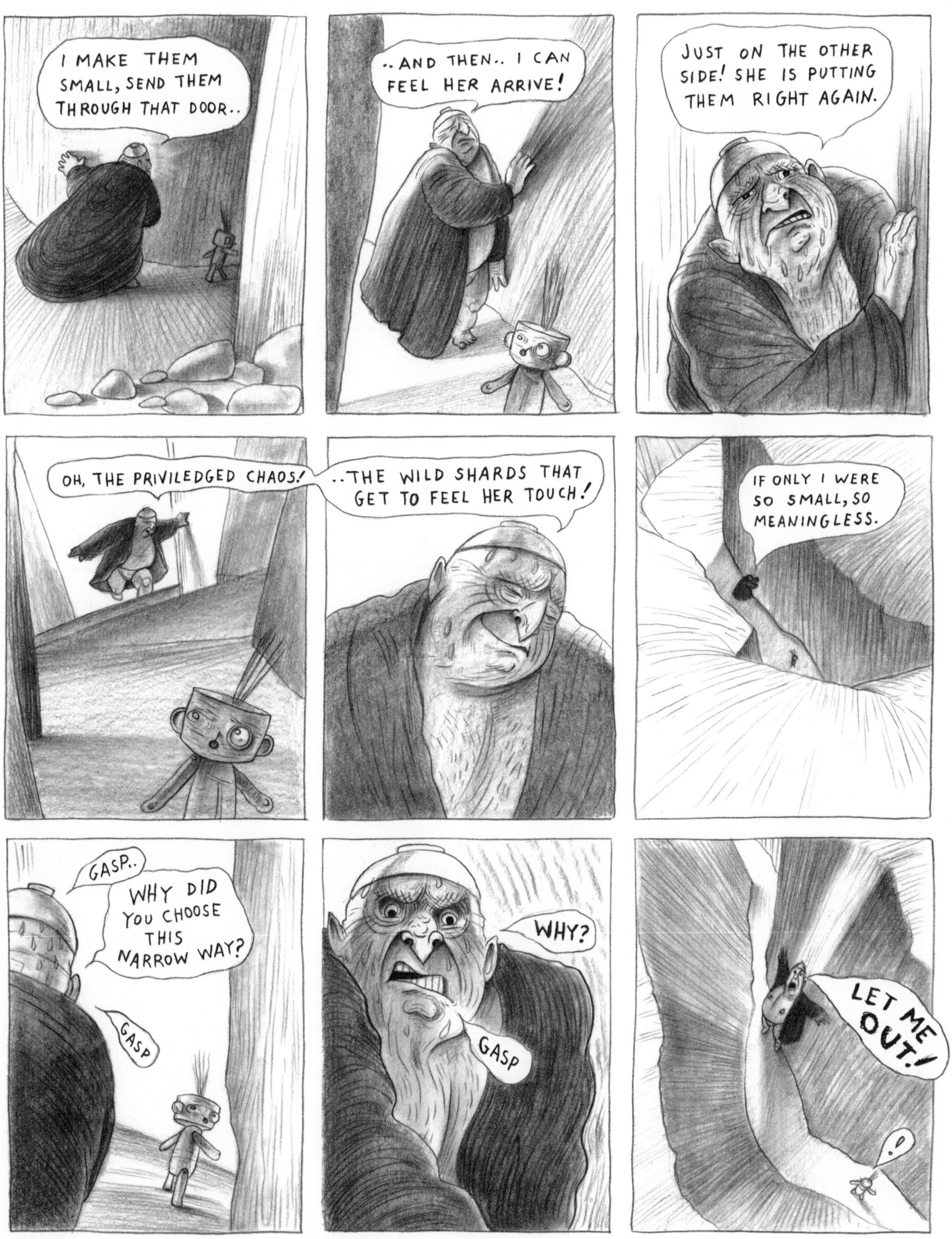
I MAKE THEM SMALL, SEND THEM THROUGH THAT DOOR..
..AND THEN.. I CAN FEEL HER ARRIVE!
JUST ON THE OTHER SIDE! SHE IS PUTTING THEM RIGHT AGAIN.
OH, THE PRIVILEDGED CHAOS!
..THE WILD SHARDS THAT GET TO FEEL HER TOUCH!
IF ONLY I WERE SO SMALL, SO MEANINGLESS.
GASP..
WHY DID YOU CHOOSE THIS NARROW WAY?
GASP
WHY?
GASP
LET ME OUT!
!

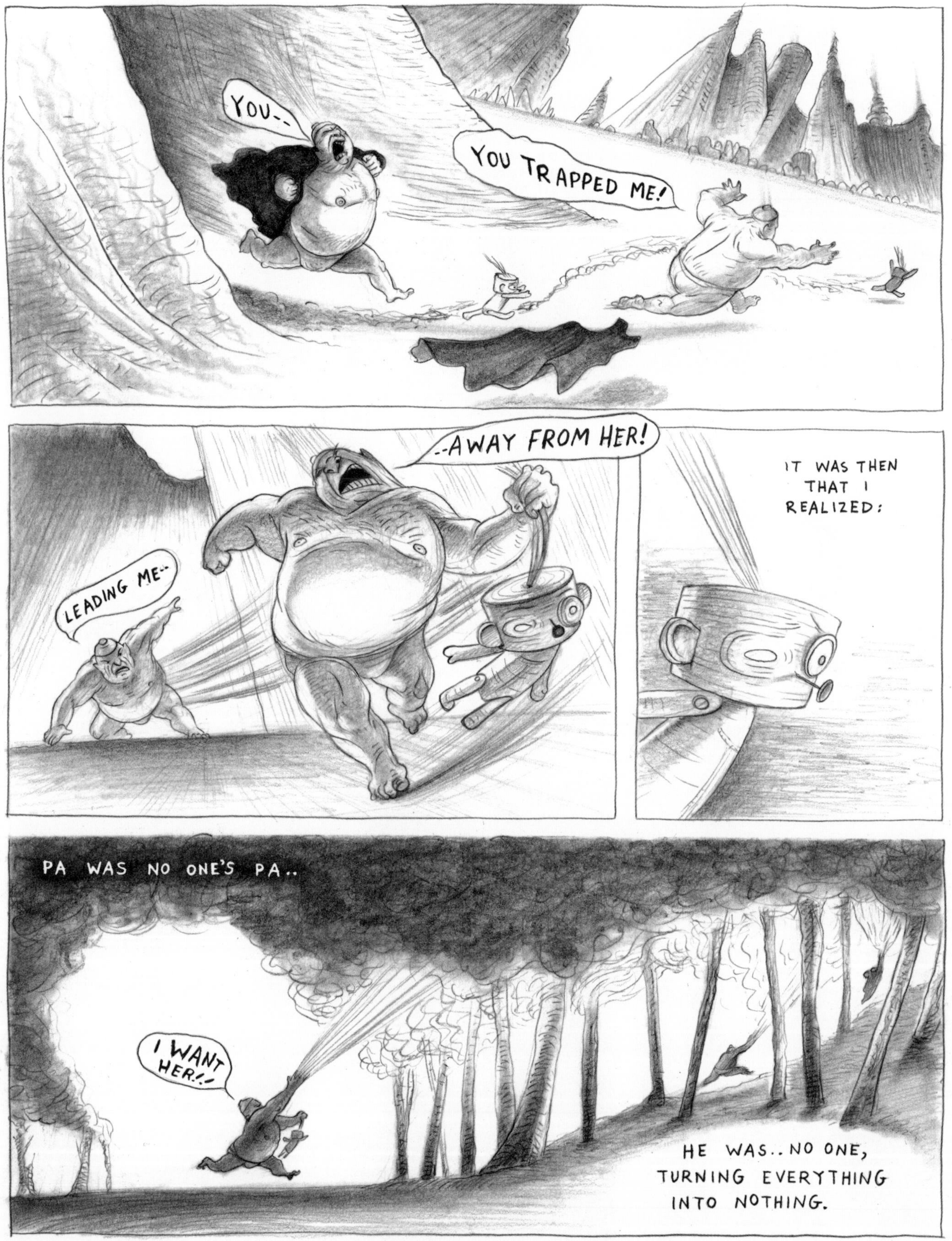
YOU--
YOU TRAPPED ME!
--AWAY FROM HER!
LEADING ME--
IT WAS THEN THAT I REALIZED:
PA WAS NO ONE'S PA..
I WANT HER!!
HE WAS..NO ONE, TURNING EVERYTHING INTO NOTHING.

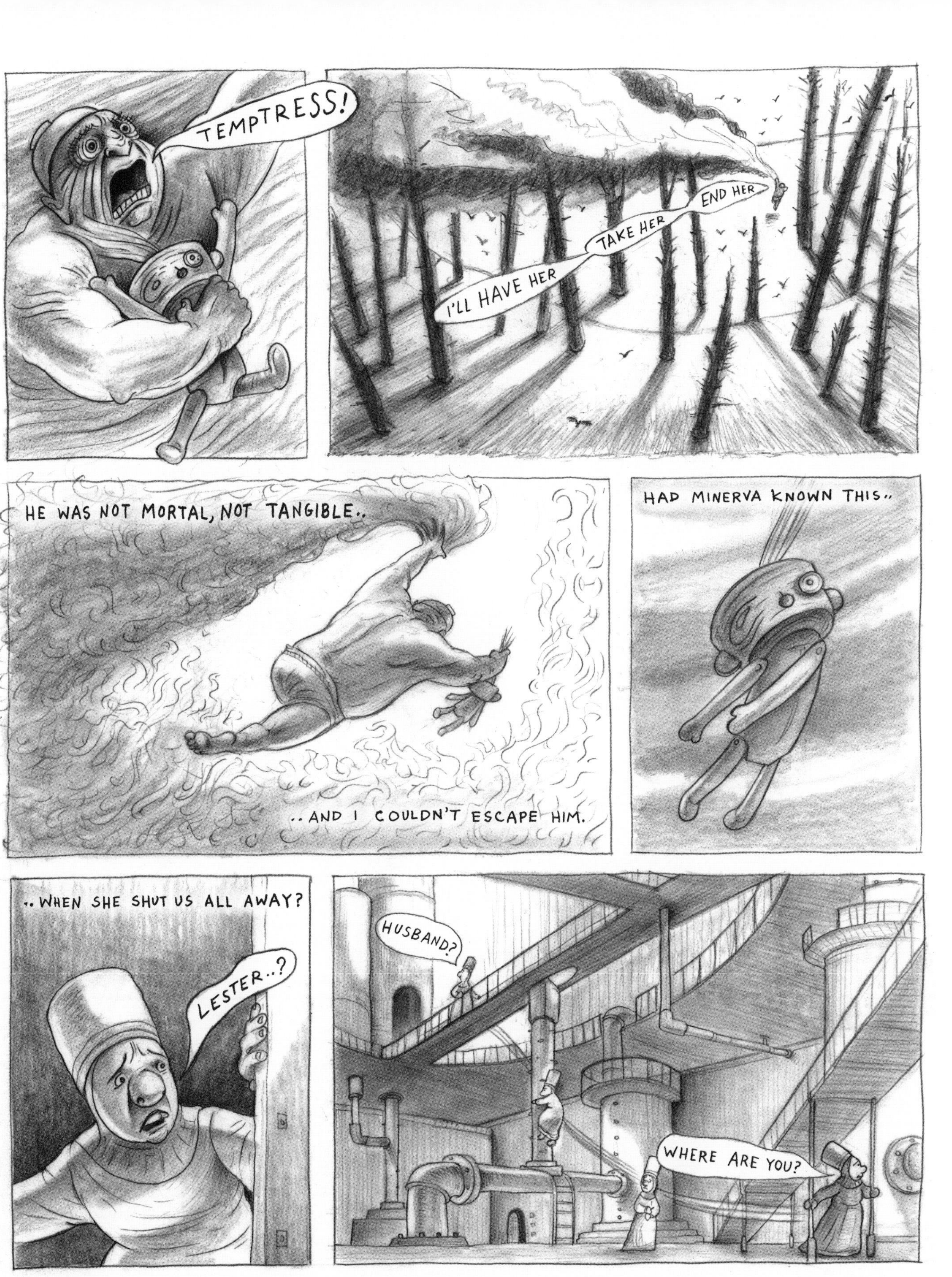
TEMPTRESS!
I'LL HAVE HER
TAKE HER
END HER
HE WAS NOT MORTAL, NOT TANGIBLE..
..AND I COULDN'T ESCAPE HIM.
HAD MINERVA KNOWN THIS..
..WHEN SHE SHUT US ALL AWAY?
LESTER..?
HUSBAND?
WHERE ARE YOU?

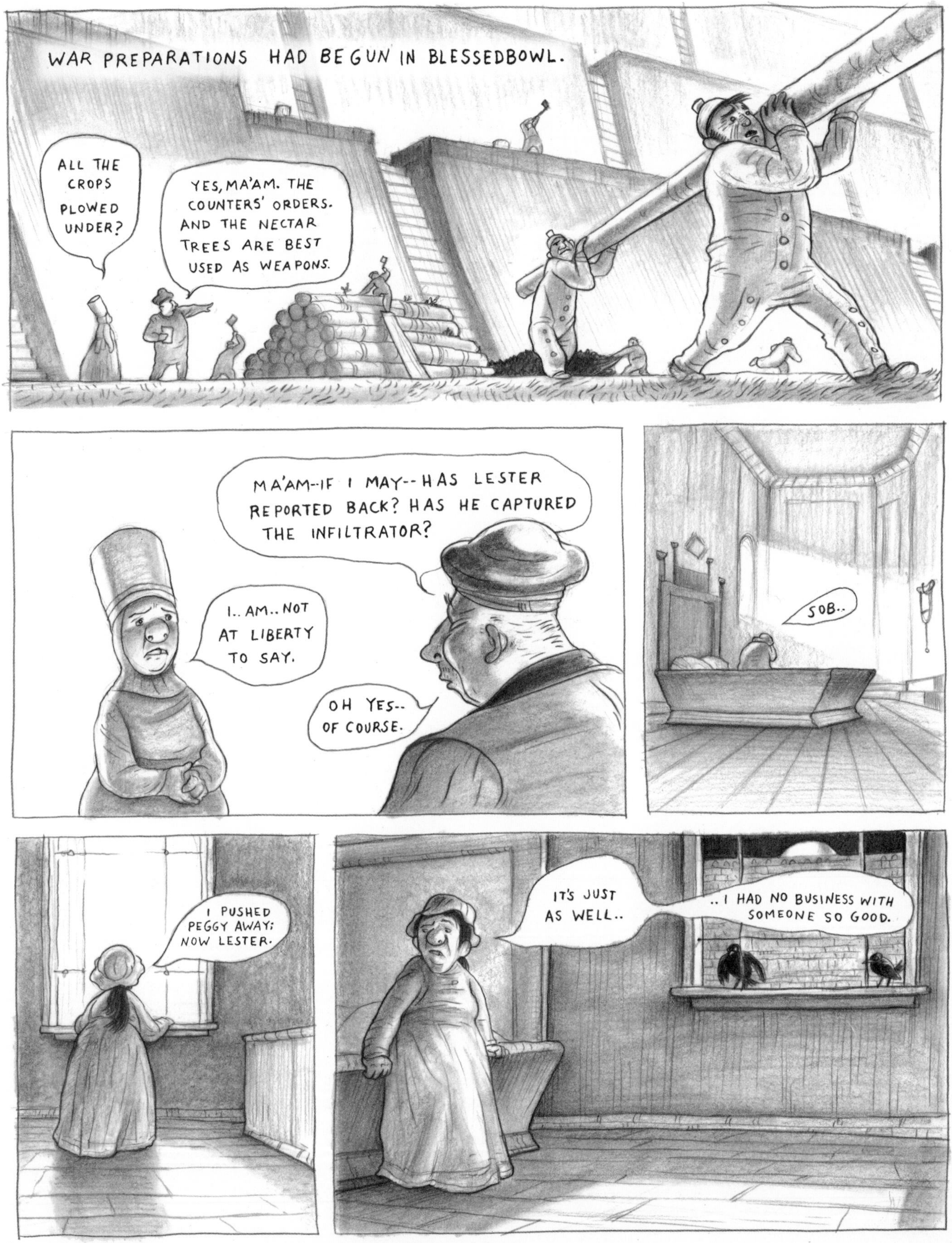
WAR PREPARATIONS HAD BEGUN IN BLESSEDBOWL.
ALL THE CROPS PLOWED UNDER?
YES, MA'AM. THE COUNTERS' ORDERS. AND THE NECTAR TREES ARE BEST USED AS WEAPONS.
MA'AM--IF I MAY--HAS LESTER REPORTED BACK? HAS HE CAPTURED THE INFILTRATOR?
I.. AM.. NOT AT LIBERTY TO SAY.
OH YES-- OF COURSE.
SOB..
I PUSHED PEGGY AWAY; NOW LESTER.
IT'S JUST AS WELL..
.. I HAD NO BUSINESS WITH SOMEONE SO GOOD.

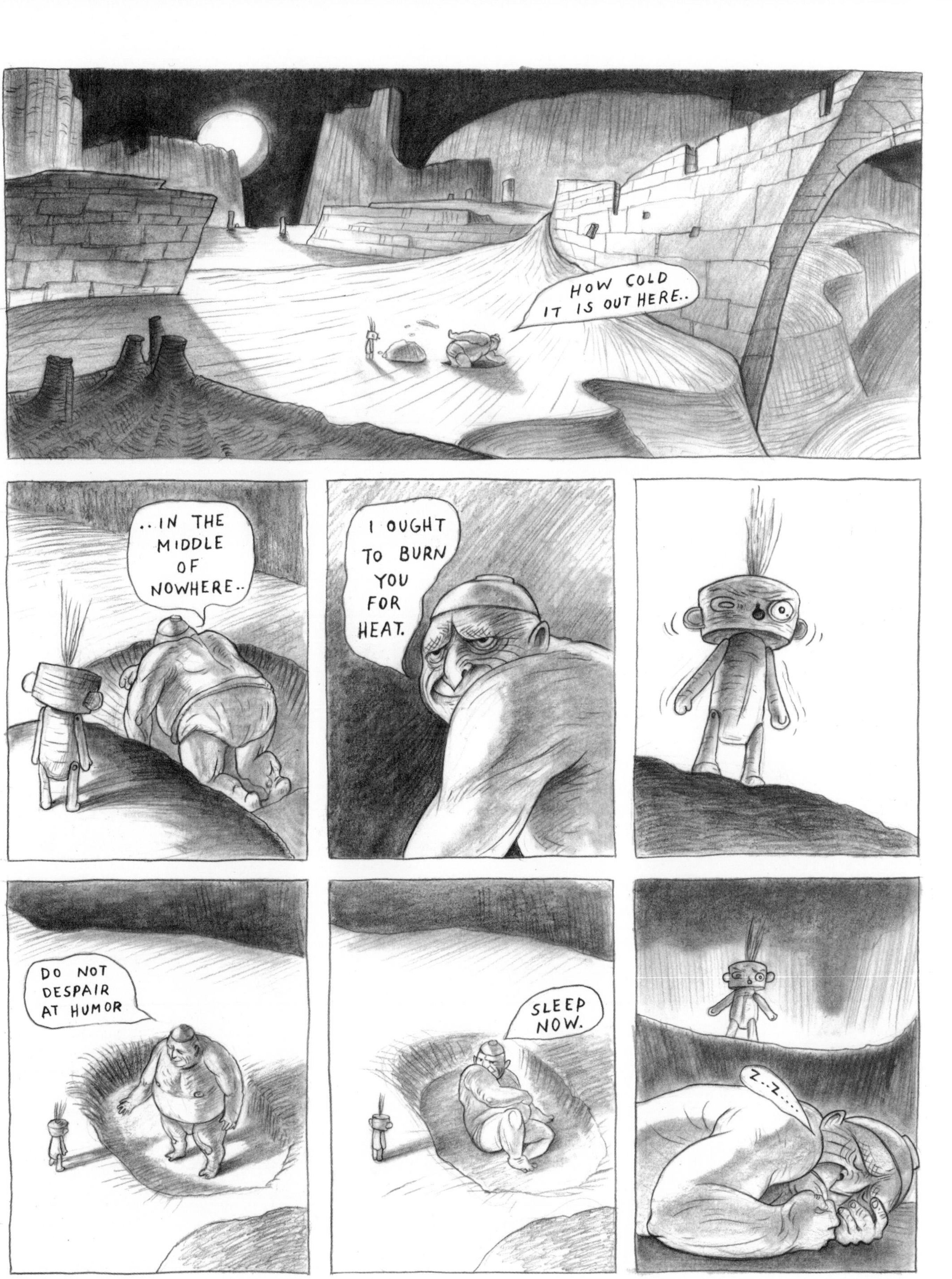
HOW COLD IT IS OUT HERE..
..IN THE MIDDLE OF NOWHERE..
I OUGHT TO BURN YOU FOR HEAT.
DO NOT DESPAIR AT HUMOR
SLEEP NOW.
Z..Z.....

I DON'T KNOW WHY I HAD THE CONFIDENCE..
..OR THE FOOLISHNESS..
ZZZ
..TO DESTROY HIM.
ZZZZZ
I SUPPOSE I JUST WANTED TO GO HOME.
ZZ
ZZZ
ZZ
ZZ
WHY?
ZZ
WHY DO YOU ALWAYS LEAVE ME..
WHERE..DID..YOU..GO..
ZZ
?!
DEAR GIRL...
ZZZ

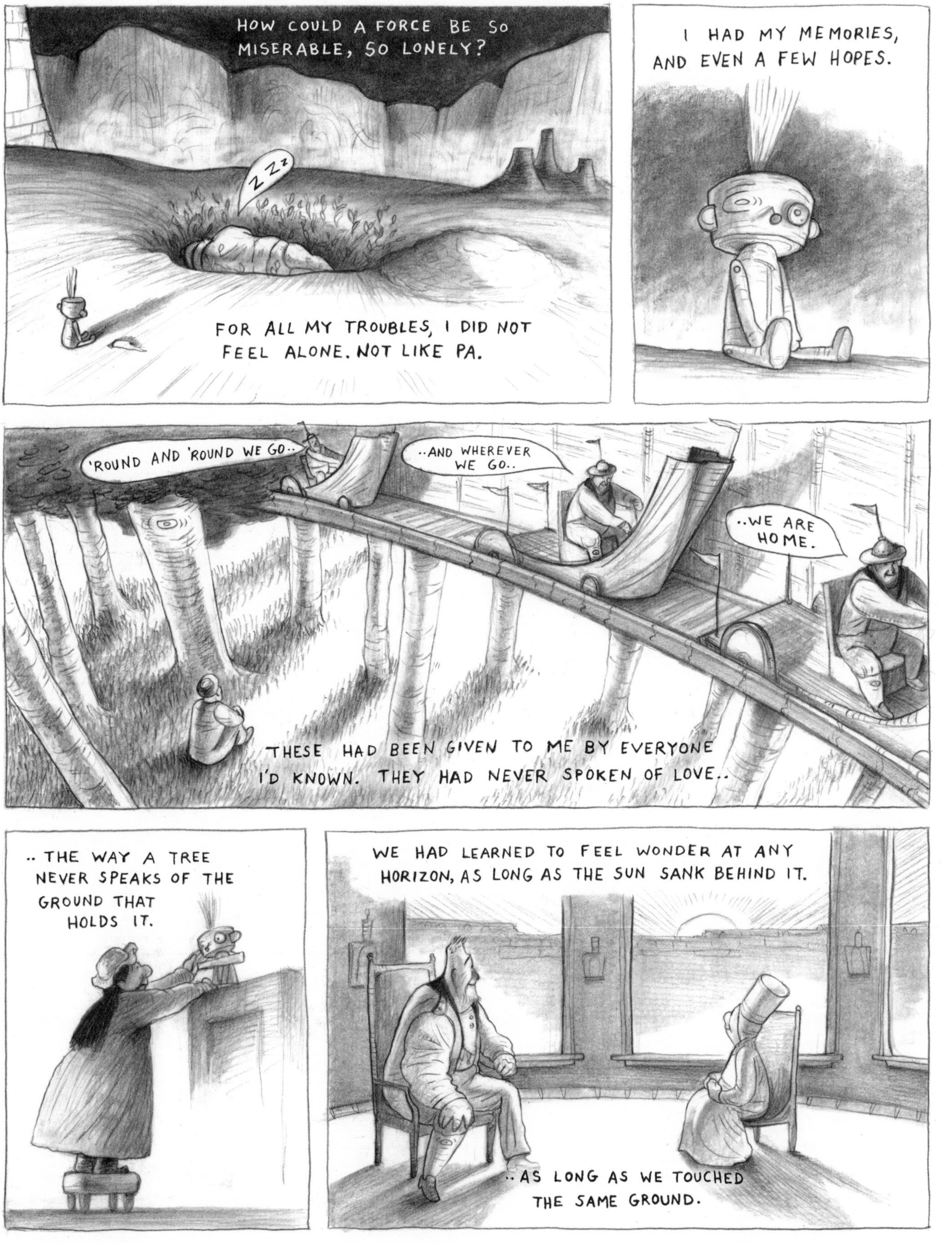
HOW COULD A FORCE BE SO MISERABLE, SO LONELY?
ZZZ
FOR ALL MY TROUBLES, I DID NOT FEEL ALONE. NOT LIKE PA.
I HAD MY MEMORIES, AND EVEN A FEW HOPES.
'ROUND AND 'ROUND WE GO..
..AND WHEREVER WE GO..
..WE ARE HOME.
THESE HAD BEEN GIVEN TO ME BY EVERYONE I'D KNOWN. THEY HAD NEVER SPOKEN OF LOVE..
.. THE WAY A TREE NEVER SPEAKS OF THE GROUND THAT HOLDS IT.
WE HAD LEARNED TO FEEL WONDER AT ANY HORIZON, AS LONG AS THE SUN SANK BEHIND IT.
..AS LONG AS WE TOUCHED THE SAME GROUND.

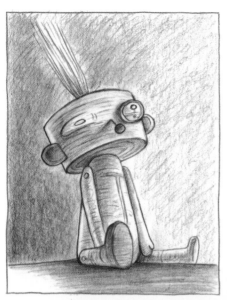

I SUPPOSE PA WAS LOOKING FOR HOME, TOO.

PLEASE

THE GIRL IN THE LIBRARY..

I ALMOST PITIED HIM.

I.. NEED TO SEE HER..

..BEFORE I DIE..

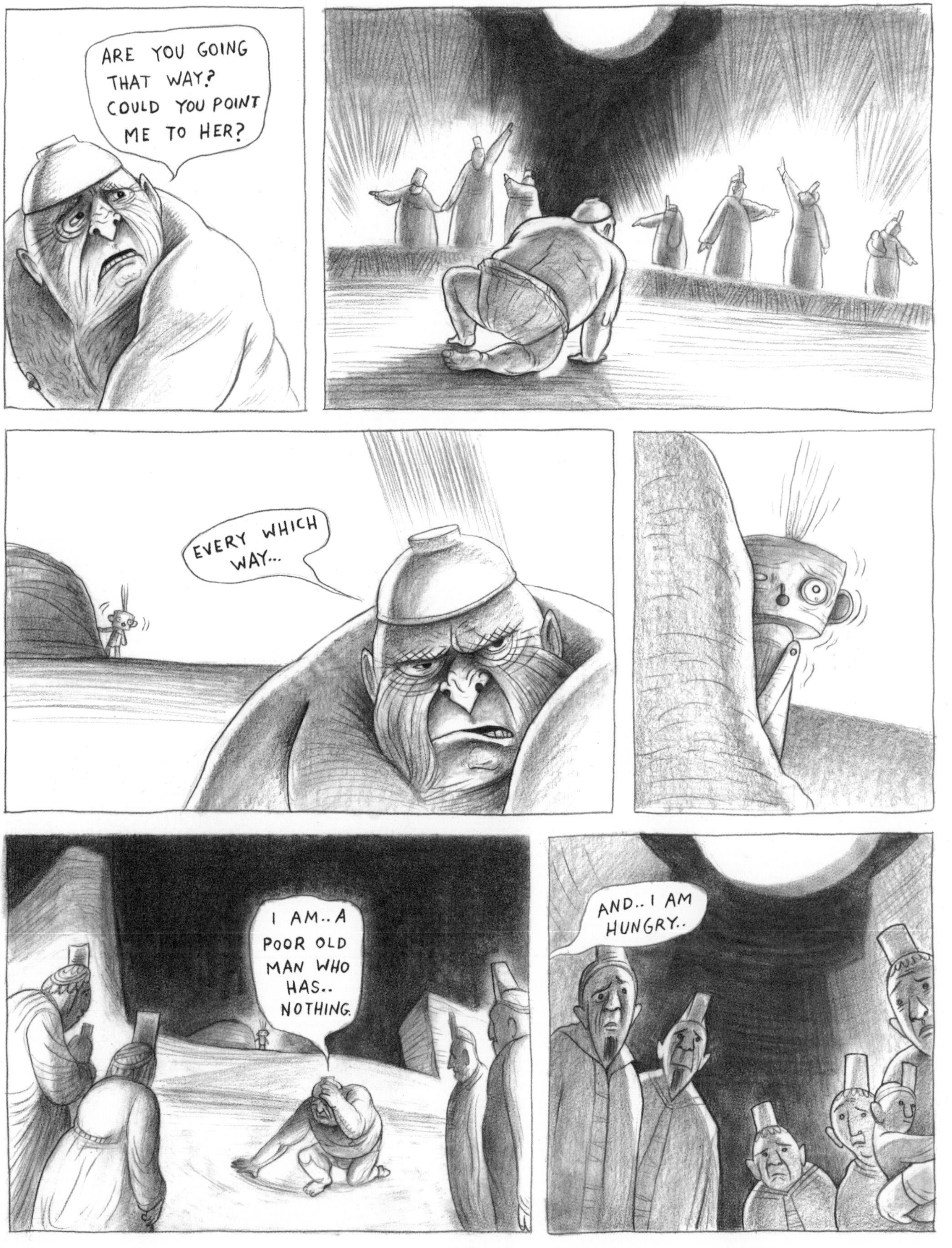
ARE YOU GOING THAT WAY? COULD YOU POINT ME TO HER?
EVERY WHICH WAY...
I AM.. A POOR OLD MAN WHO HAS.. NOTHING.
AND.. I AM HUNGRY..

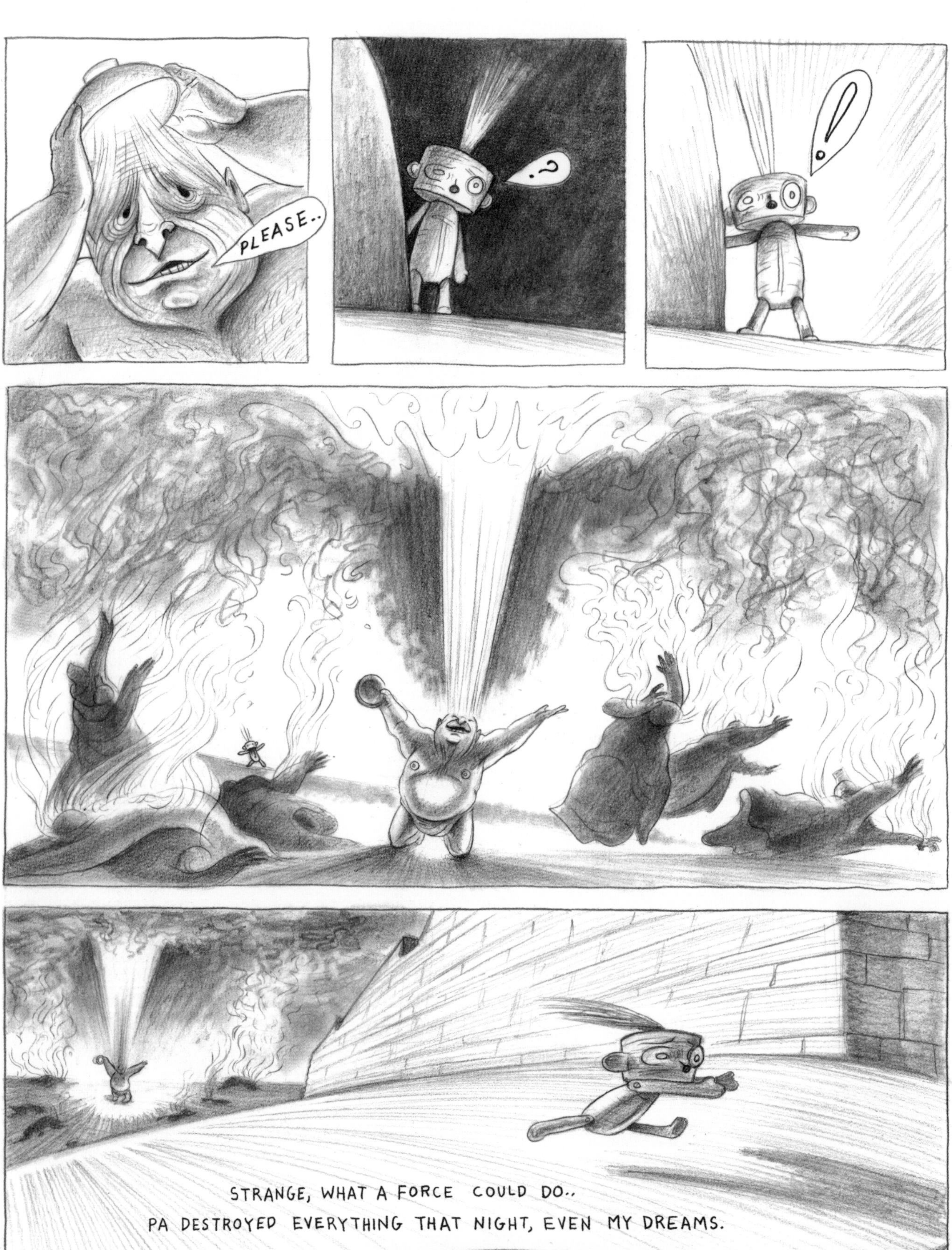
PLEASE..
?
!
STRANGE, WHAT A FORCE COULD DO..
PA DESTROYED EVERYTHING THAT NIGHT, EVEN MY DREAMS.

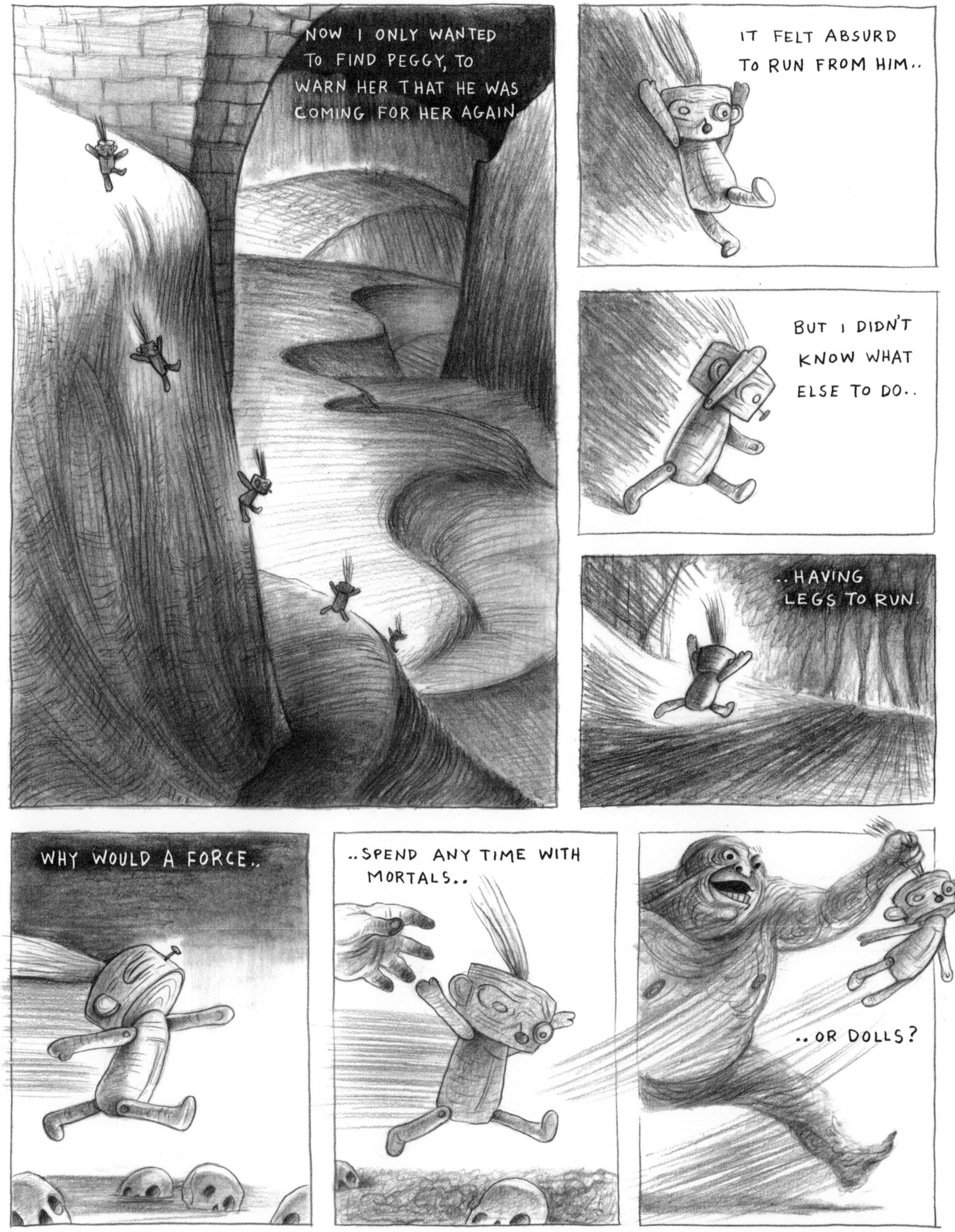
NOW I ONLY WANTED TO FIND PEGGY, TO WARN HER THAT HE WAS COMING FOR HER AGAIN.
IT FELT ABSURD TO RUN FROM HIM..
BUT I DIDN'T KNOW WHAT ELSE TO DO..
..HAVING LEGS TO RUN.
WHY WOULD A FORCE..
..SPEND ANY TIME WITH MORTALS..
..OR DOLLS?

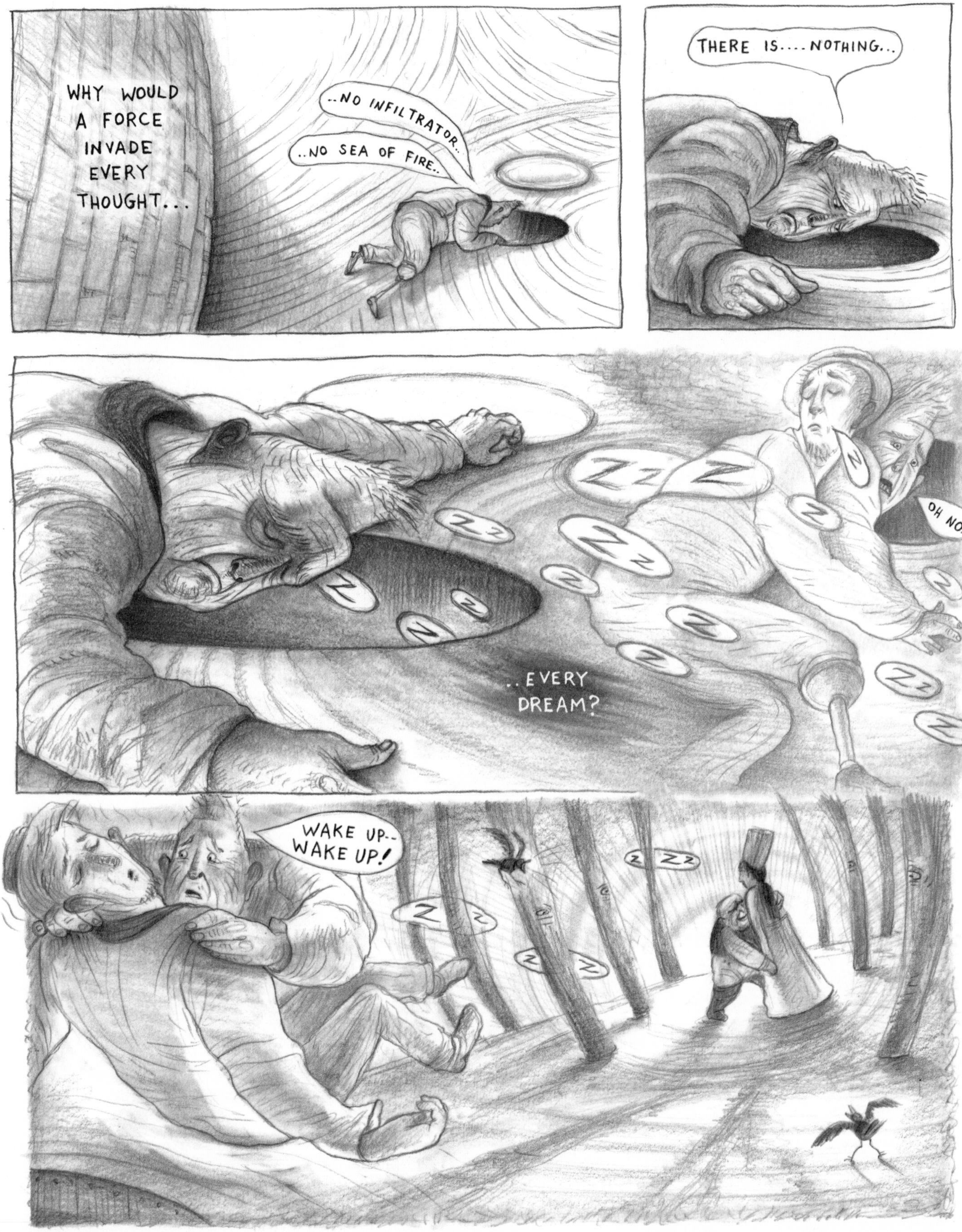
WHY WOULD A FORCE INVADE EVERY THOUGHT...
..NO INFILTRATOR..
..NO SEA OF FIRE..
THERE IS.... NOTHING...
OH NO.
..EVERY DREAM?
WAKE UP-- WAKE UP!

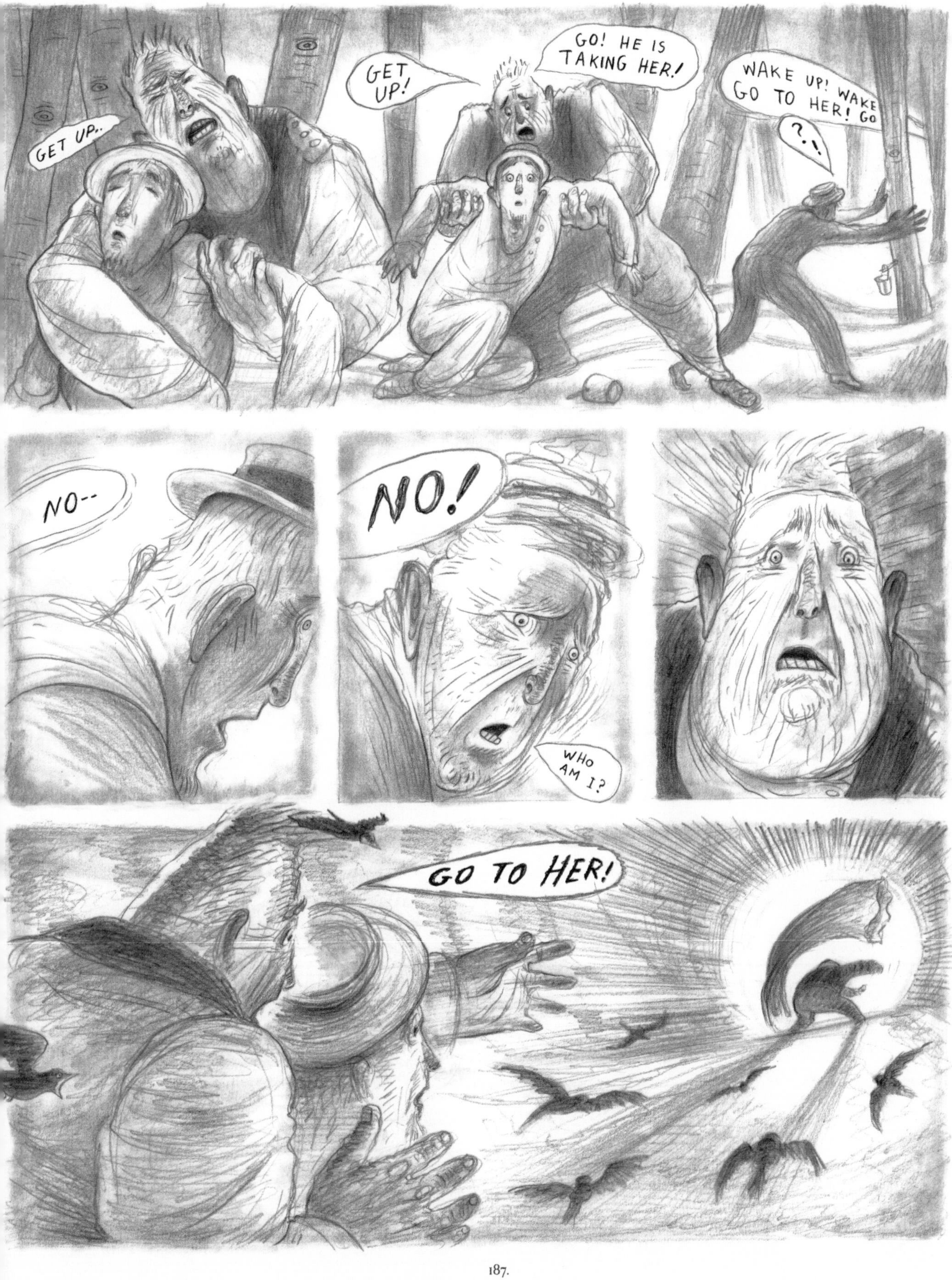
GET UP..
GET UP!
GO! HE IS TAKING HER!
WAKE UP! WAKE GO TO HER! GO
?.!
NO--
NO!
WHO AM I?
GO TO HER!

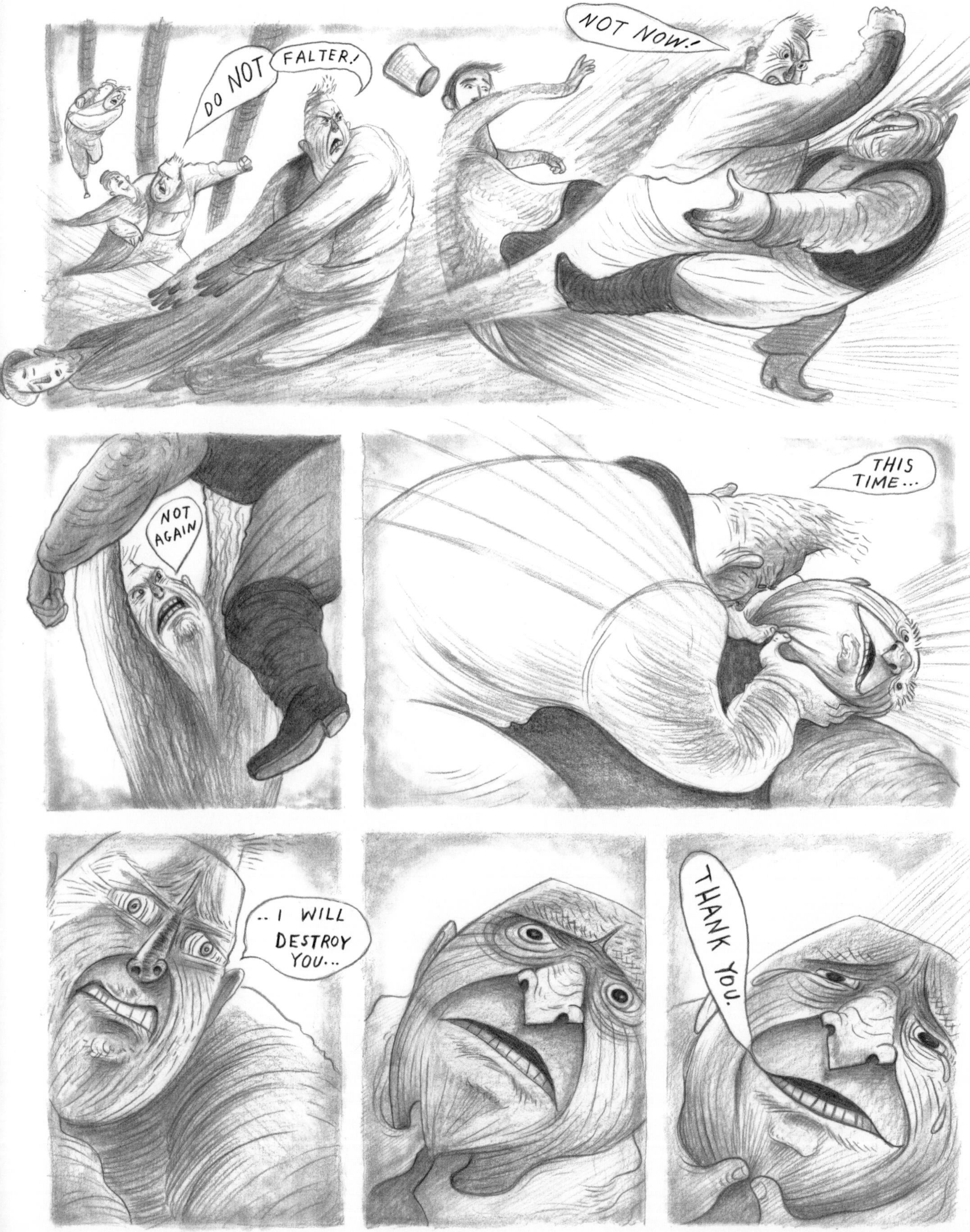
DO NOT FALTER!
NOT NOW!
NOT AGAIN
THIS TIME...
..I WILL DESTROY YOU...
THANK YOU.

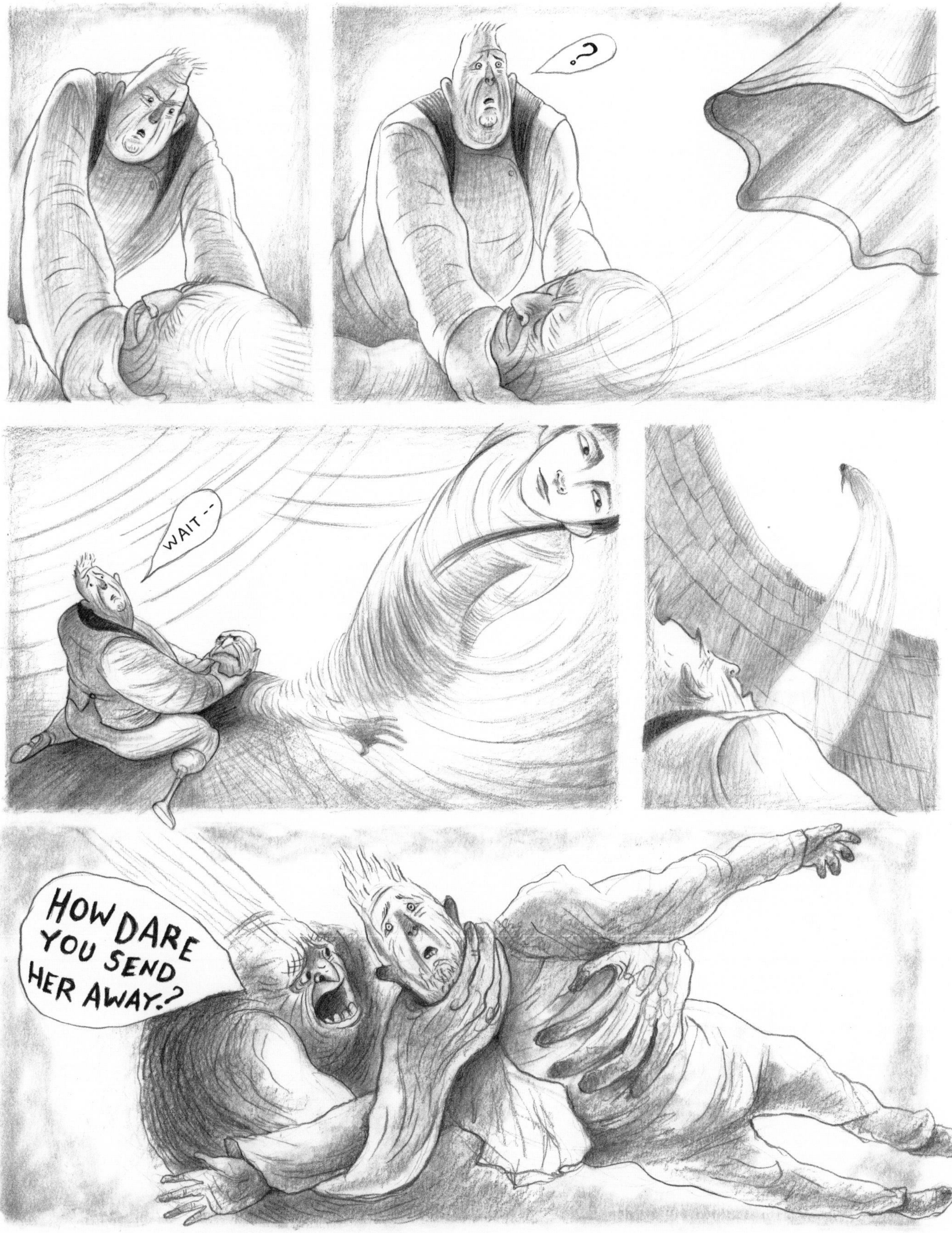
?
WAIT --
HOW DARE YOU SEND HER AWAY.?

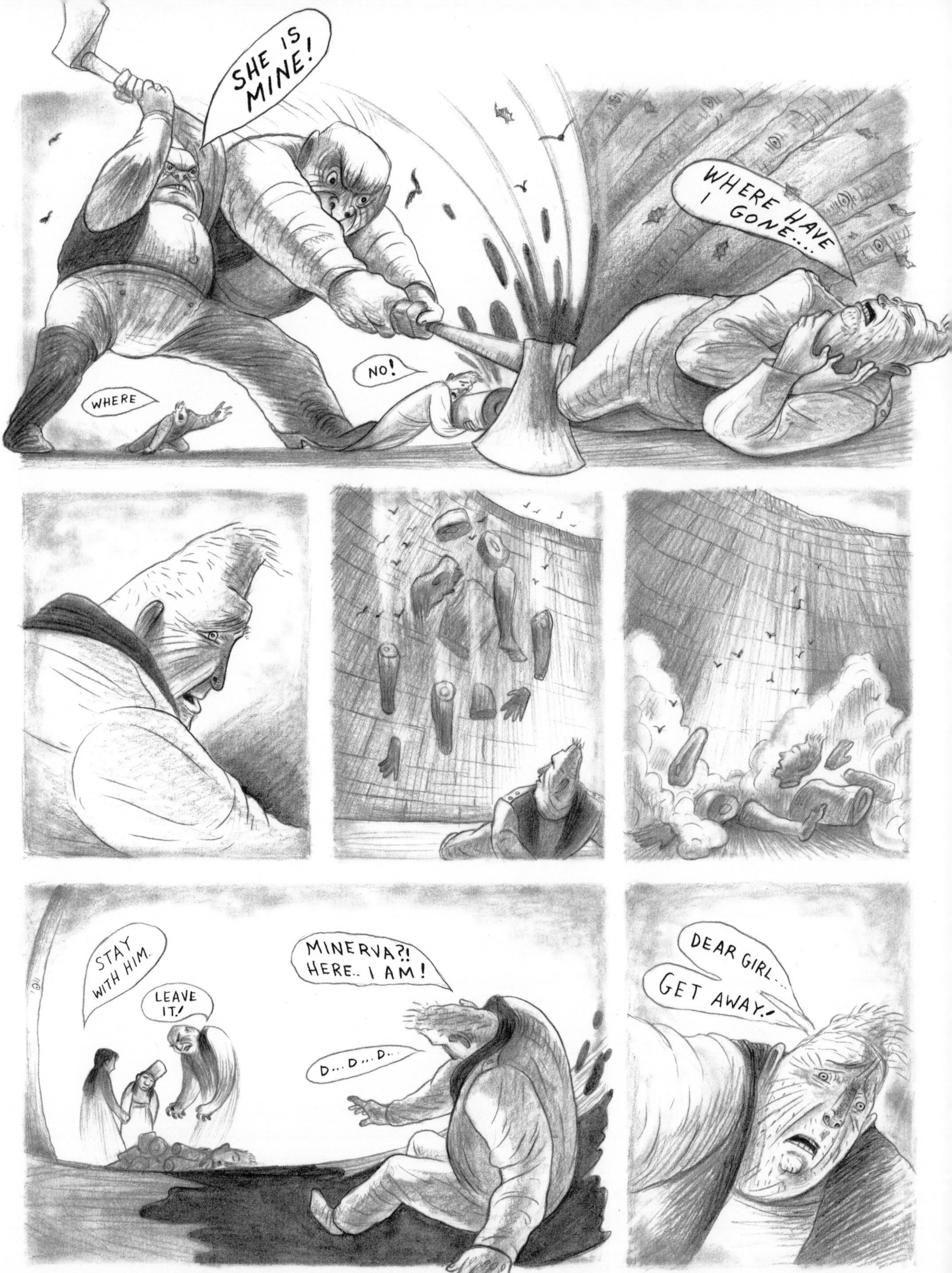
SHE IS MINE!
WHERE HAVE I GONE....
NO!
WHERE
STAY WITH HIM..
LEAVE IT!
MINERVA?! HERE.. I AM!
D... D... D..
DEAR GIRL...
GET AWAY!

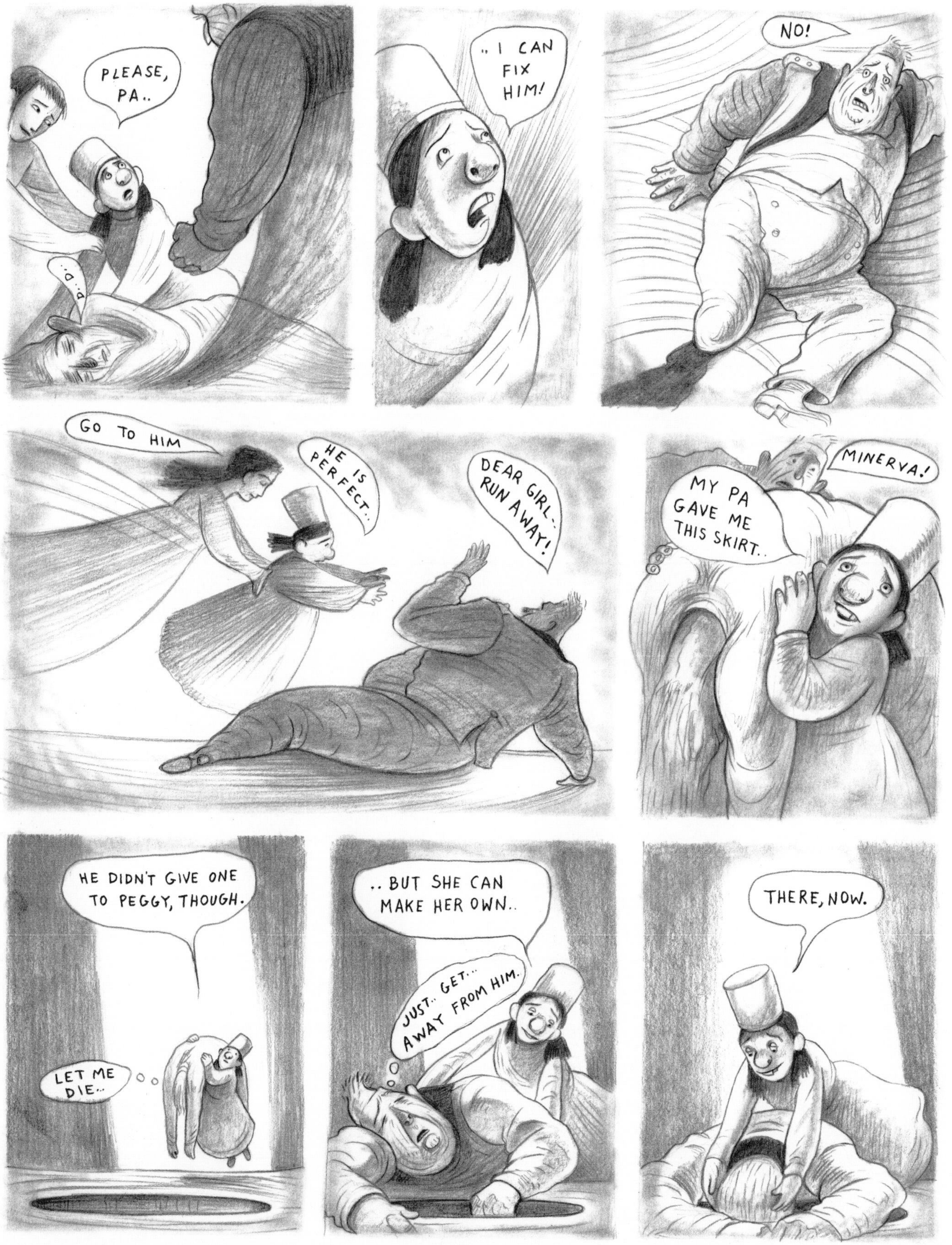
PLEASE, PA..
D.. D..
.. I CAN FIX HIM!
NO!
GO TO HIM
HE IS PERFECT..
DEAR GIRL.. RUN AWAY!
MINERVA!
MY PA GAVE ME THIS SKIRT..
HE DIDN'T GIVE ONE TO PEGGY, THOUGH.
LET ME DIE..
.. BUT SHE CAN MAKE HER OWN..
JUST.. GET.. AWAY FROM HIM.
THERE, NOW.

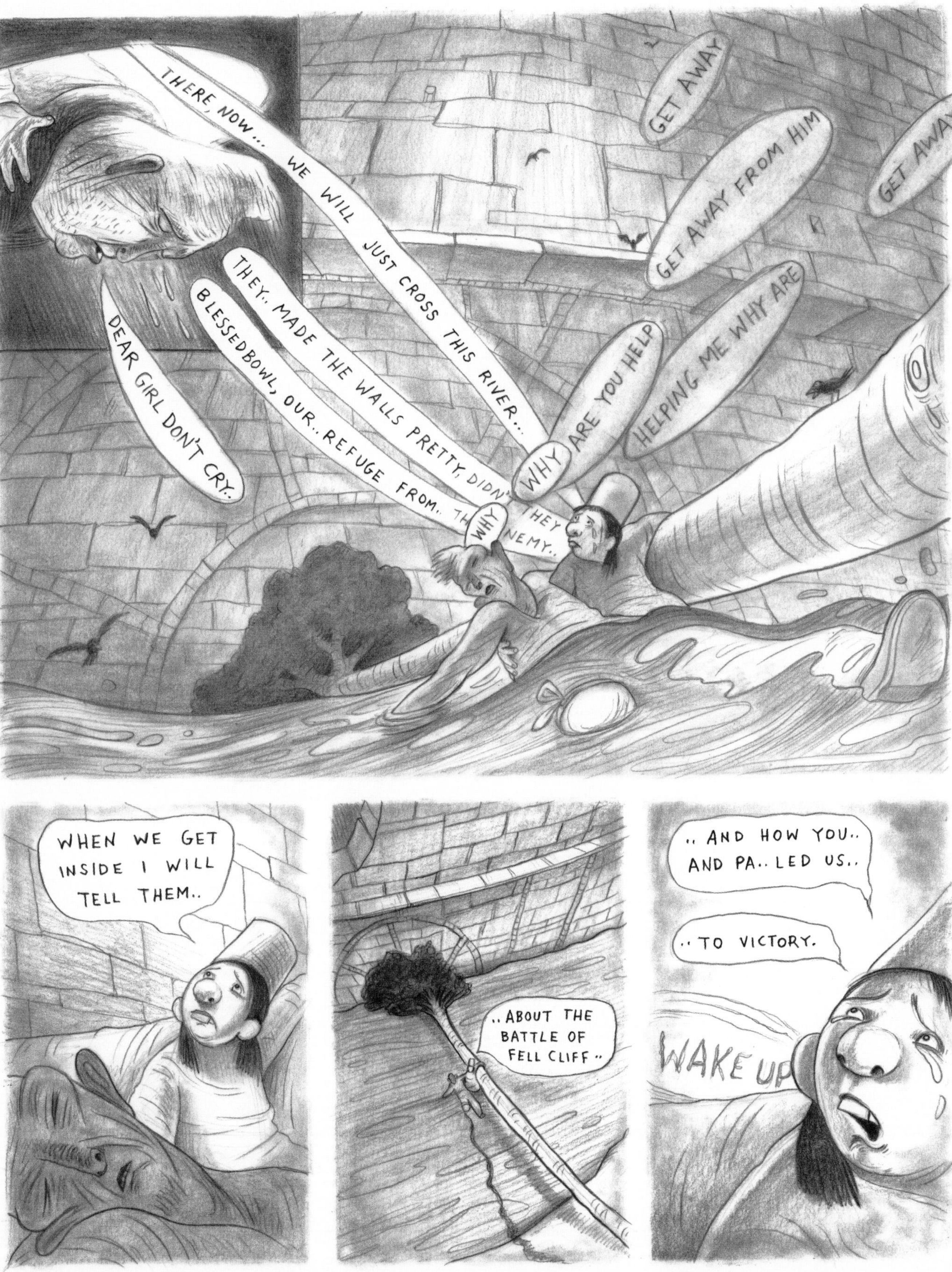

THERE, NOW... WE WILL JUST CROSS THIS RIVER...
THEY.. MADE THE WALLS PRETTY, DIDN'T THEY
BLESSEDBOWL, OUR.. REFUGE FROM.. THE ENEMY..
DEAR GIRL DON'T CRY..
WHY
WHY ARE YOU HELP
HELPING ME WHY ARE
GET AWAY FROM HIM
GET AWAY
GET AWAY
WHEN WE GET INSIDE I WILL TELL THEM..
..ABOUT THE BATTLE OF FELL CLIFF..
.. AND HOW YOU.. AND PA.. LED US..
.. TO VICTORY.
WAKE UP

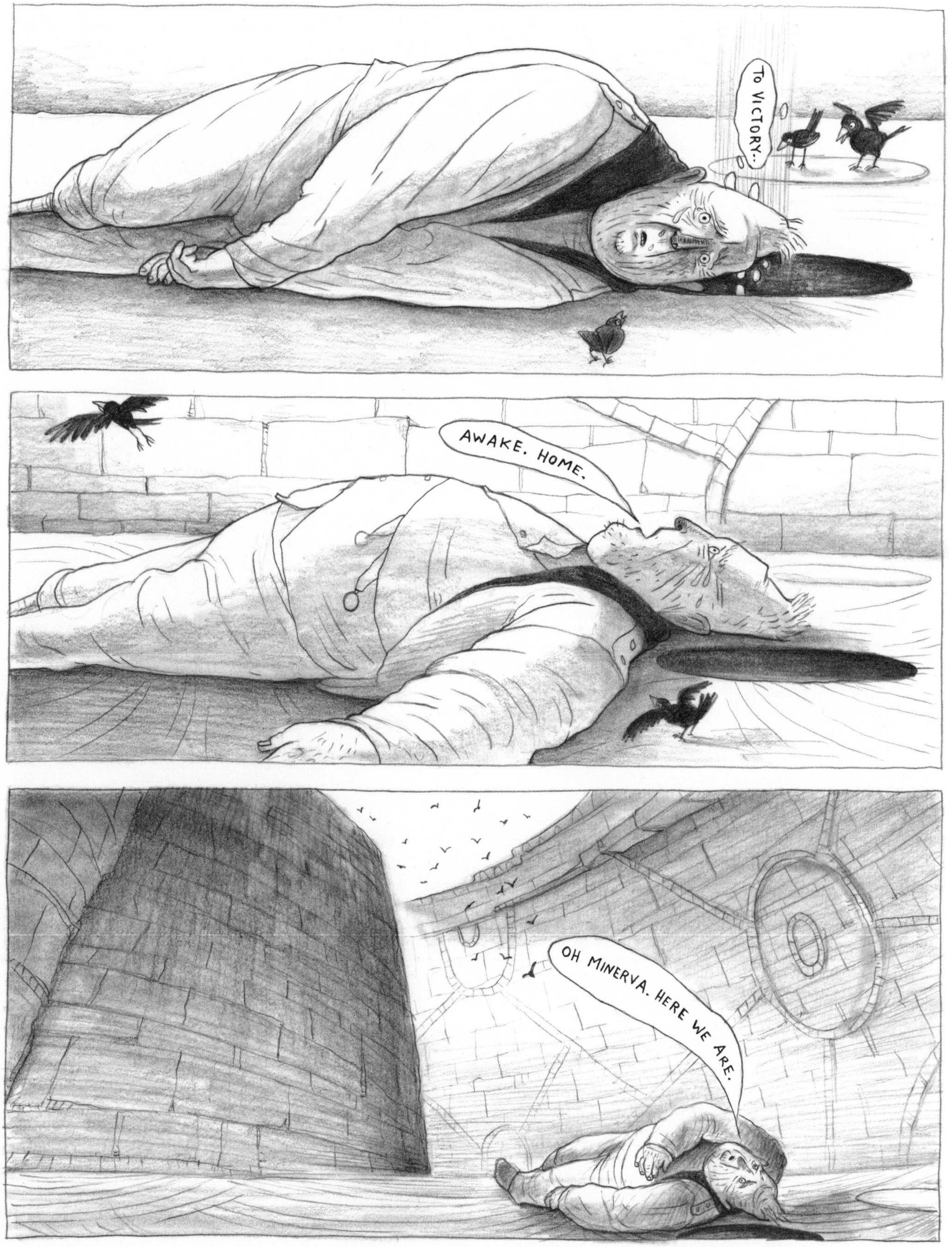
TO VICTORY..
AWAKE. HOME.
OH MINERVA. HERE WE ARE.

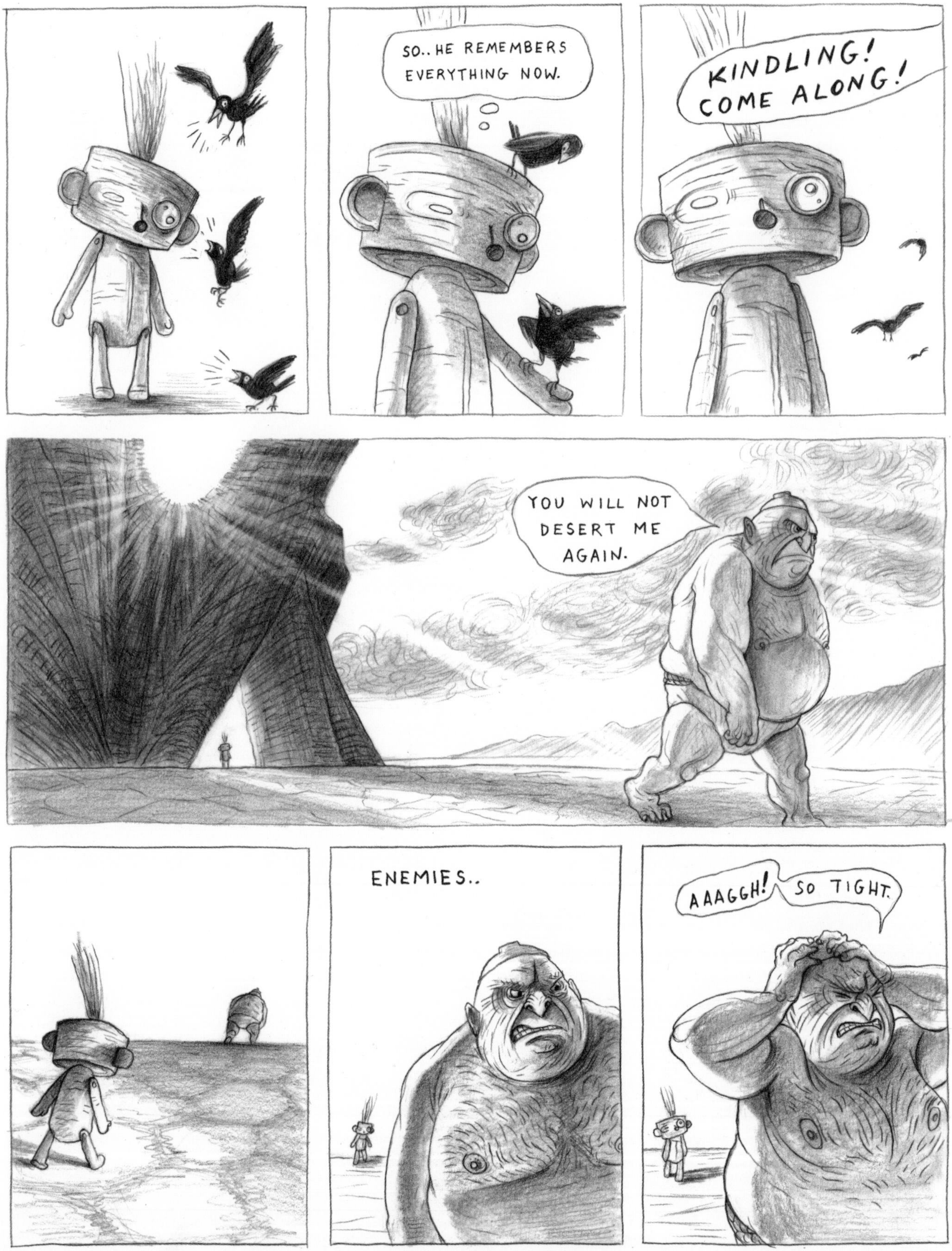
SO.. HE REMEMBERS EVERYTHING NOW.
KINDLING! COME ALONG!
YOU WILL NOT DESERT ME AGAIN.
ENEMIES..
AAAGGH!
SO TIGHT.

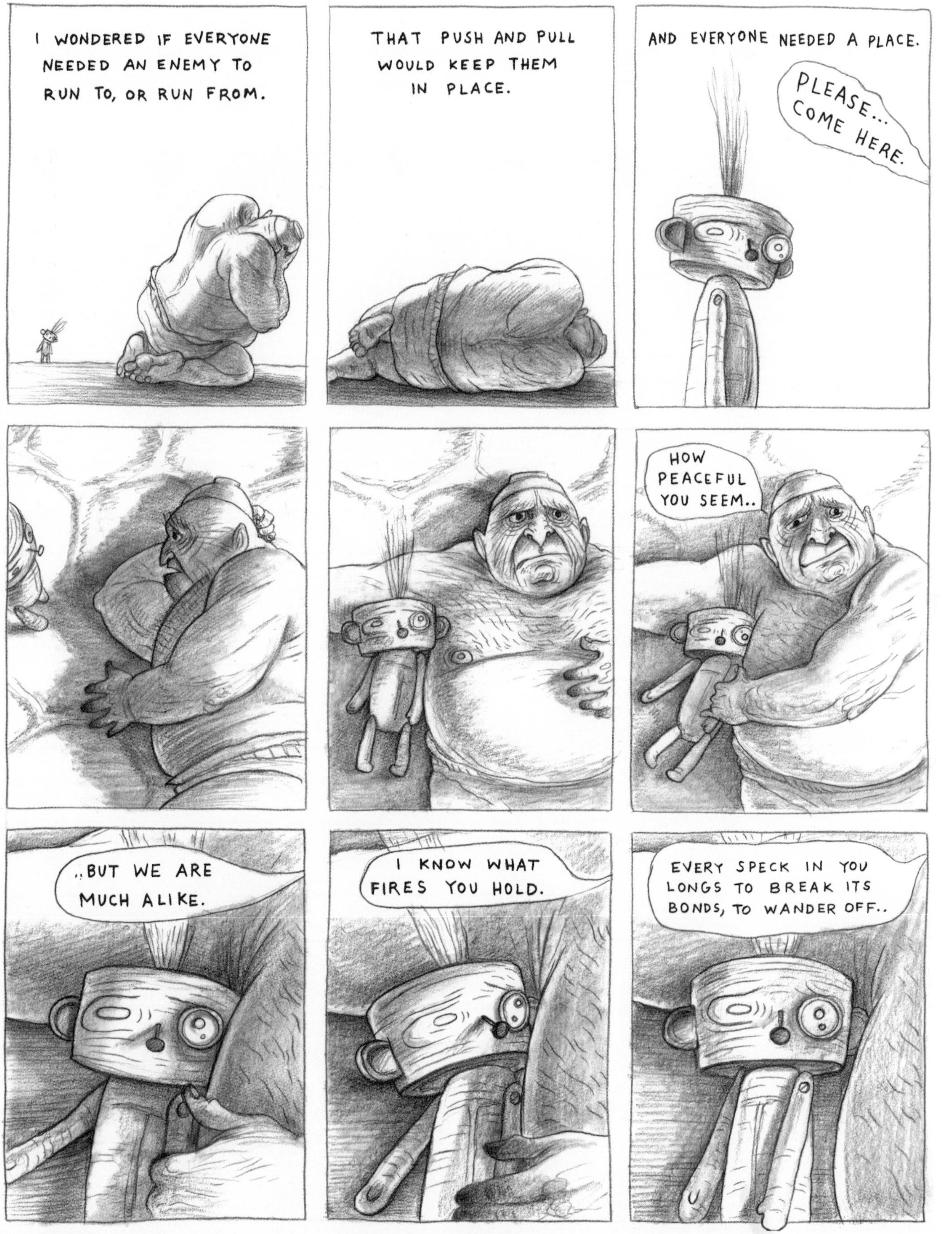
I WONDERED IF EVERYONE NEEDED AN ENEMY TO RUN TO, OR RUN FROM.
THAT PUSH AND PULL WOULD KEEP THEM IN PLACE.
AND EVERYONE NEEDED A PLACE.
PLEASE... COME HERE.
HOW PEACEFUL YOU SEEM..
..BUT WE ARE MUCH ALIKE.
I KNOW WHAT FIRES YOU HOLD.
EVERY SPECK IN YOU LONGS TO BREAK ITS BONDS, TO WANDER OFF..

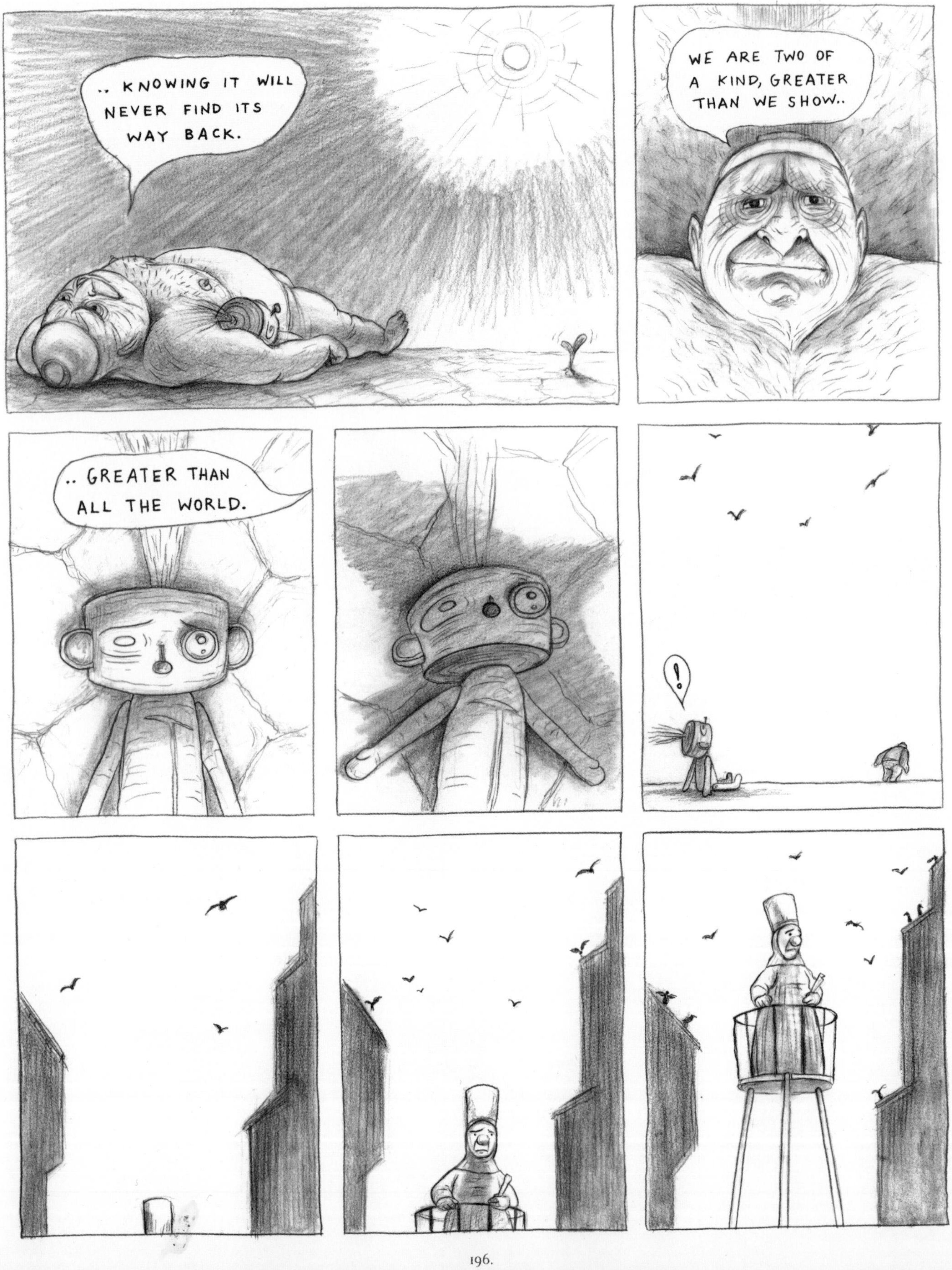
.. KNOWING IT WILL NEVER FIND ITS WAY BACK.
WE ARE TWO OF A KIND, GREATER THAN WE SHOW..
.. GREATER THAN ALL THE WORLD.
!

MINERVA HAD LOOKED HIGH AND LOW..

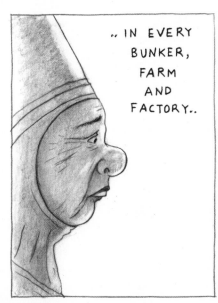

.. IN EVERY BUNKER, FARM AND FACTORY..

A MAN WITH ONE LEG AND A DOLL COULD NOT HAVE GOTTEN FAR..

.. BUT, SOMEHOW, LESTER HAD.

TRUER MEMORIES HAD TAKEN HIM FROM HER, WHICH WAS ONLY FAIR, SHE KNEW.

HOW I WANTED TO COMFORT HER, TO TELL HER EVERYTHING!..

..BUT THE CERTAINTY OF DOOM HAD PUT HER AT EASE.

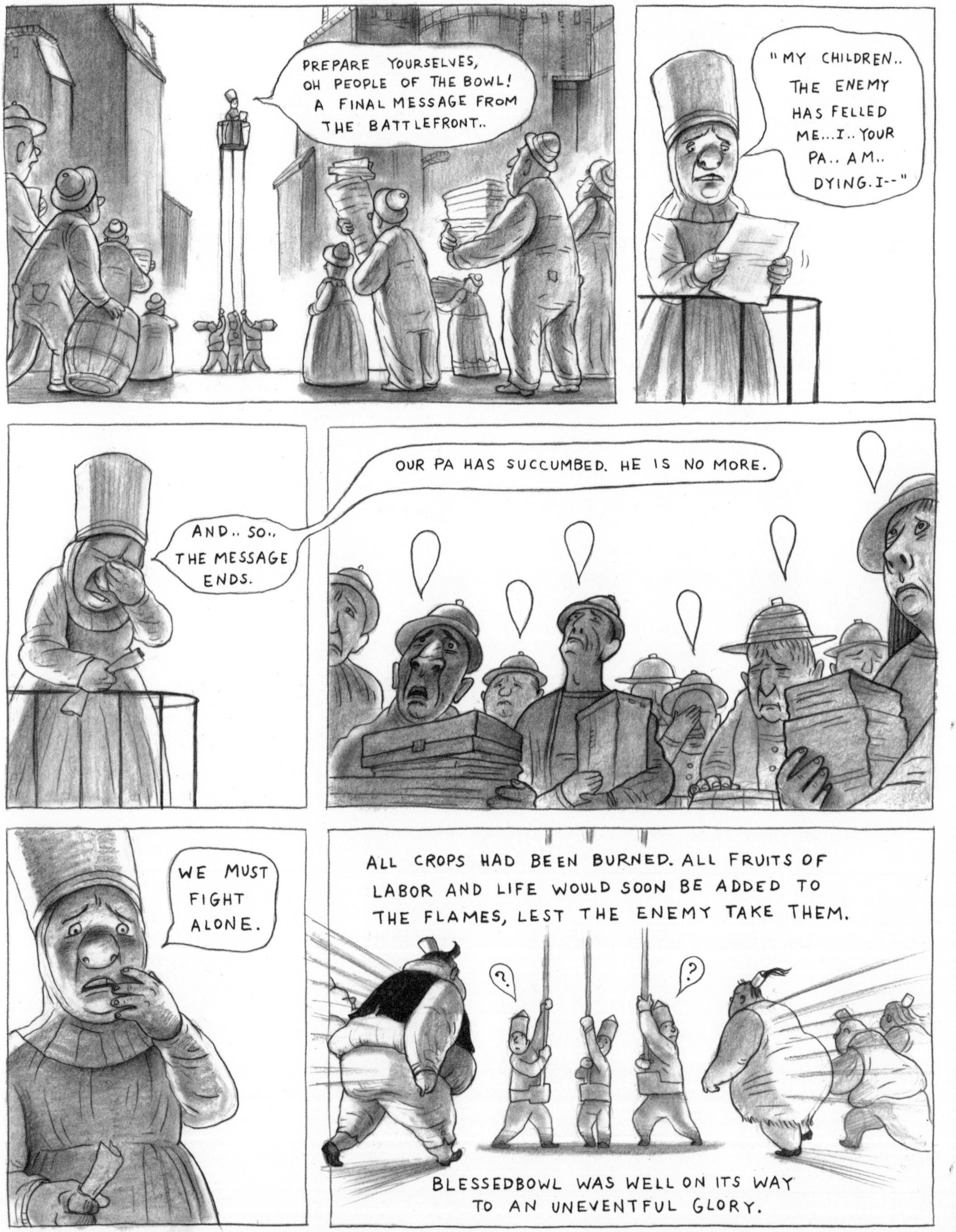
PREPARE YOURSELVES, OH PEOPLE OF THE BOWL! A FINAL MESSAGE FROM THE BATTLEFRONT..
"MY CHILDREN.. THE ENEMY HAS FELLED ME...I.. YOUR PA.. AM.. DYING. I--"
AND.. SO.. THE MESSAGE ENDS.
OUR PA HAS SUCCUMBED. HE IS NO MORE.
WE MUST FIGHT ALONE.
ALL CROPS HAD BEEN BURNED. ALL FRUITS OF LABOR AND LIFE WOULD SOON BE ADDED TO THE FLAMES, LEST THE ENEMY TAKE THEM.
?
?
BLESSEDBOWL WAS WELL ON ITS WAY TO AN UNEVENTFUL GLORY.

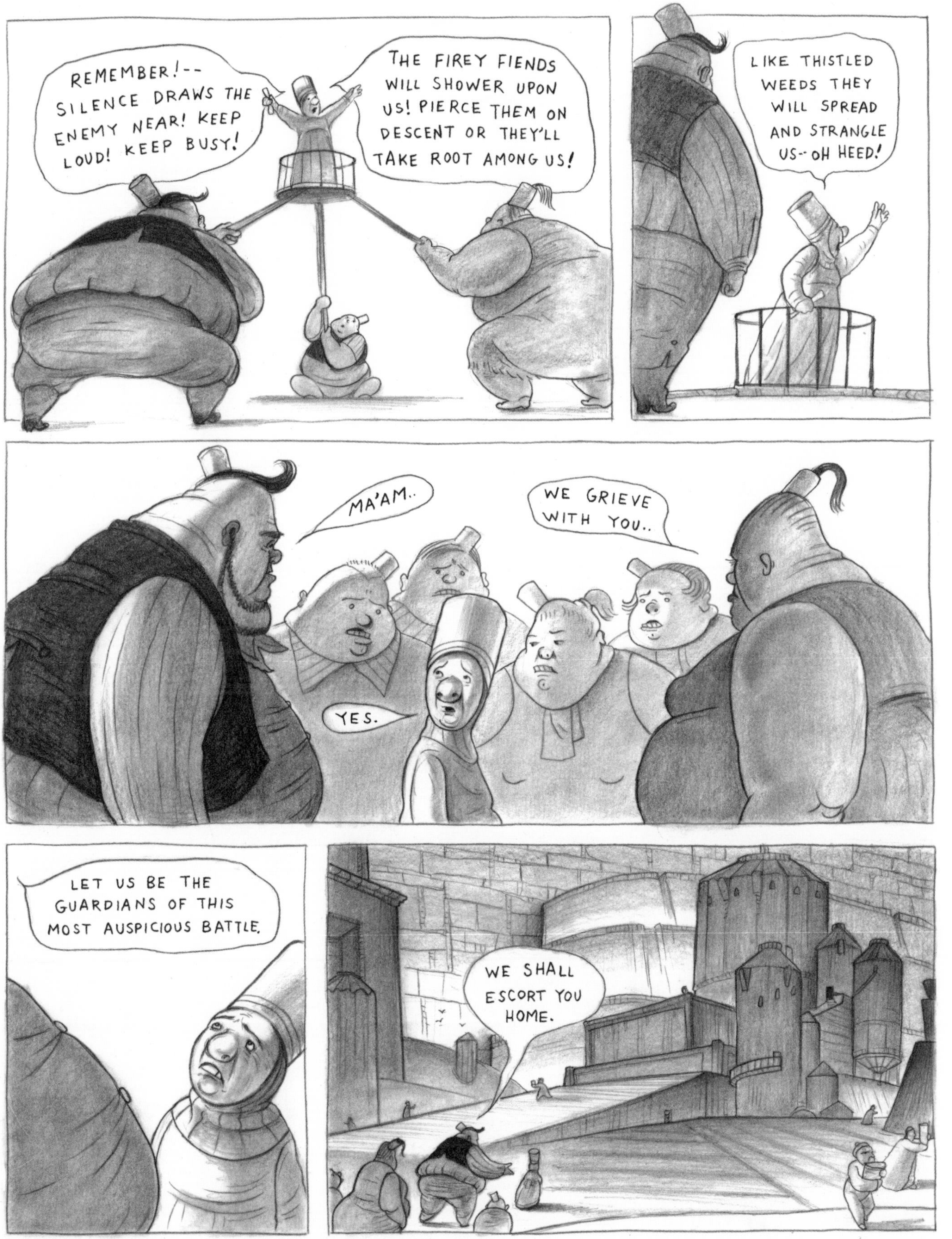
REMEMBER!-- SILENCE DRAWS THE ENEMY NEAR! KEEP LOUD! KEEP BUSY!
THE FIREY FIENDS WILL SHOWER UPON US! PIERCE THEM ON DESCENT OR THEY'LL TAKE ROOT AMONG US!
LIKE THISTLED WEEDS THEY WILL SPREAD AND STRANGLE US-- OH HEED!
MA'AM..
WE GRIEVE WITH YOU..
YES.
LET US BE THE GUARDIANS OF THIS MOST AUSPICIOUS BATTLE.
WE SHALL ESCORT YOU HOME.

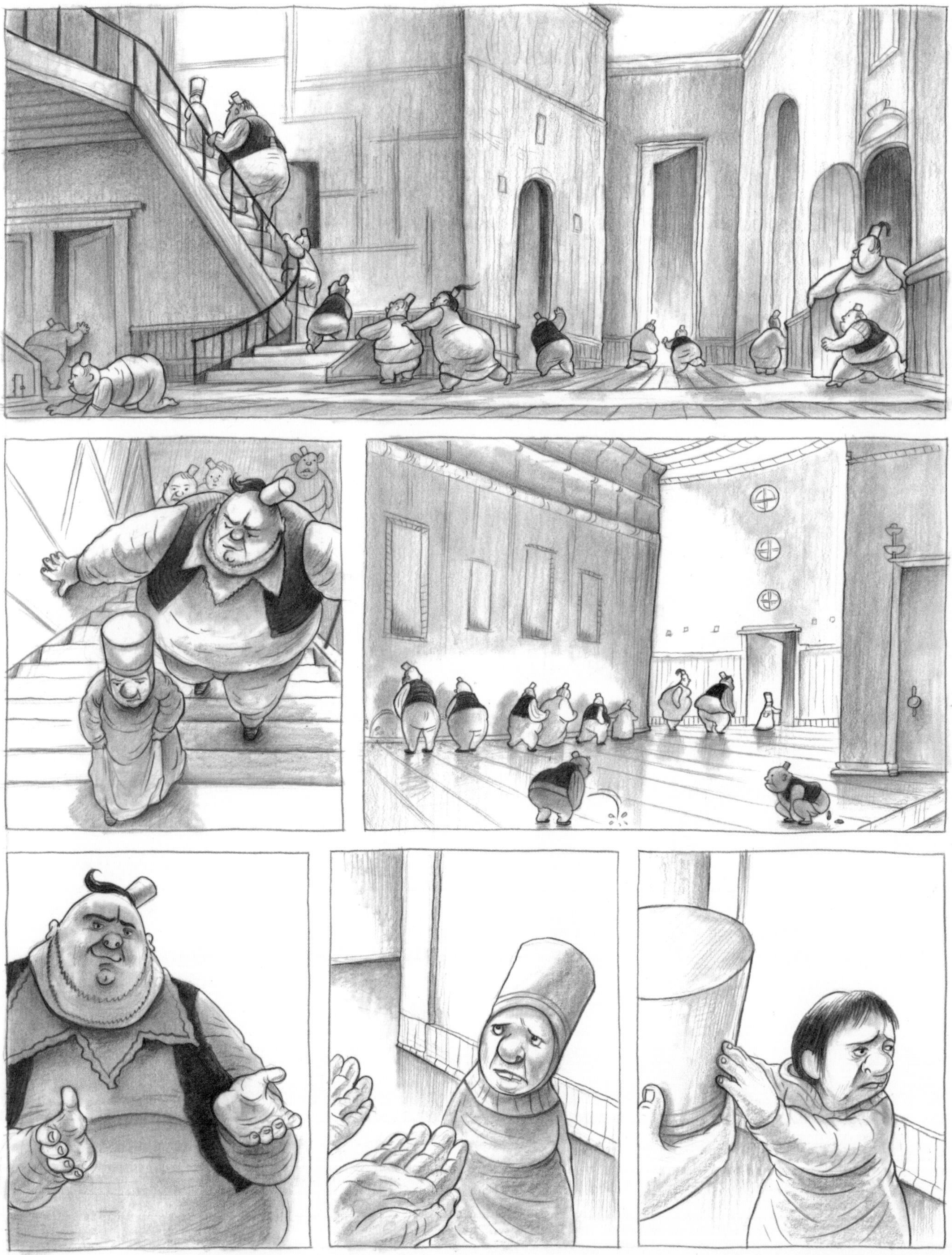

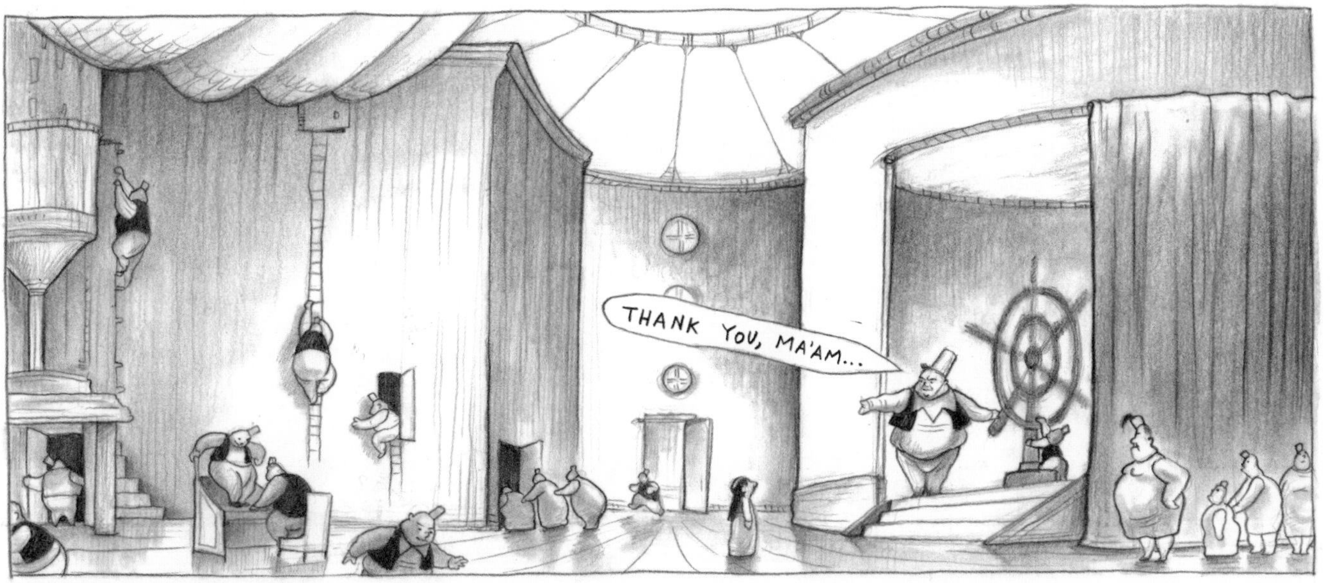
THANK YOU, MA'AM...

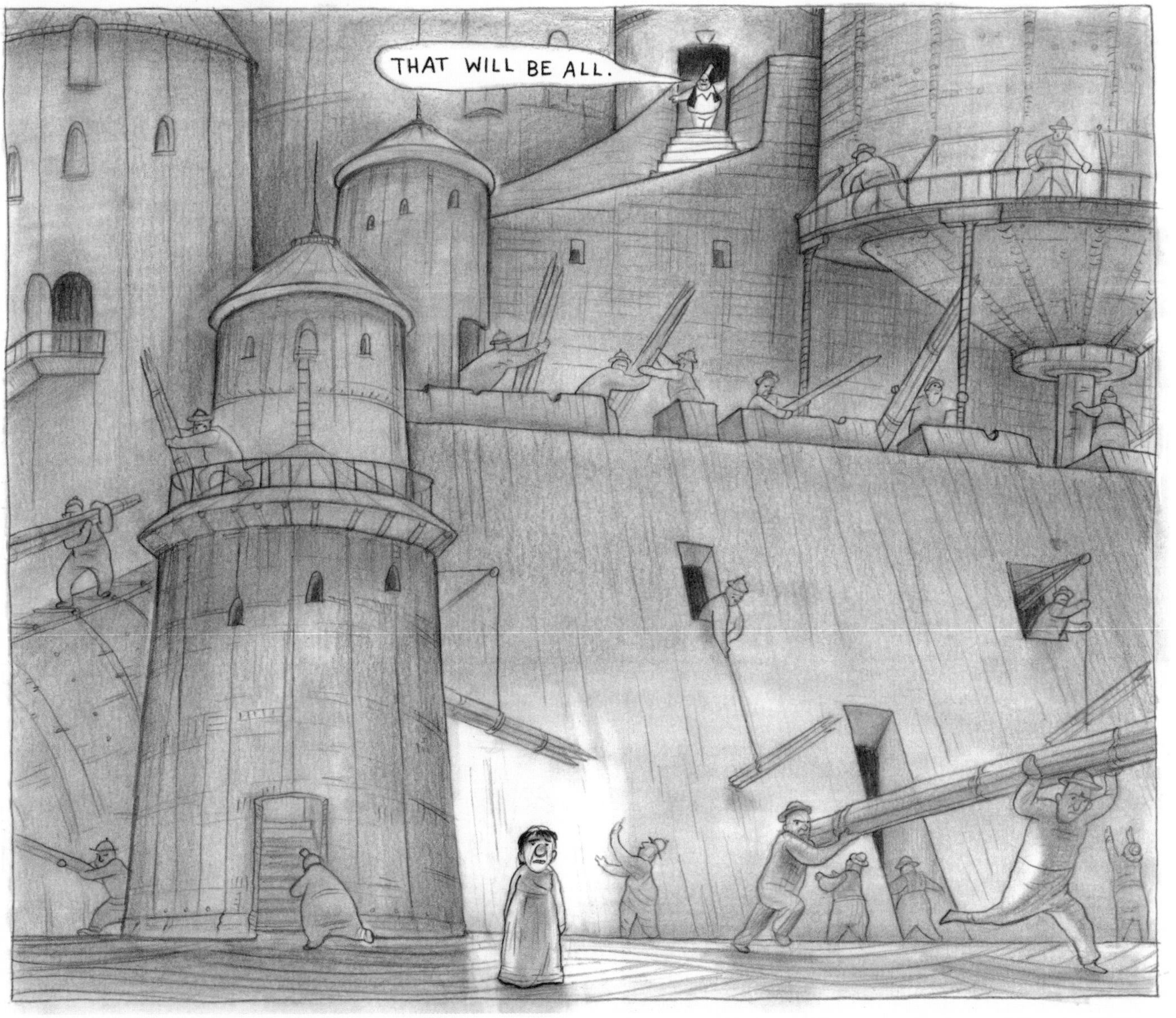
THAT WILL BE ALL.

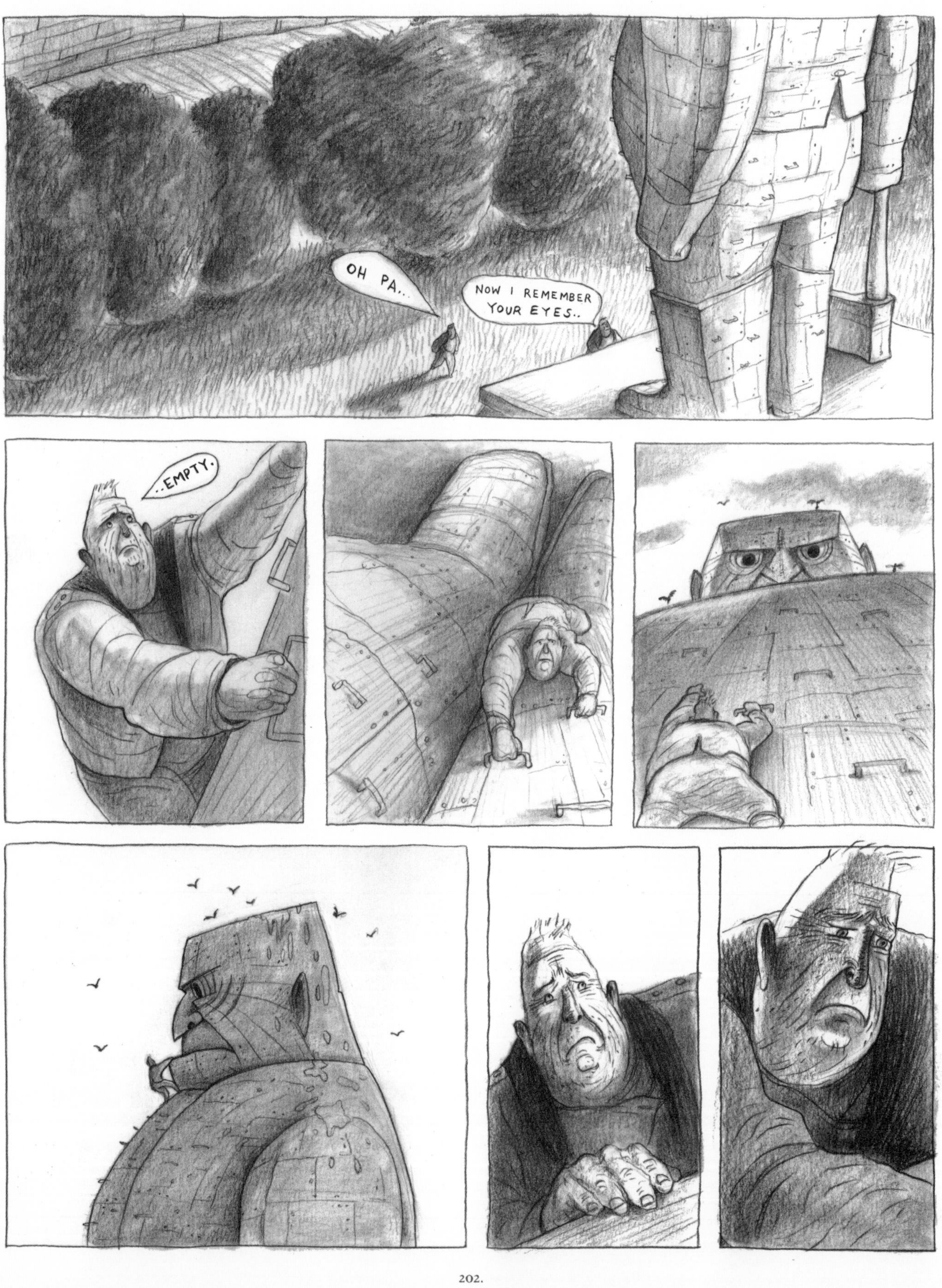
OH PA..
NOW I REMEMBER YOUR EYES..
..EMPTY.

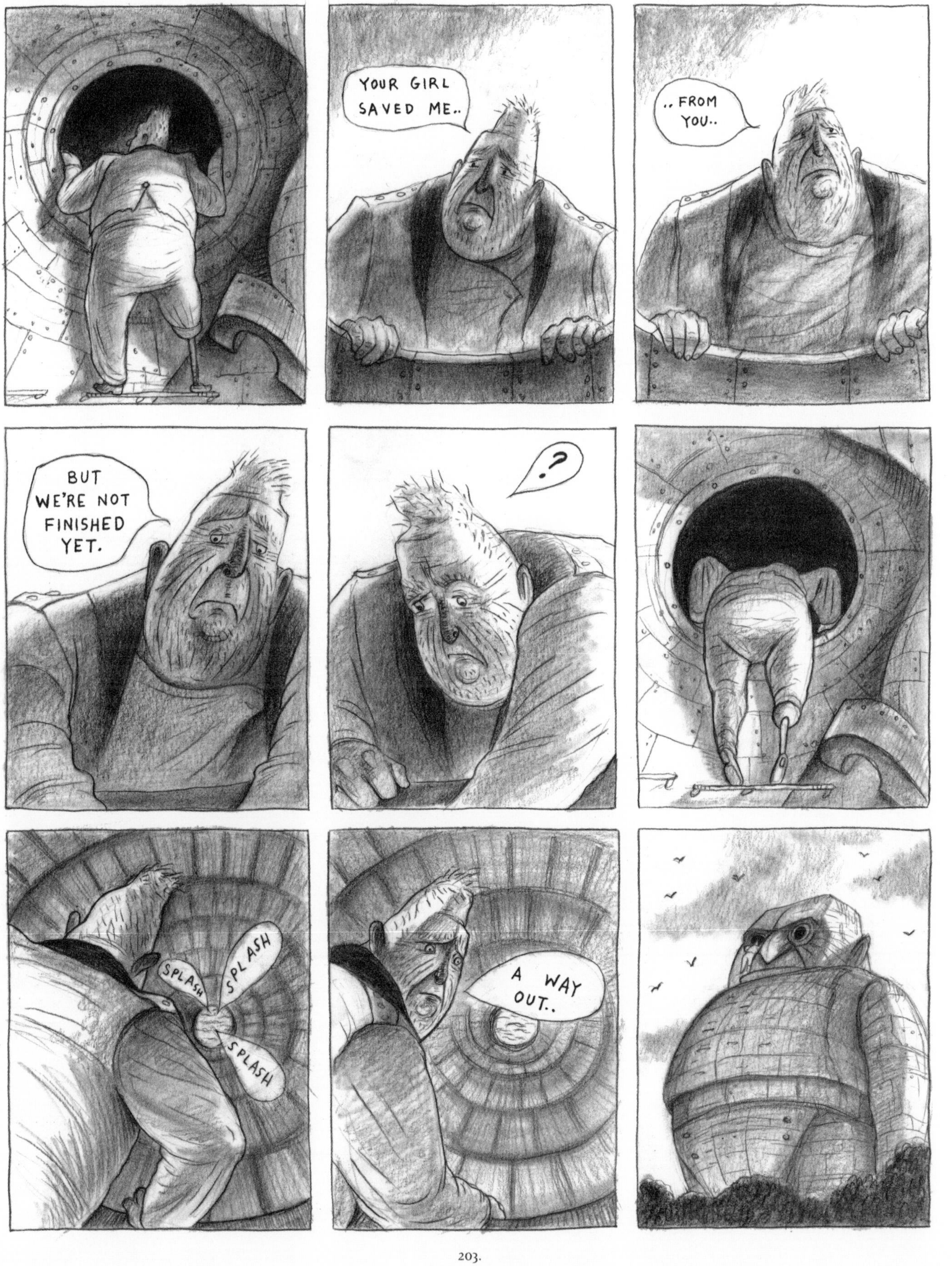
YOUR GIRL SAVED ME..
.. FROM YOU..
BUT WE'RE NOT FINISHED YET.
?
SPLASH
SPLASH
SPLASH
A WAY OUT..

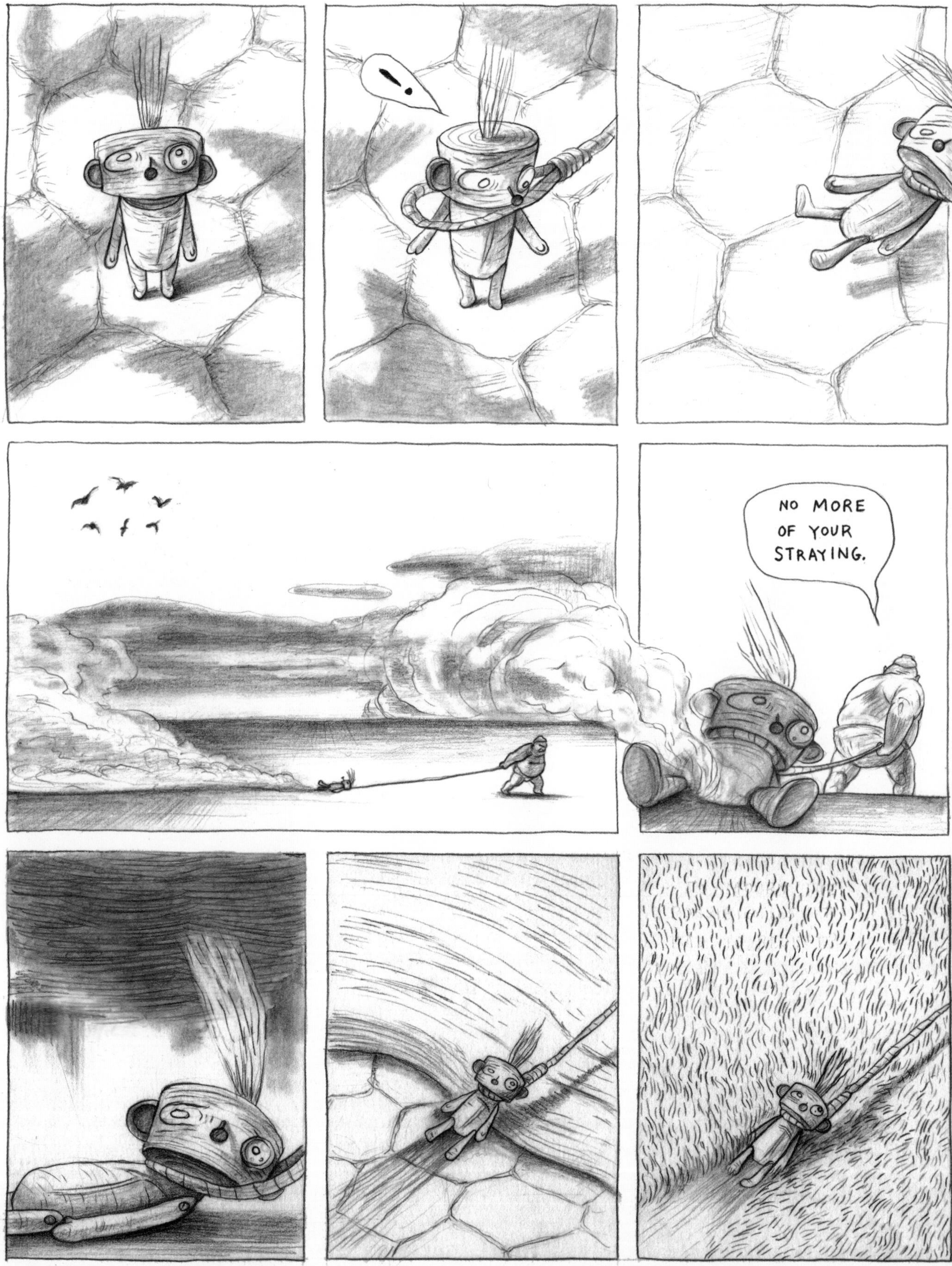
!
NO MORE OF YOUR STRAYING.

YOU FLOAT. TAKE ME ACROSS THE RIVER.

I DISTRUST THE WATER SO MAKE IT QUICK.

FAIL ME AND I WILL BURN YOU TO OBLIVION.

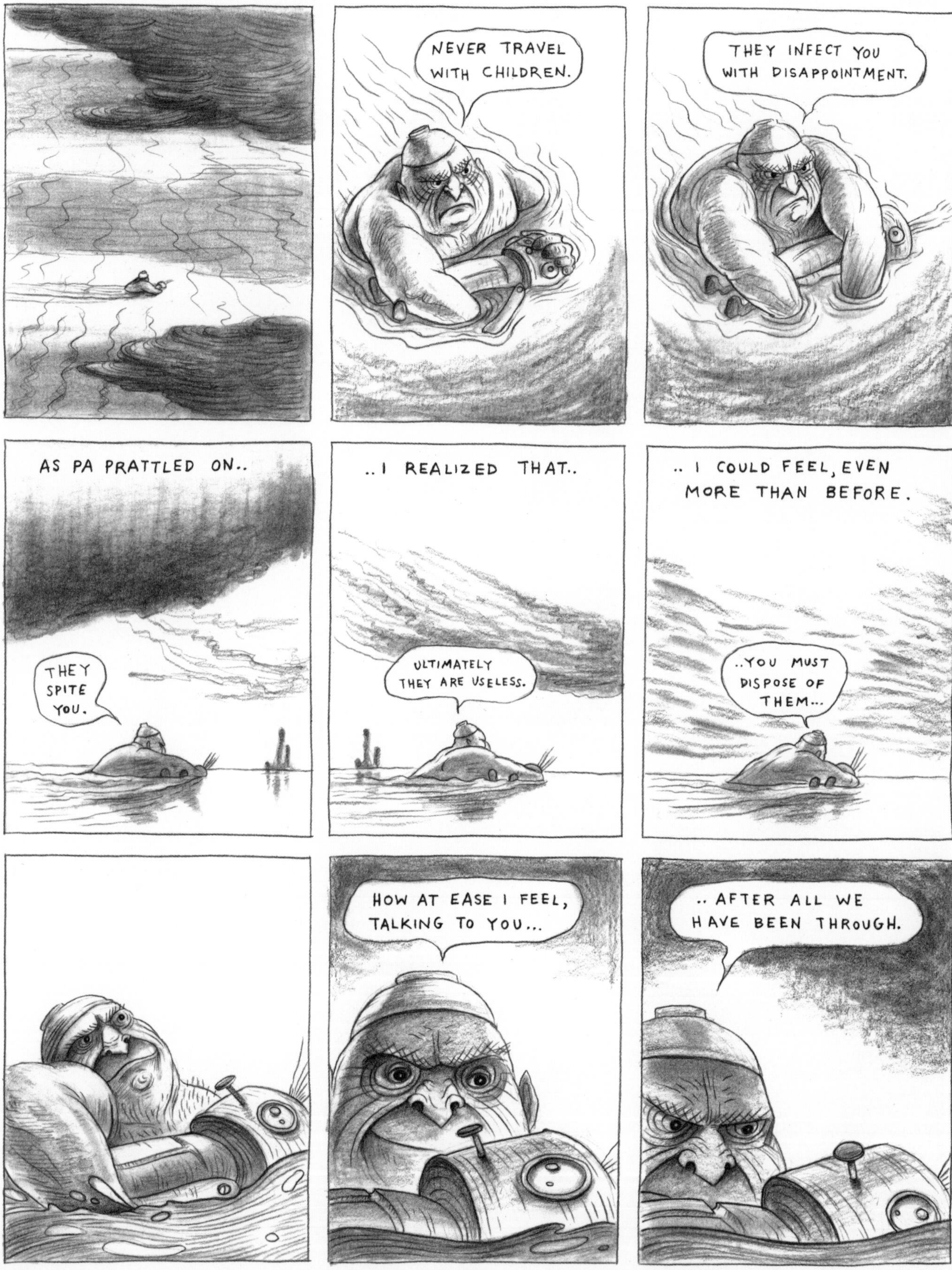
NEVER TRAVEL WITH CHILDREN.
THEY INFECT YOU WITH DISAPPOINTMENT.
AS PA PRATTLED ON..
THEY SPITE YOU.
..I REALIZED THAT..
ULTIMATELY THEY ARE USELESS.
.. I COULD FEEL, EVEN MORE THAN BEFORE.
..YOU MUST DISPOSE OF THEM...
HOW AT EASE I FEEL, TALKING TO YOU...
.. AFTER ALL WE HAVE BEEN THROUGH.

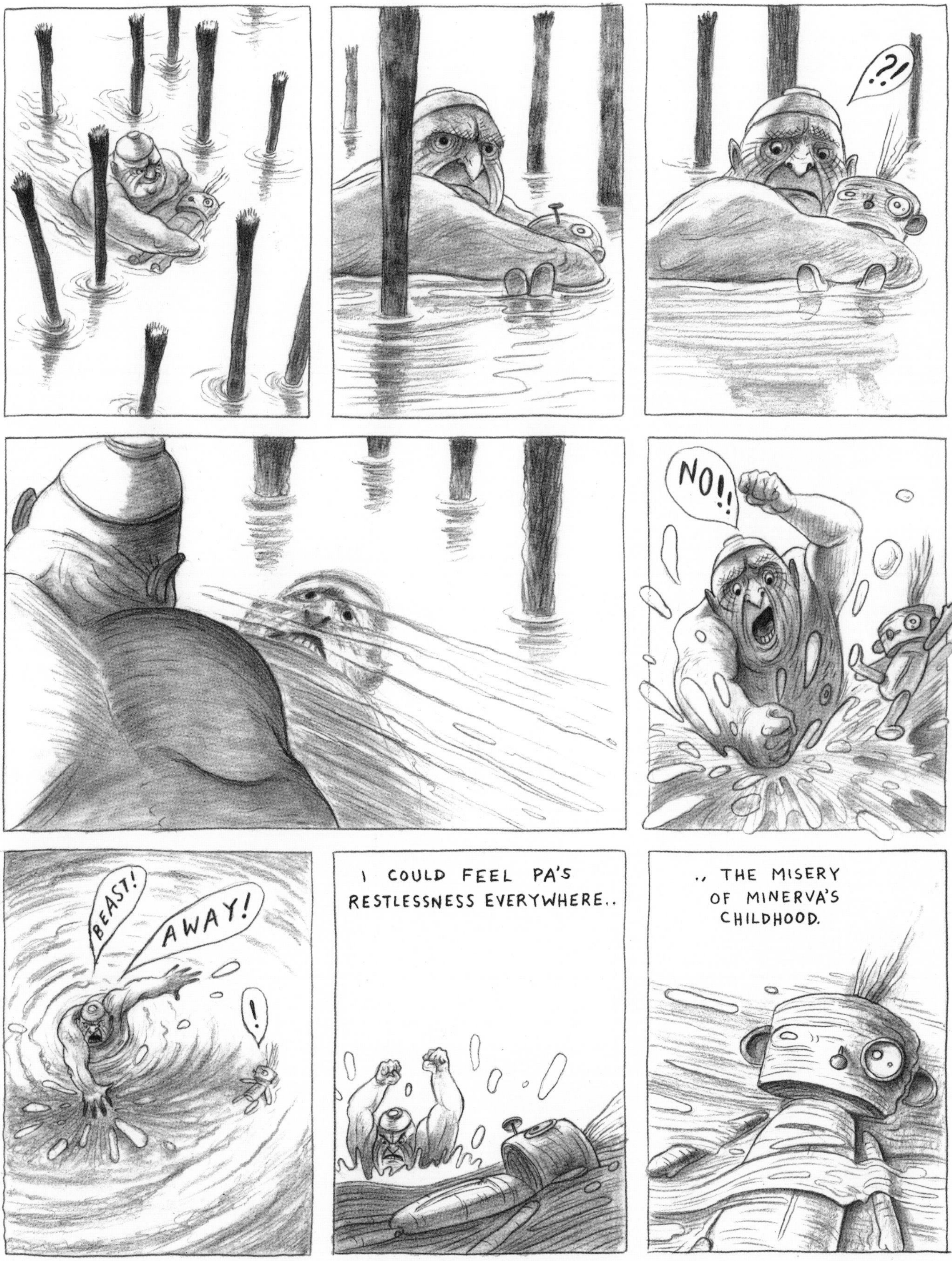

?!
NO!!
BEAST!
AWAY!
!
I COULD FEEL PA'S RESTLESSNESS EVERYWHERE..
.. THE MISERY OF MINERVA'S CHILDHOOD.

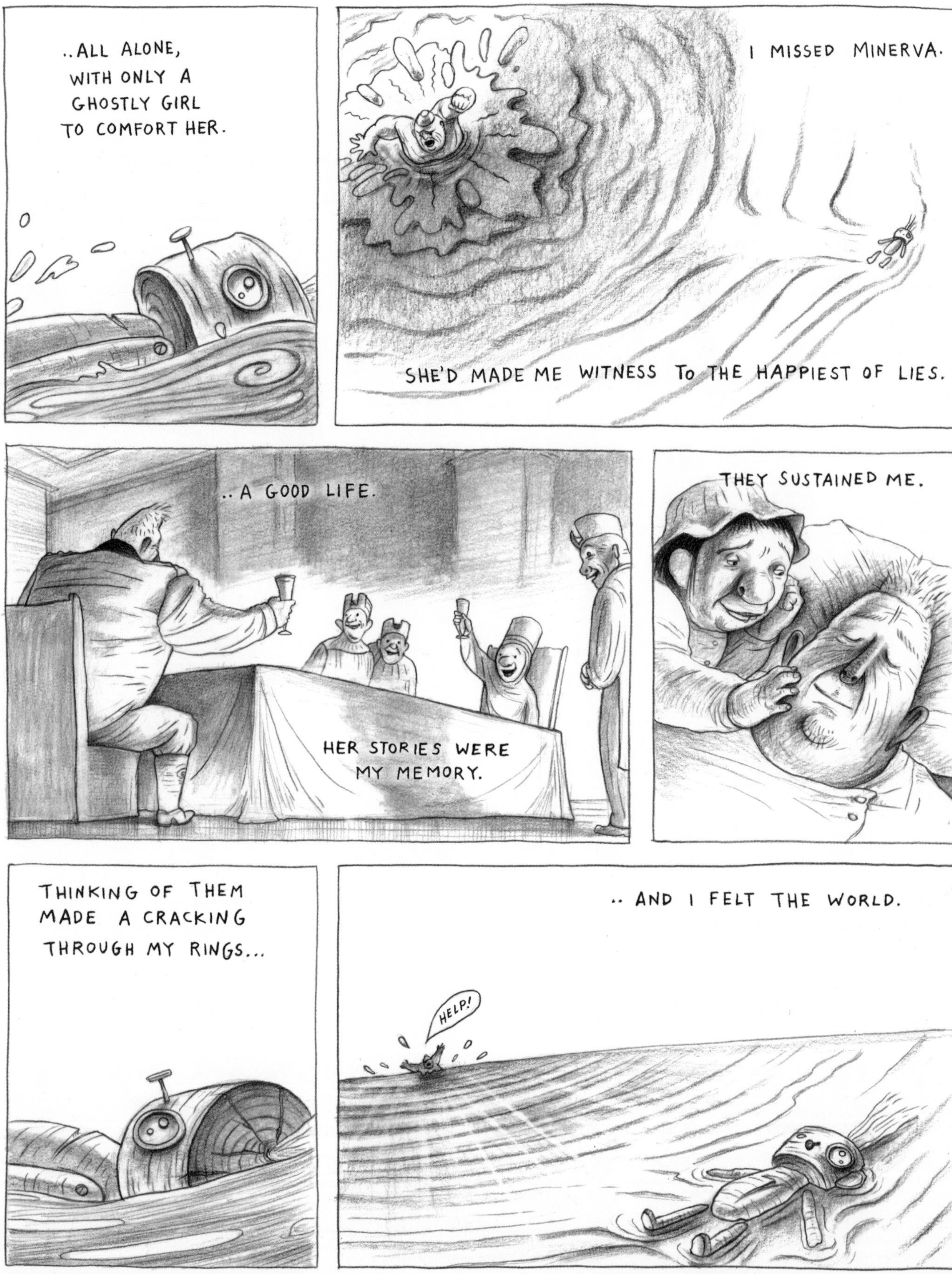
..ALL ALONE, WITH ONLY A GHOSTLY GIRL TO COMFORT HER.
I MISSED MINERVA.
SHE'D MADE ME WITNESS TO THE HAPPIEST OF LIES.
..A GOOD LIFE.
HER STORIES WERE MY MEMORY.
THEY SUSTAINED ME.
THINKING OF THEM MADE A CRACKING THROUGH MY RINGS...
.. AND I FELT THE WORLD.
HELP!

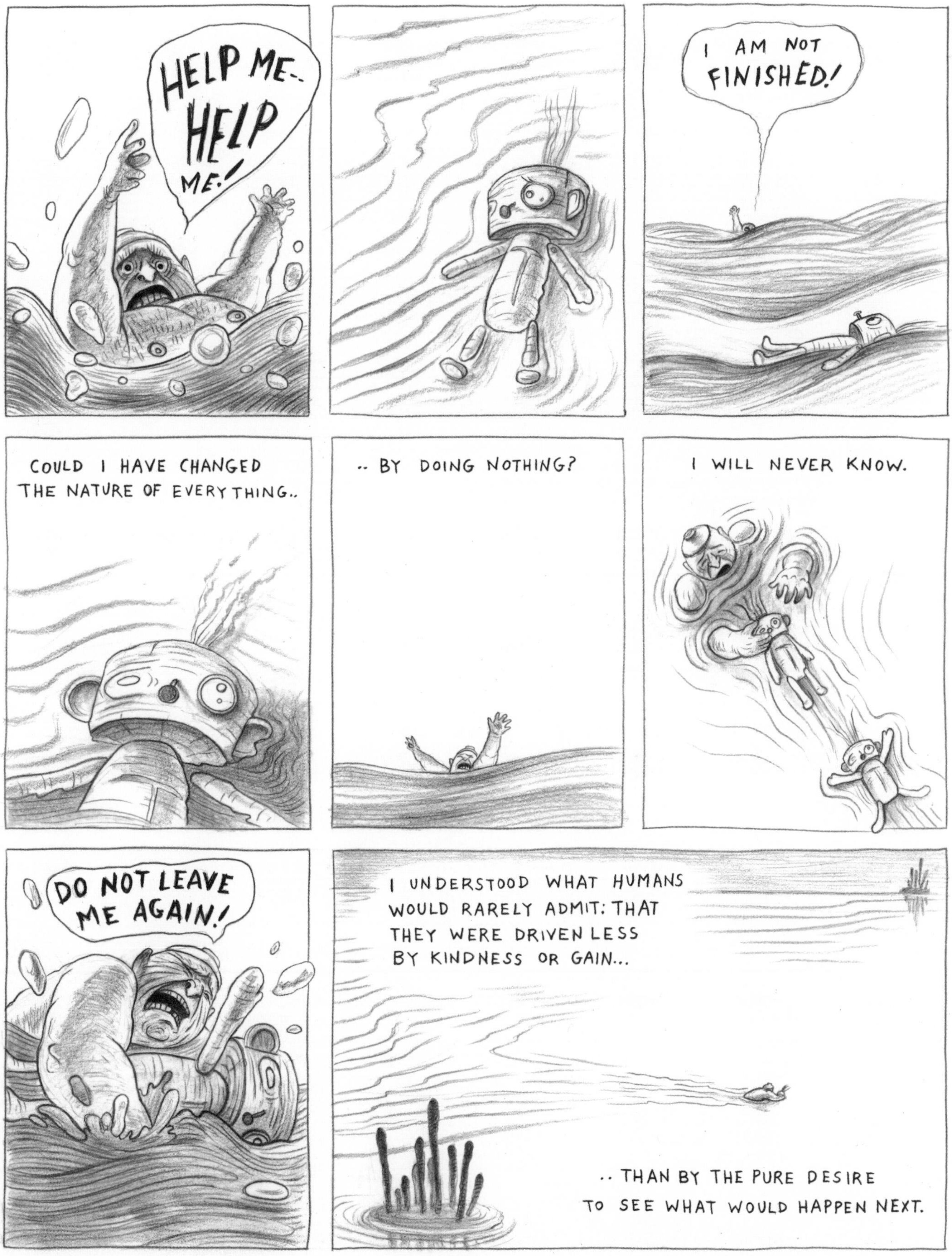
HELP ME-- HELP ME!
I AM NOT FINISHED!
COULD I HAVE CHANGED THE NATURE OF EVERYTHING..
.. BY DOING NOTHING?
I WILL NEVER KNOW.
DO NOT LEAVE ME AGAIN!
I UNDERSTOOD WHAT HUMANS WOULD RARELY ADMIT: THAT THEY WERE DRIVEN LESS BY KINDNESS OR GAIN...
.. THAN BY THE PURE DESIRE TO SEE WHAT WOULD HAPPEN NEXT.

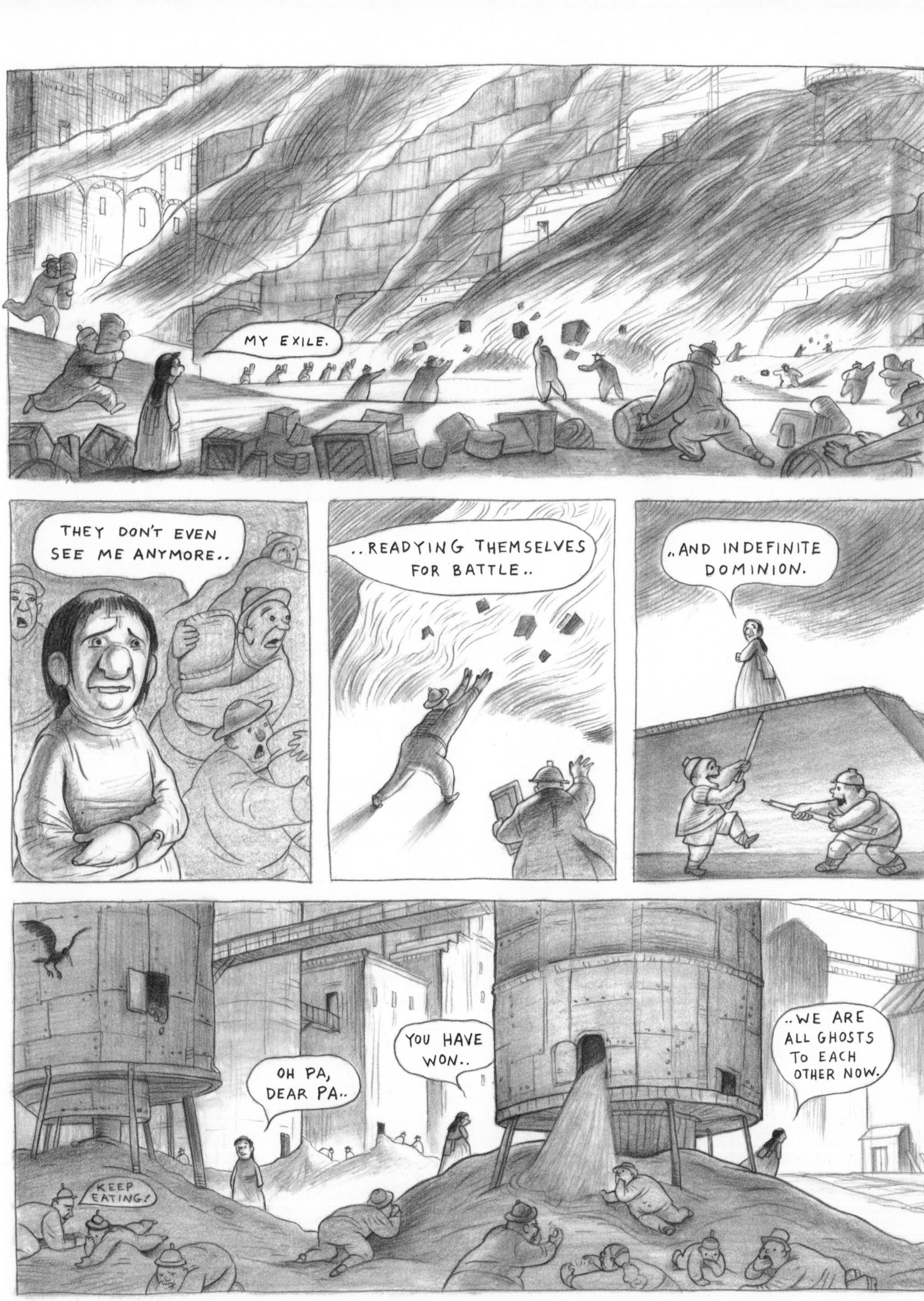
MY EXILE.
THEY DON'T EVEN SEE ME ANYMORE..
..READYING THEMSELVES FOR BATTLE..
..AND INDEFINITE DOMINION.
KEEP EATING!
OH PA, DEAR PA..
YOU HAVE WON..
..WE ARE ALL GHOSTS TO EACH OTHER NOW.

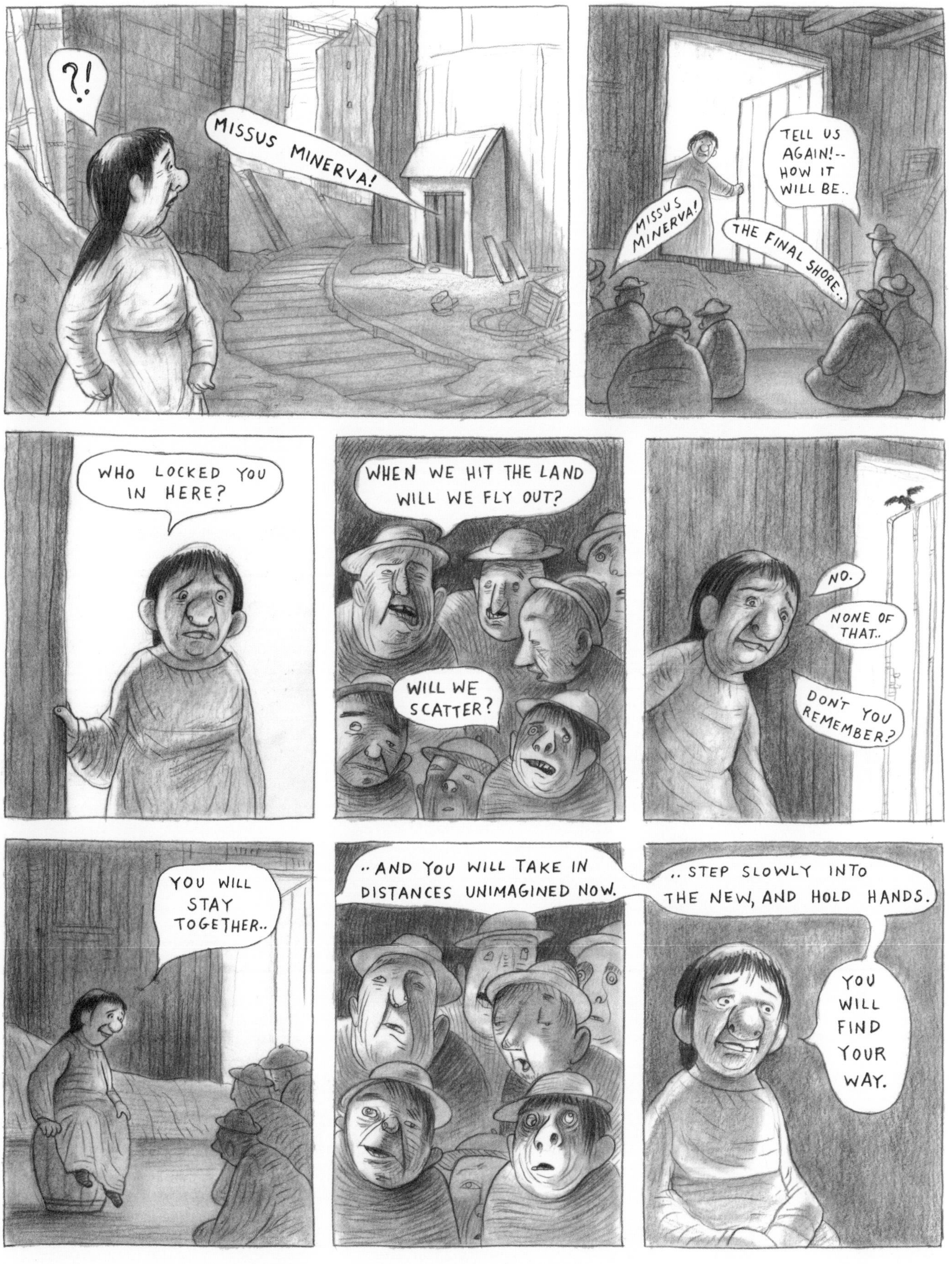
?!
MISSUS MINERVA!
MISSUS MINERVA!
TELL US AGAIN! -- HOW IT WILL BE..
THE FINAL SHORE..
WHO LOCKED YOU IN HERE?
WHEN WE HIT THE LAND WILL WE FLY OUT?
WILL WE SCATTER?
NO.
NONE OF THAT..
DON'T YOU REMEMBER?
YOU WILL STAY TOGETHER..
.. AND YOU WILL TAKE IN DISTANCES UNIMAGINED NOW.
.. STEP SLOWLY INTO THE NEW, AND HOLD HANDS.
YOU WILL FIND YOUR WAY.

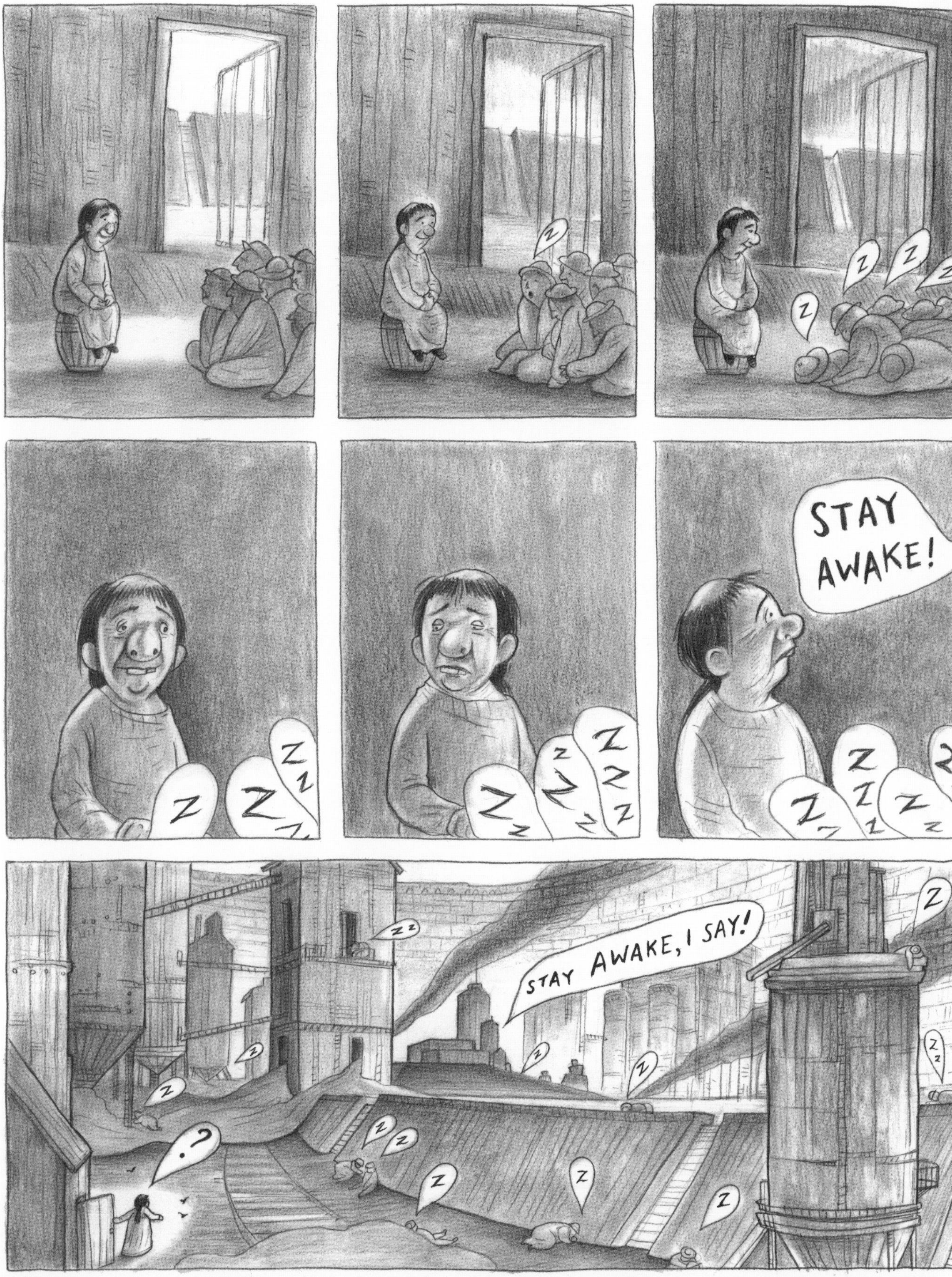
STAY AWAKE!
STAY AWAKE, I SAY!

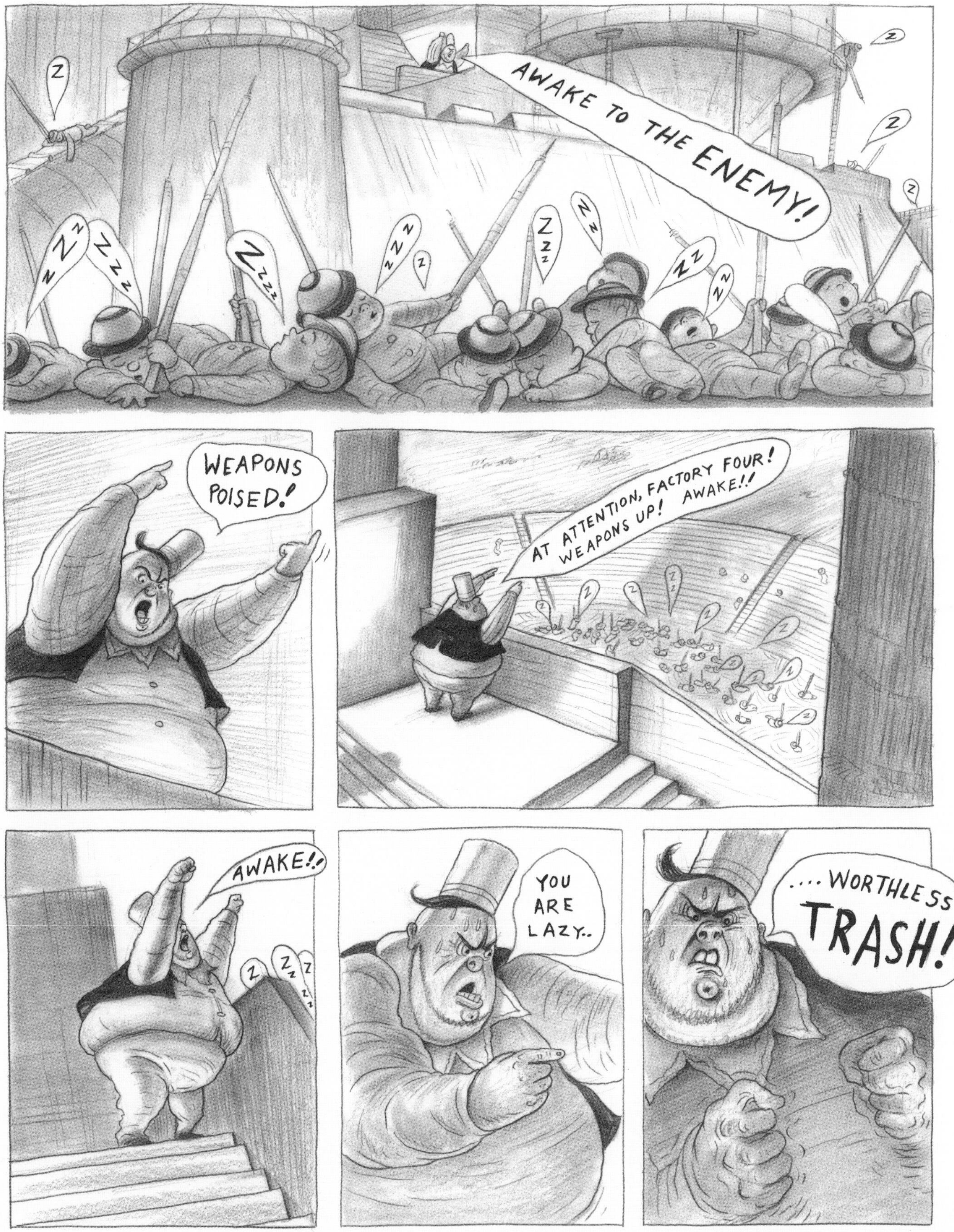
Z
Z
Z
Z
ZZZ
ZZZ
Zzzzz
ZZZ
Z
ZZZ
ZZ
ZZ
ZZ
AWAKE TO THE ENEMY!
WEAPONS POISED!
AT ATTENTION, FACTORY FOUR! WEAPONS UP! AWAKE!!
AWAKE!!
Z
ZZZZ
YOU ARE LAZY..
....WORTHLESS TRASH!

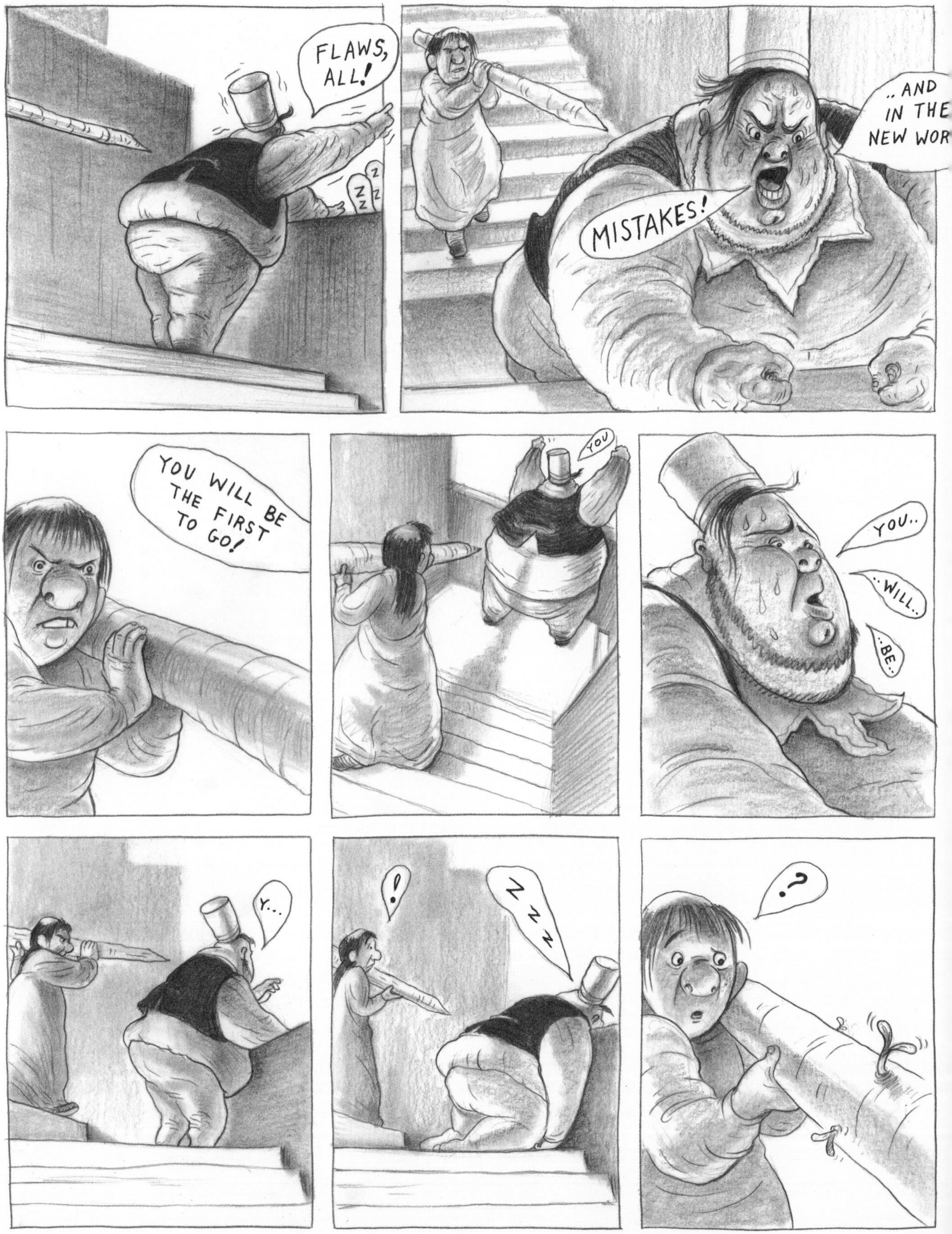
FLAWS, ALL!
ZZZ
MISTAKES!
..AND IN THE NEW WOR
YOU WILL BE THE FIRST TO GO!
YOU
YOU..
..WILL..
..BE..
Y...
!
Z Z Z
?

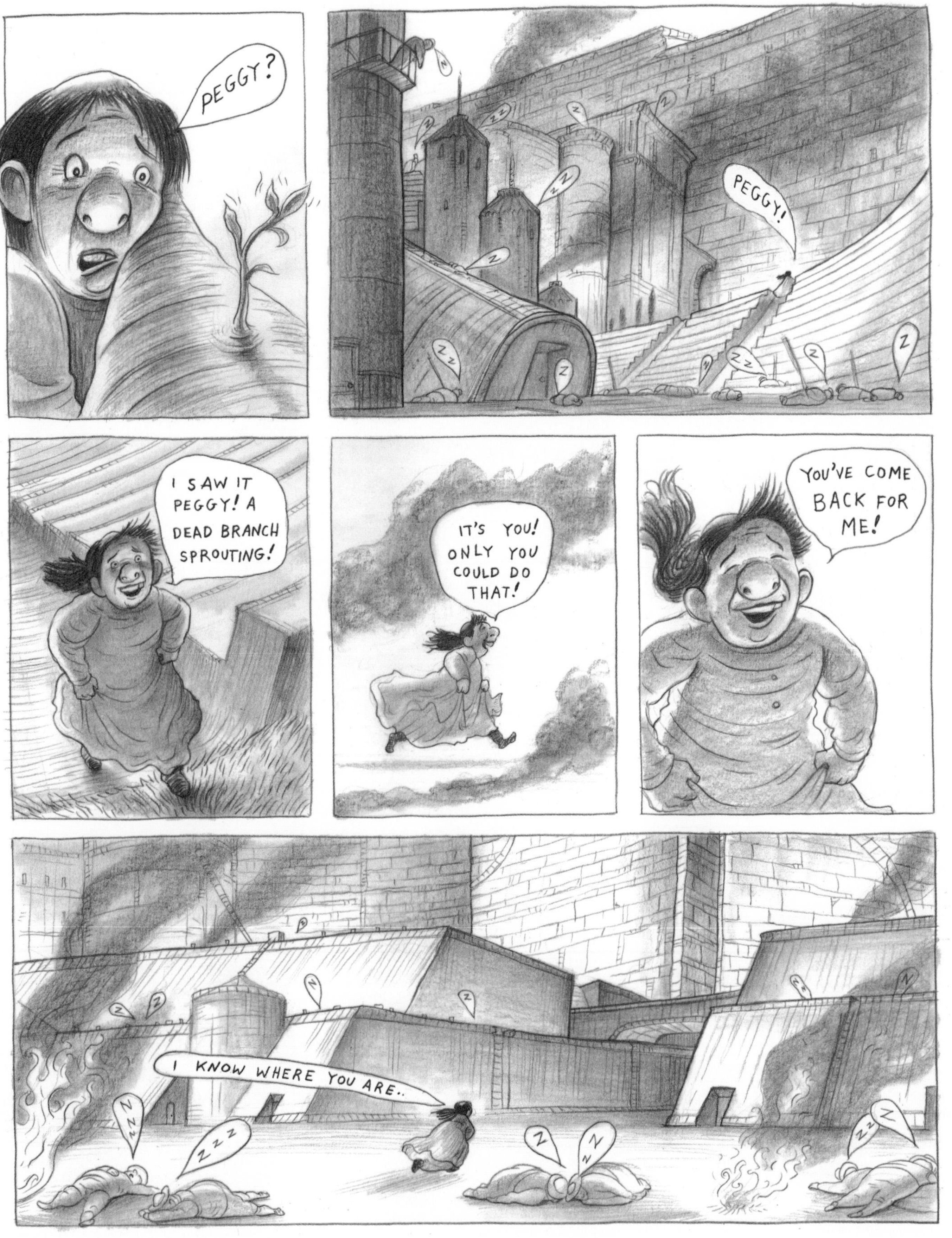
PEGGY?
PEGGY!
I SAW IT PEGGY! A DEAD BRANCH SPROUTING!
IT'S YOU! ONLY YOU COULD DO THAT!
YOU'VE COME BACK FOR ME!
I KNOW WHERE YOU ARE..

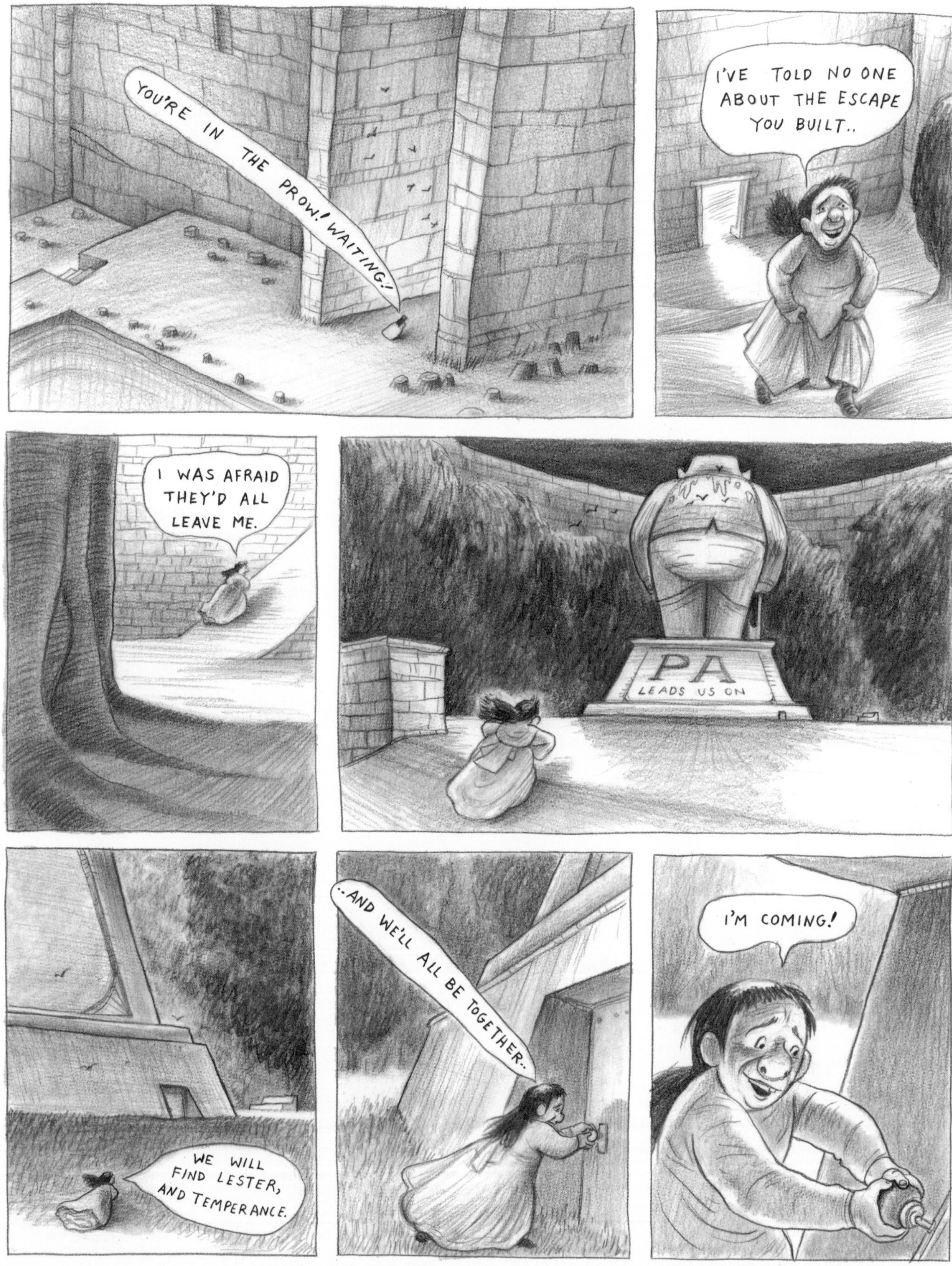
YOU'RE IN THE PROW! WAITING..
I'VE TOLD NO ONE ABOUT THE ESCAPE YOU BUILT..
I WAS AFRAID THEY'D ALL LEAVE ME.
PA
LEADS US ON
WE WILL FIND LESTER, AND TEMPERANCE.
..AND WE'LL ALL BE TOGETHER..
I'M COMING!

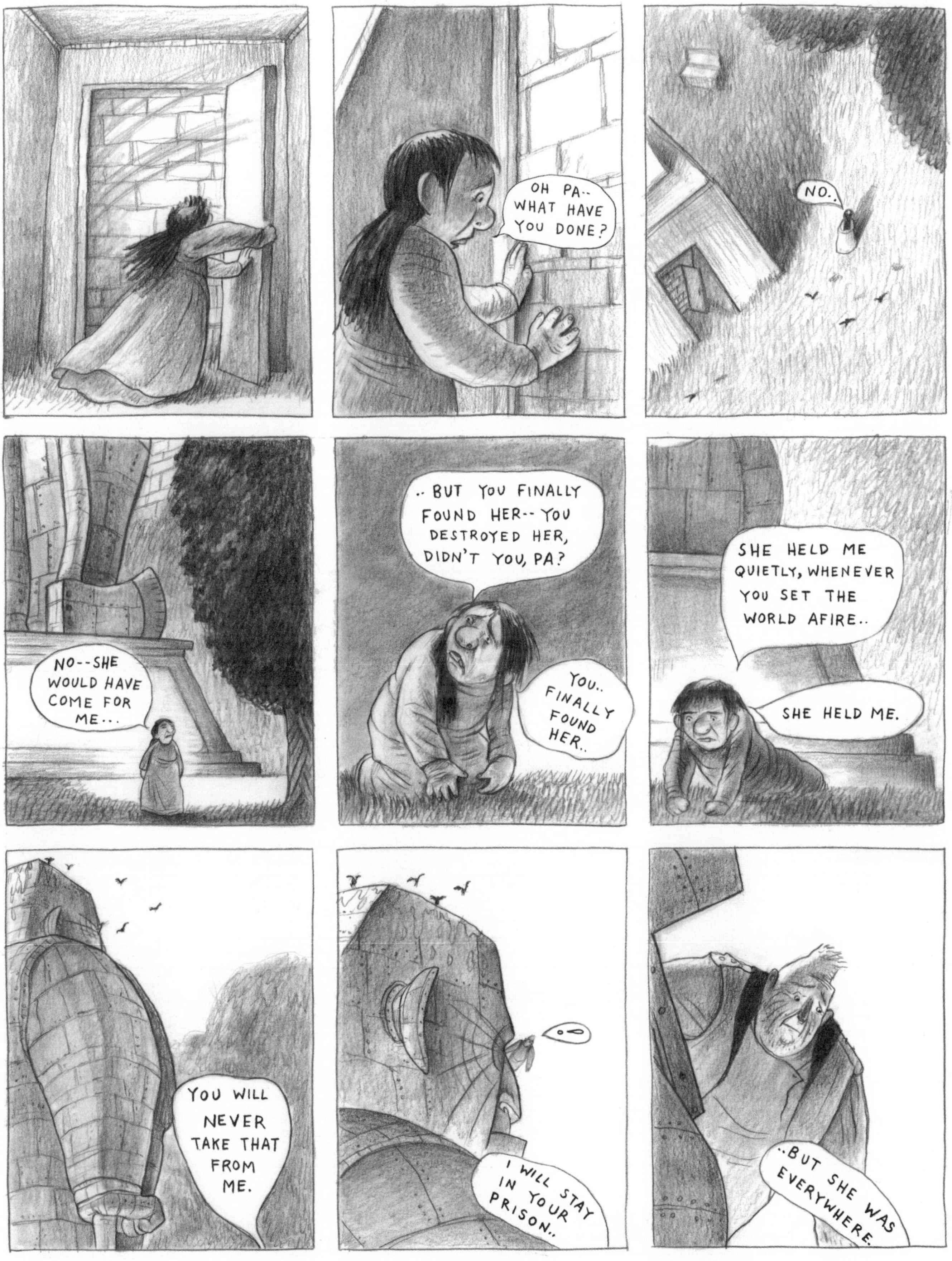
OH PA-- WHAT HAVE YOU DONE?
NO..
NO--SHE WOULD HAVE COME FOR ME...
.. BUT YOU FINALLY FOUND HER-- YOU DESTROYED HER, DIDN'T YOU, PA?
YOU.. FINALLY FOUND HER..
SHE HELD ME QUIETLY, WHENEVER YOU SET THE WORLD AFIRE..
SHE HELD ME.
YOU WILL NEVER TAKE THAT FROM ME.
I WILL STAY IN YOUR PRISON..
..BUT SHE WAS EVERYWHERE.

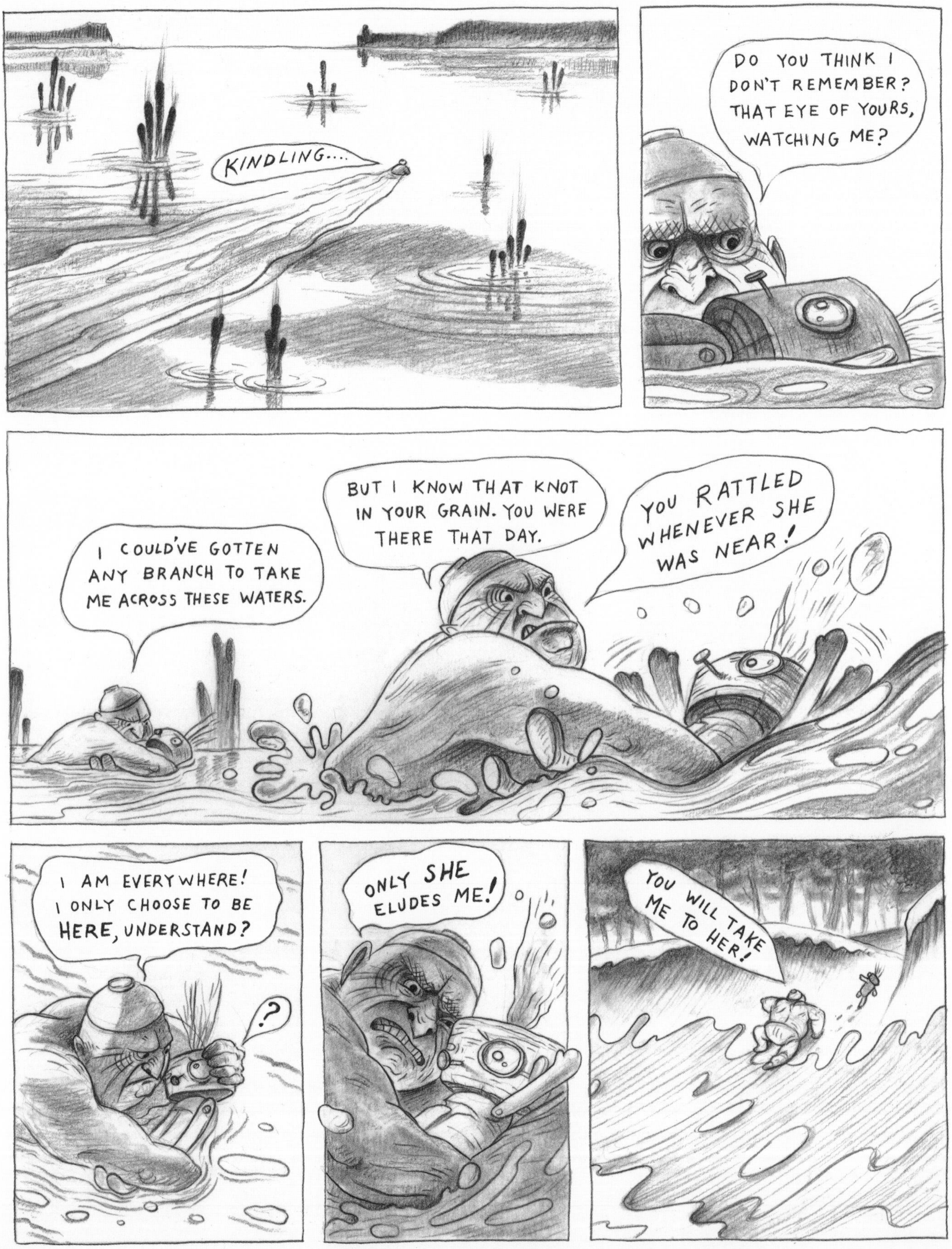
KINDLING....
DO YOU THINK I DON'T REMEMBER? THAT EYE OF YOURS, WATCHING ME?
I COULD'VE GOTTEN ANY BRANCH TO TAKE ME ACROSS THESE WATERS.
BUT I KNOW THAT KNOT IN YOUR GRAIN. YOU WERE THERE THAT DAY.
YOU RATTLED WHENEVER SHE WAS NEAR!
I AM EVERYWHERE! I ONLY CHOOSE TO BE HERE, UNDERSTAND?
?
ONLY SHE ELUDES ME!
YOU WILL TAKE ME TO HER!

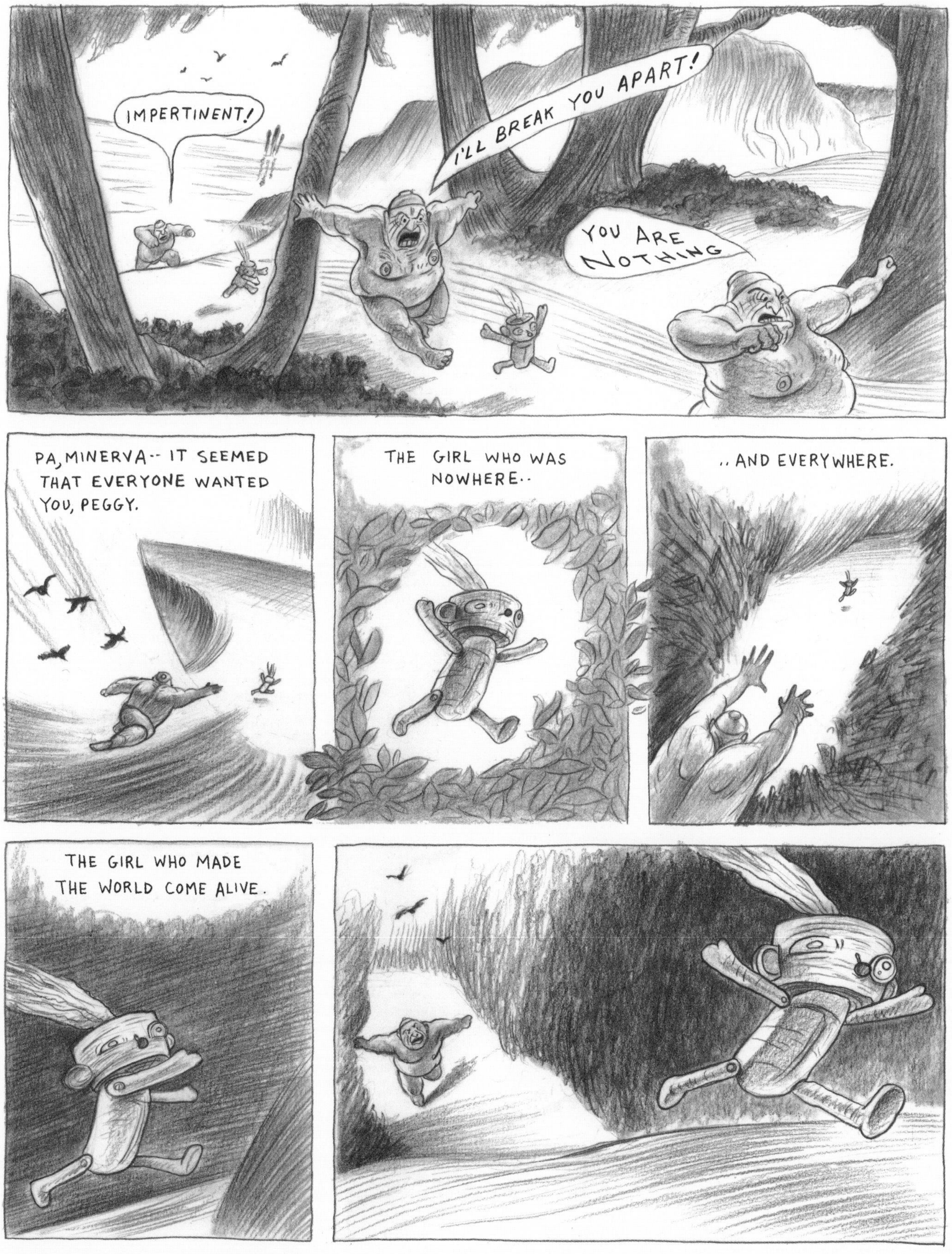
IMPERTINENT!
I'LL BREAK YOU APART!
YOU ARE NOTHING
PA, MINERVA-- IT SEEMED THAT EVERYONE WANTED YOU, PEGGY.
THE GIRL WHO WAS NOWHERE..
.. AND EVERYWHERE.
THE GIRL WHO MADE THE WORLD COME ALIVE.

I RECOGNIZED THIS QUARRY..

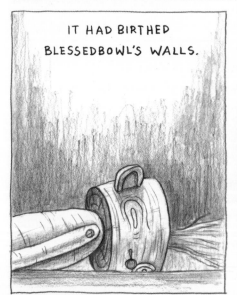

IT HAD BIRTHED BLESSEDBOWL'S WALLS.

I KNEW THE STONES..

.. AND LOVED THEM.

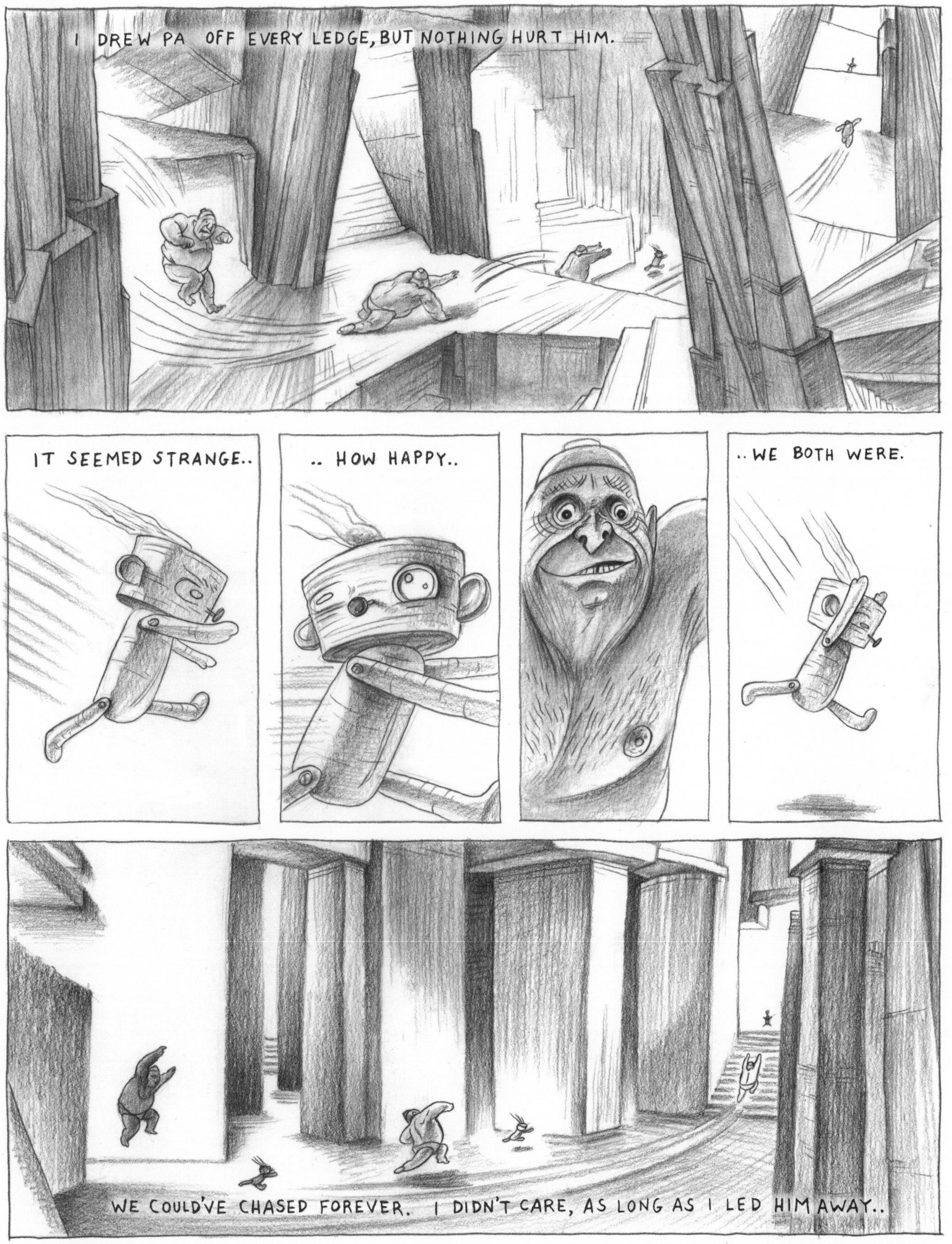
I DREW PA OFF EVERY LEDGE, BUT NOTHING HURT HIM.
IT SEEMED STRANGE..
.. HOW HAPPY..
..WE BOTH WERE.
WE COULD'VE CHASED FOREVER. I DIDN'T CARE, AS LONG AS I LED HIM AWAY..

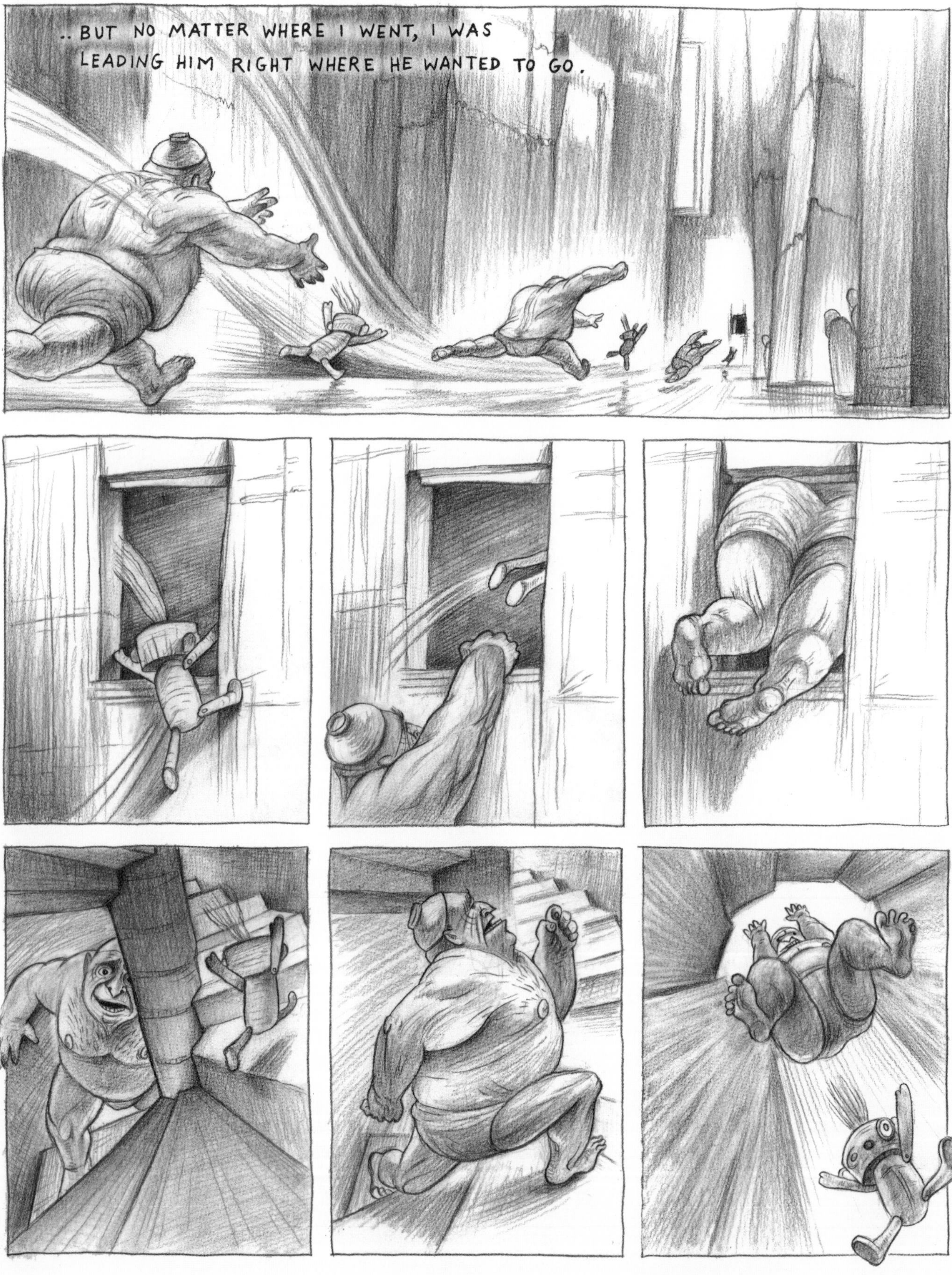
.. BUT NO MATTER WHERE I WENT, I WAS LEADING HIM RIGHT WHERE HE WANTED TO GO.

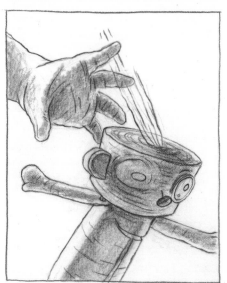

.. LEADING HIM TO YOU.

MY GIRL!

MY GIRL!

PEGGY!
?!

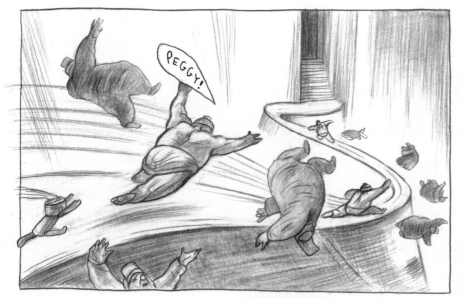

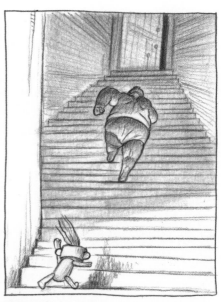

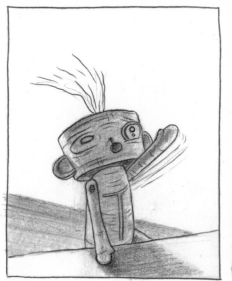

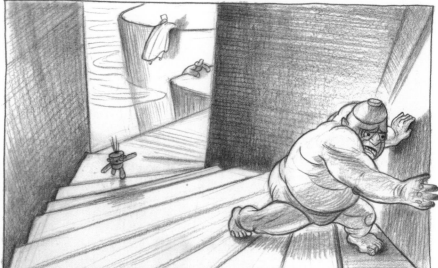

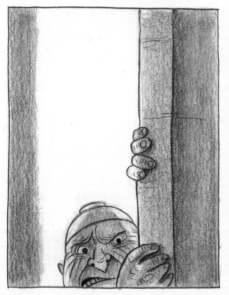

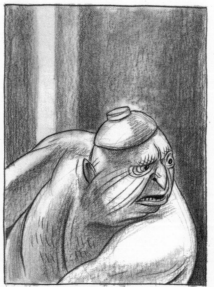

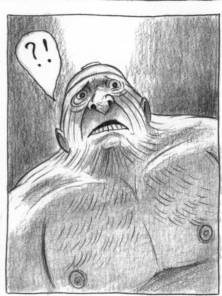

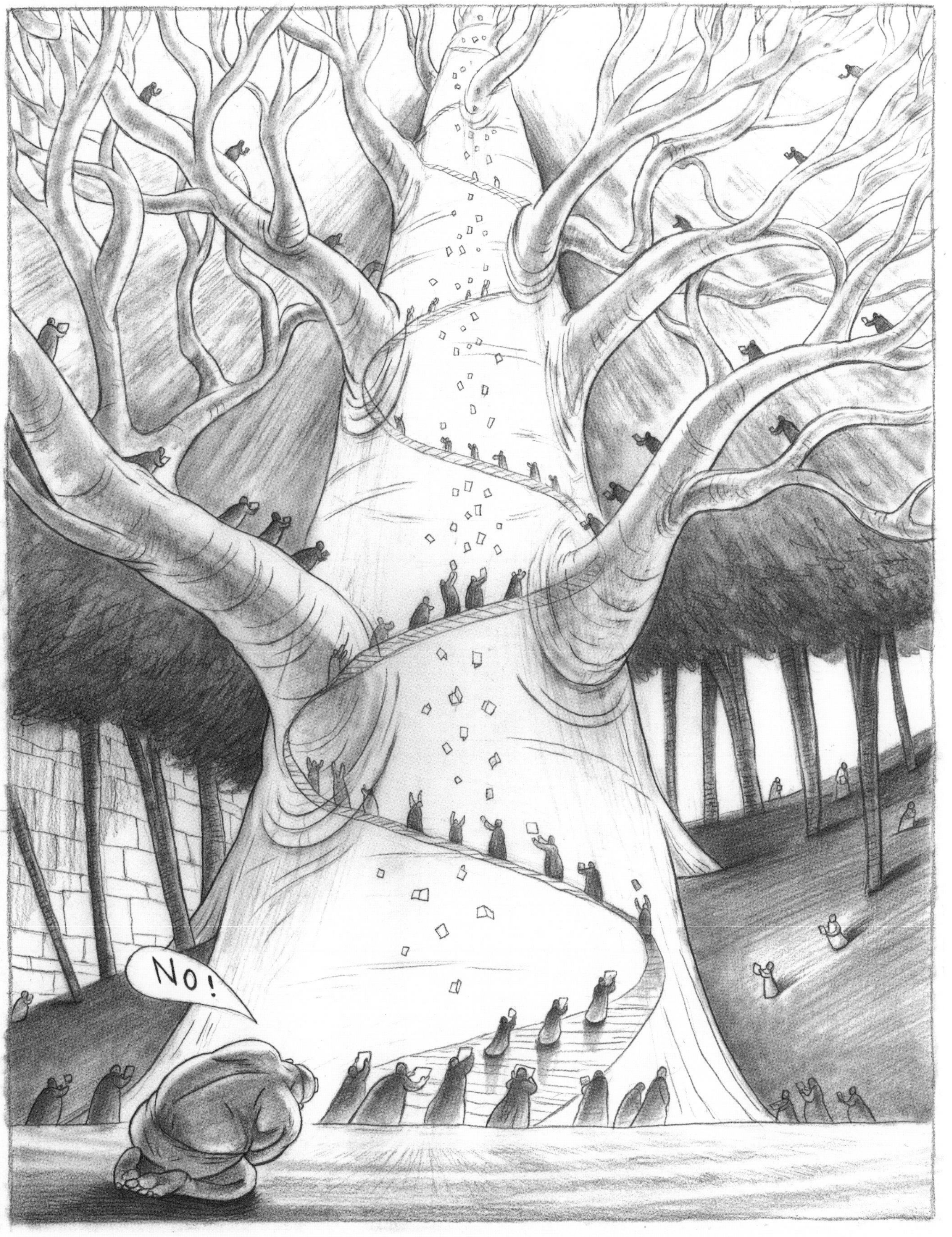
No!

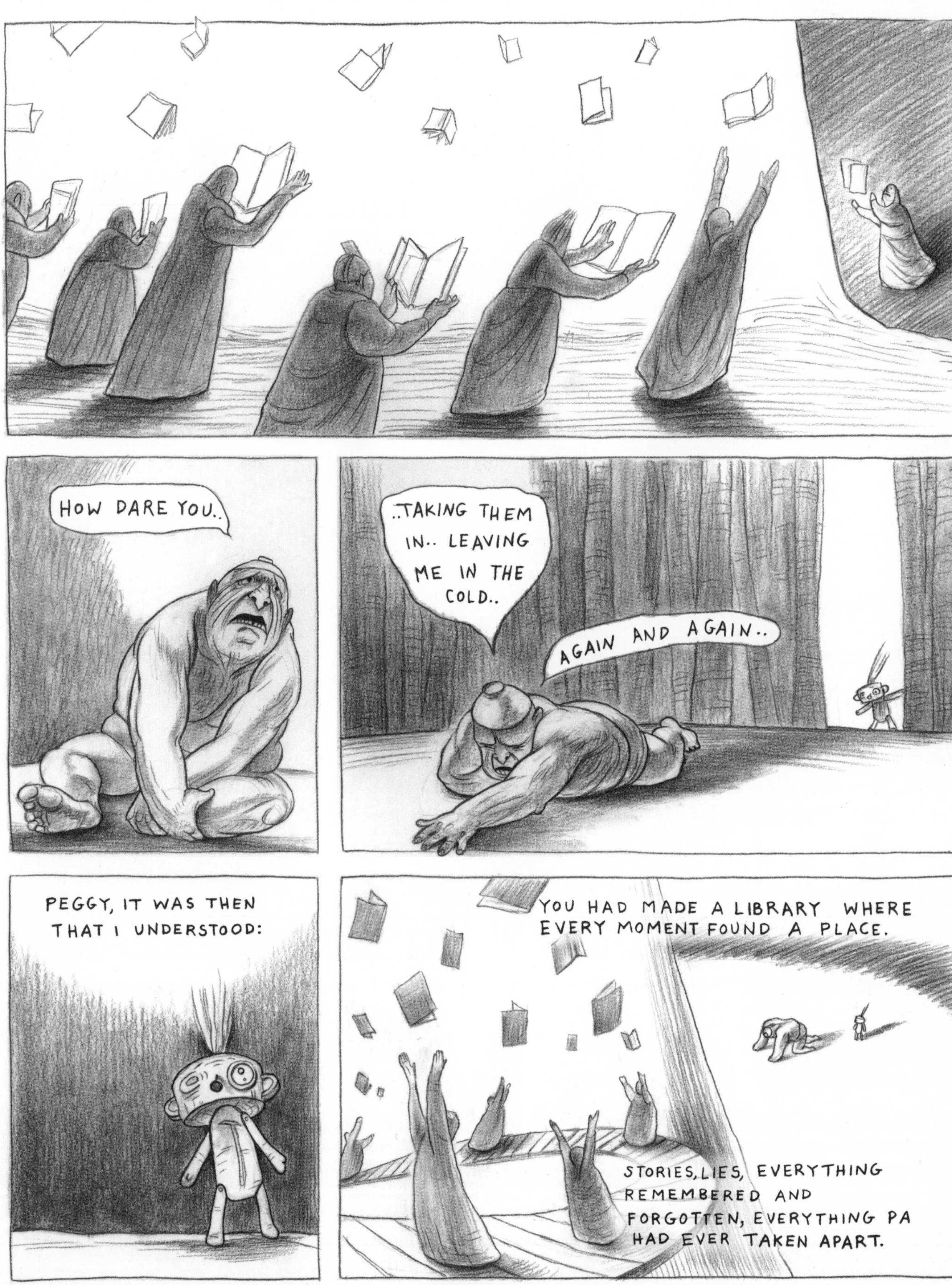
HOW DARE YOU..
..TAKING THEM IN.. LEAVING ME IN THE COLD..
AGAIN AND AGAIN..
PEGGY, IT WAS THEN THAT I UNDERSTOOD:
YOU HAD MADE A LIBRARY WHERE EVERY MOMENT FOUND A PLACE.
STORIES, LIES, EVERYTHING REMEMBERED AND FORGOTTEN, EVERYTHING PA HAD EVER TAKEN APART.

YOU TOOK IN EVERY LAST VAGABOND, LETTING IT FLOAT OUT OF REACH, TO RE-ROOT ITSELF IN SOME DISTANT SOIL.

TO PA IT WAS AN UNBEARABLE MESS.

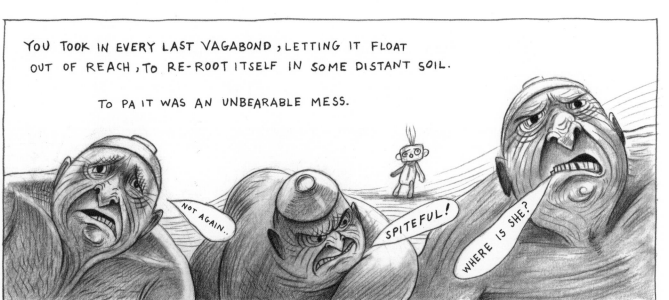

NOT AGAIN..

SPITEFUL!

WHERE IS SHE?

SHE IS MINE!

HELP ME.

OH PEGGY..

WHY WAS I SO HOT-HEADED?

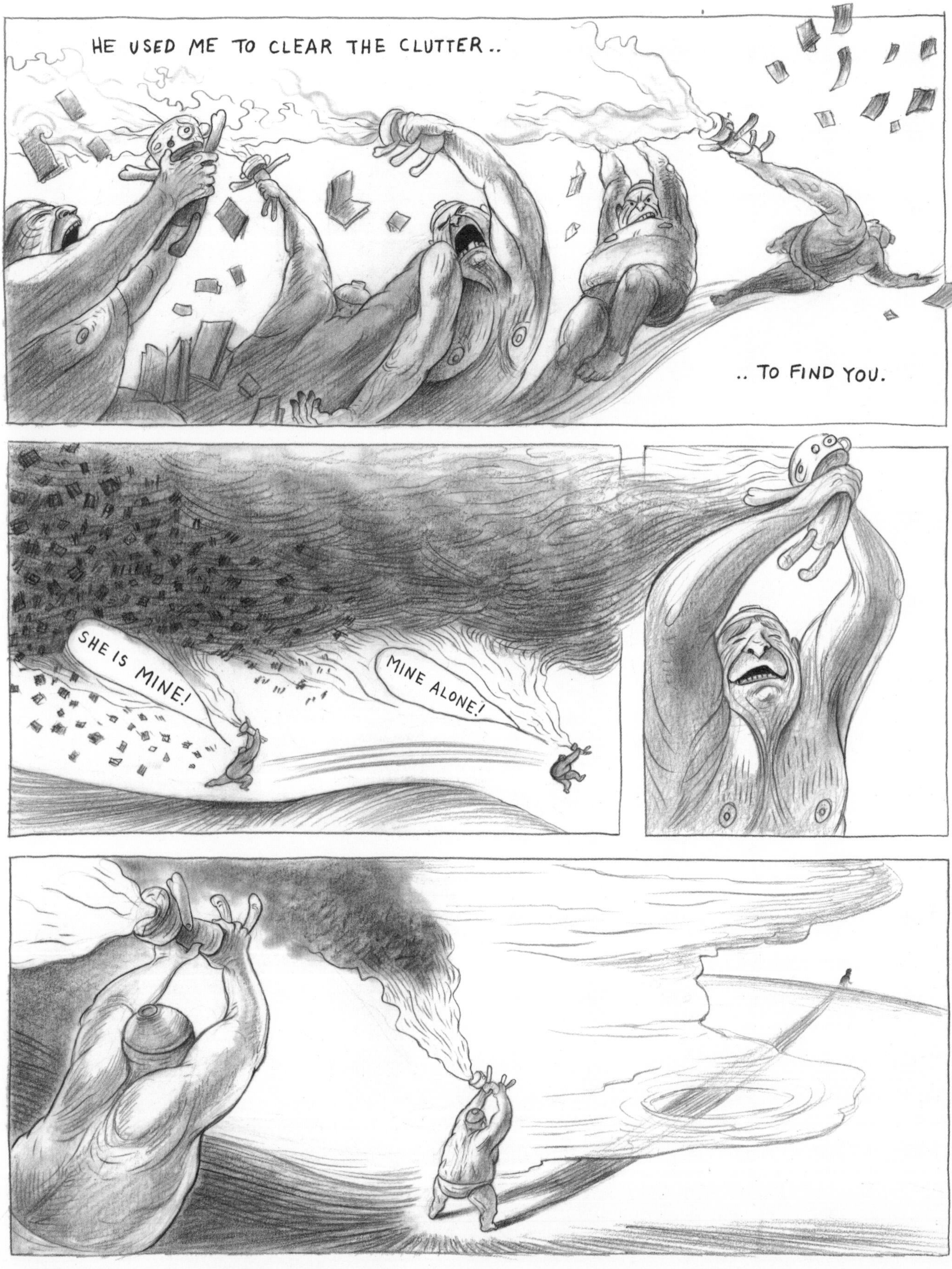
HE USED ME TO CLEAR THE CLUTTER..
.. TO FIND YOU.
SHE IS MINE!
MINE ALONE!

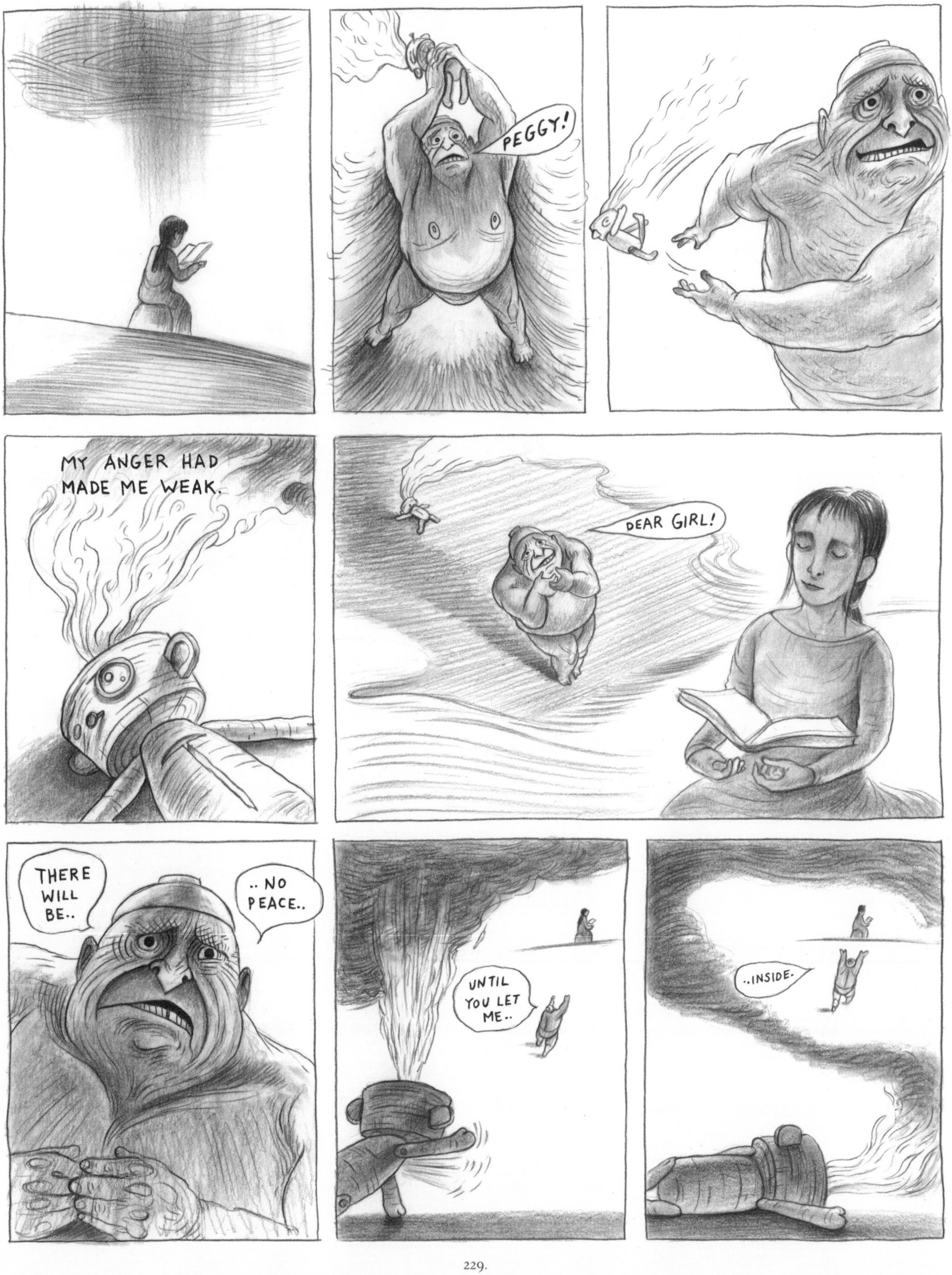
PEGGY!
MY ANGER HAD MADE ME WEAK.
DEAR GIRL!
THERE WILL BE..
.. NO PEACE..
UNTIL YOU LET ME..
..INSIDE.

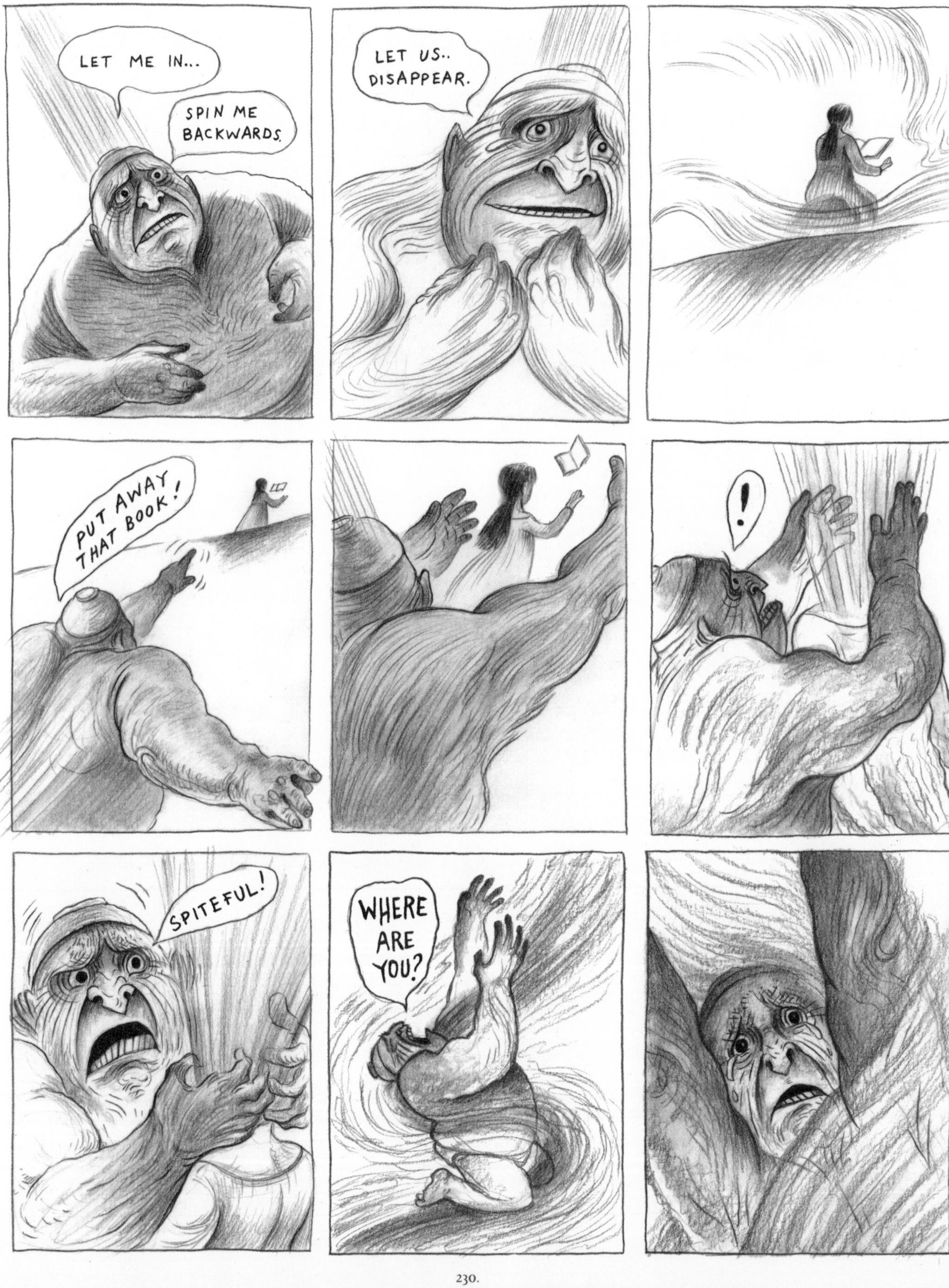
LET ME IN...
SPIN ME BACKWARDS.
LET US.. DISAPPEAR.
PUT AWAY THAT BOOK!
!
SPITEFUL!
WHERE ARE YOU?

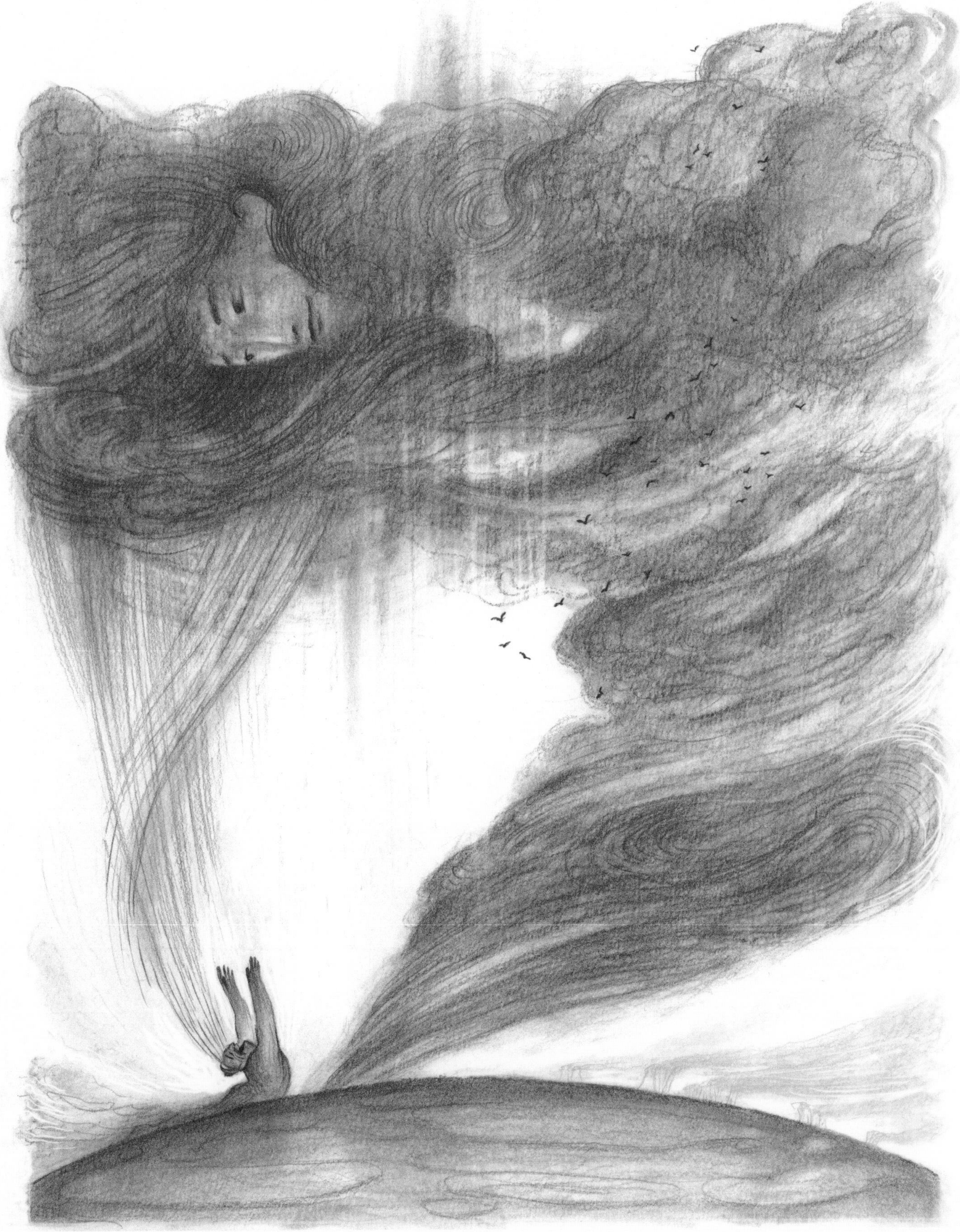

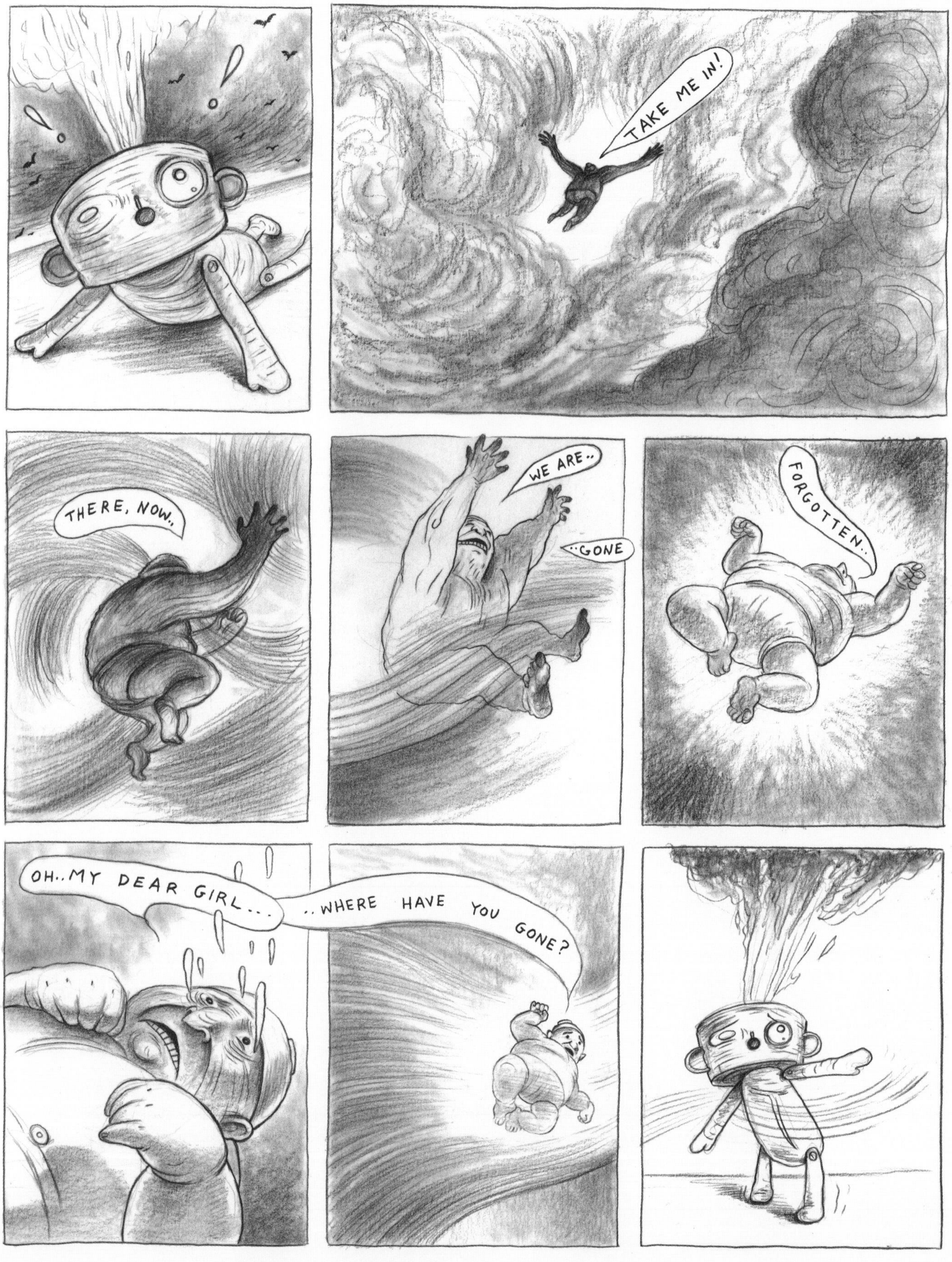
TAKE ME IN!
THERE, NOW..
WE ARE..
..GONE
FORGOTTEN..
OH..MY DEAR GIRL...
..WHERE HAVE YOU GONE?

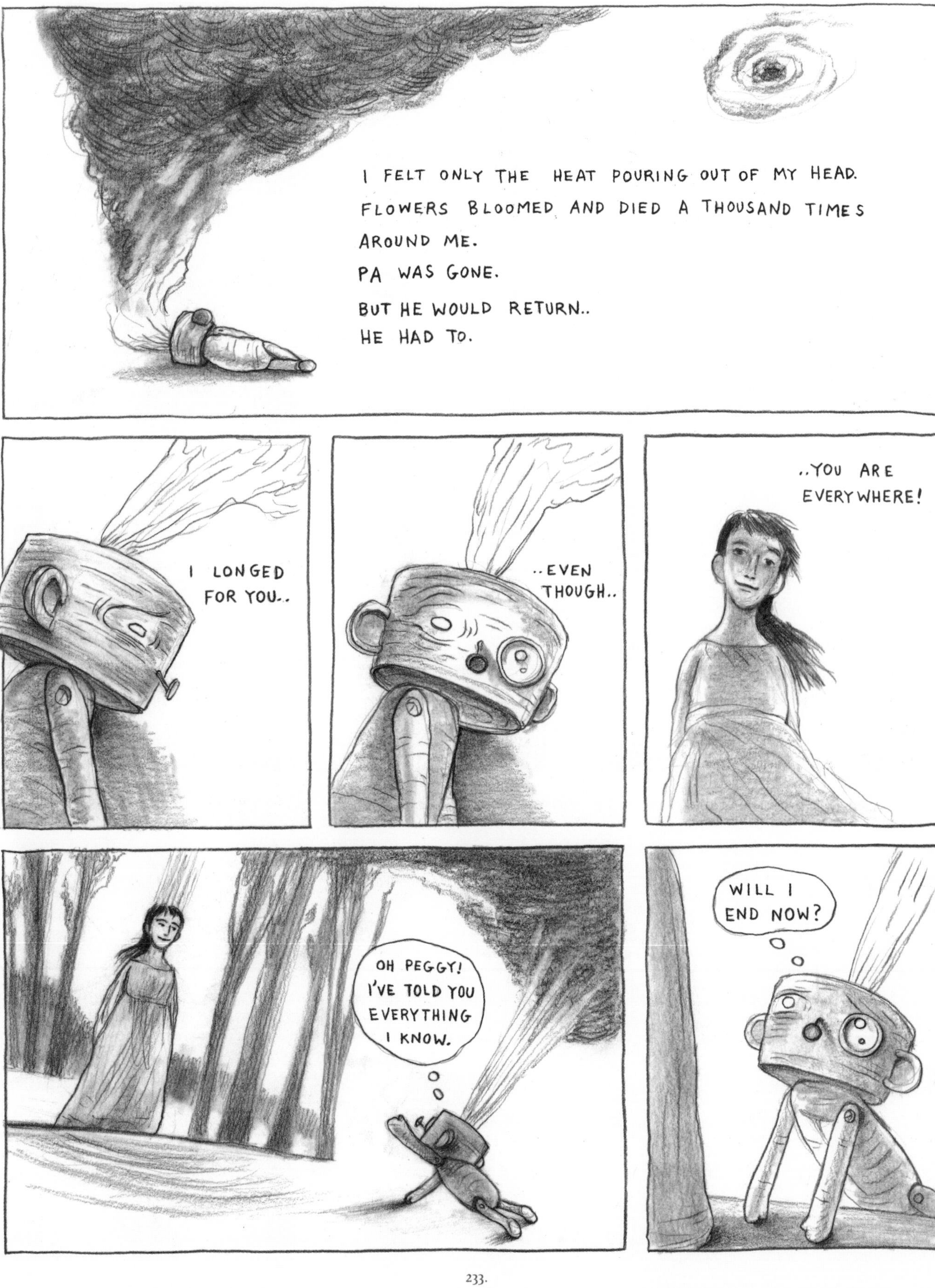
I FELT ONLY THE HEAT POURING OUT OF MY HEAD.
FLOWERS BLOOMED AND DIED A THOUSAND TIMES AROUND ME.
PA WAS GONE.
BUT HE WOULD RETURN..
HE HAD TO.
I LONGED FOR YOU..
..EVEN THOUGH..
..YOU ARE EVERYWHERE!
OH PEGGY! I'VE TOLD YOU EVERYTHING I KNOW.
WILL I END NOW?

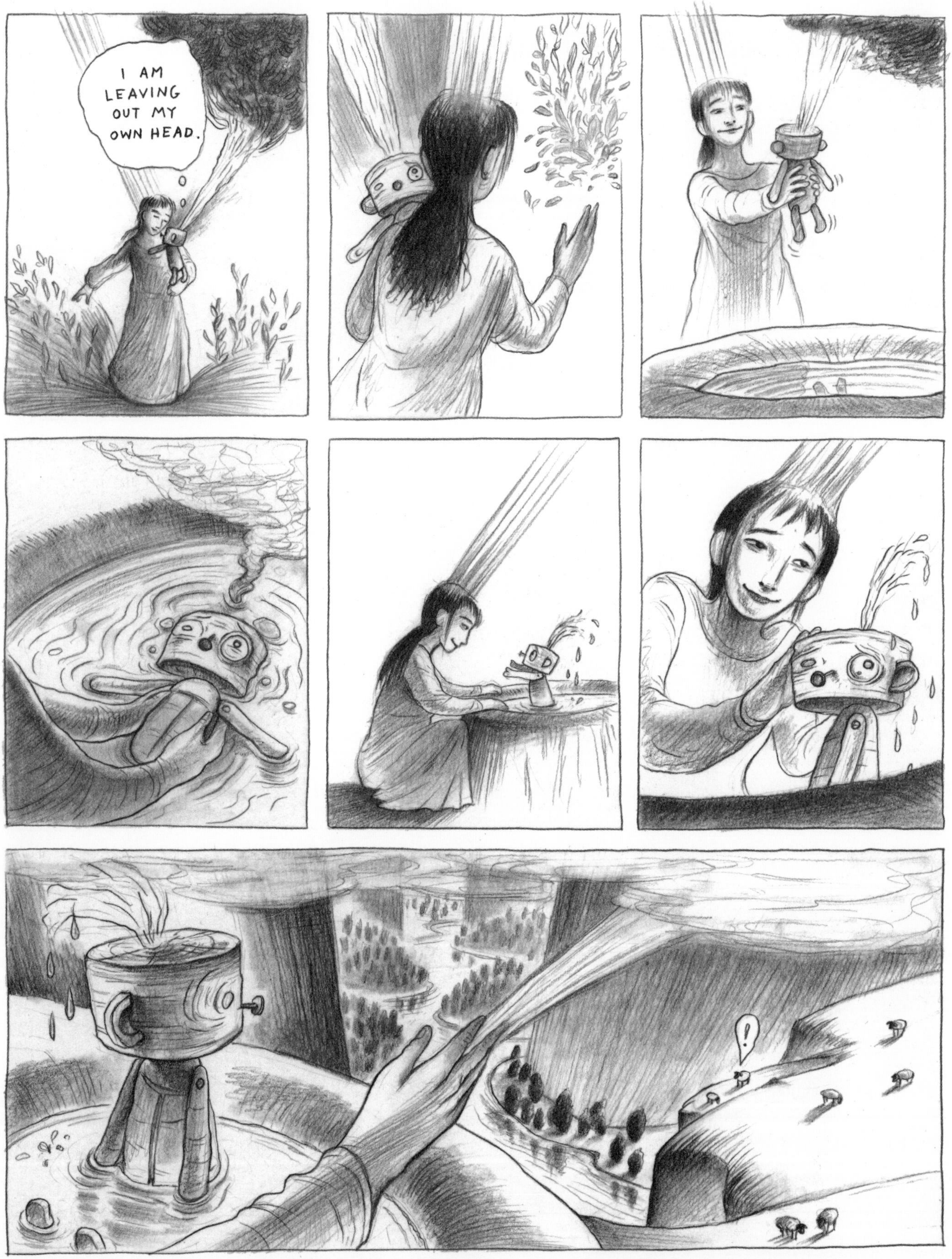
I AM LEAVING OUT MY OWN HEAD.
!

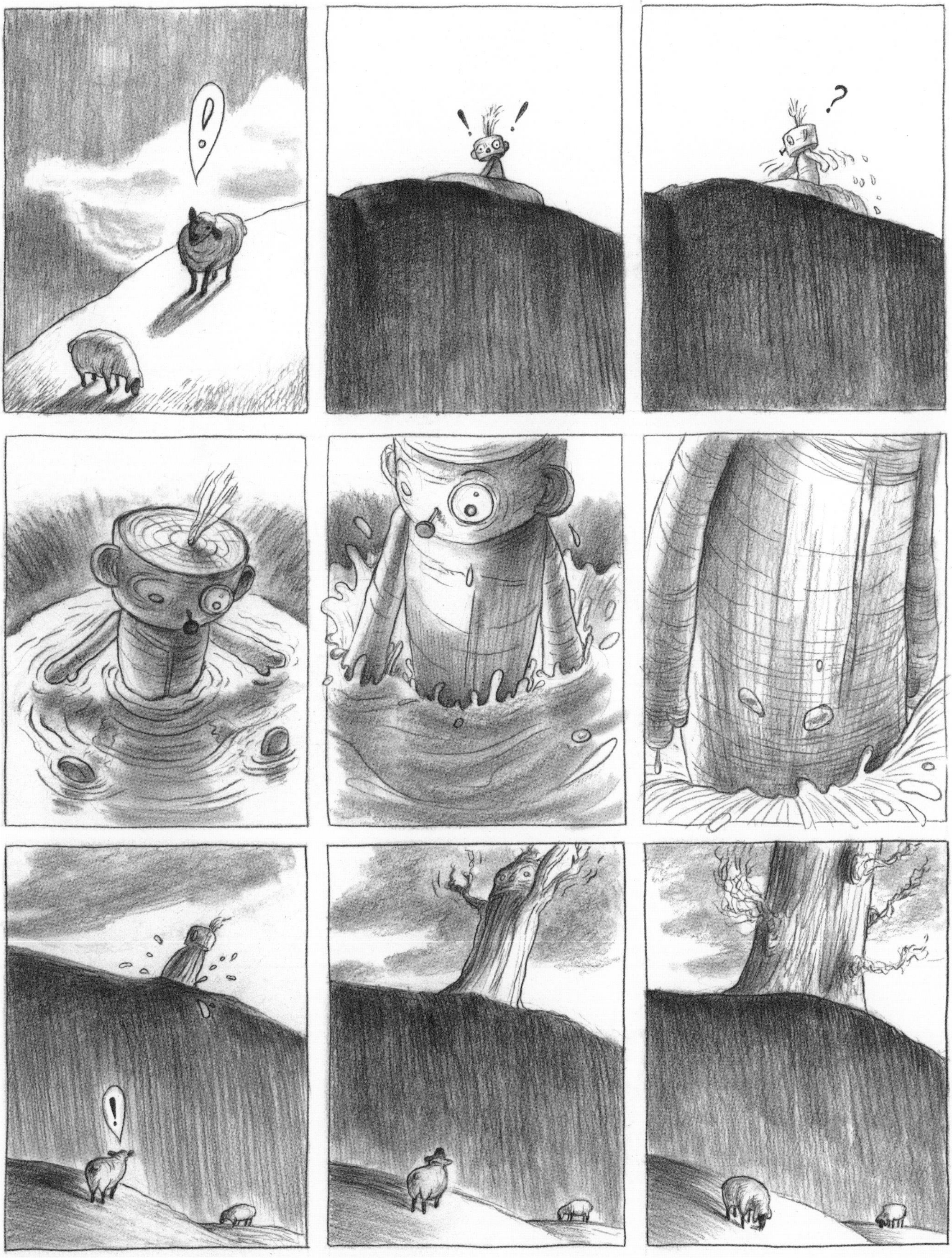
!
! !
?
!

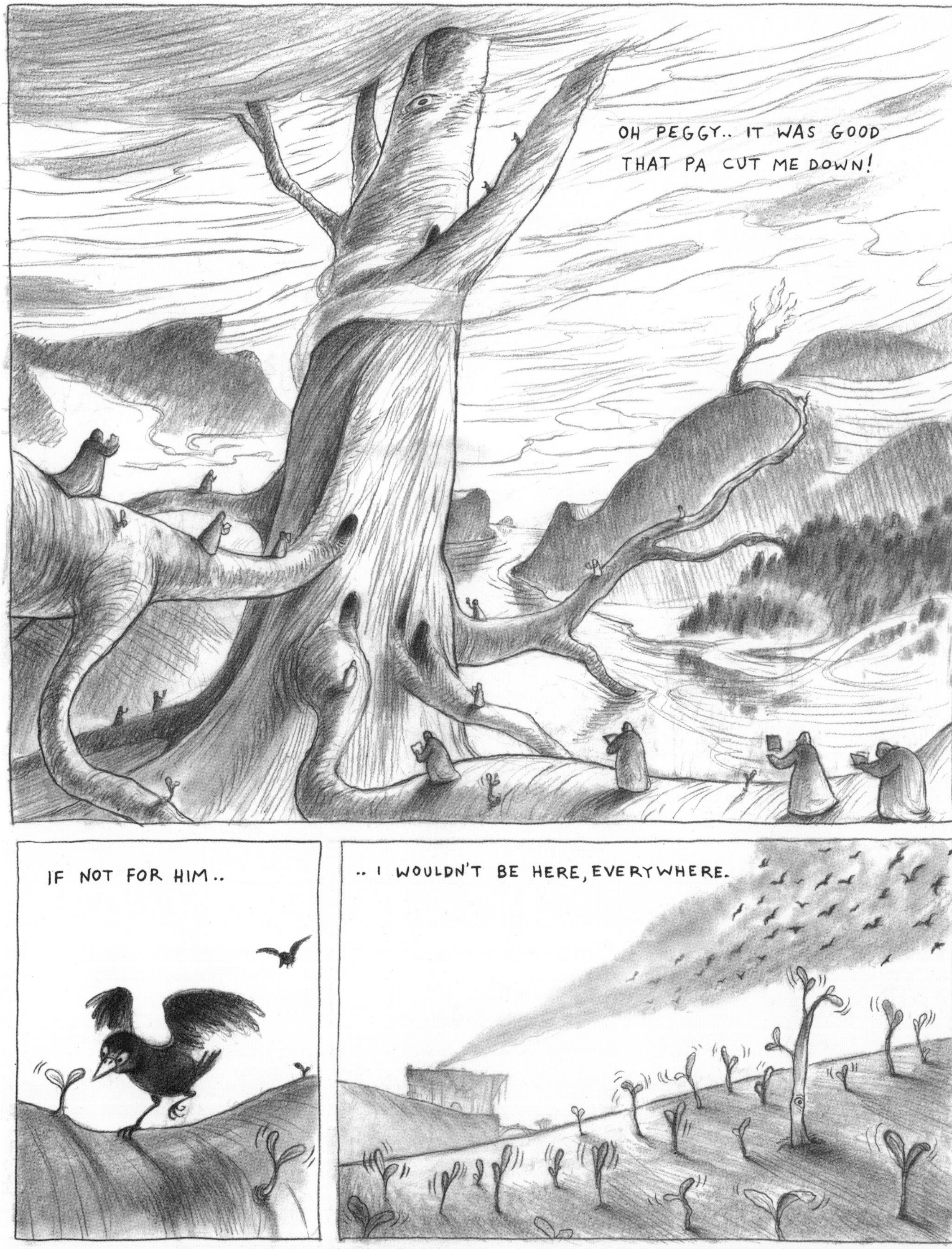
OH PEGGY.. IT WAS GOOD THAT PA CUT ME DOWN!
IF NOT FOR HIM..
.. I WOULDN'T BE HERE, EVERYWHERE.

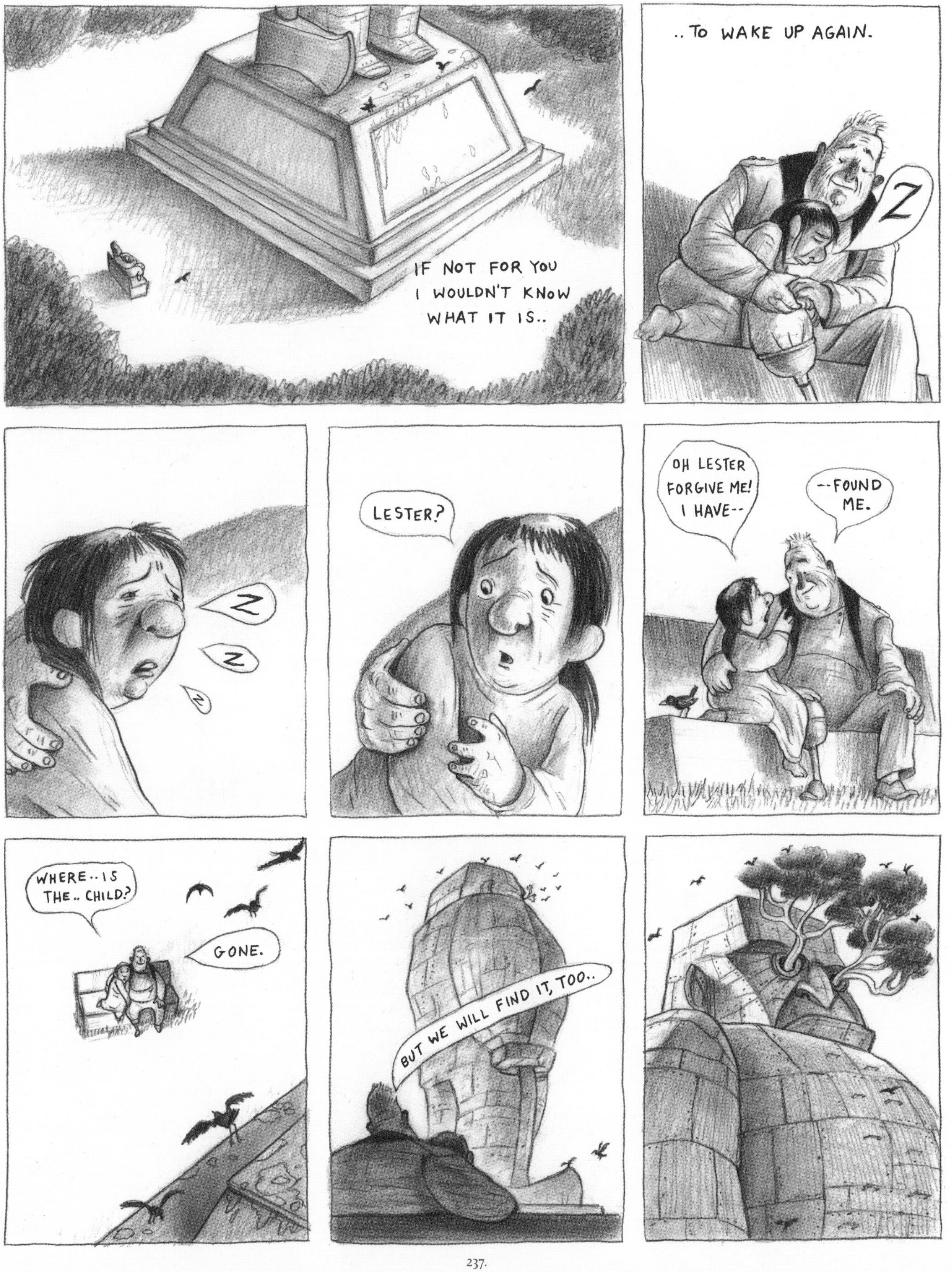
IF NOT FOR YOU I WOULDN'T KNOW WHAT IT IS..
.. TO WAKE UP AGAIN.
Z
Z
Z
Z
LESTER?
OH LESTER FORGIVE ME! I HAVE--
--FOUND ME.
WHERE.. IS THE.. CHILD?
GONE.
BUT WE WILL FIND IT, TOO..

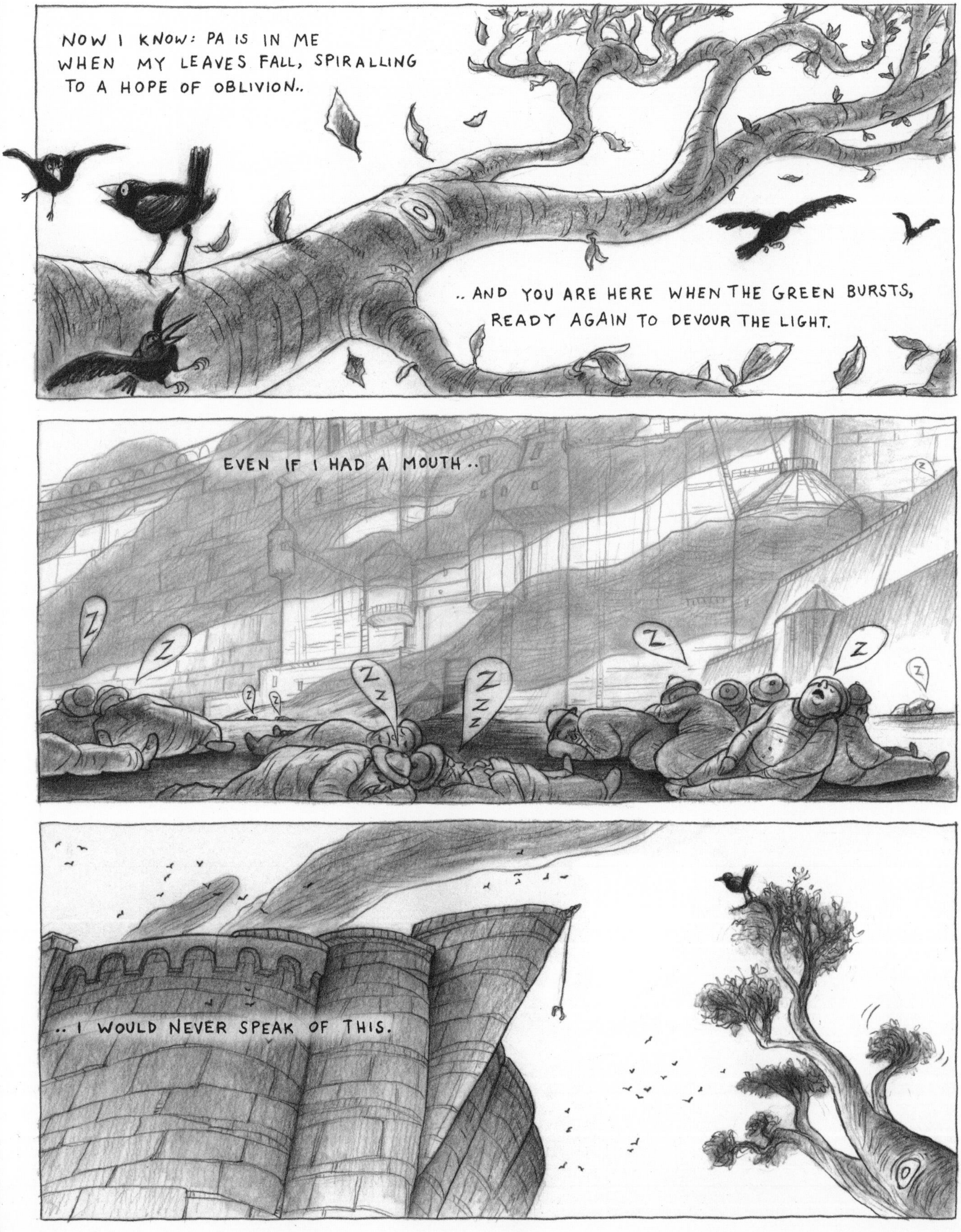
NOW I KNOW: PA IS IN ME WHEN MY LEAVES FALL, SPIRALLING TO A HOPE OF OBLIVION..
.. AND YOU ARE HERE WHEN THE GREEN BURSTS, READY AGAIN TO DEVOUR THE LIGHT.
EVEN IF I HAD A MOUTH ..
.. I WOULD NEVER SPEAK OF THIS.

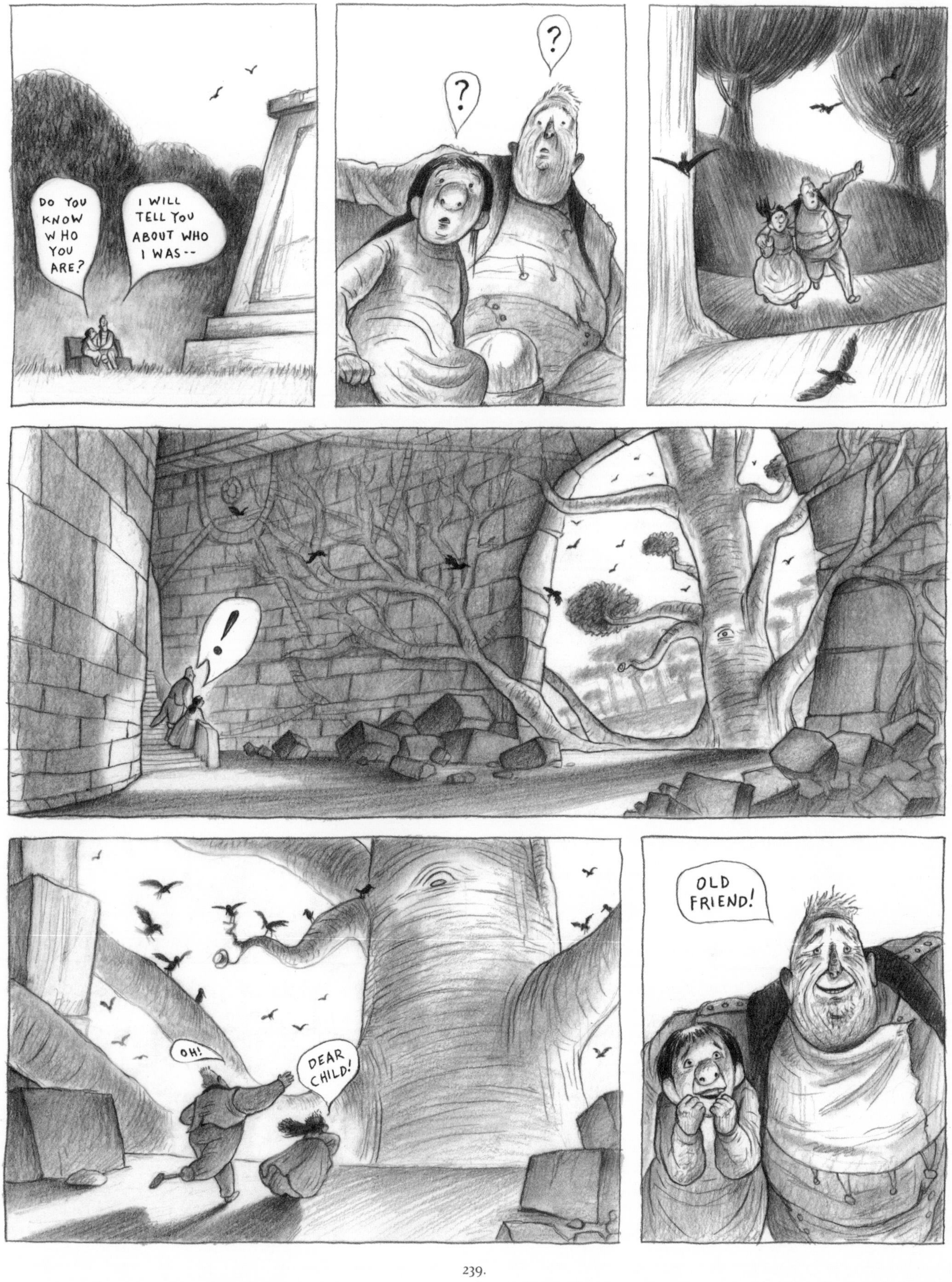
DO YOU KNOW WHO YOU ARE?
I WILL TELL YOU ABOUT WHO I WAS--
?
?
!
OH!
DEAR CHILD!
OLD FRIEND!

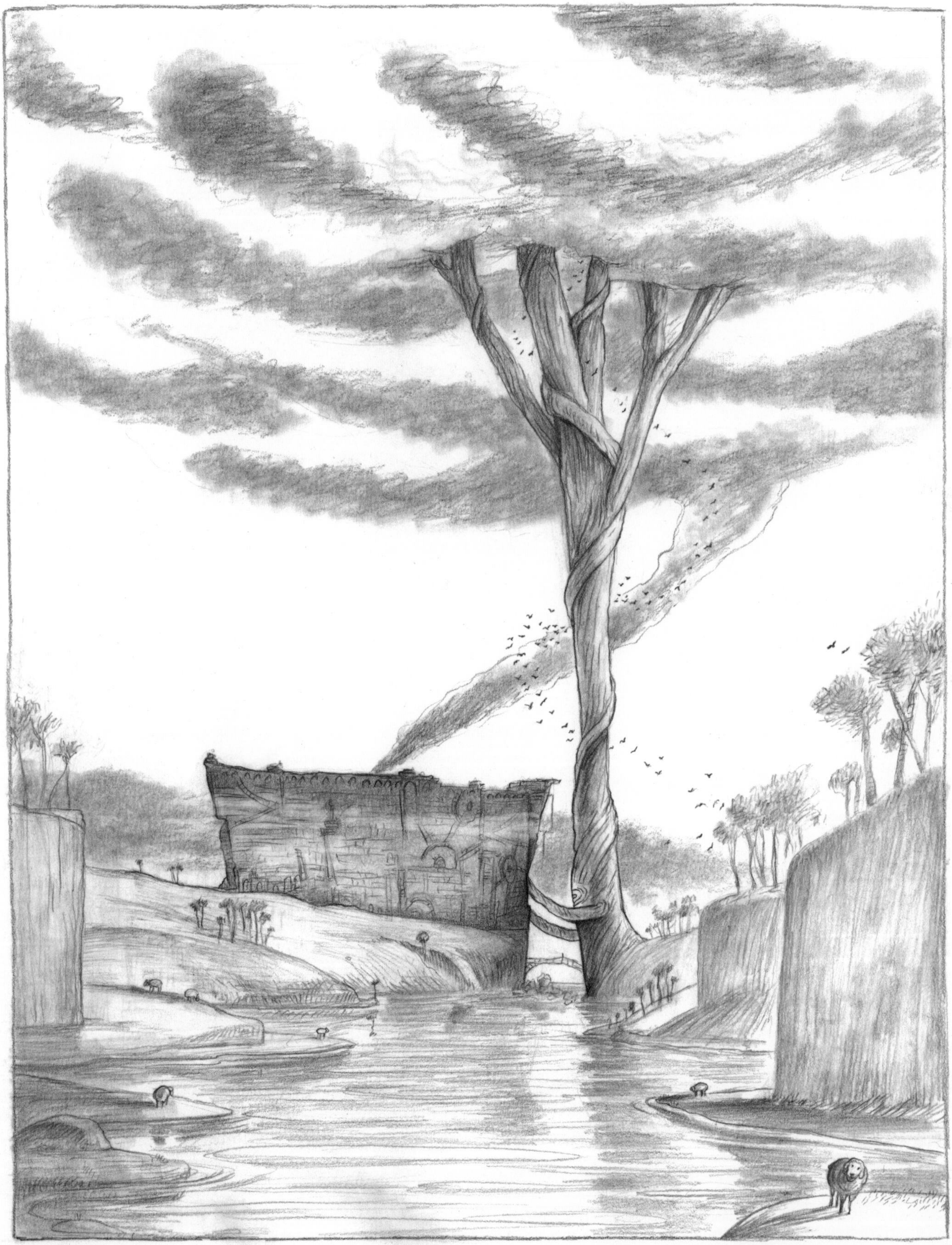